PRAISE FOR *RETHINKING HOPI ETHNOGRAPHY*

Just as a long tradition of ethnographic research and writing may be coming to an end at Hopi, Peter Whiteley argues that its continuation there, freshly conceived and fully informed by modern Hopi sensibilities, can serve a number of useful ends and purposes. This is a candid and thoughtful book, careful and articulate, which deserves the close attention of fieldworking anthropologists everywhere.

Keith Basso, University of New Mexico

Piw naat i' Hopit qatsitwiyat piptsankyangw qa suupwat tutuvenyukiltiqe antsa aqwhaqami Hopit qatsiyat aw tutuqayyaqamuy, pu' put qatsit yesqamuy, amumi pu' piw alöngötwat ang töqti. Niiqe i' pu' tutuvenyuki nan'ivo itamuy sòosokmuy u'nana, itam qa naakyaptsivewat naanami taywisqw put ep itamuy nan'ivo ökwhana. It ang paas tungwayaqam sosomatsnen ep hìitawat yaw qa su'antsatskiwqat ang naaviptsayani.

This is yet another book containing more than one perspective on Hopi culture by which, in effect, it speaks to things different than expected by those who study, and by those who live in, the lifeway of the Hopi. That being so, this book now cautions all of us on both sides of this [interest in Hopi] that our regard for each other is wanting in mutual respect, and for that it voices an admonition. Those who read this book heedfully will see themselves in some of the improprieties inferred in it, if they are discerning.

Emory Sekaquaptewa, University of Arizona

SMITHSONIAN SERIES IN ETHNOGRAPHIC INQUIRY

William L. Merrill and Ivan Karp, Series Editors

Ethnography as fieldwork, analysis, and literary form is the distinguishing feature of modern anthropology. Guided by the assumption that anthropological theory and ethnography are inextricably linked, this series is devoted to exploring the ethnographic enterprise.

Advisory Board

Richard Bauman (Indiana University), Gerald Berreman (University of California, Berkeley), James Boon (Princeton University), Stephen Gudeman (University of Minnesota), Shirley Lindenbaum (City University of New York), George Marcus (Rice University), David Parkin (Oxford University), Renato Rosaldo (Stanford University), and Norman Whitten (University of Illinois)

RETHINKING HOPI ETHNOGRAPHY

PETER M. WHITELEY

SMITHSONIAN INSTITUTION PRESS
WASHINGTON AND LONDON

Grateful acknowledgment is made for permission to reprint the following material. Chapter 2 originally appeared in two parts as "Unpacking Hopi 'Clans': Another Vintage Model Out of Africa?" and "Unpacking Hopi 'Clans,' II: Further Questions about Hopi Descent Groups," in the *Journal of Anthropological Research* vol. 41 (1985), 359-74, and vol. 42 (1986), 69-79. Chapter 3, "The Interpretation of Politics: A Hopi Conundrum," first appeared in *MAN* (n.s.) vol. 22 (1987), 696-714. Chapter 4, "*Hopitutungwni*: 'Hopi Names' as Literature," first appeared in *On the Translation of Native American Literatures* (1992), Brian Swann, ed., Washington, D.C.: Smithsonian Institution Press, 208-27. Chapter 5, "Burning Culture: Auto-da-fé at Oraibi [Orayvi]," first appeared in *History and Anthropology* (1992), vol. 6, no. 1, 46-85. Chapter 6, "The End of Anthropology (at Hopi)?" first appeared in *Journal of the Southwest* (1993), vol. 35, no. 2, 125-57. The core of Chapter 7 first appeared as "*Paavahu* and *Paanaqawu*: The Wellsprings of Life and the Slurry of Death" in *Cultural Survival Quarterly* (1996), vol. 19, no. 4, 40-45.

COPY EDITOR: Marsha A. Kunin
DESIGNER: Linda McKnight

Library of Congress Cataloging-in-Publication Data
Whiteley, Peter M.
   Rethinking Hopi ethnography / Peter M. Whiteley.
     p. cm. — (Smithsonian series in ethnographic inquiry)
   Includes bibliographical references and index.
   ISBN 1-56098-857-6 (alk. paper). — ISBN 1-56098-882-7 (pbk. : alk paper)
   1. Hopi Indians. 2. Hopi philosophy. 3. Ethnology—Methodology. I. Title. II. Series.
E99.H7W49 1998
973'.049745—dc21   98-6011

British Library Cataloguing-in-Publication Data available

Manufactured in the United States of America
05 04 03 02 01 00 99 98   5 4 3 2 1

♾ The paper used in this publication meets the minimum requirements of the American National Standard for Information Sciences—Permanence of Paper for Printed Library Materials ANSI Z39.48-1984.

For permission to reproduce illustrations appearing in this book, please correspond directly with the owners of the works, as listed in the individual captions. The Smithsonian Institution Press does not retain reproduction rights for these illustrations individually, or maintain a file of addresses for photo sources.

FOR JANE CAMPBELL

[E]thnography is anthropology, or it is nothing.

Marshall Sahlins

We cannot . . . characterize behavior independently of intentions, and we cannot characterize intentions independently of the settings which make those intentions intelligible both to agents themselves and to others.

Alasdair MacIntyre

However initially attractive, even apparently "true" the idea might be that all our narratives are partial fictions, the wholesale enthusiastic acceptance of that way of thought removes both interest and power, in the end, from both art and the moral life.

[I]t now becomes necessary to reconsider the idea of truth, hard truth, and its possibility. . . . I do believe language has denotative as well as connotative powers.

A. S. Byatt

La valeur éminente de l'ethnologie est de correspondre à la première étape d'une démarche qui en comporte d'autres.

Claude Lévi-Strauss

CONTENTS

PREFACE AND ACKNOWLEDGMENTS

The papers collected here were written over a decade's span, and they draw upon research that began five years earlier. I cannot do justice to the thanks I owe many individuals and institutions for indispensable support, wisdom, aid, and comfort over that period. Specific acknowledgments are included with the endnotes. Here, I want to thank most particularly Sarah Lawrence College, which, since 1985, has given me an academic home that is both challenging and broadening: Its small-scale, convivial interdisciplinarity and participatory teaching have significantly influenced my critical thinking. Colleague Arnold Krupat has been an abiding fount of insight, intellectual inspiration, and warm friendship. The late Lina Brock was also a defining voice for my own anthropological sensibility.

To the following I owe profound gratitude for many kindnesses great and small, intellectual and otherwise: the late Harry Basehart, Keith Basso, Karen Blu, Willem and Jo Brans, John Martin Campbell, Susan Horsley Campbell, Guy Cooper, Kate Crehan, Timothy and Cornelia Eland, Armin Geertz, Paul Henley, Stephen Hopkins, Louise Lennihan, Hartman and Tsianina Lomawaima, David Major, Vernon Masayesva, Rev. Richard McKeon, Peter Nabokov, Shuichi Nagata, the late Alfonso Ortiz, Triloki N. Pandey, Scott Rushforth, Marshall Sahlins, the late Rev. Charles Scott, the late Abbott Sekaquaptewa, Emory Sekaquaptewa, Louise Stiver, Brian Swann, Stephen Turner and Monono Matsaba, Phillip and Judy Tuwaletstiwa, John R. Wilson, and Barton

Wright. For reasons discussed in Chapter 1, most Hopis prefer ano-
nymity, but my gratitude is extended to many people—for their hospi-
tality, for guiding my understanding, and for insisting on the autonomous value of Hopi thought against any propensity to romanticize or
objectify.

Previously published chapters have mostly been allowed to stand,
"warts and all." New introductions update some matters, and there are
a few revisionary insertions. I have cleaned up some infelicities of
expression, and I am most grateful to Marsha A. Kunin for finding and
fixing many more. Spellings of Hopi personal names (except where they
are surnames with set spellings) and place-names have been altered to
conform to present standards for writing Hopi. While I argued in
earlier work for retaining spellings such as *Oraibi* (now *Orayvi*), I now
lean, with some ambivalence, toward standardization. My ambivalence
concerns spellings long established in historical and anthropological
literature and in official discourse. But while *Oraibi* is an old convention, other names exhibit so many variations that an orthographic
standard seems, on balance, desirable. (There are a few minor variants
in the orthography herein from that of the Hopi dictionary [*Hopi
Dictionary—Hopìikwa Lavaytutuveni: A Hopi-English Dictionary of
the Third Mesa Dialect,* University of Arizona Press, 1998]. The dictionary appeared as the present work was going to press—unfortunately too late to permit corrections.)

To Daniel Goodwin and Bob Lockhart of Smithsonian Institution
Press I am particularly indebted for their consistent care, attention, and
encouragement. For permission to republish, I am most grateful to the
Journal of Anthropological Research for Chapter 2, "Unpacking Hopi
'Clans': Another Vintage Model Out of Africa?"; the Royal Anthropo-
logical Institute of Great Britain and Ireland for Chapter 3, "The
Interpretation of Politics: A Hopi Conundrum"; Smithsonian Institu-
tion Press for Chapter 4, "*Hopitutungwni:* Hopi Names as Literature";
History and Anthropology, and Gordon and Breach for Chapter 5,
"Burning Culture: Auto-da-fé at Oraibi [Orayvi]"; and the Mennonite
Library and Archives, Bethel College, North Newton, Kansas, for the
text included within Chapter 5, "A Hopi Indian Finds Christ," prepared by Rev. John P. Suderman; the *Journal of the Southwest* for
Chapter 6, "The End of Anthropology at (Hopi)?"; and Cultural Survival Inc., for "*Paavahu* and *Paanaqso'a:* The Wellsprings of Life and
the Slurry of Death," which forms the basis of Chapter 7.

I also want to thank Jane Campbell, to whom the book is dedicated and without whom I find it impossible to imagine life, in an anthropological vein, or in any other. As both kin and affine to anthropologists, she is unillusioned of their claims, and for that reason, among others, she has provided a continually fine critical eye on writing she considers generally less worthwhile than Edith Wharton's.

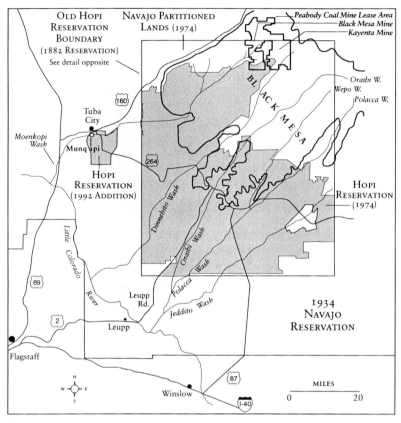

The Hopi Reservation and Environs

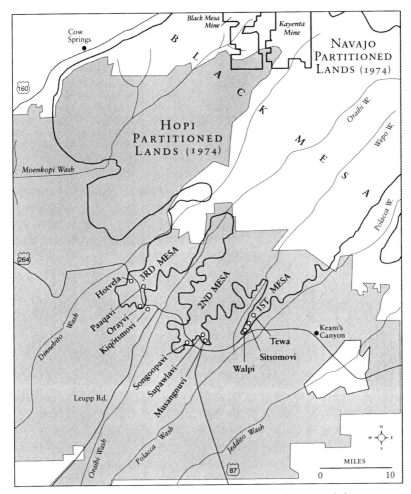

The Old 1882 Hopi Reservation, showing the Hopi Villages and the 1974
Navajo-Hopi Land Settlement Act partition.

INTRODUCTION
The Predicament of Hopi Ethnography

As they were then [1540, the first Spanish exploration], so they are in our own day, one of the most interesting peoples in the world. Their religion, system of government, apparel, manufactures,—no less than the romantic positions of their villages, appeal to the curiosity or sympathy of almost every class of travelers, archaeologists, divines, men of letters, or ordinary sight-seers.

> Capt. John Gregory Bourke,
> *The Snake Dance of the Moquis of Arizona,* 1884

In a society like the Zuni whose members believe that outsiders, and in particular anthropologists, cause conflict and dissention [*sic*] among them, discontent and protest against such outsiders are inevitable and destined at times to assume grave proportions. This whole atmosphere of mistrust, coupled with the events of history, is germane to and must influence any interpretation of the view which the natives have of anthropologists and their works.

> Triloki Nath Pandey,
> "Anthropologists at Zuni," 1972

Ethnography has reached a precarious point, perhaps a terminus, at Hopi. The very idea, for example, of a formal fieldwork project, hatched as a theoretical "problem" in a university setting, underwritten by an exogenous granting agency, and without internal consultation, is no longer conceivable. The hypostasized academic envelope of detachment, purporting to inoculate metropolitan ethnography from local

1

Figure 1.1. View in Orayvi, 1890s, looking north. Photographer not identified (possibly Charles Carpenter). Courtesy of the Field Museum of Natural History, Chicago (Field Museum Negative #185).

vectors of representation and interest, is irreversibly permeated. Hopis, ever more encompassed by the world system, are in general keenly aware and deeply mistrustful of anthropological research as, fundamentally, commodification—of themselves, their ideas, and their practices. That academic commodification appeals to intellectual rather than material accumulation matters little when the social relations of research production substantially duplicate everyday commodification of Hopi culture by non-Hopis within and beyond the U.S. Southwest. And indeed intellectual knowledge as cultural capital is readily comprehended by Hopis, who traditionally manage knowledge by protocols of secrecy and privilege, which highlight the folly of readily ceding it to others (see Chapter 3).

From the plenitude of outside interest over the last century, cultural representations—which internally are in many cases *instruments* of value effectuated by conscious social labor (in ritual)—have been transformed, by an outside world oblivious to, or scornful of, their instrumentality, into mere symbols. Within the Hopi community, the governance of ritual knowledge's instrumentality entails a symbolic wealth sui generis. But such wealth is consistently attached to its capacity to transform material conditions. The cultural capital of ritual knowledge (a currency of power and a medium of hierarchy) scarcely circulates. It is maintained within tightly circumscribed lines of inheritance: Hopi *navoti* (traditional power/knowledge) adheres to particular social persons (referred to as *a'ni himuytaqa*, "a powerful person," or *pavansinom*, a "class of powerful people," among other terms), and is fundamentally untransactable.[1] Western commodifications of Hopi culture detach knowledge from its sentient agents and put it into (relatively) free circulation.[2] In response, and as a measure of their involvement in the world system,[3] Hopis too now treat their cultural forms as property, and jealously guard rights of ownership—not simply to protect against the erosion of cultural sovereignty, but in recognition of the determining effects of the market. In short, Hopis have come to participate, in various respects, in the commodification of their own culture as a result of the conjuncture with capitalist circulations, of which academic knowledge is a form (cf. Bourdieu 1988, 1994).

Intellectual property laws are a major interest at present as a means of exercising control over Hopi representations,[4] particularly in the Hopi Tribe's Office of Cultural Preservation.[5] Founded in the late 1980s, this branch of Tribal government has become the key intercessor in academic research, and the main guardian of intellectual sovereignty against raiders of Hopi symbolic capital. It polices its gates with increasing vigor. The rules for research that it promulgates (as well as occasional pronouncements of privacy rights in *Hopi Tutuveni*, the Tribal newspaper) are directed at protecting Hopi knowledge and practices, which are considered a complex of both individual and communal intellectual property. The chief intent of these rules vis-à-vis outside researchers is control and exclusion, and they have successfully prevented much proposed research considered intrusive. For outside researchers of avowedly benign intent, the results can be frustrating. Distressed that her requests to interview Hopi women about attitudes toward abortion (as part of a regional sociological comparison) were continuously temporalized, a recent researcher demanded to see a Tribal Bill of Rights and challenged her own rejection in terms of a denial of First Amendment rights to free speech for Hopi women. In some ways Hopi remains a closed society (in Popper's sense), and discursive protections enable collective sovereignty and tradition to meaningfully continue within the overarching hegemony of the U.S. nation-state. There is a fundamental clash with the free-for-all individualism of Western openness—in ideological terms, anyway—regarding knowledge circulation. Pandey (1972:335) historicizes this pattern:

> How should we interpret such reactions? Is this part of the general dis-trust in which anthropology is held nowadays in some developing socie-ties? I take this reaction as a *quest for equality,* and as these people want to get rid of the intolerable inequality inherent in their colonial past, they have developed this negative attitude to anthropology, which is seen as a study of past customs and beliefs rather than of predica-ments in which they find themselves. (emphasis added)

Protectionist tendencies toward cultural knowledge mirror, and at some level seek to emulate, the academic castle, with its own elaborate rules of access and mystification. In the anthropological wing, Hopis typi-cally experience these rules as excluding them from control of their own representations once these are transmitted to outside ethnographers. Transcribed into ethnographic records, Hopi knowledge and practice enter a blind, where sight—and even more certainly, oversight—is denied to the producers. Descriptively reduced to fieldnotes, subject to arcane judgments, and manipulated for argument or theory that is, to say the least, "experience-distant," graphed Hopi images—many of which, to repeat, are *instrumentally* valuable within their own set-tings—are lost not so much in as *by* translation, released to an alien bureaucracy of academic knowledge. (For my own position in this regard, see below.) While frequently sending its emissaries into Hopi life, the academic castle has largely denied Hopis a circulating presence within its borders. The Cultural Preservation Office's declaration that anthropologists' fieldnotes and photographs in museums or university archives are Tribal property, and require Tribal permission for access or use, is a direct attempt to breach this boundary and invert the terms of exclusion. Public calls by Tribal officials and others for "no more research," for example at a conference convened to assess relationships between Hopis and outside researchers (see Sanner 1996), reflect the same pattern. These are further associated with larger Native American pressures for sovereignty—cultural, political, and intellectual.

If such antipathies now flourish at Hopi, a virtual Rorschach of anthropological developments since the inception of the field, parallel exercises of cultural sovereignty are prevalent elsewhere too. National and "Tribal" agencies analogous to the Cultural Preservation Office— smaller equivalents of the French Ministry of Culture, with its stern gaze on Anglophone pollutions—are burgeoning in other cultural settings considered archetypal provinces of ethnography. As Sahlins (1993:3) puts it:

> The cultural self-consciousness developing among imperialism's erst-while victims is one of the more remarkable phenomena of world history in the later twentieth century. "Culture"—the word itself, or some local equivalent, is on everyone's lips. Tibetans and Hawaiians, Ojibway, Kwakiutl, and Eskimo, Kazakhs and Mongols, native Australians, Balinese, Kashmiris, and New Zealand Maori: all discover they have a "culture." For centuries they may have hardly noticed it. But now, as the New Guinean said to the anthropologist, "If we didn't have *kastom,* we would be just like white men."

This transvaluation of indigenous cultures is likely to persist, so long as cultural capital is useful for political gains unobtainable by direct resistance to the state (Jameson 1986; Lowe and Lloyd 1997), or even as the necessary basis of solidarity for effective direct resistance (Sahlins 1993:18). Of course, many parts of the world, nation-states or their internal entities, have historically made anthropological research difficult, and regarded anthropologists as little better than spies for some imperium or other. Difficulties of obtaining permissions to work among indigenous peoples in, say, Brazil or Irian Jaya, have become notorious over the last two decades. And formal ease of access to many Native North American communities has in the past been guaranteed by their status as internal colonies of the U.S. nation-state. Increasing sophistication in matters of political autonomy by Native communities is partly responsible for the greater difficulties of access for external ethnographers. But the grounds of intellectual exclusion differ in some respects from the policing of civil boundaries elsewhere in the world: As with Hopi, the attention in many Native communities is toward the protection (and recuperation, via the Native American Graves Protection and Repatriation Act) of knowledge as metaphysically instrumental property rather than the protection of long-breached geopolitical boundaries. If religious knowledge, in particular, is alienated, millennial disaster threatens and the ontological foundations of the Hopi ecumene are jeopardized. (For the encompassing reach of Hopi cultural structures, see below.)

The shifting of hegemonic battlegrounds from control over directly strategic material resources (although assaults on these in Native communities are strongly persistent—see Chapter 7) to "culture" as commodified intellective form, fundamentally repositions the ethnographic

RETHINKING HOPI ETHNOGRAPHY

project. The possibilities for a Palestinian ethnographer of an Israeli community, or vice versa, seem remote, and exclusion here is founded in pragmatic antagonisms. But the "culture wars," to nudge this term into a slightly different register, are being fought on more metaphysical grounds, where violence is largely allegorical and discursive rather than practical (cf. Jameson 1986, Lavie 1990). Beyond tribal communities in Native North America, a parallel protectionism has emerged within the academy (e.g., Cook-Lynn 1997, Krupat 1996, Littlefield 1992, Warrior 1994) where non-Indian academics are urged by some Native scholars to simply "keep out." Disciplinary balkanization in universities among Native Studies, Cultural Studies, and Anthropology both reflects and reinforces this identitarian intellectual separatism.[6]

Anthropology's shortcomings as a plurally inclusive intercultural discipline come into sharp relief in this trend. The reasons for indigenous resistance to cultural commodification by academic ethnography are several (I take some up again in Chapter 6), but at base they are the result of the social and political estrangement of anthropology as a research-university discipline from the perspectives and situated interests of its subjects. This estrangement coexists uneasily and paradoxically with anthropology's stated will-to-knowledge as a global democratic virtue. Anthropology has often advertised itself as a bridge to intercultural understanding, but the bridge has typically been one-way, and the advertisements depend upon systematic effacement of historical intentionalities. The epistemology of the ethnographic closet[7] reflects a willful ignorance that is a self-reproducing and necessary condition for the instantiated desire to know the Other as object rather than as presence in genuinely intersubjective dialogue. This imputation of un-known Otherness infuses the gathering of knowledge with hierarchy (as Foucault and Said have persuasively demonstrated)—of subject and object, knower and known, transcriber and transcribed: It is this hierarchy, and its resemblance to formal political-economic subjection, that is the fundamental target of Native cultural resistance. The clash of representational interests and the epistemic and practical projects these are tied to pivots on questions of cultural knowledge as instrumental form, intellectual property, and political capital.

HOPI ETHNOGRAPHY: A HISTORICAL PALIMPSEST

Amongst the most interesting and important aborigines of North America are the Pueblo or Village Indians of Arizona and New Mexico. Their importance . . . [is that] in their institutions they form a link or in-

Figure 1.2. *Leenangw,* the "Flute ceremony" at Orayvi, probably 1897, under close ethnographic scrutiny by, at right, H. R. and Martha Voth. I am unable to identify the white man in the foreground (it may be Sumner Matteson). Photographer not identified (possibly Charles Carpenter). Courtesy of the Field Museum of Natural History, Chicago (Field Museum Negative #177).

termediate stage between the barbarous tribes to the north and the civilized Indians of Mexico, Central America, and Peru.

Sir James Frazer, *Totemism and Exogamy,* 1910

If Hopi ethnography has come to some sort of an end, the trajectory of its demise may be of more than ordinary interest, since anthropology practically begins at Hopi and Hopi is substantially represented, both descriptively and analytically, in virtually every theoretical paradigm since Morganian evolutionism. The first formal descriptions, by Army Surgeon P. G. S. Ten Broeck, appear in Schoolcraft's (1851–57) famously transitional proto-anthropological compendium—part marvelous speculation, part naturalistic reportage—from a visit in 1852, shortly after the appearance of Morgan's own founder ethnography, *League of the Ho-de'-no-sau-nee or Iroquois* (1851). Since then, a partial list of those who have conducted at least some ethnographic work at Hopi reads like a metonymic who's who of earlier disciplinary history within the United States: John Wesley Powell, John Gregory Bourke, Frank Hamilton Cushing, Matilda Coxe Stevenson, Jesse Walter Fewkes, George A. Dorsey, Elsie Clews Parsons, Robert Lowie, Clyde Kluckhohn, Julian Steward, Daryll Forde, Leslie White, Fred and Dorothy Eggan, Mischa

Titiev, Edward Kennard, Georges Devereux, Benjamin Lee Whorf, Ernest Beaglehole, Laura Thompson, and so on. If we add to this field the Pueblos in general, of whom the Hopi have frequently been treated as a type in anthropological writing, we could include, among many others, Franz Boas, Alfred Kroeber, and Ruth Benedict.[8] And I have not listed those at Hopi, like Alexander Stephen and H. R. Voth, whose field ethnography is the most comprehensive, but who have achieved less visibility in the canon of disciplinary history.

Several major anthropological expeditions to Hopi, both specifically and as part of a larger Southwest focus, were mounted (earlier equivalents to the collective systematic attention by Harvard, for example, to Chiapas, !Kung, and Gê): including the Hemenway expedition (1880s to 1890s, notably sponsoring Fewkes's work for the Smithsonian) and the Archer M. Huntington expedition (1915-16, sponsoring Lowie's work on social organization coordinate with Kroeber's work at Zuni). In 1932 Leslie White, of the University of Michigan, led a team of anthropologists—Fred Eggan, Mischa Titiev, Georges Devereux, Ed Kennard, and Jess Spirer—from the Laboratory of Anthropology in Santa Fe. Several of these became illuminati of the discipline. The Harvard Peabody Museum's Awatovi excavation project (field seasons from 1935 to 1939) also deployed numerous scholars, including Watson Smith, Joseph Brew, Ross Gordon Montgomery, and Charles Avery Amsden.

The proliferation of Hopi studies in the 1930s and 1940s also coincided with a change in Indian administration under the leadership of Commissioner John Collier, the Indian Reorganization Act, and some specific developments at Hopi involving reduction of the Hopi Reservation by three-fourths via the assignation of several "grazing districts" to the Navajo (with results ongoing in the Hopi-Navajo land dispute). Collier himself met several times with protesting representatives—both traditional and newly elected to the incipient Tribal Council—at Hopi and in Washington (Whiteley 1989). Yet he refused to budge on Hopi confinement to "Grazing District Six" and on massive stock reduction to Hopi herds. As a direct result, the fledgling Tribal Council folded, and along with more "traditional" resistors, Roger Quochwytewa, governor of Kiqötsmovi (the most "progressive" village, one that had lent strong support to the Council), spent time in jail. In 1942-43, Collier's future wife, Laura Thompson, under joint sponsorship by the University of Chicago's Committee on Human Development and the Bureau of Indian Affairs, led a team of more than fifty scientists (and

Figure 1.3. Missionary/ethnographer H. R. Voth in the Snake kiva (probably late 1890s), prior to the public Snake Dance, with unidentified Hopi man. Voth is remembered for sometimes forcing his way into kivas when denied admission to esoteric rites. Photograph by Sumner Matteson. Courtesy of the Milwaukee Public Museum.

see below), assembled to address issues of Hopi culture and personality relationships—in the midst of the material crisis induced by Collier's failure to protect Hopi land rights. Field investigators comprised psychologists, anthropologists, sociologists, and others, who worked mainly at First Mesa, and in the Third Mesa communities of Orayvi and Kiqötsmovi. Together with advisors directly involved in training or oversight of the fieldwork, researchers included several existing or ascendant luminaries in anthropology, psychology, and sociology, such as Lloyd Warner, Bruno Klopfer, Ruth Underhill, Ruth Benedict, Erik Erikson, Irving Hallowell, Kurt Lewin, D'Arcy McNickle, Margaret Mead, Morris Opler, Dorothea Leighton, Ray Birdwhistell, Conrad Arensberg, Felix Cohen, Solon Kimball, Alexander Leighton, Gordon Macgregor, and Edward Spicer (in addition to some, like Fred and Dorothy Eggan and Clyde Kluckhohn, mentioned above).[9]

From the 1940s to the present, other active outside ethnographers are Alfred Whiting, John Connelly, Frederick Dockstader, Charles and Florence Voegelin, Edward Dozier, Arlette Frigout, Shuichi Nagata,

Barton Wright, Maitland Bradfield, Bruce Cox, Joann Kealiino-homoku, Richard Clemmer, Louis Hieb, Alice Schlegel, Ekkehart Malotki, David Shaul, Armin Geertz, myself, John Loftin, and Hans-Ulrich Sanner. Hopi anthropologists Emory Sekaquaptewa, Laverne Masayesva Jeanne, Frank Dukepoo, and Hartman Lomawaima also began to practice over the last three decades.[10] And local institutional sponsorship of ongoing ethnological research has occurred since the 1920s, most notably by the Museum of Northern Arizona, under the leadership of Harold S. Colton; its periodicals, *Plateau* and *Museum Notes,* feature a whole series of ethnographic interpretations by, notably, Katherine Bartlett, Alfred Whiting, Colton, and Edmund Nequatewa.

In this cumulative ethnographic palimpsest, the Hopi appear as exemplars in a legion of theoretical paradigms: cultural evolutionism (in, for example, Morgan 1877), animism (Frazer 1890), totemism (Durkheim and Mauss 1963 [1908]), cultural ecology (Forde 1931, 1934, Steward 1937), psychosocial evolutionism (Mauss 1938), culture and personality (Thompson 1950, D. Eggan 1943), action anthropology (Thompson and Joseph 1944), psychoanalytic anthropology (Aberle 1951, D. Eggan 1956), structural-functionalism, with a dash of historical particularism (F. Eggan 1950), linguistic relativism (Whorf 1956, strongly opposed by Malotki 1983), structuralism (Lévi-Strauss 1955, 1966), descent versus alliance theory (F. Eggan 1964), symbolic anthropology (Ortiz 1972, Hieb 1979a), gender and feminist anthropology (Schlegel 1977), activist anthropology and world-systems theory (Clemmer 1978, 1995), religious hermeneutics (A. Geertz 1987), history of sexuality/race/colonialism (Gutiérrez 1991), cultural materialism (Levy 1992), and structure-and-agency (Whiteley 1988, Rushforth and Upham 1992). Specifically, the Hopi are credited with inhabiting or exemplifying, among other abstractions: the Stage of Middle Barbarism (Morgan 1871), sociocentric totemic classification (Durkheim and Mauss 1963 [1908]),[11] animistic totemism and transmigration (Frazer 1890, 1910), paradigmatic matrilineality (F. Eggan 1950, Lévi-Strauss 1949, Schneider and Gough 1961), timeless language (Whorf 1956), Apollonian psychological tendencies (Benedict 1934,[12] Thompson 1950), and, contrarily, psychological repression and anxiety (D. Eggan 1943, Aberle 1951), epistemological bricolage (Lévi-Strauss 1966:passim), gender equality (Schlegel 1977, Gutiérrez 1991),[13] endemic political factionalism (Clemmer 1978), phenomenological constructivism and postmodern irony (A. Geertz 1990 and 1994, respectively), and cultural hegemony and agential intentionalism (Whiteley 1988, and see Chapter 3). Probably the most widely taught ethnographic autobiography until Marjorie Shostak's *Nisa*, Don Talayesva's *Sun Chief* (Simmons 1942) continues to be pedagogically scrutinized for its psychological intent (of both editor and subject) as well as its cultural content. And if we were to add secondary anthropological utilizations of Hopi images, the implications of Hopi ethnography expand exponentially.

Because of its relative geographic proximity to metropolitan U.S. universities, the negotiation of Hopi imagery via ethnography has further, ancillary contexts. Brief visits to Hopi rituals by local and long-distance anthropologists, both established and aspirant, have been de rigueur for the last century. Fred Eggan used to speak of a fleeting visit from Bronislaw Malinowksi, among others, while at Orayvi in the 1930s. Fred himself unfurled his bedroll on my floor during my first fieldwork in 1980-81, and toward the end of that period I was incongruously thrilled to encounter Alfonso Ortiz escorting Clifford Geertz at the *Sa'lako* ceremony in Songoopavi—and not a little disconcerted, in my liminal state between ethnography as practical experience and as explanatory practice, when they asked me for some impromptu ritual exegesis. The supposedly autonomous topos of the ethnographer's work in the pristine field, so cultivated by Malinowski, and so jealously emulated since (e.g., recently, Descola 1996), has not been even a plausible fiction at Hopi since the 1880s. Not only are there the usual colonial officials (BIA agents and the like), missionaries, and traders—to be first textually situated and then distanced from the ethnographer's superior technical insight (as in Malinowski's famous introduction to *Argonauts of the Western Pacific*)—but there is scarcely elbow room among a gaggle of ethnographers, some of whom go to great lengths to avoid noticing each other.[14]

Indeed the present problems of ethnography are attended, and certainly exacerbated, by a flurry of monographs, autobiographies, coffee-table books, volumes of old photographs with new interpretations, reprintings of older ethnographies, dissertations and theses, and other ethnographic work over the last two decades, which would suggest that ethnography is anything but terminal.[15] Several large, long-term research projects with a Hopi focus include: the University of Arizona's Hopi dictionary project;[16] the 1934 Reservation case trials; joint projects between the Cultural Preservation Office and, for example, the National Park Service at Glen Canyon and Grand Canyon; and archaeological projects at Black Mesa (University of Southern Illinois),

Homol'ovi (Arizona State Museum), and Walpi (the Museum of Northern Arizona). The Hopi-Navajo land dispute (in the 1882 Hopi reservation) has generated research and writing, though most of it has been heavily biased in favor of the Navajo.[17] Several conferences have convened Hopi scholars, including the Tricentennial symposium in 1980 (commemorating the Pueblo Revolt),[18] a 1982 Advanced Seminar on "The Hopi Indians" at the School of American Research in Santa Fe,[19] and a number of major museum exhibits across the country and internationally.[20] A series of photographic projects[21] and full-length documentaries[22] have been undertaken since the 1970s. And Hopi filmmaker Victor Masayesva Jr.'s developing oeuvre has engaged numerous Hopi topoi.[23]

Para-ethnography on Hopi (see also Chapter 6)—often garnering a wider audience than the writings of anthropologists—has proliferated since the late nineteenth century. Better-known authors, from a variety of genres, include Charles Lummis (1958 [1903]), Aby Warburg (1939 [1923]), D. H. Lawrence (1924), Edward S. Curtis (1922), John Collier (1962), Frank Waters (1963), Peter Matthiessen (1984), Tony Hillerman (1982),[24] and Leslie Marmon Silko (1991). Popular art films (Godfrey Reggio's *Koyaanisqatsi* and *Powaqqatsi*) relocate simulated Hopi representations in a truly postmodern play of extraterritorial transmutations. The immediate antecedent for the latter is Waters's *Book of the Hopi*, probably the most widely selling book on Hopi culture, despite its notorious confabulation of fact and imagination (see A. Geertz 1983; McLeod 1994). Such popular materials have formed the basis of a virtual Hopi cult (Chapter 6), particularly among U.S. New Agers and in Germany (Kelly 1988).[25] In my first (preanthropological) trip to the Snake Dance in 1978, a fellow tourist assiduously pored over his Waters while waiting for the dance to come on; evidently Hopi was an already parsed culture, and any search for *this* Other came with its own how-to. At present (summer 1997), controversies—especially at Third Mesa over the publications of New Age savagist Thomas Mails (1996, 1996a)—reproduce a long-standing dislike for Waters's work in particular. The formal ethnographies, with their guild jargons, at least have the virtue of being less squarely in the public eye.

The social history of academic, intellectual, aesthetic, and popular interest in the Hopi by the metropolitan and the not-so-metropolitan West co-occurs with a continuous pattern of political and economic domination. This has occasionally been underwritten by coercive force:

The U.S. military's last visit in numbers was to Hotvela in 1911, though a pattern of local and long-distance incarcerations for cultural and political resistance was common into the 1940s (see, e.g., James 1974), including imprisonment of several Hotvela men in a federal penitentiary during World War II for refusing selective service. Hopis have not been silent on such matters, and there is a rich documentation of Hopi resistance and testimony on land encroachment and enforced culture change dating back more than a century (e.g., Whiteley 1989).

The proliferation of representations amid the overall context of national and world-system domination situates contemporary ethnography in a conjuncture that is intensively intertextual and political, and this conditions all interactions between Hopis and outside researchers. The desire in any writing, though ethnography has its own particularities on this account, is origination. Any latter-day ethnographer who seeks to claim new discursive ground on Hopi culture must attend—as well as to Hopi practices s/he observes and perspectives s/he learns—to the received panoply of texts on Hopi, which come freighted with multiple anthropological premises. My work is necessarily more revisionary than originary, but it attempts to engage Hopi analytical perspectives with an aim that is both restorative and corrective. The present volume cannot claim a Hopi viewpoint, but my principal concern is how Hopi perspectives, insofar as I understand them, construct, create, and constrain social life, and how these may most fruitfully be conjoined with social theory for a more fully intercultural mode of explanation. My argument is that for a variety of reasons, theoretical and pragmatic, analytical and political, anthropology needs to use local knowledge as local *theory*. The conscious conjunction of theory should aim toward *analytical* hybridity and cosmopolitanism, with intersubjective and intercultural approximation as the ultimate social goal. It is this sort of project that Arnold Krupat has dubbed "ethnocriticism"—an explicitly ethical scholarly engagement:

> Ultimately, ethnocriticsm, multiculturalism, and cosmopolitanism are all oriented toward materializing their values on the sociopolitical level, contributing to the possibility of institutionalizing . . . the polyvocal polity. (Krupat 1992:3-4)

For Krupat, ethnocriticism seeks "To alter or ambiguate Western narrative and explanatory categories. . . ." Putting this into practice requires:

Figure 1.4. *Tsu'tiikive,* the "Snake Dance." Walpi, 1897. Photograph by Ben Wittick. Tourists and ethnographic photographers at this ceremony became a major presence by the turn of the twentieth century, particularly at Walpi (see also Dilworth 1996). J. G. Bourke's *The Snake Dance of the Moquis of Arizona* (1884), the first ethnographic monograph on Hopi, was accompanied by several other accounts in popular monthly magazines. In the late 1880s, Ben Wittick began to commercialize Hopi ethnographic images, and was soon followed by numerous others, including A. C. Vroman, George Wharton James, Emory Kolb, F. H. Maude, and Edward S. Curtis. Library of Congress (LC-USZ62-101155).

> . . . real engagement with the epistemological and explanatory categories of Others, most particularly as these animate and impel Other narratives. The necessary sorts of movement, therefore, are not only those between dominant western paradigms but also those between western paradigms and the as-yet-to-be-named paradigms of the Rest.
> (Ibid.:113)

The primary paradigm I seek to put in play here is what I have elsewhere termed Hopi hermeneutics (Whiteley 1988). The play rests upon certain epistemological convictions, which, were it not for the madness of the postmodern moment, seem simple truisms that would be needless to state. The first is an existential realism about human social life. The second is a belief that language can indeed describe experience, both individual and collective. Those who regard "existence," "essence," and "experience" as *only* naturalized categories may now predictably yell "Naturalism!" and "Essentialism!", though such epistemic sloganeering is a shallow path of infinite regress. Third, cultural ideas are intersubjective in Wittgenstein's sense and they get expressed and acted upon in objectively describable social practices. Fourth, this intersubjectivity must—because of irrefutable species conditions of Homo sapiens sapiens—be potentially extensible across linguistic barriers; in short, just as there can be no private language, I am suggesting that there can be no private culture, whose key saliences and engagements are de jure incommunicable to others. I believe that forms of Hopi understanding can be effectively rendered into English (if the rendering is sufficiently attentive and sensitive), ultimately because I reject a solipsism of culture as much as a solipsism of the self. Now, this raises all sorts of questions about what a "unitary," "bounded" "culture" might be, and such questions have in recent years largely obviated the use of culture in this located, "village-based" sense (Clifford 1997:21). Anthropologists have lately been targeting formally identical questions at the "self" (often guided, even if not consciously, by the influence of Lacan [1966-71]): what its "borders" are, that it can have no "essence," that it is unstable and shifting—like signification itself—and fundamentally that the conception of unitariness is Western ideology and is decidedly *not* shared by the Rest.[26] And while there may be "people without culture" and certainly are "people between cultures" (Rosaldo 1989), the general idea of, say, Hopi culture, seems to correspond well with an identifiable complex of ideas and practices with persistent cores of meaning—amidst transformations, reproductions, and changes—that a particular group of people claims for its own, and associates with a distinctive language, form of social dwelling, history, and territory. While diaspora, transnationalism, and deterritorialization militate against a holist view of culture, this should not require that the model, as paradigmatic, be jettisoned, rather than qualified and resituated.

My main point in analogizing "culture" to "self" is that inasmuch as the intersubjectivity of discourse vitiates the possibility for a genuinely private language, incommunicable even in principle to others, the intersubjectivity of cultural ideas fundamentally implicates the necessary conditions (if not the sufficient ones) of intertranslatablity. For effective translation, which remains the overriding contribution of anthropology, we need to find, to paraphrase Clifford Geertz, the right locutions for their logic (see Chapter 3). But to deny that this is possible, for fear of being accused of the cardinal postmodern sins of naturalism and essentialism, leads ultimately to a requirement that certain human beings be excluded from the species. For reasons epistemological and pragmatic, political and moral, as well as from the simple fact of interpersonal experience,[27] I am not prepared to do this, no matter how sophisticated antireferentialist treatments (surely, like so many deconstructive moves, a practical oxymoron) of language may have become.

ESTRANGEMENT

Despite the marked increase in formal attention to situated perspectives, especially via the influence of Native American critics like Vine Deloria Jr., and Gerald Vizenor, and more lately by postcolonial interventions (at least those of metropolitan academics like Spivak, Said, Bhabha, or Trinh),[28] much anthropological writing seems ever more estranged from the lives of textualized subjects (cf. Spiro 1996). Indeed some anthropologists actively argue for this estrangement as a guarantor of disciplinary seriousness. (Hastrup 1995, for example, makes the case that "Native anthropology" is a "contradiction in terms," and she privileges an elite anthropological discourse cloistered from its subjects' critical engagements.)[29] Earlier in the century, anthropology's fledgling entry into the academy was marked by a strenuous discursive emulation of hypothetico-deductive natural sciences. Radcliffe-Brown's program for kinship studies will serve as an example:

> In the study of social institutions such as the study of kinship, the theoretical social anthropologist regards any particular social system as supplying him with a body of factual material which he can use for formulating or testing theory. But on the other side theoretical knowledge can be used to give an understanding of the features of some particular system. In the light of the general theoretical knowledge that has resulted from the comparative study of societies of diverse types the scientist may undertake the analysis of a particular system so that any single feature is seen in its relation to other features of that system and in its place in the system as a whole. The value and validity of any such study of a particular system will obviously depend on the extent and soundness of the general theoretical concepts by which it is directed. (Radcliffe-Brown 1950:3)

At present, the balance of discipline envy has shifted to the continental literary/philosophical arena. Anthropologists tendentiously ape the involutions of oracular Parisian theory (cf. Leach 1982:56)—by spotting everywhere deterritorializations, simulacra, incommensurabilities, nomad thoughts, double movements, and the like—which, whatever else they may be, are drastically under-informed by attendance to the lived perspectives of people outside global metropoles. So, a current star of the anthropological firmament, Vincent Crapanzano, refigures the antihumanistic prose of Radcliffe-Brown in a postmodern register:

> Insofar as the self is an arrested moment in a continuous dialectical movement, and insofar as such arrested moments depend upon language, the constitution of "self" requires a guarantor of meaning, or at least of the conventions of meaning, a Third, that permits, within limits, the play of desire. It is not a real or imaginary being but a function that can be embodied in real or imaginary beings, in king or fetish, in even their anatomical parts (the eye, for example, in Victor Hugo's "La Conscience" . . .), indeed, in conscience itself. More abstractly, the function of the Third may be symbolized by such notions as the law, convention, reason, culture, tradition, language, or tact. It may be conceived as the (absent) interlocutor in those silent but forceful secondary, or shadow, dialogues that accompany any primary dialogue. . . . The institutionalization, ritualization, and internalization of the representations—the embodiments and symbolizations—of the Third mask their instability and project an illusory stability that is now perhaps shaken in our "post-modern" era. The representations of the guarantor of meaning are themselves implicated in the dialectical play of desire, convention and resistance, becoming the ultimate stake in the negotiations between ego and alter. Who has the fetish has the power! (Crapanzano 1992:93)

The use value of this kind of analytics, like much postmodernism, lies principally in an intellectual aestheticism that encloses a hermetic sphere of academic endeavor (cf. Spiro 1996). And however brilliant its surfaces, these glitter at the expense of increasing, and increasingly problematic, alienation from the subjects of its study.[30]

There are of course exceptions to disengaged solipsism and alienating prose forms in contemporary academic ethnography that still have important general arguments to make.[31] And productive counters to elitist theory disengaged from the world are found in practicing or applied anthropology, which must continually embrace the moral as well as the intellectual side of the ethnographic endeavor (e.g., Reed

1997).[32] Yet the project of an "ethnotheory" that honors the locally conceptualized continues to be elusive; Basso (1996) or Tsing (1993) may well come closest to this. Certainly my own language here is partly in the jargon of disciplinary anthropology (though I have written for other purposes in different registers; e.g., 1988a, 1989, 1992). My aim, however, is to conjoin this with a closer approximation of Hopi conceptions, so that these enter more nearly into, in order to transform, critical social theory. To requote Barth (see Chapter 3):

> We should capitalize on our unique advantage: that our "object of study" can help us actively to transcend our categories by teaching us their own. This means recognizing that the actors' categories provide a way to understand reality, *as well as* being part of that reality. In practice, probably most of the productivity of the anthropologist derives from this source, even though his arrogance as a professional academic, and his defensiveness when his *own* reality is being threatened by the enchanted world of another culture, both militate against such learning. (Barth 1981:9–10)

THE ETHNOGRAPHER AND THE FIELD: A SORT OF LIFE (WITH APOLOGIES TO GRAHAM GREENE)

It may be relevant to state some of the terms of my own conjuncture, both with anthropology and specifically with fieldwork. I do so with some ambivalence: the authorial self foregrounded in recent ethnographic writing obviates dry abstraction with autobiographical detail and local color in often salutary ways. But the authored self is as much a puppet as the "ventriloquist's dummies" of self-declared dialogical ethnography. And the attendant confessionals frequently occupy a plane of profundity more in keeping with Adrian Mole than with Augustine. What do reflexive ethnographers *not* tell us about their motivations, feelings, personal histories, fieldwork experiences, inchoate immediate or long-term doubts, and structured positionalities? What do they *not know* about themselves? The apparent ease of introducing the ethnographer as self into the text is, beyond style, more problematic than has been openly imagined.

I began as an undergraduate in anthropology in 1972, the year before Talal Asad's landmark *Anthropology and the Colonial Encounter* was published. At that time, anthropology was far more marginal in British public consciousness than it was in that of the United States. I discovered social anthropology at Cambridge, happily imagining a broader exposure to different cultural realities than the more Eurocentric disciplines offered. Like many undergraduates, I was disappointed by theoretical obfuscation of intercultural dialogue to a largely self-referential discourse of abstracted cultural distillations and reified ideas, of which particular cultures were largely instantiations. While I look back now with nostalgia at Meyer Fortes's lectures on Kariera kinship, at the time (and my vision certainly had its callow elements) anthropological theory seemed more obstacle than means to humanist curiosity in global peoples. The potential of anthropology to open gates and build bridges seemed stifled by a formalism that reduced the vitality and agency of its subjects to structural automata. That the British school insisted upon a commonsensical social empiricism and skepticism—in frequently voiced contradistinction to French cerebralism on the one hand, and North American ideal/material naturalisms, on the other— was hardly the sufficient antecedent to an intercultural meeting of the minds (although such empiricism and skepticism make for an important and necessary recognition of a shared human condition—abandoned by postmodernists—that still informs my anthropological imagination).

But disappointment was accompanied by increasing intellectual fascination, especially in Edmund Leach's lectures on structuralism and Christianity, a tradition I had been rather vaguely raised in. In my final year (1974-75)—and somewhat against the Cambridge grain (which tended to sneer at its culturalism)—I picked up Clifford Geertz's *The Interpretation of Cultures* and was elated that here at last was the combination of imaginative sweep, humanistic orientation, and philosophical focus on lived sociocultural experience that I sought. While sympathetic to some streams in the torrent of recent criticism of Geertz, I remain, in part, an unrepentant Geertzian interpretivist (see Chapter 3, especially), particularly via the subsequent influence of Alfonso Ortiz. In retrospect, the main influences on my own anthropological thinking began to crystallize at this point: British structuralism and sociological empiricism (with an unapologetic Giddensian realism), Lévi-Straussian structuralism especially as mediated by Leach, Geertzian interpretivism and symbolic anthropology, as well as an abiding interest in philosophy of mind and action.

I chose graduate school at the University of New Mexico for several reasons: access to cultural (contra social) anthropology; because it was a little unorthodox, but with a strong reputation; and for its location in a sociocultural and geographical environment that intrigued me.

Though I scarcely knew of his work hitherto (I planned initially to undertake fieldwork in Amazonia), I quickly fell under the spell of Alfonso Ortiz, whose dual embodiment of scholastic brilliance and Pueblo identity, and his vigorous defense of an ethically engaged anthropology, were very persuasive forces.[33] Alfonso's direct introduction of students to Pueblo ritual performances—at Jemez, San Felipe, and San Ildefonso, for example—opened a window onto a world that remains a personal fascination. As he liked to put it, here you could catch your anthropology "on the hoof," not as some disembodied textual reduction of people distantly removed (and, ipso facto, exoticized) from the more metropolitan universities. This, amid a cultural and political balance in the general composition of the New Mexican populace—Hispanic, Indian, and Anglo[34]—rendered the anthropological study of culture relevant and vital, and genuinely dialogical, unlike the pragmatically otiose British model. But the offer of a prestigious grant took me in 1978 to Oxford University with plans to undertake fieldwork in Amazonia. The sense of culture shock, both generic, after life in the rough-hewn tricultural democracy of New Mexico, and academic, in terms of an elitist scholasticism, was profound—clearly, any imagined sense of self I might have accumulated as a true-blue British expatriate was delusionary. The Institute of Social Anthropology[35] reproduced the same fractured, para-imperial imagination of the Other (Barbara Pym's [1955] delicious novel of social crisis in anthropology (see Epilogue)—three decades before it became one in the discipline—is especially evocative in this regard) that my experience in New Mexico seemed to have irreversibly displaced. And for me, personally, the displacement turned out indeed not to be reversible.

Throughout 1977 and 1978, fledged from Ortiz's guiding hand, I had followed the Corn and Saint's Day dances around the Rio Grande Pueblos, visiting all and becoming gradually more comfortable as attentive, hopefully polite tourist, invited to eat at Pueblo tables, and learning a little of Pueblo mores. This still seemed more cultural tourism than ethnography (the line is inevitably blurred—see Chapter 6), but it was becoming an increasing addiction. About a week prior to my return to England, I went to the Third Mesa Hopi village of Hotvela for the Snake Dance, and was, like so many before, absolutely transfixed.[36]

I arrived at dawn, and after the zigzagging Snake race from five miles out in the Dinnebito Valley, I waited all day for the dance to come on. I had not bothered to read available accounts, simply seeking the experience without preconception as far as possible. The tourist presence built throughout the day, gradually swelling to dwarf Hotvela's tiny plaza. Around four o'clock in the afternoon, while I was still glued to the spot staked out eight hours earlier, the Snake and Antelope societies emerged from their kivas into performance. The depth of their seriousness, the intensity of inward concentration, was utterly palpable. My own presence and that of other tourists faded from relevance: This was no commodified spectacle of the exotic for a conjunctural American audience; its profound religiosity was tangible, sensible. Within half an hour of the dance (which lasts about forty-five minutes), a soft rain began to fall from a sky that had been burningly cloudless throughout the day.

The memory of this, and the rest of my quasi-ethnographic experiences in New Mexico, confronted an Oxford of antihumanistic sterility and explorer Othering of its subject I could no longer endure. And from my earlier background, Oxford anthropology seemed pathetically out of step with contemporary Britain. I grew up in Leicester, a provincial city in the industrial Midlands, surrounded by a rural county known principally for foxhunting and Stilton cheese. Difference was largely a matter of class, local allegiance, and town versus country, until the 1960s when the urban population was transformed by substantial South Asian and West Indian immigration. Ethnic and racial difference, while on the fringes of my teenage consciousness, was largely remote from my experience: I was sixteen when the first lone black pupil was admitted to my exclusive high school. But the working world—of factories, shops, and farm labor—which I entered intermittently from my midteens on, increasingly opened up a more heterogeneous reality that was a frank relief from the parochial tedium of lower middle-class white life in a provincial British suburb. Conformity meant management-track employment in a bank or office, joining the Conservative club and the Anglican Church, and dancing to apolitical Motown at the local discothèque. Unlike the young Graham Greene, suburban boredom never tempted me to Russian roulette. My own way of escape was via American blues music and mild soccer hooliganism (almost unrecognizable from the harsher violence that developed later), running against rival packs of teenage hoodlums from Manchester United, Nottingham Forest, and the like. They were tougher towns: We usually lost. Controlled doses of ethnic and working-class difference thus offered an attractive tonic to the mundane "learning-to-manage" (borrowing from Paul Willis 1977) paradigm of provincial, lower-middle, white socialization. When, after Cambridge, I spent a year as a milkman and delivery driver in some shabbier corners of East End and northeast London—multiracial, largely working-class, and polyglot— what had been the exotic evolved into consociate experience. Jamaican, London Jewish, as well as white Protestant bosses; Gujarati, Nigerian, and cockney coworkers; and nights "down the pub" in a largely amicable, sometimes frayed, multiracial mix (this was reggae capital Stoke Newington, Hackney, and pre-yuppie Islington, not skinhead East Ham or Millwall)—all of which gradually became for me the natural model of British society. And this contrasted not only with my own largely monochromatic childhood, but strongly also, to get back to the point, with the evident imperialist nostalgia of Oxford's anthropology.

At New Mexico, too, I had been exposed to plural scholarship, where politically naive constructions of anthropological interest—in American Indians, especially—were forever subverted. As Elizabeth Grobsmith puts this (referring to Vine Deloria's celebrated critique in *Custer Died for Your Sins*): "Those of us 'raised on Deloria' have had built into our knowledge of our discipline issues of ethics and morality, legality and propriety, jurisdiction and self-determination" (Grobsmith 1997:45). I was "raised" more directly on Ortiz than Deloria in this regard, but the ethical implications were equally clear; their respective moral positions vis-à-vis anthropology differed, I always felt, more in angles of vision than in substance.

I resolved to return to the University of New Mexico and attempt to work at Hopi—a perilous route for two reasons: first, the well-known Pueblo antipathy to anthropologists. Second, within the preferred terms of the discipline, this was neither "overseas" nor "virgin territory" but an overworked vein, hardly the ground for inscribing a career-minded innovation.[37] Neither factor was sufficiently dissuasive.

Beginning with *Powamuy*, "Bean Dance," in February 1980, I began to make the two-hundred-fifty-mile trip to Hopi from Albuquerque every weekend I could. With an introduction from Fred Eggan to Eugene Sekaquaptewa, who served as a sort of cultural broker for many outsiders, I ended up at a gathering in Paaqavi, where several older people discussed (with periodic translations for my benefit) their chagrin at the passing of traditional knowledge, and how valuable a written history would be. The proverbial lightbulb soon flashed, and a short while later I presented a proposal to the village's governing body to write such a history for my doctoral dissertation. It was debated and submitted to a village-wide survey. Three months later I was invited to move into the village. Initial progress was slow; I worked every day on the language and on a historical household census with Herschel Talashoma, a Badger clan man then in his forties, who is an expert storyteller with a superb knowledge of oral history, and who had worked with other academics. Otherwise, moments of partial inclusion within Hopi sociality (though I strove, and still strive, to avoid wannabe-ism)—the most poignant for me was being singled out for presentation with special, colored *piiki*, "wafer bread" by an *Angaktsina*, "Long-Hair Kachina" during a Home Dance—were brief interludes in an overall experience of marginalization and exclusion. Older people typically averted their eyes or looked through me, pointedly not noticing my presence; when they did acknowledge me, it was usually in the form of a lightly parodic, "hail fellow, well met" simulacrum of the way white people often condescendingly relate to Indians in the border towns of Winslow, Flagstaff, and Holbrook.

Harry Kewanimptewa, a septuagenarian Spider clan man, who had long been involved with village leadership, was recommended as very knowledgeable, but he had been ill in hospital and I was advised to wait. He also had something of a curmudgeonly reputation. When, after he returned home, I went over to his house, he was overtly hostile: "We don't want any white men in this village. What are you doing here? You should just get out of here. Go and see David Monongye; he likes white people."[38] I explained the history project, which, despite the village survey, he showed no knowledge of. "Well, my daughter's going to college, why can't she do it? We don't want any white men around here. You're just going to make a lot of money off your book." Even then, there was a glint in his eye, and he seemed to telegraph that he was testing my resolve, although this was by no means clear. Later on I learned that he possessed a virtually clairvoyant capacity (culturally celebrated and highly valued) to anticipate precisely my thinking at the opening of a new encounter; I would go to see him, for, say, the first time in a week, with some specific questions in mind, and before we had completed the pleasantries, he would begin to address some of those specific questions. I have no desire to fetishize or exoticize here, but this was something about him and some other, particularly older, Hopis that I have experienced repeatedly and am unable to explain rationally.

Three weeks after the first abortive meeting, I was walking past his house. He called me over gruffly to help pitch hay from a horse trailer with his grandson, and later on he took me out to his ranch and began to talk in an extraordinary variety of registers. Thus began a relationship that (even though he passed on in 1985 and other relationships have been significantly longer and more fully socially inclusive) remains a central model of my Hopi education. He was acutely intelligent, a purist profoundly committed to underlying Hopi values (not in the throwaway form of some of the more popularized Traditionalists), about which he was deeply knowledgeable. He was an acerbic, equal-opportunity critic of U.S. domination, white mores, and Hopi individuals who failed to live up to the rigorous demands of Hopi ethics.[39] He had some trouble with English, and, like many men of his generation, associated this with the sting of his own incapacity (a perception reinforced by the denigrating regime of Sherman Institute, the BIA Boarding School in Riverside, California, where he spent six years), rather than triumphal resistance to hegemony, in the way that younger anthropologists and Native studies scholars sometimes like to imagine. His English, however, was a great deal better than my incipient Hopi. We evolved a bicultural dialogue that brought understanding progressively nearer; he drew upon English analogs, frequently social or biblical,[40] as I slowly became better at locating Hopi ones. He talked about a lot of issues in Hopi history; his father, Kuwannömtiwa, had led the second split of Orayvi to found Paaqavi, and, on his mother's side, as Spider clan heir, Harry had been initiated into the Blue Flute society as assistant to his aged uncle, Lomahongiwma, principal leader of Orayvi's Hostiles before Yukiwma. He attached his narratives to *places,* and he started to take me to important sites,[41] both local and distant, to situate their particular saliences: like Walpi, where we were cordially greeted by his clan mother, the Flute clan matriarch, who remembered his visits from half a century before in company with his father—a diplomatic intermediary between villages and the Indian Agency; Orayvi, where we received a brusque reception from the then *Kikmongwi,* "village chief," who announced that he did not want any more books, after the trouble caused by *Book of the Hopi;* Songoopavi, where Harry's Bear and Bluebird clan relatives were both hospitable and tutelary, situating contemporary events in relation to mythological antecedents; Kawestima (Betatakin and Keet Seel), the planned destination of the Fire and Spider clan people who left Orayvi at the split; Pisisvayu, the Colorado River, of manifold cultural and religious significance to Hopis; Ganado, the site of a Walpi battle with Navajos that led to the establishment of a boundary, by the public placement of skulls and Navajo presentation of a *tiiponi,* "palladium," to mark their good-faith negotiation (the boundary is long since transgressed by Navajo immigrants into Hopi land, though many Hopis continue to remember it); and so on. I drove, Harry talked—and talked, until he thought I had understood. He talked flat fact and traditional prophecy, though with a wry mysticism that was anything but credulous. "Do you believe it?" he would challenge. On some counts, he was a skeptic, "X is going over to Grand Canyon to find the real *sipaapuni* ["place of emergence"]; he's not going to find it—that's all symbolic."[42]

My relations with other individuals and families broadened throughout the year, especially via agricultural work. This was the domain of Hopi practice, mostly male, that was and remains the most socially carefree; when a Hopi man goes to his field, he can forget the trials and tribulations of small-town life surrounded by the irresistible demands of kin, and engage in a praxis that is fundamentally defining of individual male existence: The field's product is one's *natwani,* the exterior reflection of one's inner intentionalities, a frame of the self's autonomy and pleasure in work. In countless episodes, I have probably learned more of what it means to be Hopi from hoeing weeds, setting traps, and thinning clumps in cornfields—and from the talk while all this is going on—than from the myriad ceremonial events I have had the good fortune to attend, although these remain defining moments of Hopi religious and aesthetic sensibility.

Personal relationships in such contexts mean a great deal to me and undergird the ethnographic observations and analyses appearing in the following chapters. But I hesitate to venture further into these in print, even though textualizing personal experience with Other subjectivities has become the mode in ethnographic writing. There are two reasons. First and foremost, because the Hopi individuals in question would not welcome it (Harry Kewanimptewa, I believe, would not have minded what I have said, though *his* perspective on *me* would have made a nice counterpoint): It would breach the delicate fabric of privacy, dignity, and trust that is vital if I am to be regarded, at base, a friend as much as an interloper (the latter is occasionally made abundantly clear when I inadvertently cross certain lines). One of the reasons I sought to work at Hopi was that I was fundamentally interested in a long-term relationship, including repeat visits that would mark a more lasting engagement, and *moral* as well as intellectual commitment. Alfonso Ortiz and Keith Basso, each in his own way, served as models in this regard, and I remain uneasy with the Oxbridge (among others) model of the explorer-academic parachuting in to a local community, only to return to the ivory tower after serving the requisite term of exotic interaction.

The second reason I eschew textual reflexivism and personalization past a certain point is that, partly from my British training (a tradition strongly upheld in graduate school particularly via the influence of Harry Basehart and Louise Lamphere), I retain an abiding interest in the forms and processes of social life, together with a basic referentialist credo that these can be represented discursively. Too much recent narrative ethnography lapses into narcissism or romanticism, and far from genuinely humanizing its subjects, crafts them into textual puppets that dance to the tune of the ethnographer as auteur.

Some of the most productive sessions of my earlier fieldwork involved senior men and women in colloquy, discussing aspects of the past, both memorate and traditionally narrated. In these sessions, and in many individual conversations, a Hopi theory of society and history began to emerge via political discourses on leadership and a philosophy of action involving—as central elements—planning, intending, and conscious prosecution. Attribution of events, like the Orayvi split, to the decision-bound actions of leaders, endowed Hopi history and praxis with an overarching sense of deliberacy. Increasingly, I realized that a single text for village history and dissertation would be impossible: The clash of local and global demands was too great. So I wrote two texts (subsequently published as 1988a, 1988b). For the external world, Hopi history required situating in Hopi social and cultural contexts, and above all in its constituted historicity. Assessing the dynamics of Hopi social structure, political leadership, senses of the self, aesthetics, and the interpenetration of culture and nature became crucial for a cultural historiography that would remain true, insofar as possible, to its source. It is to this same situating of the Hopi historical and social imagination that the present essays collectively tend.

Keith Basso has commented regarding recent anthropological attention to other histories that a principal question, rarely addressed adequately, concerns *whose* historical imagination is being pondered: "Ethnographers, to be sure, must worry long and hard about how *they* imagine history . . . , but they must also try to discern how history gets imagined by the people whom they study." Basso concludes that historicities may be sufficiently different as to be "incompatible and even irreconcilable" (Basso 1996:154–55). Though somewhat haphazardly, this may also be a lesson emerging from the Sahlins-Obeyesekere debate (e.g., Obeyesekere 1992; Sahlins 1995; Borofsky 1997). With regard to Hopi history-making, my argument is that ethnography, as at base a medium of translation between constituted orders of meaning and experience, should work to establish the salient terms of Hopi historical imagination. As Basso incisively demonstrates for the Apache, points of irreconcilability can then be more identifiably situated within a fabric of what *can* be approximated, reconciled, and hopefully understood. It is toward such cultural approximation that this work, the cumulative result of my own thinking about the Hopi historical, social, and moral imagination, is aimed.

After the initial fourteen months of fieldwork, I continued to visit Hopi periodically. From 1983 to 1985, while working in Flagstaff, I again rented the house in Paaqavi where I had stayed during my earlier fieldwork. This remains one of my favorite images of dwelling in Hopi space.[43] Inside, the walls were whitewashed adobe covering rough-hewn sandstone; outside, the back wall was built about four feet deep into the earth, to make the house "cool in summer, warm in winter." The floor was pounded earth with a much-worn linoleum covering. It had cold running water and an old potbelly stove, but that was the extent of the amenities (unless you count the mice, for which I had to import a fearsome feline from Songoopavi). The roof was the old-fashioned kind: roughly trimmed pine beams overlain by rabbitbrush beneath a layer of clay, with smaller cut pine branches spaced to keep the brush from falling. It had been built by "Nice Man" Masahongniwa (see Simmons 1942:passim), and now belonged to his granddaughter. Nice Man was a *pas tsu'wungwa*, "*real* Snake clan man," and a *kwaani'ytaqa*, "One-Horn society man," who used to perform his ritual obligations solo, after other initiates had ceased public processions around the village. He was also a *tsu'wimkya*, "Snake society initiate," from Orayvi, before moving to Paaqavi at the split. They say that after Nice Man died, a rattlesnake was found in the house, and refused to leave. Munzro, an old Snake man from the north side of town (whom I knew in his declining years), had to be called in to persuade the rattler it was time to go. Some of Nice Man's house prayer-feathers were still attached to the nutbrown rabbitbrush. Waking up to that ceiling gave a sense of being within productively engaged, but not disfigured, nature—a light touch of the deliberate aesthetics of Hopi praxis, which carefully constructs woodpiles and stone-house villages in resemblance of the natural landscape. The villages on the mesa tops, like Walpi or Musangnuvi, evince one aspect of this; at first it is hard to tell where the mesa ends and the house walls begin.

I returned to Nice Man's house as often as I could from 1983 to 1985, and then in 1985 for two uninterrupted months of research on ethnogeography.[44] Since then, I have visited Hopi every year, except for

1993 and 1994, for a month or two, but the major context of my ethnography has shifted further into practice. In 1988 I was called to work as an expert witness on the 1934 Reservation case, a long-term legal contest between Hopis and Navajos for areas outside the boundaries of the 1882 Hopi Reservation (where most of the land disputes have centered). In 1991 I was asked to prepare an ethnohistoric and ethnographic report for water rights adjudication, which is still in negotiation. This contracted work, where I was not funded by an outside research agency, but directly by the Hopi Tribe or the federal government underwriting the Tribe's interest, has been congenial because of its explicit application of anthropological knowledge to a context determined socially useful by local interests.

Much of this fieldwork, on contemporary and historic land-use patterns—farming, grazing, foraging, and religious use—has been unerringly routine: walking canyon fields, visiting stock tanks and ranch houses, examining distant cattle corrals, sorting through dust-caked files in a woeful Nissen hut outbuilding of the Tuba City BIA Agency, charting locations for gathering colored sands, and so on, though some of the more recent work on religious uses has been highly interesting. My earlier fieldwork had been mostly confined to Third Mesa, with occasional visits to First and Second Mesas (particularly for ceremonies) and conversations with *kyavakvit,* "members of other villages." The 1934 case has involved extensive work at all the villages, and the level of cooperation has been extraordinary given the sensitivity of some of the information; indeed this demonstrates the degree of felt jeopardy to Hopi traditional sites as a result of Navajo encroachment. While the material generated is restricted from publication, it has significantly deepened my understanding of Hopi social forms in relation to a vitally continuing religious system. Again, in contrast to current theoretical celebrations of hybridity, borders, transnationalisms, and collages of the traditional and the modern, an autonomously Hopi cultural life is strongly persistent and profoundly vigorous. Although there are shifts of meaning occurring for some Hopis —away from the religious per se, for example, toward a more aestheticized engagement in cultural praxis—ritual performance remains largely *un*transformed into a commoditized register and continuingly instrumental on its own terms. Indeed, it is because of the persistence of traditional commitment that the crisis of Hopi springs and water supplies (Chapter 7) is as much a *cultural* as a natural resource issue.

The following essays thus draw upon field and archival research extending over sixteen years from 1980 to 1996; the fieldwork itself now totals a little less than three years. Chapters 2 and 3—on clanship and polity—were based on research and conversations from 1980 to 1985. Chapters 4 and 5—on personal names and altar-burning—include a longer period, 1985 to 1991. Chapter 6—on representations—adds experiences from the second phase of the 1934 case, and was written while I was on sabbatical from Sarah Lawrence College in 1992. Chapter 7, on water, draws upon experiences through 1996, including work for the Hopi Water Resources Program (1996) and as a consultant on the BBC film *The Hopi Way* (1995).

My own position on circulating Hopi images (see above) is as follows. I remain committed to an ideal of intercultural dialogue. For that to lead to the transformation of inequalities constructed around cultural and racial difference, it is crucial for intercultural knowledge to continue to circulate. Until Native Americans are genuinely humanized in the national society's consciousness, and cease to be stereotypically oblated in various ways, the likelihood of genuine social equality and cultural pluralism is slim. I believe that anthropological knowledge—as Alfonso Ortiz underscores (Chapter 6)—can be used "humanely and ethically." Edward Said's position on criticism can well guide anthropology toward explicitly ethical engagement: "Criticism must think of itself as life-enhancing and constitutively opposed to every form of tyranny, domination, and abuse; its social goals are noncoercive knowledge produced in the interests of human freedom" (Said 1983:29).[45]

Likewise, Abbott Sekaquaptewa—a highly sophisticated Hopi politician, with a passionate commitment to the defense of Hopi interests[46]—addressing ethnographic publication on Hopi, put it this way: "so long as it positively enhances their lives, their understanding." (His is the anonymous voice that is identically quoted in Chapter 6.) He associated this with the ethical commitment Hopis incurred at emergence to spread the beneficial effects of their teachings, an aim reproduced in ritual practice and intended to benefit all life, including all kinds of human beings, rather than Hopis alone.

If the social goals Said and Sekaquaptewa identify are to be approximated, any barriers constructed around knowledge must be established with great care so that their aim to protect does not lead to oppression, either within Hopi society, or, reactively, from agencies of the dominant society. Again, Said (1983:290) argues against discourse that serves "'as an agent of closure, shutting off human investigation, criticism, and effort' to achieve understanding" (in Krupat 1989:11). But borrowing authority from a leading postcolonial scholar to support my own view will not easily settle the problem of "speaking for Others" (Chapter 6). Clearly, I am speaking here also for *myself,* and as a white male ensconced in a college setting, I am as open to the charge that I am expropriating Hopi images for my own gain, an intellectual form of "whiteshamanism" (e.g., Rose 1992), perhaps, as any other non-Native anthropologist. Elizabeth Cook-Lynn's (1997) position on this, which calls for an identitarian Native reappropriation of Native studies from white academic colonists, is hardly sympathetic to mine. Such arguments, as Arnold Krupat (1996) has lucidly argued, entail a double-bind: White scholars cannot be asked to simultaneously learn from Native knowledge and stay away from Native studies. Against this double bind, all I can do is proclaim good faith and hope to demonstrate through my writings the virtue of intercultural understanding as a necessary condition for plural social equity.

With a continuous pattern of disrespectful intrusions into private areas of Hopi life, especially religious, however, restrictions on the circulation of some knowledge are eminently reasonable. My circulation of Hopi images attempts to steer clear of private matters, while trying to give a sense of the depth, nuance, and complexity of Hopi thought and practice that will serve the ultimate goal of understanding recommended by Said.

STRUCTURES OF INTERPRETATION

"Structure"—that well-worn, still slippery term—is a key analytical metaphor in this book. My sense is significantly informed by Sahlins (e.g., 1985), that is, I see "structure" as an order of cultural value and protocol received from the past and engaging action via events. It is encompassing, "total" in Mauss's sense, including the social order, the natural order, phenomenology, metaphysics, and cosmology; it proposes modes of interpretation, assignments of cause and effect, the terms of explanation, and the forms of art. It is then a realist and holist view of structure that emphasizes its systematicity; it is not a constructivist view (Lloyd 1993). With the partial exception (and implications) of some of Lévi-Strauss's remarks, more encompassing, more culturally attentive notions of structure have largely been neglected in Hopi anthropology in favor of principally sociocentric versions, and of these, especially the Durkheim/Radcliffe-Brown sort, via the work of Fred Eggan and his students.[47] Several of the essays that follow include some arguments with Fred's landmark *Social Organization of the Western Pueblos,* one of a handful of truly indispensable anthropological works of the twentieth century. But Fred was an avowed and unregretting structural-functionalist, with both the virtues and limitations this approach entails. The limitations fundamentally have to do with explanatory adequacy—in the scientific sense—for Hopi ideas and practices.[48]

An exception to sociocentric ethnographers is someone whose work has largely fallen by the wayside in the historical canon of Hopi anthropology: Laura Thompson. Building on the inchoate, sometimes intractable but penetrating insights of Whorf into the Hopi language, as well as systematic culture-and-personality research, Thompson articulated a sense of Hopi worldview and metaphysics that, while idealized and somewhat problematic in its political context (see above), comes closest to my sense of structure—both abstractly and empirically. It also comes considerably closer to Hopi conceptions than other anthropological systemizations of Hopi thought and practice. Thompson's work was criticized, especially by materialists (e.g., Manners 1952, Clemmer 1995), and the Hopi part of the multitribe Indian Personality project has virtually disappeared from the discipline's collective memory.[49] Thompson's holistic notion of "structure" appears as immanent "cosmic Law," a conception much influenced by Kluckhohn's (e.g., 1944) "pattern assemblages" and "covert" or "implicit" culture, uniting conceptions of nature, society, and causality:[50]

> The Hopi conceive the cosmos as a complex, ordered structure regulated by an inherent logical Principle. According to Hopi ideology, all phenomena relevant to Hopi life—including man, the animals and plants, the earth, sun, moon, and clouds, the ancestors and the spirits— are interdependent through an innate, dynamic Law. According to this Law, the various orders and suborders of the over-all universal scheme work together for the common weal by exchanging values or services, which are essentially equivalent but not identical. (Thompson 1945:540-41)

This ideal whole is composed of interdependent "higher orders" linking humanity with nature and transecting empirical classification:

> Such a higher order, for example, may include a group of men related by kinship (namely, a clan), a species of animals, of birds, of plants, or supernatural beings, of elements, etc. It also may have other attributes, such as direction, color, sex, etc. These century-long established, cross-

classified higher orders may be thought of as forming a sort of super-society which functions as a universal nature-man cooperative. They form the backbone of the system of interdependent relationships which gives basic structure to the universe. (Ibid.:541)

Thompson clearly perceives a dialectic, in Hopi consciousness, between structure and individual action:

In this system each individual—human and non-human—has its proper place in relation to all the other phenomena and each has a definite role in the cosmic order. The scheme does not operate mechanically, however, on account of the special role played by man. Whereas, according to Hopi theory, the non-human universe is controlled automatically by the reciprocity Principle,[51] man is a responsible agent who may or may not completely fulfill his function in it. . . . [M]an has a margin of choice and also man has the power to elicit response. Indeed the Hopi believe not only that man can positively affect the functioning of the external world of nature to a limited extent, but that in the measure that he fails to do so, the harmonious functioning of the universe will be impaired. . . .

Moreover . . . to be effective [in relation to nature], man must participate in the universal scheme not only at the overt behavioral level—that is, by performing certain rites at prescribed intervals in certain ways—but he must participate also at the emotional and ideational levels—that is, by a concentration of his psychical energy on praying or willing. In the Hopi language, the word for "to pray" also means "to will."[52] . . . The individual's success in life, the welfare of the tribe, and to a certain extent the smooth functioning of the whole cosmic order, depend on man's carrying out the rules, in cooperation with his non-human partners, wholeheartedly and with an effort of the will.

Hopi traditional philosophy, therefore, ascribes to man a purposive, creative role in the universe, a role which is dependent on the development of his volition. The universe is . . . a harmonious, integrated system operating on the principle of immanent justice, and in it the key role is played by man's will. (Ibid.:541-42)

And again:

To the Hopi, as to modern psychiatry, man is a complex psycho-physiological whole. Moreover, the Hopi believe that each individual is a responsible agent through the creative development of his will, and Hopi interest in the whole man centers in the psychophysiological development of the will. Man is a sculptor who can mold himself from within.

This assumption is the basic adjusive and generative postulate of their cosmogony. (Ibid.:543-44)

But Thompson does not imagine a free market of individual egotists, and "dividual" sociality—in Marilyn Strathern's (1988) sense—is centrally present:

> The Hopi's ideal is to live, to the utmost of his powers, for society as envisaged in Hopi terms—i.e., the pueblo unit composed of groups of human beings in association with their non-human partners, interacting correlatively in fulfillment of the Law. And hence one who approaches most nearly the ideal would be the individual who is most completely socialized. (Ibid.:544)

Thompson's style is of its historical moment, her account is overly idealized, and she mostly deals with Hopi ideology (rather than, say, the praxis of factionalism), conveniently neglecting the material causes of "the Hopi crisis" of the early 1940s from livestock decimation and territorial reduction by John Collier (cf. Clemmer 1995:176). Notwithstanding all this, Thompson here sketches a Hopi model of structuration that accords with my own experience of Hopi discourse and action. The emphasis on personal responsibility to an embracing order of society and nature is pervasive in everyday Hopi talk and is centrally inculcated in ritual initiation.

This model—a Hopi structurationism if you will—may allow an egress from the reified oppositionality of structure and agency in social theory. And here we may move Whorf's influence on Thompson into a new analytical register. One of Whorf's (1956:passim) well-known emphases was the processual, "eventing"-based phenomenology of Hopi linguistic forms (producing a predominance of verbs), versus the "entity"-based model of Standard Average European languages (with their predominance of nouns). In this light, Hopi theory rests upon a dialectical mutuality of "structure" (perhaps "structur*ing*" is truer to the conception) and "eventing," instrumentalized by willed action that mobilizes latent structural potentialities through conscious and extraconscious intentions (see below). In short, Hopi metaphysics overcomes the great divide between structure and agency produced by the epistemological bias of Western theoretical languages privileging, inter alia, entities rather than processes. I shall return to Hopi structuration. But first, a fuller situating of individual and collective *intentions* may shore up this way of escape from debilitating dualism.

AGENCY AND INTENTIONALITY

The key question—in many ways for any realist social theory—occurs in the dialectics of structure and agency, society and individual, objective and subjective, synchrony and diachrony. Curiously, Saussure (e.g., Culler 1986), whose legacy has been to effectively reify the interplay of *langue* and *parole* into inescapable reproduction, provides a way out from the "prison-house of language" into history and change. *Parole*, "the individual side of language, the individual act," Saussure indicates, "is always individual, and the individual is always its master" (Saussure 1966:13-14). This aspect of his theory is widely dismissed, for example by Roman Jakobson, who argued for the conjoint sociality and individuality of both *langue* and *parole* (Jakobson 1990:80-109) particularly in terms of the intersubjectivity of speech acts. Yet the effacement of Saussure's emphasis on individual agency (in language), reflects a widespread trend in social theory that favors collective abstract forces—collective representations, institutions, traditions, models, discourses, practices, polyvocality, etc.—against the possibilities for humanistic determination, which is to say intentional actions by individuals and groups. This anti-individualist pattern finds numerous recent examples that often position themselves against an antithetical strain perceived as dominant in Western social thought. Arguing against "prevailing notions of individual agency, intentionality, and truth in Western speech act theory" (Graham 1995:141) exemplified by Habermas and Searle, Laura Graham reproduces this anti-individualist move with a favoring of "discourse, meaning and intentionality [as] contextually situated and intersubjectively produced" (ibid.:167), with authorization from Bakhtin, Vološinov, and Vygotsky. Yet her transition from language to social action is telling: In Xavante men's councils "the locus of political action resides in emergent social interaction, not in any single agent as in the idealized model of Western democratic tradition" (ibid.:166). The argument against individual agency and intentionalism in social life thus appears as a cultural critique of Western ideology: it is, then, an ideological argument (and see Chapter 5). Frequently, this pattern of argument takes the negativist "Not-Us" form (as Clifford Geertz [1988:102-28], writing of Benedict, puts it) that highlights the Other's difference from the supposed atomism and alienation of individuated Western consciousnesses.

Yet how much authentic individualism is really present in Western social theories of greatest influence in anthropology? Structural-functionalism? Culture and personality? Structuralism? Marxism? Practice?

Cultural materialism? Not a very promising group for the anti-individualist argument. Talcott Parsons and G. H. Mead—arch perpetrators of individualist theory—in fact oversocialized their conceptions of individual actors into virtual chess pieces (cf. Pomper 1996, citing Wrong 1961), and Habermas (e.g., 1990 [1983]) is not much different in this regard. Or, if we look to transactionalism, rational-choice theory, or game theory, for cases of methodological individualism, or to the few glimmers of individual agency in Bourdieu's practice theory (e.g., Munn 1992:106-7), here too, instead of individual moral careers with biographical histories, we tend to see the agent as depersonalized bourgeois-economic man in a behaviorist suit. So the individual, as individuated self, far from being an analytical sacred cow in social theory, is more the reverse—even qua individual, s/he is rendered into structured positionality.

PROBLEMS OF SELF/SUBJECT AND INNER STATES IN CULTURAL ANALYSIS

Il est évident, surtout pour nous, qu'il n'y a jamais eu d'être humain qui n'ait eu le sens, non seulement de son corps, mais aussi de son individualité spirituelle et corporelle à la fois.

Marcel Mauss, 1938

Though surrounded by Western hegemony, Hopi thought remains in some ways as philosophically removed from the Western mainstream as it is possible to imagine. And yet a thoroughgoing, culturally foregrounded intentionalism marks an acting self as centrally within Hopi ethics and sociology as does the intending self in Aristotelian theory of will (e.g., Kenny 1979) or in Husserlian phenomenology (e.g., Ricoeur 1967).[53] (I will return to this shortly.) Recent anthropological denials of autonomous selfhood in numerous non-Western cultures I find both perplexing and troubling, insofar as they may lead to an implication denying agency to non-Western . . . well, "subjects" may not be the word. Or then again, it may. Despite the heralded "death of the subject" (e.g., Jameson 1991:14-15), Debbora Battaglia's (1995) critique of essentialist transcultural projections of a Western self, for example, blithely reproduces "the subject" as a foundational category.[54] The terms of "subjecthood" as opposed to "selfhood" typically remain underexplored in the new phenomenological anthropology. The flurry of ethnopsychological interest in disproving a universal selfhood, especially since the rediscovery of Mauss's famous essay on the person (Carrithers,

Collins and Lukes 1985), has emphasized the "dividual" features of sociality (Strathern 1988, Ochs and Capps 1996). An ethnographic, collectivist Other is here being constructed in opposition to the Western "self" conceived as unitary whole, markedly manifest in bourgeois possessive individualism and averse to collective engagement or identification.[55] Four decades ago, in a landmark inquiry into culture and the self, Irving Hallowell (1955:75, quoting Chien 1944) began with a foundationalist credo: "[E]veryone, with the possible exception of infants, some philosophers, and some psychopaths, is aware of one's self." To this dire list, we must now add numerous non-Western "subjects," especially Melanesians—or, at least, some of their ethnographers.

Yet analytical philosophy—for a change, perhaps—does not seem so confused on this score. Rom Harré, for example, argues:

> The question of whether there is a referent for the theoretical concept of "the self" other than the unity of the unities of experience need never be raised in psychology. . . . [I]ts aetiology begins for each of us with the public concept of a person; any metaphysical or noumenal self, pulsing away beyond all possible experience, is quite redundant. (Harré 1984:99)

Using examples from ethnography (especially Eskimo and Maori), Harré (1984:85) argues that "what every society recognizes as human individuality in the form of persons in the Strawsonian [1958] sense of embodied agent, that is, it has a common primary structure" differs from "wide variations in secondary structure, that is the degree of singularity with which persons organize their experienced thoughts, feelings, premonitions and plans as their own." While confronting that variation in specific cases, Harré affirms, "it would be hard to prove that there was a tribe quite without selves" (ibid.). In short, whether or not selves under some secondary rhetorical or ideological terms are cross-culturally commensurable, the primary constitution of a person as embodied agent presupposes a degree of reflexivity and intentionality that is a species characteristic, rather than a cultural fluke.

The genuine tendency of noncapitalist economies to produce and reproduce social life collectively is attended superstructurally by doxa of communitarian interest. Indeed this is a marked emphasis at Hopi, too, and flagrant pursuit of individual ambition over the social good is abhorred and likely to result in accusations of—that prime discourse of excessive individualism and antisociality—witchcraft (see Chapters 3 and

5). There are clear differences here from Western ideologies that sanction, to mix a few metaphors, "following one's bliss," with "dog eating dog" "all the way to the bank." (Indeed, it may not be pure chance that ethnographies of the dividual self—reflecting a search for alternatives to agonistic atomism—emerge during the "greed works" Reagan/Thatcher 1980s, although the influence of Lacan [1966-71] and Foucault [e.g., 1982] looms large also.) Anthropologists may have forgotten this, but there are, of course, many streams of value in Western thought and practice (and see Ochs and Capps 1996) that this simplistic oppositional analytic—Western selves as consistent wholes, non-Western persons as synecdochic relationals—fails to take into account.

Let me give two brief examples from Western master narratives, one theological, the other psychoanalytic. The Episcopal eucharist formally and substantively aims to produce "one body in Christ" among its communicants and more broadly all its "members"—an etymological derivative from a somatic domain intrinsically constructed around part-whole synecdoche. From the 1928 prayer book, the postcommunion prayer reads: "We are very members incorporate in the mystical body of thy Son, which is the blessed company of all faithful people" (Episcopal Church 1944:83).[56] The message signally evokes a partible, relational notion of selfhood rather clearly suggestive of Marilyn Strathern's notion of dividuality. While from one point of view this may involve a form of false consciousness, it is nonetheless clearly counterdiscursive to naked individualism in Western thought.

For psychoanalysis, I merely want to assent to Richard Rorty's characterization that Freud effectively remade the self into "a tissue of contingencies, rather than [the contrast is with Plato, Kant, and Nietzsche] an at least potentially well-ordered system of faculties" (Rorty 1989:32). Again, this view accords rather well with a sense of self composed of detachable strands of relationality within and between bodies (Strathern 1988:349ff.). Such examples, from two mainstreams of Western discourse—and they might easily be multiplied[57]—suggest that the "unitary whole" self is neither an encompassing ideal nor a practical reality. Sociality and dividuality, and fragmentation and contingency are not marginal but major elements of Western commonsense, theological, and psychological theories of the self. Contemporary anthropologists, in carving out an ethnographic discourse of the self against perceived essentialisms, seem almost wilfully underinformed about psychological and philosophical perspectives on selfhood in the West. They have not so much *identified* an essential holistic-unified, possessive individualist self as *produced* it via a straw-man mode of negativist argument designed to show its inadequacies as a cross-cultural explanans. What they have not done is an adequate ethnography of the multiple Western senses of the self (in its "secondary" usages, in Harré's terms). Neither have they typically gone beyond bourgeois white commonsense thought to examine the selfhood and sociality of, say, Yorkshire coal miners, Italian factory workers, African-American rural laborers, Nuyorican seamstresses, and so on (not to mention recent Third World transplants to First World countries—are their self-praxes now of the West or the Rest?).

And yet, while the term "self" may now be beyond rescue as a neutral analytic, the foundationalist persistence of an apparently unproblematic "subject" in its stead (cf. Kondo 1990:38) reveals that querying the self through the "rhetorics of self-making" (in Battaglia's terms) is no more than a semantic quibble. Indeed, this "subject"/"self" opposition is, under another description, merely Harré's distinction between primary and secondary selfhood. The supposed anthropological deconstruction of universal selfhood is typical of many deconstructive moves: *declaring* instability of meaning, or false centers in need of decentering, via critical assertions whose very utterance depends upon referentiality and an at least temporarily stable center of vision. In short the recent anthropology of selfhood seems to be based on epistemological inversion: "our" individuality versus "their" dividuality, "selves" present in the West versus absent in Melanesia, Bali, or wherever else. It further reflects a pervasive theoretical Orientalism (in Said's sense), wherein Western individual agency is contrasted with the Other's passivity (deriving from an absence of effectual selfhood). Dumont's famous contrast (1970) between Western individuals and Indic synecdoches, for example, reappears in Todorov's (1984) analysis of the Mexican conquest, effected by Cortes's individualistic improvisations, for which Montezuma's rote fulfillment of ritual protocols and incapacity for self-motivated imaginative action, associated with an incapacitating Aztec theory of history (nothwithstanding the recency of Aztec imperial expansion), were no match.

A variant of this pattern occurs in recent querying of "inner states" and "intentions" cross-culturally (Rosen 1995; see also Duranti 1994). Here the philosophical question, in nicely Cartesian fashion, has shifted from "self" to "mind." Lawrence Rosen indicts "the false positivism of assuming that an inner state always exists" (Rosen 1995:5). Yet the contrary assumption—that inner states do not exist in other cultures unless they are shown to—I find as morally indefensible and politically alarming as positing an absence of selves. Moreover, it is a rather curious resurrection of neo-Cartesian doubt about (O)/other minds (e.g., Wagner 1995). While much human action is not intentional and does not merit a search for causes in individual plans, clearly a good deal is; problematizing the construction of inner states, which is a good thing to do, should not, however, lead to an assumption of their culture-specific absence, unless the "science of man" is prepared to countenance intraspecific differences of rather extraordinary magnitude.

Beyond the denial of universal selves and/or minds, a second influence on the theoretical loss of individual agency is the fashion for totalizing social theories. In practice theory, structural history, variant strands of Foucauldian discourse theory, and evolved forms of cultural studies[58] as reworked in anthropology (not to mention more grounded materialisms), subjects and selves are mere effects: of discourse, structure, language-game, conjuncture, relations of production, etc. "Practice" merely reproduces the aseptic reification of collective consciousness from prior paradigms (see S. Turner 1994). An emphasis on individual selves and minds as engines of social action, historical transformation, or poetic relationality seems a positively quaint and suspiciously essentializing recommendation against these modish totalizations. But it is precisely such full acknowledgement of, and engagement with, Other minds that ethnography must bring to broader social theory if it is to advance beyond the alienation and estrangement that the Hopi case highlights.

HOPI STRUCTURATION

Tunatya, "intending," "intention," is the central concept in Hopi philosophy of action. In *Deliberate Acts* (Whiteley 1988), I highlighted this as part of a triune principle of intentionalism strongly emphasized by an older Hopi informant (Yoywayma[59] of *Honngyam,* the "Bear clan"). The conversation occurred toward the end of my first fieldwork, and we were both, I think, saddened by the imminent truncation of a relationship that had become in some ways quasi-paternal. It was one of those fabled epiphanous ethnographic moments, when a clear light suddenly beams through to grant a new threshold of insight. He said it unexpectedly, pedagocially, kindly, almost conspiratorially, as if he were giving me the key to a code: *"tunatya, pasiwni, okiw antani*—this is the cornerstone of the Hopi way." As I have come to learn more of Hopi, this axiom seems ever more dense, and its ripples of significance expand ever farther. *Tunatya,* explained with a characteristic horticultural metaphor, refers to a "seed of thought" — the germ of an idea, we might say — that occurs in one's "field" of consciousness. *Pasiwni,* "planning," means bringing together and setting into motion all the necessary technical and symbolic resources to germinate the seed and bring it to fructifying life. *Okiw antani,* "let it be this way," refers to proper mental attitude and is also a prayer that sanctifies the intending to deific forces. Fundamentally, then, this configures a picture of intentionality and action by conscious agents in relation to an encompassing metaphysics of universal causality (see Whiteley 1988).

When the Hopi first emerged from below into this, the fourth world, they greeted Maasaw, the demigod, liminal between humanity and deity, whom they asked to lead them. He refused, pointedly noting that they could not be led since they clearly already had their own intentions — echoing the Edenic fall, with the human choice of self-determination. In Chapter 3 an elderly *Paaqapwungwa,* "Reed clan man," gives voice to another major social metaphor that "Hopis are like clowns and Kachinas — they plan out life" — again foregrounding conscious engagement in social action. This intentionalist principle frequently appears in Hopi assessments of the human condition; when a Coyote clan friend was visiting in New York City, his response to the madding crowd, was "just imagine — all these people, each with their own intentions." Often, with irony and cultural reflexivism, Hopis jokingly accuse each other (or me) of acting intentionally after an inadvertent or accidental occurrence. The awareness of an over-determining paradigm of intentionalist explanation such jokes reveal suggests a skepticism (and see Whiteley in press) and critical rationalism at work in everyday explanations, too, as well as a decided lack of mystical-causal solemnity (and these jokes are not particular to a generation, gender, or more or less acculturated group of people).

Whorf characterizes *tunatya* as the fundamental idea of Hopi metaphysics:

> If we were to approximate our metaphysical terminology more closely to Hopian terms, we should probably speak of the subjective realm as the realm of HOPE or HOPING. Every language contains terms that have come to crystallize in themselves the basic postulates of an unformulated philosophy, in which is couched the thought of a people, a culture, a civilization, even of an era. Such are our words "reality, substance, matter, cause," and . . . "space, time, past, present, future." Such a term in Hopi is the word most often translated "hope" —

tunatya—"it is in the action of hoping, it hopes, it is hoped for, it thinks or is thought of with hope," etc. Most metaphysical words in Hopi are verbs, not nouns as in European languages. The verb *tunatya* contains in its idea of hope something of our words "thought," "desire," and "cause," which sometimes must be used to translate it. The word is really a term which crystallizes the Hopi philosophy of the universe in respect to its grand dualism of objective and subjective; it is the Hopi term for SUBJECTIVE. It refers to the state of the subjective, unmanifest, vital and causal aspect of the Cosmos, and the fermenting activity toward fruition and manifestation with which it seethes—an action of HOPING; i.e. mental-causal activity, which is forever pressing upon and into the manifested realm.[60] (Whorf 1956:61–62)

Tunatya and *pasiwni,* in combination with *natwani,* an exteriorization of self, suggest that—as for Husserl—intentionality and its worldly engagement is the defining feature of a conscious self. *Naap* is the generic Hopi term for "self" and in its stem form *naa-, na',* or *na-* frequently appears as a third-person singular reflexive. *Natwani* derives from *na-* plus *tuwanta,* "to try, attempt, make an effort toward." *Natwani* thus includes the notion of "self-practice." Taken together as part of an ideational complex, the three terms—*natwani, tunatya, pasiwni*—strongly suggest a sense of what we might call "self" and "mind" as quite central in Hopi ontology.[61]

Hopi ethics prescribe modesty, self-effacement, interpersonal and environmental responsibility, industry, courtesy, circumspection, and humility. *Natwani,* the worldly reflection of one's self-practice and conduct, may refer to crops, children, or other fruits of personal effort; if these turn out well, they accrue to the individual's virtue as *hopi* (an ethical term at least as often as an identity marker). Ethically constituted and judged selves in intersubjective relationship thus agentially engender and perpetuate moral community. In short, agency and intentionality are foregrounded in Hopi discourse, and as they continue to be reflected—as "intentions"—in Hopi English, are diagnostic of the human condition, of personhood and selfhood (see also Chapters 4 and 5).

Hopi intentionalism and sensibilities of agency are situated within a different metaphysics than Western secular humanism, however, and in this respect reveal the limitations of rational-mechanistic structure-and-agency models for intercultural explanation. Sociological structuration models rest upon a rationalist theory of action and choice-making by rather wooden agents (see Munn's [1992:106] critique of Giddens, for example), with a great deal of social production the result of unintended consequences. Clearly, many effects of intentional actions are unintended by-products, and it is unimaginable that much social transformation could result from intentional planning, given the preference for stochastic forces that pervades our explanations of events. But Hopi philosophy of action includes supernatural agencies, cosmic forces, and fateful processes as well as goal-oriented human pursuits. Hopi ontology issues in agency via conscious thought and deliberate act, but these operate within a metaphysical landscape where intentionalism itself is less an exclusively interior thought process than a force-field behind a continuous coming-into-being, in Heidegger's sense; this is the manifesting-manifested paradigm Whorf identifies in Hopi phenomenology. Perhaps the clearest example is Hopi ritual effort, through prayer and liturgy (preplanned through *tiingavi,* the ritual equivalent of *pasiwni*), to bring rain or other beneficial circumstances. When it becomes manifest, rain—the animate presence of spirits of the dead—is called into being by the individual and collective mental and spiritual effort of the participants. This sense of intentionalism, or, more appropriately, meta-intentionalism, involves a willed (and religiously trained and practiced) entrance into universal forces of creation and transformation. This metaphysics of intentionality distinguishes Hopi senses of both structure and action from sociocentric rational-mechanical counterparts in Western social theory.

Consciousness, as Marx maintained, is the mediating force between structure and action. In Hopi theory, however, the universe itself as well as individual agents within it (human beings, eagles, coyotes, deities, spirits), is intentional. The idea that all is a coming-into-being (Whorf is surely corrrect about Hopi metaphysics, if not about time itself), the continuous movement from manifesting to manifested, but that all was cosmically planned, indicates a metanarrative of predestination. Accounts of predestination abound in Hopi discourse, often with references to *navoti* (literally "knowledge," "teachings") as a body of prophecies originally given to Hopi leaders upon their emergence into *tutskway'qatsi,* "life on earth." Major events are incorporated into structures of conception in the conjunctural manner Sahlins (e.g., 1981, 1985) envisages: They occur as the fruition of intention-bearing seeds set at the founding of the present epoch (the "fourth world") or even before. In this light, structure, rather than the frozen precipitate of past cumulations of collective consciousness, is agential, ripe with intentional force, and events/eventings are the products of originary universal intendings: they are the manifesting forms of what has always been latently present.

This meta-intentionalism undergirds Hopi explanatory schemata. Explanation of specific events, however, deploys a more direct sense of intentional action by conscious agents, which is not so much mystical as pragmatic, often rigorously so in its psychology of individual motivation. There are thus two intentionalisms in Hopi metaphysics and etiology, perhaps best rendered in the opposition between essence and matter that Alfonso Ortiz regards as fundamental to Pueblo worldview:

> [T]he general Pueblo conception of causality is that everything—animate and inanimate—counts and everything has its place in the cosmos. All things are thought to have two aspects, essence and matter. Thus everything in the cosmos is believed to be knowable and, being knowable, controllable. Effective control comes only from letter-perfect attention to detail and correct performance, thus the Pueblo emphasis on formulas, ritual, and repetition revealed in ritual drama. Among human beings, the primary causal factors are mental and psychological states; if these are harmonious, the supernaturals will dispense what is asked and expected of them. If they are not, untoward consequences will follow just as quickly, because within this relentlessly interconnected universal whole the part can affect the whole, just as like can come from like. Men, animals, plants and spirits are intertransposable in a seemingly unbroken chain of being. (Ortiz 1972:143)

Individual intentions, then, while the mark of conscious, agential selves, are ultimately not the private properties of rational-mechanical individual organisms, but are more fragments of individuated consciousness broken off from a great chain of intentional being. But if all, at the level of essential metanarrative, was intended, the manifesting-manifested trajectory is not a lockstep matching of event to structure. These individuated fragments of consciousness, granted subjectivity and life, have free will—particularly in their capacity for moral action—to perform acts adherent to models of the social good, or, conversely, to depart from this to further selfish interests.

Thus considered as entailing a cultural theory of structuration, Hopi social and metaphysical thought offers new grounds of explanation. While social theory may balk at ultimate predestination, the continuous interplay of agential structur-ings and event-ings, manifesting via individual and social consciousness—fundamentally processes rather than entities—offers a potential solution to the trichotomous problem of frozen structures, disembedded agencies, and detached events.

THE INTENTIONALIST STANCE

In much recent argument, anthropologists seem to have given up on their greatest strength—the irreducibility of their lived and shared experience in fieldwork *with* people in a multiplicity of places. Now, it seems, theory guides ethnography to find Derridean decenterings, abstract flows of power, consciousnessless agency, and discursive bodies everywhere—in the Amazon, Melanesia (a particular culprit), and so on. But what anthropologists should be insisting upon, surely, in the experienced actualities of other social thoughts and lives, is a critical counter-hegemony against these recursive, self-regarding theories happily and ignorantly entrapped in metaphysically Eurocentric questions (cf. Hastrup 1995).

My point is that anthropology seems to have forgotten its mission in social and philosophical theory: pluralist cultural critique engendering multifaceted reflexivism *among* systems of thought rather than endogenous self-reflection. In this respect, again, anthropology should positively celebrate its inherent liminality between epistemologies rather than seeking to tag along after a fashionable philosophical or literary-critical paradigm. Why have anthropologists given up this historic mandate—the legacy of Boas, Malinowski, Mead, Evans-Pritchard, and indeed Lévi-Strauss? Clifford Geertz's heuristic borrowings from Ryle and Wittgenstein (among others); Edmund Leach's argument for topological models; Lévi-Strauss's inquiry into mentalities; S. J. Tambiah on magical reason; Mary Douglas's cultural systematics; Whorf's linguistic relativism; Sahlins's interrogations of practical reason and history; and Marilyn Strathern's dividuality[62]—all have been part of a robust dialogue with Western philosophy, not a capitulation to its hermetic claims. Some rather productive philosophies of the twentieth century have taken critical inspiration from anthropology: Freud and Wittgenstein, for example, from Frazer; Susanne Langer and Alasdair MacIntyre from ethnography in general; Peter Winch from Evans-Pritchard; Richard Rorty from Clifford Geertz; and Harold Taylor from Mauss. As if in sinking awareness of creeping desuetude (how long has it been since "Anthropology" was hip enough for Charlie Parker to title a piece after it?), anthropologists currently scramble to disassociate themselves from a past depicted as *only* colonial, rather than celebrating its persistent intellectual fragmentation of colonial structures (often unwitting, to be sure) that has, certainly since Boas and Mead, been anthropology's signal contribution.

Fundamentally, anthropologists should be seeking in their theory less to align themselves with a linguistic/philosophical episteme that disavows referentiality (the "all that is solid melts into air" school of representation), than to show, through an absolute dependency on ethnography as translation, the instrumental necessity of treating languages as referential. And more than this, cultural translation is predicated upon interlinguistic referentiality to a major degree. In privileging difference, anthropologists tend to obfuscate cross-cultural commonalities—in such areas as production, reproduction, and organization—that are readily commensurable and translatable. One cannot speak (well, not with much social value anyway) of Cree hunting, Balinese water management, Dogon metaphysics, Nuer politics, Kayapo resistance, Trobriand matriliny, or Kawelka gender, without the conviction that the peoples, places, and endeavors thus indexed exist, or recently existed, in real time and space. Further, their very presence within a universe of anthropological discourse results from painstaking ethnographic transactions utterly dependent on a shared sense of potential approximation between the subjects and concepts involved. Neither is this any innovation of formal ethnography: It is simply the basis of intercultural communication since the origins of cultural difference itself. Cultural understandings between individuals are built to a significant extent by a joint reliance on translinguistic references to the experienced phenomenal world. Hopi and English may differ on temporality, materiality, mentality, and how to distinguish "blue" from "green," but they do not differ substantially on categories like heads, hands, domestic versus wild animals, plants, walking, sitting, killing, birthing, mothering, distributing—or on many of the accompanying premises necessary to sustain or engage the phenomena or actions indicated. In short, a cross-cultural intersubjectivity of the experienced phenomenal world strongly suggests parallel systems of referentiality in many conceptual domains; indeed, this is the sine qua non for much intertranslatability, and the precondition for more fine-grained, context-sensitive translations (see Chapter 5, especially).

Field ethnography is constitutively dependent on the actuality and conscious recollection of co-presence—of interpersonal engagement, of an (at least partial) meeting of minds. Because of this, in contrast, say, to philosophy, literary theory, cultural studies, or even history, the necessary epistemological condition of ethnography is antisolipsistic. Field ethnography's very conception vouchsafes human conjuncture: unless in the fictional paraethnography of a Carlos Castañeda, it thus guarantees presence—of the ethnographer as a human being and of other human beings. And its gradual progress depends on the genuine possibilities and learned protocols for interaction among those human beings. In short, ethnography is intrinsically—even when it goes wrong—a moral endeavor, that, of necessity, existentially acknowledges (at some level) the common humanity of its subjects.[63] Anything less is a dereliction of responsibility to subject communities, as well as to the larger goal of intercultural and interpersonal understanding (cf. Reed 1997:24-25).

CONCLUSION

Structures—linguistic, economic, political, ritual, and "total" in the Hopi sense emphasized above—frame individual and several lives and events, and elucidation of them must remain a key goal of anthropological analysis. Hopi clanship, ritual hierarchy, aesthetics, and organization of nature are doxically patterned, and adherence to such patterns is both habitual and self-reproducing. Denying the palpable existence of such structurings of thought and action—on the grounds of instability of linguistic meaning, perspectivalism, or shifting histories, signs, centers, or borders—is evasion; postmodernism may be principled evasion (or it may not), and it may train critical scrutiny upon important supplemental questions, but inasmuch as it is used to substitute for existentially realist appraisals of human social forms, ideas, and processes, it remains scholastic mystification.

Structures, however, are fundamentally inflected by culture. If anthropologists had followed Leach's recommendation (1961) for topological flexibility of analytical categories, entailing an interstitial language of explanation, such cultural inflections need not have been seen as antagonistic to theory. Instead the virtual abandonment of kinship, for example (though see Peletz 1995; Faubion 1996; Godelier 1998), might not have been so necessary as David Schneider (1984) envisaged, and the radical transformation of explanatory concepts Sahlins (1996) suggests might not either. Culture, then, is an interplay of structures that are mutually determining, co-existent, logically implied in each other, correlative and covariant—the order of the cosmos, of nature, of descent, of polity, economy, and ritual. To be true to their object, a genuinely cultural *explanation* cannot espouse monadic determinants. Hopi structures are multiplex, as Laura Thompson argued, and among them there is a tendency toward holism, though not a perfect fit (as she would have wished) and in this slippage—as well, obviously, as in colonial domination—lies the seeds of larger structural transformation. And while structures are dialectically realized in agency, agency has some autogeny, particularly via individual intentions that reassemble fragments of meaning, bricolage-like, from manifested structures into *innovative* forms (and this is where, in the absence of a return to given structures, I depart from Lévi-Strauss [1966]). This autogeny must be granted before we can escape stultifying totalizations and nihilist/solipsist perspectives to see social life as a noncircular dialectical process between structure and individual agential engagements.

Such is the guiding argument of this book, together with the emphasis on specificity and cultural inflection of structures in their local contexts. Each chapter represents an argument with a particular set of anthropological concepts and with received ethnographic wisdom. The separate arguments occur within a larger trajectory focused on Hopi sociality, identity, and history. Each chapter variously foregrounds Hopi conceptions and consciousness of action, and critiques theory that fails to conjoin Hopi reality. The aim is to deploy Hopi conceptions critically in relation to broader questions of sociality, polity, subjectivity, agency, representation, and nature. My call for dialogue does not address rhetorics of ethnographic representation, but rather a dialogics of *cultural explanation* that seeks to integrate local and global *analysis*.

In Chapter 2, "Unpacking Hopi 'Clans,'" I argue that a reductionist theory of (Hopi) social structure minimizing the natural, cosmological, and religious underpinnings of the clan system, fundamentally does not "get" the meaning of clans in Hopi practice or perspective. In "The Interpretation of Politics" (Chapter 3), I consider structures of Hopi power and inequality, and how these resist understanding by ingrained political theory that excludes ritual value and the orchestration of metaphysical agencies. "Hopitutungwni—Hopi Names" (Chapter 4) negotiates the poetic and social import of Hopi personal names and their signification of Hopi subjectivities. In the process Maussian theories of selfhood, and poststructural literary theory that effaces authorial intention, are found radically wanting. In Chapter 5, "Burning Culture," I argue that social and historical theory that disallows intentional actions by conscious, socially positioned subjects as directly consequential of sociocultural change—indeed of *history*—cannot effectively explain an apostate Two-Horn priest destroying his altar to produce an epochal rupture of axial cultural structures. In "The End of Anthropology" (Chapter 6), my argument is that the dehistoricized presumptions of ethnography falter amidst the trafficking and conflictual uses of representations in their contemporary Hopi context and in Hopi consciousness of these. I urge an anthropology more fully cognizant of its moral implications as the basis of a crucial pragmatic and theoretical reformation. And, in "Paavahu and Paanaqso'a" (Chapter 7), Vernon Masayesva and I address Hopi conceptions and concerns about water that lead to an all-too-sensible apocalypticism in the face of colossal resource waste by a multinational mining company.

The central, unifying idea in these essays is a truism: that Hopi society is made up of people (however theorized—"subjects," "agents," "persons," "selves," "individuals") who consciously think about—as well as unconsciously reproduce, their practices, culture, history, politics, intercultural relations—and act on the basis of that thought. Such thoughts and actions reflect structured engagements centrally conceptualized in ritual, but that ramify throughout quotidian discourse, social schemata, personhood conceptions, aesthetics, history, and social criticism. My underlying argument is that listening to Hopi views, examining some of their consequences and implications, and situating these in reciprocal relation to theory, allows a more powerful transcultural understanding—of society, polity, poetics, history, representation, sovereignty, and environment. In seeking such understanding, my ethnography attempts to do most honor and least violence to Hopi thought and practice, and most tribute to morally engaged critical cultural analysis.

2

UNPACKING HOPI "CLANS"
Another Vintage Model Out of Africa?

Structural-functionalism, the prevailing mid-twentieth-century anthropological theory, provided an organicist framework for interpreting
social formations that is perhaps unsurpassed in its comparatist productivity. "Society" was a structure of interrelated institutions, each of
which functioned toward the smooth operation of the whole. Structural-functionalism has long been debunked, but there is a curious
theoretical half-life for the understanding of particular cultures; the
theory's passing seems to go unnoticed in the continuing reliance on
ethnographic descriptions couched in its idioms. Fred Eggan and, to
some extent, Mischa Titiev, attached Hopi social structure to a structural-functionalist model. Owing to the extensive use of their work in
secondary texts, the model has adhered to the social forms in question
beyond its theoretical life span.

My argument here is that Hopi "structure," in the encompassing
sense outlined in Chapter 1, is not effectively addressed by structural-
functionalist descent-theory models. Hopi social structures, especially
clans, are not corporate entities formed around joint estates in property
(economic, ritual, or jural), and to transform them into such entities—
especially via "the lineage principle"—is to misconceive Hopi doxa and
praxis. I am thus seeking to dislodge the received sociocentric model in
order to point to Hopi cosmological and historical conceptions of clans,

and to prepare the way for considering the forms of political action addressed in Chapters 3 and 5.

This chapter is also situated within the accumulated anthropological interpretations of Pueblo social organization. Since 1871, when Lewis Henry Morgan used the Pueblos as a significant example in *Systems of Consanguinity and Affinity of the Human Family,* anthropological discourse on Pueblo kinship and totemism has burgeoned. Frazer (1910), Kroeber (1919), Lowie (1929), Parsons (e.g., 1933), Eggan (1950), and Lévi-Strauss (1966) developed questions of "totemic" social organization into variously abstract conceptual models. Kroeber famously argued for a pan-Pueblo conceptual scheme that superseded present-day local variations. He displaced the cultural-historical approach of Fewkes (e.g., 1900) and Mindeleff (e.g. 1891), rejecting indigenous explanations of clan origins, histories, migrations, and differences.

Anthropological conceptualization of Pueblo culture was thus shifted into a more cognitive, even protostructuralist mode, since schemata of natural association and opposition are clearly seen by Kroeber as a template—"good to think" in Lévi-Strauss's terms—for the articulation of social distinctions. But this formalization entailed a serious loss of indigenous perspectives; Kroeber was in effect saying—several years prior to Malinowski—that clan "histories" were legitimating mythological charters motivated by current interests, and were irrelevant, or simply false, as history. Kroeber's sense of structure, however, is important, and conditions numerous subsequent explanations. Eggan, in turn, replaced Kroeber's culturalist scheme with a rigorous emphasis on a model of social relations via the injection of Radcliffe-Brownian mechanics, particularly the lineage principle. Eggan also put some cultural history back into the equation, especially in the comparison of distinct Pueblo systems. Eggan's use of history is to explain broader differences between Eastern and Western Pueblo, however, rather than to restore, say, Hopi perspectives to anthropological interpretation. Jerrold Levy (1992) has recently reproduced, in large part, Eggan's structural-functionalist interpretation of Hopi descent groups (see Whiteley 1994), eliding substantive differences among clans to preserve the apparent logical systematicity of his model. Like Levy, Richard Clemmer (1995:311-17) has reinscribed Eggan's view and has also assailed my analysis, but his attack is too inchoate and fragmentary to rebut here.

While the obsessive literalism of Fewkes's reading of Hopi clan histories disabled his investigations, and he has been dismissed by anthropologists now for almost a century, that he took clan histories seriously remains ethnographically salutary. Indeed, these distinctive histories remain as vital in present Hopi discourse, attached to the same historical migration routes and commemorative sacred places, as in Fewkes's time. They continue to define Hopi social identity and ritual practice. And while, to some extent, they speak in metaphor, the literal association of Mesa-based clans with specific ruins—particular event-based histories, cosmological entitlements, and forms of power—centrally animates Hopi thought about clan significance.

PART 1

The Hopi Indians of Arizona are "one of the best known tribes in anthropological literature" (Fox 1967:88).[1] Their society has been used to inform countless anthropological treatises, and it has become enshrined in anthropological thought as embodying definitive theoretical features. For example, regarding their mode of reckoning descent, Lévi-Strauss (1949:121) uses the phrase "des sociétés aussi matrilinéaires que les Hopi." Exactly what he means by "as matrilineal as" is not clear, but his confidence in the nature of Hopi descent reckoning is apparent. Others have made equally confident characterizations of Hopi social structure. For instance, Fox (1967:89) states that it is constituted by "an organization of genuine descent groups." This characterization identifies an embedded series of matrilineal units—households, lineages, clans, and phratries—similar to the coordinate levels of lineage segmentation described for the Nuer (Evans-Pritchard 1940). Moreover, the Hopi provide more than a merely average example of a unilineal system. Plog (1978:362–64) classifies Western Pueblo social organization as "strongly lineal" and states that the matrilineal clan is "a self-contained and self-sufficient unit."

These conventional views of Hopi social structure were established largely by Fred Eggan and Mischa Titiev in the years following World War II. Eggan's theoretical perspective derived directly from the teachings of Radcliffe-Brown at the University of Chicago in the 1930s and was strictly structural-functionalist. His admiration for Radcliffe-Brown's thought is evident throughout the text of his earlier published works (e.g., Eggan 1949, 1950). For example:

> The most important structural principle among the Hopi . . . is the principle which Professor Radcliffe-Brown has recently referred to as the solidarity and unity of the lineage group. . . . Perhaps the most

significant aspect of the Hopi lineage is its function of conserving and transmitting, not only the social and ritual heritage, but property rights, houses, and ceremonies as well, from one generation to the next. Professor Radcliffe-Brown has used the analogy of a corporation conserving an estate, and has pointed out the advantages of unilineal descent in achieving that goal. Among the Hopi the women of a lineage or clan act as trustees with reference to land and houses, holding them in trust for the generations to come. (Eggan 1949:142-43)

Titiev, on the other hand, had an evolutionist bent, perhaps due to the influence of his colleague Leslie White (Titiev 1943). In 1932 White led the first field party from the Laboratory of Anthropology in Santa Fe to Hopi. The party, comprised of White, Titiev, Eggan, Edward Kennard, and Jess Spirer, succeeded in laying the basis for the most significant anthropological studies of the Hopi for many years to come.

Titiev and Eggan conducted a good deal of their Hopi fieldwork together at Orayvi in 1933 and 1934. The benefits for their common interest in social structure seem to have been considerable. For Eggan the structural key is the "lineage principle," while for Titiev it is segmentation, but there is great consistency between their respective descriptions of Hopi society. In both *Old Oraibi* (Titiev 1944) and *Social Organization of the Western Pueblos* (Eggan 1950), social structure is conceived of as a body of interrelated institutions.

Titiev and Eggan supplanted prevailing theories of Pueblo social structure (e.g., Kroeber's *Zuni Kin and Clan,* 1919, and Parsons's numerous writings on the Pueblos, e.g., 1933) with a more rigorous conception. They held that Hopi society consisted primarily of unilineal descent groups. This configuration, Eggan maintained, represented one end of a continuum of Pueblo types, stretching from the Hopi and Zuni in the west to the Rio Grande Tewa in the east. Among the Rio Grande Tewa, the opposing type featured a dual organization of non-kin-based ceremonial moieties. In between, the "Keresan bridge," a structural mixture found in variant forms among eastern and western Keres Pueblos, was held to incorporate elements of both extremes.

Fox's (1967a) account of Cochiti, and Ortiz's (1969) of San Juan, have reoriented our thinking on the historical development of Keresan and Tewa social organization, respectively. Nevertheless, Eggan's ethnographic analysis of Hopi society has remained largely without challenge. Fox (1972:73) attributes this to the "convincing and overwhelming nature of his theory [which was] simply accepted by most specialists." Moreover, the influence persists; a recent brief, authoritative summary of Hopi social organization (Connelly 1979) perpetuates many of Eggan's conclusions.

The Development of Descent Theory

Since publication of Eggan's and Titiev's primary works on the Hopi, theoretical views on the significance of kinship have passed through some dramatic transitions. In 1974, for example, Needham came to the radical conclusion that not only was kinship theory meaningless, but that the very phenomenon of kinship was nonexistent. Today, studies of social structure are overshadowed by more ardent quests for "meaning" or "material causes." Assaults on descent theory have come from several quarters. (Kuper 1982 provides a good summary.) One source that was significant for the present inquiry was New Guinea ethnography of the 1960s and 1970s. Serious problems were encountered in attempting to analyze Highland New Guinea societies with schemata developed primarily to explain African lineage-based systems. Barnes's seminal paper (1962:5) on these issues concluded that "it has become clear that Highland societies fit awkwardly into African moulds." Analytic concepts that were supposedly culture-free and susceptible of wide application had, in fact, been developed inductively from specific cultural contexts. Difficulties arose with the attempted application of these concepts to other, quite distant, cultural contexts.

In spite of these problems, the structural-functionalist school continued in a trend toward rigidification of the concepts of lineage theory. The demand for analytical precision led to increasingly specific statements of the nature of unilineal descent groups. In the 1950s, M. G. Smith, for example, gave lucid expression to the dogma emanating from the structural-functionalist school:

> Lineage groups are conceived of as segmentary in structure and corporate in function. Where unilineal descent obtains without groups of this character, there are no lineages in the sense of this theory. Lineages are thus corporate groups of a segmentary character defined in terms of unilineal descent. (Smith 1956:39)

The segmentary aspect of unilineal descent systems had been emphasized in Fortes's and Evans-Pritchard's *African Political Systems* (1940) and in other works by these two authors (e.g., Evans-Pritchard 1940; Fortes 1945, 1953). Unilineal descent groups were seen as jurally exclusive units arranged in a nested series of coordinate levels of complementary opposition.

The concept of corporateness, deriving primarily from Maine (1861), also began to receive more attention. A descent group's corporateness rested in its joint control of some estate—either in persons or things. Radcliffe-Brown set this out as follows:

> It is convenient to speak of such a group as the Kariera horde as a "corporation" having an "estate." . . . By an estate is here meant a collection of rights (whether over persons or things) with the implied duties, the unity of which is constituted either by the fact that they are the rights of a single person and can be transmitted, as a whole, or in division, to some other person or persons, or that they are the rights of a defined group (the corporation) which maintains a continuity of possession. (Radcliffe-Brown 1952:34)

Furthermore, Radcliffe-Brown (1952:34) stressed the real property aspect of the estate: "The corporate estate of a Kariera horde includes in the first place its rights over its territory. The continuity of the horde is maintained by the continuity of possession of the territory, which remains constant, not subject to division or increase."

Others, such as Fortes (1953) and Goody (1961), have maintained and expanded these ideas. Goody's discussion of descent group corporateness added greater precision to the definition. Rejecting a less restricted usage, he stated: "I would reserve the term 'corporate,' to distinguish those UDGs [unilineal descent groups] in which rights in material objects are vested, or, more precisely, within which property is inherited" (Goody 1961:5). Goody received praise for thus "sharpening the tools" of anthropological analysis, and his ideas gained considerable acceptance (ibid.:13–21). However, while the concepts of descent theory were being ever more sharply honed, there was a simultaneous attempt to expand their sphere of application. This was an important aim of Fortes's 1953 paper, "The Structure of Unilineal Descent Groups." He suggested that, beyond the limited group of African societies previously in the spotlight, unilineal descent groups formed a modal type in the organization of human societies and thus provided a tool for broad cross-cultural comparison. He listed examples of such societies (Fortes 1953:24), placing the Hopi (he cites Eggan) explicitly in the same category as the Nuer, Beduin, Yakö, Tallensi, Gusii, and Tikopia.

A few voices were raised against this extension by Fortes (1953:39) of his "limited number of principles of wide validity." Fried (1957:8), in particular, questioned the utility of lumping together the societies

mentioned. Complaints about other aspects of descent theory continued to multiply. Since the 1960s, however, anthropological attention
has shifted away from these debates, though descent theory is not yet
dead. No enduring paradigm has replaced it, and the continuity of its
influence is revealed in periodic reassessments and revisionist conceptual schemes. As Verdon (1983:20) notes, "Classical descent theory
outdid all its rivals by the richness of the ethnography it inspired, and
by the great number of comparative hypotheses it generated." In contrast, Adam Kuper (1982:92–93) has stated: "My view is that the
lineage model, its predecessors and its analogs, have no value for
anthropological analysis. . . . [A] century of often very nimble manipulation of the basic model has yielded no profit. The efforts of generations of theorists have served only to buy time for the model in the face
of its long-evident bankruptcy."

The descent theory model persists, however, in anthropological consciousness, if only as an object for retrospective blame or praise. Although contemporary reconsiderations of social structure in substantive
ethnographic cases may conflict with earlier descent theory ethnographies, we must continue to take account of the latter. The sheer perva-
siveness of descent theory in well-established ethnographies makes this
necessary.

Descent Theory and the Hopi: Problem Areas

Of particular concern in this chapter is the explanatory adequacy of
descent theory for Hopi society. Let me therefore state certain major
premises of the theory with which I take issue in this regard. They are:
(1) that many societies are constructed of unilineal descent groups and
may thus be compared using a common theoretical framework; (2) that
unilineal descent groups are necessarily corporate; (3) that corporateness is based on possession of a joint estate, which is equated with
productive property; (4) that, in societies where unilineal descent
groups are the operative social units, they provide a structure of political action that is based on segmentary opposition; (5) that descent
groups of coordinate levels are structurally and functionally
isomorphic.

Time and Ethnography

My argument with these premises will be explored in more depth later.
However, there is at least one obvious problem with using classical
descent theory as an explanatory system for Hopi society: The Hopi

have refused to remain frozen in the ethnographic present of 1932 through 1934. Extensive social and cultural change has occurred over the last fifty years: The erosion of much traditional Hopi practice and belief, and their partial displacement by Anglo-American analogs, has resulted in Hopi redefinition of important cultural and social structural features. Formerly, for example, the ownership of a specific ceremony by a clan was a key demarcator of group identity. At present, with the decline of many ceremonies (at First and Third Mesas, at any rate), this source of identity has switched from demonstrative symbolic action to historical association. Similarly, a dramatic decline, especially since the 1960s, in subsistence agriculture in favor of participation in the cash economy has had a critical impact on social structure. It is important, then, to distinguish between different interpretations of the same Hopi reality: that is, the situation from 1932 to 1934, on the one hand, and differences in Hopi society deriving from half a century of social change, on the other.

I should emphasize, at this point, that my focus is primarily upon Third Mesa.[2] While anthropologists have occasionally recognized differences between the three Hopi Mesas, the acknowledgment is typically cursory, with a resultant neglect of variations that are in fact pervasive. Twentieth-century social change at Third Mesa shows some significant contrasts with the patterns at First and Second Mesas. For example, at the turn of the twentieth century, Orayvi, the only Third-Mesa village, had, by far, the largest population of the Hopi villages, accounting for at least half the total population in census records from 1885 to 1900. A corollary of this larger size was a significantly larger number of matrilineal "clans" than the other villages. (See Eggan 1950:65–66 for clan composition of the various villages.) It is probable that differences in socioeconomic organization between the Mesas partly result from the consistently greater population at Orayvi.

In 1906, however, Orayvi split over political differences between two major factions. More than half the population (the so-called Hostiles) left to found the new villages of Hotvela and Paaqavi.[3] In time, three other villages (deriving from the "Friendly" faction) became increasingly established as separate entities from the mother village: Lower Munqapi, Upper Munqapi, and Kiqötsmovi.

Hopi Social Structure: Orayvi

According to the view established by Eggan and Titiev, Hopi social structure is composed of discrete elements that interweave to bind the whole together. Elsewhere (Whiteley 1983), I have divided the elements recognized into horizontal and vertical structures. The vertical structure comprises matrilineal descent groups of increasingly inclusive levels: household, lineage, clan, and phratry. According to the conventional view, only clans are named in Hopi; households, lineages, and phratries are considered nominal anthropological abstractions that may receive oblique Hopi reference (see Connelly 1979:539).[4] Table 1 lists the phratries, clans, households, and population breakdown for Orayvi prior to the split. (Lineages are not enumerated because Titiev [1944: 58] regards these as "the vaguest of the Hopi divisions.")

The horizontal structure that intersects the descent groups basically comprises religious sodalities and kiva groups. Fourteen religious societies have been described for turn-of-the-century Orayvi. These can be grouped into three general levels of importance:

First-Order Societies:	*Aa'alt, Kwaakwant, Wuwtsimt, Taatawkyam; Sosyalt; Mamrawt*
Second-Order Societies:	*Sakwalelent, Masilelent; Tsu'tsut, Tsöötsöpt; Lalkont; Owaqölt*
Third-Order Societies:	*Powamuy; Katsina*[5]

These levels describe general structural similarities, not strict equivalencies within categories. Usually, between the ages of six and ten, all Hopis are initiated into one of the two third-order societies. After that, they are eligible (though there is a sexual division between the societies) for initiation into a second-order society; some may never join one, others may be initiated even in old age. At roughly ages sixteen to twenty, all males, traditionally, should be initiated into one of the four "Manhood" or "Tribal Initiation" (*Wuwtsim*) societies, and most females into the *Mamrawt* (an approximate female equivalent to the *Wuwtsimt*). For males, initiation into the *Sosyalt* was then possible. In a sense, then, the *Sosyalt* is on a higher plane still, but in practice the *Wuwtsim* societies are regarded as socially the most important. Each society conducts a particular ceremony at an appointed time of the year. The ceremony is owned by a particular descent group, which should provide the chief-priest for the society. Ordinary members of the society may come from any descent group. Membership in a religious society thus creates a new set of ties for the individual: to his or her society cohorts. Kiva membership similarly crosscuts descent group ties, although it is not isomorphic with sodality membership. Eggan (1950:96)

Table 1

Orayvi Clans and Phratries (after Titiev 1944:52)

Phratry	Hopi Name	English Name	No. of Households	M	F	Total
		Clan			Population	
I	Tapngyam	Rabbit	13	33	28	61
	Katsinngyam	Kachina	2	5	6	11
	Kyarsngyam	Parrot	5	16	15	31
	Angwusngyam	Crow	1	2	0	2
II	Honngyam	Bear	5	6	13	19
	Kookyangngyam	Spider	3	16	15	31
III	Tuwangyam	Sand	9	28	31	59
	Kuukutsngyam	Lizard	4	28	30	58
	Tsu'ngyam	Snake	2	2	4	6
IV	Tawangyam	Sun	9	24	23	47
	Kwaangyam	Eagle	6	12	9	21
V	Tepngyam	Greasewood	14	37	36	73
	Paaqapngyam	Reed	7	32	17	49
	Awatngyam	Bow	4	7	8	15
VI	Masngyam	Maasaw	7	29	19	48
	Kookopngyam	Kookop ("Fire")	3	8	14	22
	Hoongyam	Cedar	0	0	2	2
	Leengyam	Millet	1	5	6	11
	Isngyam	Coyote	10	24	22	46
	Paa'isngyam	Desert Fox (Water Coyote)	10	27	30	7
VII	Pashonanngyam	Real Badger	5	14	23	37
	Masihonanngyam	Gray Badger	3	6	27	33
	Tasaphonanngyam	Navajo Badger	3	7	4	11
	Poliingyam	Butterfly	1	2	3	5
VIII	Piikyasngyam	Young Corn	7	25	20	45
	Patkingyam	Divided Water (Water-House)	7	17	19	36
	Siva'apngyam	Rabbitbrush	1	1	2	3
IX	Kyelngyam	Sparrowhawk	2	5	5	10
	Atokngyam	Crane	1	1	4	5
	Paatangngyam	Squash	2	3	6	9
Totals			30			
			147	422	441	863

notes: "Kiva membership is not primarily by clan—while men may join other ceremonies and participate in other kivas which are more congenial or more convenient, their basic affiliation is with the kiva into which they are initiated during the Tribal Initiation." Hence, kiva membership creates ties (with kiva mates) that cut across both those within the descent groups and those within the sodalities. In short, according to the conventional view, the key to Hopi social integration is a balance between discrete groups of different orders. This is achieved by the weaving together of these groups so that different combinations are brought together for different purposes. The different combinations create rights and duties that counterbalance the divisive tendencies of allegiances to just one combination. Multiple allegiances for individuals create an overall village solidarity. Eggan sums up this view:

> Hopi integration may be viewed from the standpoint of the major organizations: kinship, clan and phratry, society and kiva. Each of these organizations has various devices for increasing or maintaining its own social solidarity. Each system of organization also overlaps the others in terms of membership, so that an integration of the whole is achieved; the bonds holding individuals to household, clan, society, and kiva groupings interweave in complex fashion. (Eggan 1950:116)

The underlying assumption in this tapestry conception concerns the fundamental power of descent-group ties. Indeed, it is because of this power that the system presumably generated the interlocking mechanisms described, in order to mitigate the supposed extreme divisiveness of the matrilineal clans.

There appears to be a contradiction here, however, between the acknowledged existence of sodalities and kiva groups and the descent-theory view, wherein Hopi society is regarded as being primarily constituted by the social unit of the clan. For instance, Titiev defines the clan as follows:

> A totemically named, exogamous, unilateral aggregation of matrilineal kindred, comprising one or more lineages, all of which are supposedly descended from one ancestress. Each clan has at least one *wuya*[6] stored in the clan house. If this *wuya* forms the nucleus of a pueblo ritual, the controlling clan furnishes the officers who conduct the ceremony. It is the only kinship group for which there is a native term, and *since land is held in the name of the clan, this unit is the cornerstone of Hopi society.* (Titiev 1944:58, emphasis added)

Eggan (1950:110) also considered the clan "the outstanding unit of social organization [among the Hopi]; in Hopi conception it is 'timeless' and permanent, extending back to the period before the emergence and forward to include as yet unborn children."

Titiev regarded clan solidarity as stronger than village unity:

> Despite a nominal allegiance to the Village chief, each clan is to a large
> extent autonomous, choosing its own officers and transacting its own
> affairs with a good deal of independence. Since a clan owns land,
> houses, gardens, and water rights, it is virtually a self-sufficient unit.
> Only the rule of exogamy and the custom of matrilocal residence force
> it to cooperate with other groups. . . . Such a social system rests on un-
> stable foundations, for the more firmly people adhere to clan lines, the
> weaker must be their village ties. A Hopi pueblo is like an object with
> a thin outer shell which holds together a number of firm, distinct seg-
> ments—should the shell be cracked, the segments would fall apart.
> (Titiev 1944:69)

A Hopi Perspective on Clan Identity

In Hopi thought, clans are regarded as having been independent migra-tory units that arrived at different times and from different directions. The origin of distinctive clan names varies, but usually involves an episode with the totemic object that occurred during the clan's migra-tions.

Orayvi was first occupied by the Bear clan. Subsequently, different clans approached the village and requested permission from the *Kikmongwi* ("the village chief"—always from the Bear clan) to settle in the village. He asked what they had to contribute to the village—a contribution that frequently came in the form of beneficial power over the natural environment. Each clan performed a ceremony of some sort, and, if this was successful, for instance, in bringing rain for the crops, the *Kikmongwi* assigned them a place in the village and an area in the Orayvi Valley to farm. For example, the following was told to H. R. Voth by the leader of the Hostile faction, Yukiwma:

> One of the first clans to arrive with those mentioned was the Bow clan,
> which came from the south-west. When the village chief asked the
> leader of this clan what he brought with him to produce rain, he said,
> "Yes, I have here the Sháalako Katcinas, the Tangík Katcinas, the
> Tûkwunang Katcina and the Sháwiki Katcina. When they dance it usu-
> ally rains." "Very well," the village chief said, "you try it." So the

Figure 2.1. A contemporary Hopi painting (1981), by Ray Sumatzkuku, including several totemic icons, which illustrate the ongoing salience of clan imagery in Hopi aesthetics and social life. This conforms to a conventional
style in recent Hopi painting, popularized, for example, by the Artists Hopid
group. Clan iconography is interwoven with, and inseparable from, ritual
and mythological imagery and engagements with the natural environment.
Totemic elements here naturalistically evoke several clans, including (counter-
clockwise from bottom right): Bear, Eagle, Corn, Sun, Sun Forehead, Cloud,
Young Corn, Kachina, and Squash. Conventionalized abstract elements—for
example in the arch surrounding the *Palhikmana* Kachina bearing the bowl
of corn in the upper left—represent additional iconographic features showing the imbrication of social, ritual, and natural conceptions in Hopi
thought. Collection of the author.

Áoat-wungwa [Bow clan member] arranged a dance. On the day before the dance it rained a little, and on the last day when they had their dance it rained fearfully. All the washes were full of water. So the village chief invited them to move to the village and gave them a large tract of land. He told them that they should have their ceremonies first. (Voth 1905:24)

Thus, its mythological history and the reenactment of this in ceremony, or the reiteration of it in tradition, constitute crucial features of clan identity in Hopi thought. The ideological emphasis in this view of clanship is central and contrasts sharply with the sociological emphasis of the received anthropological view. Although Eggan and Titiev recognized the possession of ceremonial "property" as significant, the conventional view has, as noted above, evolved in a way that stresses a joint estate in land and joint economic activity as the primary components of clan unity. Let us take a look at the empirical basis of these claims.

"Clan Land" and Economic Activities: The Concept of the Joint Estate

Today the notion of clan lands is mostly vestigial at Third Mesa, owing primarily to the Orayvi split. As I have argued elsewhere (Whiteley 1988), the prevailing Hopi view of the split includes the idea that the ritual order was abolished in accordance with an agreement made by the politico-religious leaders. None of the new villages attempted to establish clan lands, since the entire basis of "clan land" in Hopi thinking has to do with the ritual order. The general term for them is *wimvaavasa,* literally "ritual/ceremonial fields."

At Paaqavi, Hotvela, and Kiqötsmovi, many men continued to cultivate areas of the Orayvi Valley that they had farmed while living at Orayvi. In addition, other fields and orchards were established closer to the new villages. All newly established fields, orchards, and garden plots were individually owned, and patterns of inheritance varied widely; inheritance through a patriline is common. This seems a major departure from the view that land-use rights are inherited within the matrilineal clan "corporation."

So-called clan lands are still recognized and farmed upon in the Orayvi Valley, but their symbolic ratification in periodic ceremonies has virtually come to an end. Claims to use-rights in certain areas on the basis of clan land are often circumvented today by reference to the split and the concomitant abolition of Orayvi's ritual order. The Tribal Council buildings below Orayvi were built on lands traditionally held in the Badger a certain area around our lands, was proclaimed to be for our use, but the extent of this area is unknown to us, nor has any Agent ever been able to point it out, for its boundaries have never been measured. We most earnestly desire to have one continuous boundary ring enclosing all the Tewa and all the Hopi lands, and that it shall be large enough to afford sustenance for our increasing flocks and herds. If such a scope can be confirmed to us by a paper from your hand, securing us forever against intrusion, all our people will be satisfied:

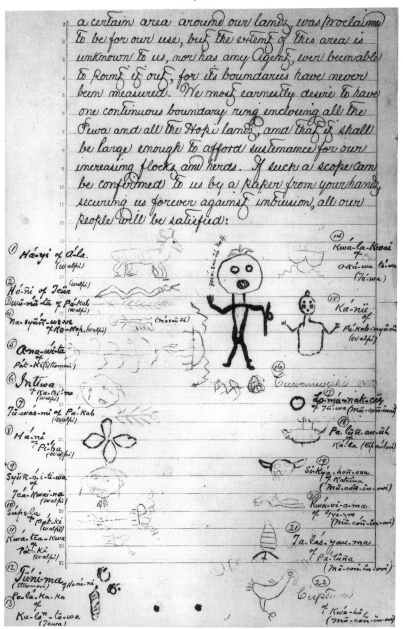

Figure 2.2. *Naatoylam*, "clan-totem images," identifying signatories (those shown are from First and Second Mesas) to the 1894 Hopi petition against allotment. The Dawes Act of 1887 sought to disestablish traditional land-holding and replace it with taxable private property. Two attempts to implement it at Hopi were resisted, leading to its abandonment in 1911 (Whiteley 1988:passim). National Archives: Record Group 75, 1894-14830L.

clan; the Hopi Civic Center stands on lands belonging to the Sand clan (both were built in the 1970s). Had the traditional system remained intact, such encroachment would have been unthinkable. As it was, heated discussions occurred, but the traditional claims were overridden. Recently, disputes at Musangnuvi (where much of the ritual order remains intact) over the laying of a pipeline on clan land produced a vigorous and successful protest by clan leaders (*Qua' Töqti* 1984:1).

Attempts to identify the location of clan lands in the Orayvi Valley have been fraught with difficulties. Some areas of farmland have been lost due to arroyo-cutting (see Bradfield 1971). Also, disputes over land were a feature of the split; subsequent opinions on the location of particular clan lands have often been politically loaded. Titiev (1944:62) includes a diagram of Orayvi clan lands, but he acknowledges that "the exact boundaries are uncertain despite the fact that the Oraibi chief was my principal informant on this question. He did not give me perfectly reliable data in all instances, and he frequently omitted important material" (ibid.:63 n.28). Furthermore, Titiev's discussion of clan lands at Orayvi prior to the split makes it clear that the nature of the holdings varied (ibid.:61–63). Some "clan lands" were granted with regard to ritual office incumbency, others were assigned on the basis of a special relationship between the clan (or its head) and the Kikmongwi in his role as head of the *Soyalangw* ceremony. Other lands apparently were assigned on a more random basis:

> Here and there, on the basis of various traditions, other clans were allotted land as they arrived at Oraibi, but even *those clans which had no legendary claims to particular plots were not left landless.* A large triangular stretch of ground near the Oraibi wash was known as "free land," on which any resident, with the chief's consent, was permitted to lay out a farm. (Titiev 1944:63, emphasis added)

The plain fact is that not all clans had "clan land." Not all clans had ceremonies or equivalent duties in the social system upon which the assignment of clan lands was mythologically predicated. Of the thirty clans listed in Table 1, Eggan (1950:103) records only eleven as owners of ceremonies. Several others had particular ritual roles or other offices, and still others had recognized social functions, such as, in the case of the *Kookop* and Coyote clans, defense of the village. Nevertheless, at least a third have no well-known social charter of this nature and no clan land; Titiev's diagram (1944:62) is rather confusing since it in-

cludes some clan names ("Turkey," "Tcip," "Bokya"—the latter two
of which I am unable to identify with any known Orayvi clan names)
not included in his chart of clans, on which my Table 1 is based. Even
so, only a maximum of twenty possible clan names are recorded in
association with farm plots.

According to my consultants, the internal distribution of clan land
at Orayvi by no means follows the nice, symmetrical pattern of lineage
and household plots that Beaglehole (1937:15-16) describes for Second
Mesa. Indeed, clan land was controlled by the leading family or lineage
segment that also controlled the particular ceremony for which the clan
was mythologically granted use of the field. Areas within the granted
tract might or might not be apportioned to other descent-group members beyond the core lineage segment, at the latter's discretion.

In this context, it is important to note that the stem word, which has
been translated as "clan land," carries the singular descent-group de-
nomination, *-wungwa*, rather than the plural, *-ngyam*, which refers to
the descent group as a whole. For example, *Kwaawungvasa*, usually
translated as "Eagle clan land," is a compound of *Kwaawungwa*,
"Eagle clan individual," and *paasa*, "field." A more precise translation
would be "Eagle clan individual's field." To be sure, there is a metonymic aspect to the term, perhaps interpretable as referring to the
apical Eagle clan ancestor who negotiated admission into the village.
The term is figuratively extended to a particular locale, and there is no
identification with a specific contemporary Eagle clan individual; neither is there any direct implication that the whole *Kwaangyam* descent
group is being referred to.

Another important factor concerns proprietary rights by sex. Anthropologists have generally agreed that "clan fields" belong to the women.
Kennard (1979:554) states: "Within each clan allotment, fields are
assigned to women of the clan, and they are planted and cultivated by
the men of the household—husbands, brothers, or sons. With the
pattern of matrilineal inheritance and matrilocal residence, fields tend
to become associated with specific households."

However, in seeking to clarify the issue of land ownership (or, more
correctly, rights of usufruct, since, in Hopi thought, *Maasaw*, an important deity, is the only being who actually "owns" the land), the
following view was presented to me. As soon as a man plants a seed
in the ground, the seed becomes the woman's property, whether this
woman is his wife, his sister, or his mother. Thus, all the plants in the
field, and all the produce from them, belong, like children in this

matrilineal society, to women. (Corn plants are explicitly metaphorized as children.)

But this notion of crop ownership is quite different from ownership of the actual plot of soil where the plants are raised. The location of the plot is, in a sense, irrelevant to women, since ordinarily they do none of the farming. From this perspective, it is men who have use-rights in the soil itself. When one man dies, the plots he has planted most of his life may pass to a son, a daughter's husband, his wife's brother's son, or someone else again. Today, at least, this seems to be a matter for decision within the nuclear-family household. The inheritor has primary subsistence responsibility to one woman, who may or may not be the woman for whom the land was formerly cultivated. The woman who acquires rights to the land's produce may be of a different clan from the first one if, for example, she is the wife of the first woman's son, who has inherited from his father the use-rights in the plot. Titiev's own account (1944:131 n.3) supports this: "In theory, only the women of a clan could hold title to land, so that a man generally farmed on the property of his wife or mother; but in practice it was not unknown for a son to inherit land from his father." Forde (1931:380) found the same situation at First and Second Mesas, where men sometimes "acquired fields from their relatives and in some instances passed them on to their daughters or even sons i.e., transferring them to individuals outside the clan." Forde (1931:382) concluded that "the Hopi system of land tenure while in theory one of clan ownership with inheritance of usufruct by females in the female line, is, in practice, subject to considerable modification."

Further, Hopi farmers maintain numerous fields in dispersed locales. Dispersion of fields is ecologically adaptive. It maximizes the chances of a good crop in this arid environment, where fields are often "moved" by the wind and where rain falls unevenly, providing moisture to some areas and leaving others completely dry.

Finally, "clan lands" refer specifically to corn fields. Especially in the past, Hopis also planted patches or fields (some were larger than some corn fields) with many varieties of beans, melons, squash, and gourds, as well as having extensive orchards of peaches, apricots, apples, and pears, and terraced gardens of various crops. Some of these plants are highly sensitive to minute variations within ecotypes and require specialized knowledge of local soil and moisture conditions. Plots for these secondary crops, as well as orchards and gardens, are all individually owned and tended, and inheritance patterns vary considerably. Titiev

(1944:181 n.3) implies clan ownership of both gardens and orchards, following his general proclivity toward accounting for economic activities in terms of descent groups, although he does acknowledge that single trees are individually owned. Inheritance may pass through a matriline, but this is a matter for individual determination. In short, the notion of these lands as "clan owned" is simply incorrect: they are *personal,* not corporate, property.

Other significant economic activities were not in the charge of the clan per se, nor even a lineage segment of it. Animal husbandry is a primary example. Titiev (1944:22) implies that a group of brothers (i.e., a matrilineal group) is the modal sheepherding unit. Elsewhere (Whiteley 1983:102-4), I have analyzed the composition of 109 sheepherding groups at Orayvi prior to 1906 (the data derive from Titiev's field notes [Titiev n.d.]). The largest single category of these groups was based on patrilateral ties, with only a maximum of 20 percent accounted for by matrilineal ties, as would be the case with brothers. Neither "clans" nor "lineages," therefore, can be regarded as the operative economic units in this activity. Similarly, cattle herding, which seems to have been important at Third Mesa since the eighteenth century (see Whiteley 1983:321-22), was not administered by clan-based groups. Horses and burros (and, today, pickup trucks), other important features of the economy, were and are individually owned. And neither hunting nor gathering were organized by clan, although rabbit hunts, in particular, involved large groups. The operative unit for at least some of these was the kiva group; this remains true in the post-*Soyalangw* rabbit hunts at Hotvela.

In sum, the concept of the Hopi clan (at least at Third Mesa) as an economically corporate unit possessed of a joint estate in property, and jointly conducting important economic activities, has not been the case in practice, either in 1900, in 1933, or today. I believe that Titiev (1944:184) took too literally an idealized Hopi view of land tenure and economic organization by clans: "In former times, while the clan system of land tenure was universally in vogue, it was customary for each group to plant and harvest as a unit, and such activities played an important part in fostering clan solidarities." The significance of this conception of joint clan activity on jointly owned property lies at an ideological level. It is a means of expressing group identity by reference to a condensed, metaphorical version of past events, in the same way as a clan is held to have been a unitary (though unilineal and exogamous) group migrating independently, prior to arrival at Hopi. Hopi oral tradition frequently condenses and encapsulates in this fashion: an effective means of preserving a large range of significant information without access to writing.

The fallacy of accepting the conventional account at face value lies in the concomitant assumption that clans are neatly divided descent groups. The problem is not really one of conflict between Hopi theory and practice. Rather, it lies in the fit between preconceived anthropological categories and a particular cultural reality. It may be that we have an African model in the Arizona Highlands.

PART 2

When we talk of lineage structure we are really concerned, from a particular analytical angle, with the organization of jural, economic, and ritual activities.

Fortes 1953:31

Among the Hopi, then, the clan is the basic kinship unit, landholding unit, and ritual unit. . . . It is the organizing unit of Hopi political and ceremonial life and provides the basis for heritable leadership and all hereditament.

Upham 1982:16

The orthodox version of Hopi social structure depicts Hopi descent groups as units that are economically, ritually, and jurally corporate. They are thus seen, particularly at the "clan" level, as strongly self-sufficient segments that are simultaneously the primary units of political action. It is suggested that the strength of clan corporateness is intrinsically destructive to the integration of society; Titiev (1944:69ff.), for example, regards clan divisiveness as the basis for the split of Orayvi in 1906. What weak integration exists is viewed as being achieved by the crosscutting ties effected by membership in religious sodalities, kiva groups, and households.

This view of descent groups rests on two major assumptions: that they are unambiguously identifiable "groups" which act corporately, and that matrilineal descent provides the strongest basis for social relationships in Hopi society. In Part 1, I questioned the economic aspects of the purported "joint estate" underlying clan corporateness. My inquiry now shifts to the ritual and jural dimensions of descent-group corporateness and to the significance of patrilateral relationships for social integration.

Ritual Knowledge and Inequality within Descent Groups

Ritual knowledge has been recognized as one kind of property that makes up a clan's joint estate. Titiev acknowledges differential access to this property within the clan. It is worth emphasizing such unequal access to ritual knowledge (which, in practice, amounts to access to political power—see Chapter 3), to counteract the common assumption of Pueblo egalitarianism. Hopis regard their society as ranked, even as composed of two "classes": *pavansinom*, "important/ruling people," and *sukavungsinom*, "common people." The key demarcation lies in the possession of socially valued knowledge, which is closely guarded in secrecy.

In ritual terms, the highest *pavansinom* are the *wimmomngwit*, or "chief-priests of the ceremonies." At Third Mesa, inheritance of these offices and the knowledge that goes with them is usually kept strictly within a descent-group segment rather than being accessible to all members of a clan. Again, as was the case in economic activities, the view of segmentary descent groups as *the* fundamental political units of Hopi society, facing off against each other at coordinate levels, is quite at variance with the actualities of Hopi political structure and action.

Some clans, such as Bear and Spider, have more prestige than others because they own important ceremonies and offices. Thus, the term *pavansinom* may be applied to these clans. But the distinctions are also made *within* the clan, so that a notion of clans ranked as whole units is inappropriate. The *pavansinom* within the Bear clan are the members of the immediate lineage segment that provides the *Kikmongwi*, "village chief," owns the *Soyalangw* ceremony, and supplies the highest ceremonial officers. Members of the Bear clan outside this lineage segment, who, therefore, do not have such access to power, are regarded in this context as *sukavungsinom*.

The *pavansinom*, then, are primarily those members of the core segments of lineages who hold principal offices in the ceremonies. Rather than the clan as a whole owning a particular ceremony as a joint estate, the core segment of a lineage—the same group that has rights of disposal over clan land—is the actual owning body. From his First and Second Mesa data, Lowie (1929:330) concluded: "Whenever the statement is made that a certain office or ceremonial privilege belongs to a clan, concrete data always show that transmission is, above all, within the narrow circle of actual blood-kin and only secondarily extends to unrelated clansmen." Parsons (1933:23) came to a similar conclusion, for she states that offices and privileges are held "not in the clan as a whole, but in a maternal family or lineage in the clan." Titiev (1944:46) also acknowledged this distinction, and he cites both Lowie and Parsons concerning this matter.

In short, ownership of ceremonies and offices is identified with the clan as a whole only by association or in severe contingency situations in which the core-lineage segment produces no heirs. Differential access to ritual knowledge, and the fact that some lineages in the clan have no access, belie the claim that ritual knowledge is part of a clan's joint estate.

The present century has seen the decline at Third Mesa of almost all ceremonial activity other than that of the third-order societies. Hence, the most important ceremonial associations have become a part of historical tradition rather than a nexus of social action. In those ceremonies which do continue, the activation of descent-group ties is clearly in evidence, but, to repeat, whole clans never operate as corporate units in ceremonial activities.

Clan Isomorphism

Hopi clans have different amounts of prestige, and some of them entirely lack ceremonial property. For example, at Orayvi, the Spider clan (or its leading lineage segment) owned the Blue Flute ceremony, the Antelope ceremony, the Warriors' society, the Stick-Swallowers' society (the last two jointly with the *Kookop* clan), a prominent office in the *Soyalangw* ceremony, the most important kiva in the village, and the chiefship of the leading branch of the *Wuwtsim* society. In contrast, the Desert Fox (a much larger clan, equivalent to Titiev's "Water Coyote" clan) possessed no clan land and seems to have had no ceremonial estate or offices in the community. Such differences suggest that to treat these groups as equivalent social units misrepresents the empirical situation.

Neither will it do to regard lineages as the apposite estate-owning corporations or as segmentary political units with parallel functional and structural attributes at coordinate levels. Some lineages or lineage segments control land corporately and own ceremonies and political offices, whereas others (comprising the great majority in pre-split Orayvi) do not.

The jural aspect of Hopi descent groups—perhaps their most often emphasized feature—also remains in question. The more developed versions of descent theory required that the estate pertain to rights in rem as well as rights in personam. However, some of the less classical versions held out for a more flexible definition. Noting that the corporate estate consisted of rights and duties "over persons or things" in Radcliffe-Brown's original formulation, Fried (1957:23) suggested that "a group is corporate if it maintains continuity of possession to an estate which consists of things, persons, or both." Implicitly then, rights in personam are the minimal criterion of descent-group corporateness. Such a view requires that we address the issues of Hopi descent-group composition and of the principles that determine group inclusion and exclusion.

"Households," "Lineages," "Clans," and "Phratries"

Eggan's and Titiev's conceptions of household and lineage are at some variance, in terms both of definition and of the respective importance each author ascribes to them. For Eggan (1950:29), the household is a matrilocal residential unit that includes inmarried affines and unmarried male kin. Eggan's "lineage" is an extrapolation from his concept of "household" or a group of households. The lineage is a less directly observable body in that it unites non-co-residential kin, but it is a more unitary body in that it constitutes a major action-group within the clan. Although lineages are unnamed units in Hopi, Eggan (1950:19), nevertheless, regards the lineage as the fundamental unit in the Hopi kinship system.

As Titiev (1944:58) defines the lineage, its precise boundaries are difficult to specify:

> Lineage—an exogamic, unilateral group of matrilineal kindred, demonstrably descended from a common ancestress. Since such demonstrations cannot always be made among the modern Hopi, and since the lineage lacks both name and *wuya* and may be scattered over several households, it is the vaguest of the Hopi divisions. Its importance lies primarily in its theoretical implications as a nascent clan, and in the tendency for inheritance to follow the lineage pattern.

In contrast, Eggan (1950:27) follows usual descent theory convention in treating the lineage as a group of individuals between whom genealogical relationships are clearly traceable. He labels as "clan" that aggregation of unilineal kin between whom genealogical links are putative but not traceable in practice.

The basic social unit for Titiev is the household, conceived of as a group of consanguineal relatives living under the same roof or, in the case of uxorilocal male kin, those continuing to regard it as their real home; it specifically excludes inmarried affines (Titiev 1944:48). Titiev's household is, then, the same unit that Eggan and others would refer to as a lineage or a lineage segment. Titiev's definition of "household" excludes affines who are palpably co-resident and includes kin who are for the most part nonresident. Hence, Titiev's basic unit is dependent primarily on a criterion of locality and secondarily on descent, while Eggan's conception of the basic unit—the lineage—is solely dependent on a criterion of descent.

Both Eggan's and Titiev's concepts present awkward problems when used to interpret actual Hopi behavior. It is difficult to distinguish what constitutes a lineage when it may comprise people who are simultaneously the sole members of a particular clan or when the same terms of reference and address are applied to clan and phratry mates clearly outside the genealogical lineage. Likewise, if the sole members of a lineage and clan are restricted to a particular household, the category terms lose their meaning as designations of empirically separable entities. Other problems arise because of sheer numbers: If the sole representatives of a clan consist of a mother and her children, then this group can be regarded as both lineage and clan, even if it consists of only two or three people. In a highly populous clan, however, lineages or households can be seen to proliferate. Titiev (1944:48) notes that "today one can find instances of one clan containing a single lineage and a solitary household; of one clan containing a single lineage but several households; or of one clan containing what seem to be several lineages whose members are scattered among a number of households."

Hence, in speaking of Hopi households or lineages as basic descent-group units, we are dealing with abstract constructs perceived by anthropologists as central principles of social structural articulation. Hopis, on the other hand, perceive lineages and households as de facto groupings, which may or may not exist within specific clans.

Clans are supposedly the only descent-group units named in Hopi, so we might expect the fewest problems with regard to their composition and identification. Our expectations would be unwarranted. Several authors have noted the practice of attributing multiple clan names to a single individual (e.g., Titiev 1944:48-49). The conflation of clan names is almost always within the same phratry, but it still raises serious questions about clan discreteness.

Let me attempt to elucidate these questions by examining some particular problems within two phratries. In phratry I, Nagata

(1970:233) points out that, while both Eggan and Titiev consider the Tobacco clan to have been long extinct in Orayvi, it is clearly represented as separate from the Rabbit clan at Munqapi. He also notes that one woman in Munqapi claims to be both Kachina clan and Rabbit clan. In Paaqavi, Rabbit and Tobacco are regarded as an inseparable clan. Similarly, although Paaqavi Rabbit/Tobacco representatives do not claim also to be Kachina clan, they acknowledge that some Hotvela people claim all three simultaneously, and they find no contradiction in this.

In the same phratry, there is a similar overlapping of Parrot, Kachina, and Crow clans. Titiev (1944:212; n.d.:27) lists one man, Polingyawma, as Parrot and Crow in different contexts. The female heads of two households are identified as Parrot and Crow, respectively (Titiev 1944:52-54), but are revealed in Titiev's census notes (n.d.:27a) as genealogical sisters—a fact confirmed by White's Orayvi genealogies (n.d.). In a 1977 census, all five of Polingyawma's grandchildren separately listed their grandfather as Kachina clan (Bacavi Village Census 1977).

Several factors account for this differential attribution of clan names. The most significant for the present purpose is that variation between self-designation and another's designation is frequent. Titiev (n.d.:27) cites a revealing quotation from his census consultant, the Orayvi *Kikmongwi*, Tawakwaptiwa, concerning Polingyawma's close lineal kin: "call selves Gyash [Parrot] but really Crow." My point is that clan identities have both positive and negative aspects; which aspect is emphasized depends on the position of the speaker. If the latter is speaking of a member of another clan or of someone who subscribes to an opposed political viewpoint, how he feels personally toward the individual under discussion is frequently relevant. Hence, in Titiev's census notes, Tawakwaptiwa (erstwhile leader of the Friendly faction) often attributes clan names to members of the Hostile faction for the purpose of highlighting less flattering aspects of their clan affiliation. Conscious, personally motivated choice in the ascription of a specific descent-group name to a particular individual is thus an important factor.

Similarly, identification of one's own descent group name when speaking to a nonmember is influenced by a number of considerations, both cultural and personal. As we have discussed, some clans have more prestige than others. Although humility is an important Hopi ideal, some people fall short of it. Many individuals identify their clan affiliations humbly, declining a prestigious identity that may be clearly perceived by others. But some individuals claim the most prestigious clan name in their phratry as their own. Individual motives are, of course, not exhausted by these two extremes.

In addition, while certain Hopi clans in the same phratry have had clear, recognizable boundaries between them through time (e.g., Third-Mesa Bear and Spider), others have not. Thus, particular lineages or lineage segments that control the clan's sacred objects may be more identifiable as comprising the "real" members of such-and-such a clan. Indeed, the term "real" is frequently applied to clans throughout Titiev's census notes; it appears to be a direct translation of *pas,* an emphatic prefix, often a superlative. The attribution of clan identities to individuals not in the prime lineage or lineage segment seems more subject to variation. The modern situation is still more fluid with the absence (at Third Mesa) of most of the traditional ritual sodalities and the correlative absence of public proof that one lineage or segment is the *pas* segment of the clan.

Phratry VII best illuminates the problems of descent-group structure. Titiev (1944:passim) lists three separate Badger clans: "Real" Badger, Gray Badger, and Navajo Badger. The origins of the latter two are subject to debate. According to Titiev's census notes, the ancestress of the Navajo Badger clan was a Navajo woman who married a Hopi man. Other versions hold that a Badger clan woman was captured by Navajos and lived among them for several years before returning to Orayvi with her children. According to White's genealogies, the Gray Badger branch derives from the extinct village of Awat'ovi, inferably from one or more Awat'ovi women who, after the destruction of Awat'ovi in 1700, were distributed among the other Hopi villages.

Queried about these divisions, a Badger clan man did recognize them, but he dismissed them as insignificant. He explained the differences in terms of the relative prestige attached to each term. "Real" Badger, *Pashonanngyam,* is considered more prestigious than the other two. Thus, members of a particular Badger lineage could attribute inferior status to another Badger clansman as a way of elevating themselves or denigrating the other. A means of internal descent-group distinction is often sought when Hopis tease and torment each other, as they often do, about this or that clan relative who is widely known for some infraction of social norms. A reply often follows the line, "Well, he's not really one of us *Pashonanngyam,* he's a *Masihonanwungwa,* 'Gray Badger individual.'" The shallow depth of recognition of actual genealogical relationships among the Hopi renders such distinctions more susceptible to debate than in those societies where genealogical accuracy is an important cultural concern.

At the time of Eggan's and Titiev's fieldwork, one well-known Orayvi woman, Sakwapa, insisted that she was a different clan from her own sons (Eggan, personal communication; cf. Titiev 1944:57). While her lineal relatives, including her own sons, regarded themselves as *Isngyam,* "Coyote clan," she claimed to be a "Yellow Fox" (a hitherto unheard-of clan). It is clear that statements of clan membership have sociopolitical significance and are not strictly regulated by genealogical accuracy. The origins of several "clan" divisions (e.g., *Piikyas-Patki, Greasewood-Reed, Kookop-Maasaw*) may be traced to disputes that very likely occurred within a group of genealogical relatives.

Hopis use a whole series of terms for categories of prestige, often mentioning color when the totem is an animal. Thus, with Badger, there are several variations on *honanwungwa,* "Badger descent-group individual." Although there is some doubt at the top end, recognized prefixes, in order of relative prestige, are as follows: *kuwan-* "brightly colored, beautiful"; *pavan-* "most important, best"; *pas-* "real"; *masi-* "gray"; *petos-* "brown, dark-colored"; *tasap-* "Navajo." The justification for considering these Badger branches as separate clans is doubtful. While there are, for example, *Honanwungvasa,* "Badger clan lands," in the Orayvi Valley, there are no separate *Masihonanwungvasa,* "Gray Badger clan lands," or *Tasaphonanwungvasa,* "Navajo Badger clan lands." Similar ascriptions occur with other descent groups, for example, Bear, Eagle, and Rabbit.

In relation to the natural world, Hopi descent groups have conceptual "rights" over an ethnotaxonomic class of natural objects. So, Badger members have exclusive rights of symbolic identification in naming practices, for example, with Butterfly, Porcupine, and certain medicinal plants (see Bradfield 1973:220–23; and see Chapter 4). Thus, it is conceivable that someone from the Badger clan could instigate a claim to being really "Porcupine descent group." If such a claim originated in the context of an ongoing social dispute, gradual establishment of "Porcupine" as a conceptually separate descent group might easily occur.

These variations in the pattern of descent-group membership demonstrate that the different clans and phratries listed by Titiev and Eggan are not isomorphic categories belonging to the same structural types. Clans are more distinct in some phratries than in others. In some cases, it is doubtful that we can refer to them as separate clans at all. In short, ascription of descent-group names in Hopi is not an unambiguous convention: It is loaded with political and social considerations that have nothing to do with genealogy.

It has been suggested in the conventional accounts that while Hopi has no terms for either lineage or phratry, the terms *-ngyam* and *-wungwa* denote "clan." The issues discussed above make these glosses seem rather arbitrary. For instance, within the Badger clan, *Honanngyam* could count either as a phratry term, including several clan branches, or, alternatively, as a single clan composed of smaller units—possibly Hopi "lineages." The notion that Hopi has no terms for "phratry" or "lineage" is really meaningless and reflects an inordinate bias toward the nominal categories of English-language anthropological usage. The fact that there are no precise terms corresponding to anthropological descent-group categories suggests that these categories may not fit the Hopi situation. The neat, geometric model of isomorphic descent groups with ordered layers of inclusion may be an inaccurate representation of Hopi social structure. Adherence to such abstract categories may, in fact, prevent us from identifying particular, concrete terms in Hopi for distinguishing supposedly unnamed categories.

The Structural Significance of Non-Descent-Group Relationships

In the conventional view, the individual Hopi is held to receive his or her social identity through membership in a series of groups—descent groups, household groups, sodality groups, kiva groups. Society is integrated through the intersection of these group boundaries, and thus individuals are tied to different groups in different contexts. Eggan (1950:passim) has also noted the importance of "kinship ties," or what Fortes would call "complementary filiation," as a component of this integrative process. However, I believe that the structural significance of these patrilateral ties has been greatly underestimated. I am particularly interested in cross-sex ties, since they are often neglected in ethnological research. In addition, an emphasis on descent groups as the primary units of social structure among the Hopi neglects the significance of dyadic bonds between individuals.

The particular Hopi relationship of interest here is between the categories *kya'a* (FZ—"father's sister") and *mööyi* (BS—"brother's son").[7] In the course of social change, some kinship relationships have lost significance, but the *kya'a-mööyi* tie remains strong both in everyday life and on ceremonial occasions (Whiteley 1983:396). This relationship is perhaps the most common focus of social amusement. A male's "aunts" (the term Hopis use in English) wash his hair at birth and name him after their descent group. From the beginning of his life they exercise a pretended proprietary sexual interest in him. Few opportunities for sexual banter are missed; the relationship clearly provides much pleasure and amusement. When the man marries, his aunts descend on their brother's (his father's) house, vociferously proclaiming their superior sexual skills, and engage in a mud fight with the boy's female relatives and his prospective bride. Their brother also comes in for a good deal of harassment for having "given away" their nephew to someone else. Though this behavior is largely symbolic, the emphasis on this relationship is maintained throughout life. When the man dies, his aunts wash his hair and prepare him for the world beyond. Eggan (1950:39) has discussed the nature of this tie and notes: "the relation between the father's sister and her brother's child is a very important one in Hopi life." However, he does not emphasize the effect of such ties at the individual level on the entire social structure.

The *kya'a-mööyi* relationship does not characterize just genealogical father's sisters and brother's sons. Since Hopi kin categories are classificatory and cover whole phratries, as well as the phratries of fictive "godfathers," the number of individuals of different descent groups who are involved in the FZ/BS relationship probably surpasses those involved in all other kinship categories. For a male, all women of his father's phratry and his godfather's phratry are his "aunts." Even with distant aunts in other villages, the relationship is one of emphatic affection and jocularity. Other classificatory relationships seem to focus in practice on those who are genealogically close, but this is not the case with the *kya'a-mööyi* tie. Women who act in the ceremonial roles mentioned will usually be close relatives of the boy's father, but this is not always so. Both sexes are eager to maximize the number of potential "aunts" or "nephews" because of the pleasurable character of the relationship.

For the "aunt," the range of individual males to whom she is *kya'a* is not limited by descent-group membership. Every male born to every man in her phratry is her *mööyi*. Since her male phratry relatives will be married into many other descent groups, the clan affiliations of her nephews are multiple. If we then include those males to whom she is a ceremonial "aunt," the relationship ramifies more widely still.

One only has to witness the closing stages of a Social Dance to see these principles activated and to see them underscored by symbolic economic exchanges. For a Social Dance, a girl, who must be unmarried, chooses her partner from among all her "nephews"; the chosen man is often genealogically distant rather than close. The honored nephew provides her with a specified kind of gift (minor household utensils are common), and at some later time she will reciprocate with woven plaques and perhaps some cooked food. Toward the close of the dance any woman from the audience, married or not, may push in front of the girl to dance with her *mööyi*. She may pick any *mööyi*, and frequently an elderly woman, much to the audience's amusement, will muscle in on several dance couples.

A discussion of the range and significance of patrilateral and fictive-patrilateral relationships is beyond my present scope. My point here is simply that the conventional view of Hopi structural integration, in which strong descent-group ties are seen as requiring mitigation by crosscutting group memberships, ignores the structural consequences of formalized cross-sex relationships that unite individuals in dyadic pairs rather than in groups. The *kya'a-mööyi* tie may give a woman formal, affectionate links with males of every "clan" outside her phratry. These ties have a critical integrating effect across the entire descent-group structure.

CONCLUSION

As I argued in Part 1, the conventional picture of Hopi social structure was much influenced by the tenets of classic descent theory. This view represents a distillation of the theoretical principles underlying unilineal descent groups. The division of Hopi social structure into households, lineages, clans, and phratries and the insistence that lineages and clans constitute distinct groups centered upon corporate estates have obscured the realities of Hopi society. That these descent group levels are potentially *observable* is not denied. That they appear in isomorphic forms with parallel functions in the total structure is quite simply not the case. Two of the primary contexts of social action—economy and ritual—have changed significantly in the twentieth century; however it seems doubtful that a rigid definition of corporateness was ever applicable to Hopi descent groups, beyond the fact that they regulate marriage by prescribing exogamy. Prescriptive exogamy marks out the major divisions—between "phratries"; within these groups, criteria of more narrow descent-group identity vary widely.

What have been called Hopi "clans" are not corporate groups—economically, ritually, or jurally—as defined by descent theory. Since there are no repeatable means of indisputably establishing the criteria of inclusion and exclusion of Hopi descent groups, it is absurd to treat them as corporate units. The supposed direct translatability of -*ngyam* and -*wungwa* into "clan" and "clan member" (where clan is a formally defined descent category), and the concomitant assumption that lineages and phratries are unnamed in Hopi, derive from a conceptual prejudice that is both theoretical and the result of an obvious bias toward the English language.

Descent theory provides a template for describing some elements of Hopi organization. However, its use is limited in scope, for Hopi society is more complex than the parameters of the theory allow. Hopis seem never to have been troubled by infractions of matrilineal principles other than exogamy. Agnatic ties, especially between fathers and sons, and affinal ties, both between brothers-in-law and between fathers-in-law and sons-in-law, were (and are) often the basis for economic cooperation, ritual sodality membership, and even inheritance of high office.[8] The example of one particularly important cross-sex patrilateral relationship (FZ/BS) indicates the cultural and structural significance of ties that transcend both matrilineality and the conventional emphasis on groups as the significant units of Hopi social structure.

Descent is an important concept for the understanding of Hopi society. However, its importance lies in the cultural use of descent as an idiom to delineate individual and group statuses and in the practical effect these statuses have upon social action, not in its supposed conformance to a rigid set of theoretical precepts about unilineal descent groups. To explore the descent idiom meaningfully and without prejudice in its Hopi contexts, a simultaneous examination of the various other Hopi idioms for identifying status and organizing action is required. I hope to have cleared at least part of the ground for such an exploration to take place.

THE INTERPRETATION OF POLITICS
A Hopi Conundrum

If Chapter 2 did succeed in clearing some of the descent-theory ground embedded in the received view of Hopi social structure, here I turn to the key matrix articulating much social life, the politico-ritual system. My critical intervention here focuses on Hopi conceptions of power (including "supernatural" power), and how these qualitatively alter the conception of politics from that envisioned by orthodox political anthropology. In brief, Hopi ritual is about control of the cosmos, which is animate, transformative, and approachable through specific symbolic action. Ritual action itself implicates a politics, in that these approaches are designed to alter the material conditions of humanity (beneficially, or indeed adversely). Hopi society deploys a systemic ritual politics (in addition to the kinship units) that is inseparable from Hopi metaphysics (and see now Kertzer's [1988] useful comparative synthesis of the ritual and the political).

The ethnographic critique here reciprocally questions rationalist premises of political theory. Anthropological representations of Hopi polity are ambiguous and contradictory: I argue that the reason lies in the epistemological disjunction of "politics" from "religion" in Western theoretical discourse, which is inadequate to systems of social inequality not assimilable to rationalist and materialist models of political structure. My theoretical recommendations tend toward Foucault's ideas on power and Gramsci's on hegemony—a move that bears the stamp of the chapter's first date of publication (1987).

The use of Foucault and Gramsci must now have a warning label attached. I agree with Stuart Hall's assessment of the productive influence of Foucault (and Gramsci) in concrete analysis, but I also question the recursive, dehumanizing effects of his totalizing vision:

> Foucault has made possible a welcome return to the concrete analysis of particular ideological and discursive formations, and the sites of their elaboration. Foucault and Gramsci between them account for much of the most productive work on *concrete analysis* now being undertaken in the field [of cultural studies]. . . . But again, Foucault's example is positive only if his general epistemological position is not swallowed whole . . . [because] Foucault so resolutely suspends judgment, and adopts so thoroughgoing a skepticism about any determinacy or relationship between practices, other than the largely contingent. (Hall 1992 [1980]:537)

And however productive, Sahlins shows that as well as an ultimate vagueness in Foucault's determination of power sources, the prolific, uncritical use of Foucault and Gramsci in recent ethnographic analysis has had a trivializing effect:

> The current Foucauldian-Gramscian-Nietzschean obsession with power is the latest incarnation of anthropology's incurable functionalism. . . . Now, however, "power" is the intellectual black hole into which all kinds of cultural contents get sucked, if before it was "social solidarity" or "material advantage." (Sahlins 1993a:15)

The effect:

> . . . is to trivialize such terms as "domination", "resistance", "colonization", even "violence" and "power." Deprived of real-political reference, these words become pure values, full of sound and fury and signifying nothing . . . but the speaker. (Ibid.:17)

Similarly, the widespread use of Gramscian hegemony via Raymond Williams's influential interpretation has been found rather seriously wanting by Gramsci specialists (see Kurtz 1996; and for more grounded readings of Gramsci see, e.g., Fontana 1993; Sassoon 1987). Still and all, I remain convinced that Hopi social control, hierarchy, and political decision-making are more effectively conjoined with the larger epistemological field of "the political" Foucault and Gramsci have now irreversibly opened in social analysis, than with alternative, narrower paradigms.

Since this chapter was first published, two other accounts of Hopi hierarchy have appeared: Schlegel 1992 and Levy 1992. The attention to Hopi hierarchy that this represents is to be wholeheartedly applauded in contrast to the equilibrium, "tribal"-level models of sociocultural integration that typically circulate. Hopi *is* a hierarchical society. But the terms of its hierarchy are constituted within a particular cultural cast that is ineffectively accommodated by Western formalist models. Levy argues for a materialist basis of Hopi inequality, which simply does not fit the culturally situated structures of Hopi power and inequality (Whiteley 1994). Likewise, Schlegel's "frontier model," while departing from materialism, fails equally to engage Hopi perspectives because of its own determinist pragmatics. Both reproduce the anthropologically usual disregard of indigenous social thought, rather than seeing it, as I attempt to here, as an essential guide to analytical understanding.

INTRODUCTION

The study of Hopi politics is riddled with contradictions. The Hopi are variously described as a theocracy and a hierarchy (Parsons 1933:53), as having "never developed a political society" (Eggan 1964:182), as an oligarchy (Upham 1982:passim), as egalitarian (Hieb 1979:181), and as having "incipient social classes" (Harvey 1972:210). In general works, the Hopi have been situated at the "tribal" level of sociocultural integration (e.g., Lewellen 1983:65), which is defined to entail a fundamental egalitarianism and the lack of hereditary leadership roles.

Whence comes such confusion? At first blush, it is tempting to seek its source in differing theoretical predilections. But, in fact, long before anthropological paradigms were a twinkle in the Enlightenment eye, similar contradictions obtained. Pedro de Castañeda, chronicler of the Coronado expedition of 1540, noted that Tusayan (Hopi) "is governed like Cibola [Zuni] by an assembly of oldest men. They have their governors and generals (sus governadores y capitanes)" (Winship 1896:489). He elaborated further on the situation at Zuni, again explicitly comparing it to Hopi:

> They do not have chiefs as in New Spain, but are governed by a council of the oldest men. They have priests who preach to them. . . .

[T]hese are the elders. . . . They tell them how they are to live, and I believe that they give certain commandments for them to keep. (Ibid.:518)

Oligarchy, theocracy, and gerontocracy might all seem appropriate inferences from this account. In contrast, however, Diego Pérez de Luxán, chronicler of the next exploration in 1583 (the Espejo expedition), reported from Orayvi: "every pueblo in this province is ruled by three or four caciques and the cacique has as little power as the ordinary Indian; hence they are all equal" (Hammond and Rey 1966:193–94).

The divergence of viewpoints among Euro-American observers of Hopi polity thus has considerable antiquity. Eggan, I believe, effectively locates the problem:

> Hopi political organization is difficult to characterize because authority is phrased in ritual rather than in secular terms and is not concentrated in any single position. There is no central authority for the Hopi as a whole. . . . Within each major village there is a hereditary group of priests or chiefs but the order of this hierarchy varies from village to village, and they have a minimum of secular authority. (Eggan 1950:506)

The key words here are "ritual," "secular," "priests," and "chiefs." Titiev (1944:59) has remarked that the loose usage of "priests" and "chiefs" for Hopi officials has rendered the terms meaningless. But the problems, I feel, go deeper still. They derive from a fundamental disjunction in the epistemological fields of Western thought, between politics and religion. Anthropologists have reflected this disjunction—implicitly and explicitly—in their analysis of non-Western societies, identifying and dividing social action accordingly. Recently the division may have begun to dissipate (cf. Fardon 1985), but conventional anthropological knowledge of cultures, constructed via earlier ethnography, continues to reflect it.

The disjunction is particularly apparent in the treatment of power—a "protean lexeme" as R. N. Adams has it (1977:xii)—which, though intrinsically ambiguous and multireferential, is a central concept in both fields. "Political," that is, secular, power concerns relationships of control within and between social groups, and it tends to be ultimately reducible to control of material production—"strategic resources" (e.g., Cohen 1970; Fried 1967; R. N. Adams 1977). Structures of political power are, then, empirical—somehow solid, measurable, and susceptible to analytical scrutiny: They conform to "our" concepts of rational activity. "Religious" power, on the other hand, concerns conceptions and experience of the numinous—power as an immanent mystical entity, inaccessible to direct analysis. "Religious" practices must be transfigured into schemes of "symbolism," which only affect political practice indirectly, and are typically treated as devices of legitimation (e.g., [recently], Bloch 1974; 1980; Ahern 1981)—expressions rather than instruments of social action. A direct role for the "supernatural" in the "political" is rejected by the rationalist convictions that inhere in ethnographic representations (even in those with avowedly relativist persuasions).

When a Hopi says the Snake Dance is for rain, for example, the ethnographer is obliged to shift from "description" to "explanation" (cf. Parkin 1982:xiv). Of course, the Hopi do not *really* dance for rain, because we all know this is impossible (e.g., Spiro 1966:113). Instead they are "dramatizing" (eminently false) religio-ecological beliefs, acting out "myths" (the double-meaning still clings), "symbolizing" social relations or sexual relations, "representing" the desirability of fertility, ideologically (i.e., with false consciousness) "legitimating" inequality, or what have you. Whatever it is they are doing, they are not engaging in instrumental acts: They have moved from pragmatic action to the domain of "meaning," which requires explanatory interpolation. Hopis, however, do not make parallel conceptual distinctions. Snake rituals activate immanent forces in a directly instrumental fashion: The clear aim is to produce rainfall. Of course, there are symbolic dimensions in Hopi exegeses also, and typically these are dense with meaning, but the ritual actions are not reducible to these. The Snake and Antelope societies directly manipulate forces which, in the community of belief, have matter-of-fact existential reality.

The bicameralization of "religion" and "politics" in Western thought, and the derivative oppositions—"sacred-secular," "rational-mystical," "natural-supernatural," etc.—in anthropological theory, are, I believe, the cause of confusion in the interpretation of Hopi polity and, perhaps, many other political systems. Ritual practices cannot be political unless they are predicated on the expression of control in economic relations, a control that must be backed by forces of brute physical coercion. Conversely, culturally recognized social hierarchies must be articulated upon control of material resources, or the hierarchies are ephemeral and society must be fundamentally egalitarian.

This poses problems, however, when the natives conceive otherwise,

have clear criteria for discriminating hierarchical structures and relations, and act accordingly. My question, then, is one of cultural interpretation, in Geertz's sense (e.g., 1973): how to translate Hopi practices
and Hopi talk about their practices into terms that least violate their
actuality: "'Translation,' here, is not a simple recasting of others' way
of putting things in terms of our own ways of putting them . . . but
displaying the logic of their ways of putting them in the locutions of
ours" (C. Geertz 1983:10).

TWO CAVEATS

I shall confine my discussion largely to Hopi society at Third Mesa,
especially in Orayvi around the turn of the century. Considerable
differences in social structure exist between the villages of the three
Mesas. It seems evident—and this accords with oral history from all
three Mesas—that Orayvi had, for a long time, a considerably more
complex political structure than the other villages. Throughout the
written historical record Orayvi (the only Third Mesa village until the
present century) is consistently described as the largest Hopi village
from Espejo's visit of 1583 on; in 1900 it accounted for roughly half
the entire Hopi population. Such size entailed a much larger contingent of matrilineal descent groups (see Chapter 2), some of which
maintained strict control of ritual sodalities and their associated ceremonies. In other villages, such control has been less strict and has in
several instances circulated among different kin groups (cf. Eggan
1950:105), entailing significantly greater fluidity of political structure
than at Orayvi.

This chapter is primarily concerned with political action defined in
Hopi society as the prerogative of males. Elsewhere (Whiteley
1988:163-65) I have argued that the sexual division of labor gives
women greater control of economic resources, while male control is
largely based in ritual. Women own houses and the products of agricultural labor, and they take a large part in the redistribution processes.
In many ways, the organization is centered in the household and the
economy is under the control of women. A more complete analysis of
the entire field of Hopi power, authority, and influence should include
the exercise of female control over production. This is beyond my scope
here, however, which is limited to a politico-ritual arena articulated by
Hopi men, but which is clearly acknowledged in the daily practices of
both sexes.[1]

HOPI POWER: STRUCTURES AND CATEGORIES

Several recent accounts of Hopi status ranking have appeared (Nagata n.d.; Upham 1982; Whiteley 1983), and E. Brandt (1985) has conducted a pan-Pueblo analysis of hierarchy. Here, I want merely to examine some central principles of Hopi stratification.

The cardinal division is between *pavansinom* and *sukavungsinom*. *Sinom* means "persons" or "people." *Pavan* has a broad semantic field, but in this context may be rendered as "most powerful" or "most important." Hopi consultants have offered semantic and morphological breakdowns for *sukavung*, but these are in doubt and I think it best to work with the English glosses Hopis usually give for *sukavungsinom*, namely, "grass-roots people," "common people." Correlatively, *pavansinom* is usually glossed "ruling people."

References to this general "class" division, a common term in Hopi-English, are extremely rare in the literature, although it is a matter of everyday Hopi discourse and seems to have clear parallels in other Pueblo societies (e.g., Tewa "Made" and "Dry Food" people [Ortiz 1969], Zuni ritually "valuable" and "poor" [e.g., Tedlock 1979:506], and Keres "cooked" and "raw" people [e.g., White 1935:167–68]). For Hopi, Nagata assigns the following passage to a footnote:

> *Pavan* means force, strength, and perhaps supernatural power (Voegelin and Voegelin 1957:C4.4), and *pavansinom* is contrasted to *shikabunsinom* or "ordinary people." The former refers to the clans owning ceremonies or members of such secret societies as *Momchit*. The people using poaka or witchcraft are also called *pavansinom* and now the Tribal Council is so called because of its power. One informant noted that the *pavansinom* tended to marry each other for fear of clan secrets being stolen by nonimportant people. (Nagata 1970:44 n.2)

Similarly, R. Brandt notes this division (although he has a different term for *pavansinom*), and provides further detail:

> The Hopi speak of themselves as a "class" society. The language contains terms marking traditional stratifications: *mongsinom*,[2] meaning "people who have the title or dignity of chiefs," and *sukaavungs sinom*, meaning "common people." If a Hopi is asked to which class a given individual belongs, he will give a definite answer depending upon the traditional tribal offices held by him or his family or his clan connections with persons holding such offices. (These offices almost always have some relation to the ceremonial system; individuals holding cer-

tain offices are usually at the same time vested with ownership of certain ceremonies and have the right to decide if and when their ceremony is performed.) . . . Members of the upper classes have prestige in the sense that the lower classes look up to them as "blue bloods" associated with the tribal leadership. (Brandt 1954:23-24)

Although Hopis can and do identify individuals who are *pavansinom* on a regular basis, criteria for occupancy of this category are more complex than the above quotations imply. While there is a sense in which all members of the Bear clan are *pavansinom* in comparison, say, to the Sun clan, the distinctions can also be made *within* the Bear clan. So, as I noted in Chapter 2, those members of the Bear clan in the core lineage segment that provides the *Kikmongwi,* or "village chief," own the *Soyalangw,* "Winter Solstice," ceremony; provide the officers for it; and are the *pas,* "real," *pavansinom* within the Bear clan. Other members of the Bear clan may be regarded, from this perspective, as *sukavungsinom.*

To enlarge sufficiently the definitions of *pavansinom* quoted, and to explain the recognition of intraclan distinctions, we must accommodate Hopi conceptions of power. *Pavansinom* merit such a designation not simply by their occupation of institutional offices, but because of the supernatural power these offices entail.

Pavansinom are primarily those members of the core segments of matrilineages who hold principal offices in the ritual order: Their authority rests in the conduct of cyclical ceremonies and is repeatedly reasserted in myth and ritual performance. The ceremony is the cornerstone of the clan's raison d'être; it records clan myth and history, and dramatically delineates the collective identity of its members. But rather than the clan as a whole, the core lineage segment is the actual owning body of the ceremony and, reflexively, head of the clan (cf. Lowie 1929:330; Parsons 1933:23; Titiev 1944:46). It is via control of a ceremony or ritual office that the apical clan segment is considered *pavansinom*. Power accrues to them through control of the specific ritual knowledge required to perform the ceremony effectively. Nonmembers of apical segments and members of clans that own no ceremonies, important offices, or highly valued ritual knowledge generally lack control over significant supernatural power and are thus *sukavungsinom.*

As Nagata points out, *popwaqt* (singular, *powaqa,* usually translated "witch"), individuals who are attributed with enormous powers and often evil intentions, may also be regarded as *pavansinom*. Further, a *tuuhikya,* "a curer who works individually," may be included in this category, although he is outside the formal ceremonial structure. His power is more achieved than ascribed, although it may be attributed to inheritance within a kin group. Because a *tuuhikya* controls effective powers, he may be regarded with respect as a *pavansino* and simultaneously with suspicion as a *powaqa* (the ambiguity is considered below). Others who routinely manifest exceptional abilities (often considered as adhering to particular lines of descent) to manipulate the world's conditions, such as in the raising of particular cultigens, may be referred to as *pavansinom* (and/or *popwaqt*) also.

In sum, the concept *pavansinom* is contingent upon conceptions of extraordinary power. The power derives from various sorts of esoteric knowledge, which carry a high social value.

FORMALLY INSTITUTED OFFICES

The *Kikmongwi* occupied the most important of a set of formally instituted offices at Orayvi. Titiev has detailed his functions and authority (1944:64–65), noting a lack of coercive power and concluding that "the Village Chief is looked upon rather as a guide and an advisor than an executive; and as an interpreter of Hopi tradition rather than as a legislator" (ibid.:65).

The *Kikmongwi* had various assistants, whose relationships with him were formally represented in the *Soyalangw* ceremony. Titiev considers members of this group the most important political leaders; he lists them in order of presentation during the *Monglavayi,* "chiefs' talk," at the close of *Soyalangw:*

> The Village Chief (kikmongwi) of Oraibi spoke first, and was followed in order by the head man of the Parrot clan; the Pikyas clan chief; the Tobacco Chief (Pipmongwi), normally the head of the Rabbit clan; the Crier Chief (Tca'akmongwi), usually leader of the Greasewood clan; and the War Chief (Kaletaka) who may be from the Badger or Coyote clan. In every respect these men are the most important officials in the pueblo. (Titiev 1944:59–60)

It is instructive to contrast this view with that of Yukiwma, leader of the Hostile faction immediately prior to the Orayvi split of 1906. Describing the mythological emergence of mankind from the world below, Yukiwma lists the leaders in order as they climb up inside the sacred reed:

So they commenced to climb up the reed, first the different chiefs, the Village Chief (Kikmongwi), who was also at the same time the Soyalmongwi, the Flute chief[3] (Lanmongwi), Horn chief (Al-mongwi), Agave chief (Kwan-mongwi), Singer chief (Tao-mongwi), Wuwuchim chief (Kel-mongwi), Rattlesnake chief (Tcu-mongwi), Antelope chief (Tcöp-mongwi), Marau chief (Marau-mongwi), Lagon chief (Lagonmongwi), and the Warrior chief[4] (Kalehtak-mongwi or Pöökong). And then the people followed and a great many went out. (Voth 1905:19)

This representation of leadership conforms with my consultants' accounts. The leaders, including the *Kikmongwi,* are referred to collectively as *Wimmomngwit,* "heads of the ritual sodalities,"[5] of which the Horn, Agave, *Wuwtsimt,* and Singers (also known collectively as the *Wuwtsim,* or "Manhood Initiation," sodalities) are accorded the most importance: In the words of one older consultant, "these [*Wuwtsim*] societies are the Hopis' government."

Titiev's main informant on Orayvi political structure and officeholders was Tawakwaptiwa (Eggan, personal communication), the *Kikmongwi,* and leader of the Friendly faction at the time Orayvi split. It is evident from Titiev's census notes (Titiev n.d.) that Tawakwaptiwa played down or ignored the roles of several major adversaries. It is also possible that my consultants (descendants of both factions, though more from the Hostile side) deemphasized the *Soyalangw* officers. But Titiev's neglect of the sodality leaders is certainly unwarranted (cf. Parsons 1933:53–54). They were not assistants to the *Kikmongwi,* but seem to have been independent participants in a group of decision-makers. Each was also the head of a particular clan, as outlined above. The *Kikmongwi*'s relationship to them seems to have been roughly primus inter pares. For example, it is well known that during periods of ceremonial performance (still today), the sodality leader's authority in the village supersedes that of the *Kikmongwi* for the duration.

Each sodality head is ritually responsible for the proper conduct of the ceremony over which he presides, and this entails control over particular supernatural forces. The sodalities have distinct functions in the annual cycle (see Frigout 1979, for summary details), but their ideal aims can broadly be characterized as the creation and re-creation of beneficial conditions in the various dimensions of the Hopi world.

The *Qaletaqmongwi* position also warrants particular examination. Titiev describes his role:

Figure 3.1. *Momngwit*. Four Orayvi leaders, 1885. Their identities are unfortunately not recorded. The blurred figure of a white woman at right may well be anthropologist Matilda Coxe Stevenson. She was present at Orayvi in 1885 in a famous confrontation (reported in the *Illustrated Police News*), when she was refused admission to a kiva (e.g., Babcock and Parezo 1988:11). It is likely that this photograph is of Orayvi leaders sympathetic to her cause (collecting ethnological specimens for the Bureau of American Ethnology with her husband James Stevenson), but it is not impossible that they are her leading antagonists. In either case, it may be the earliest extant photograph of Orayvi leaders (with the exception of an image of Tuuvi—a close ally of *Kikmongwi* Loololma—and his family at Munqapi in the early 1870s). Photographer not recorded. National Anthropological Archives (2458-A), Smithsonian Institution.

To the War chief was given the duty of maintaining the discipline, and he was the nearest approach to a policeman in each Hopi town. He had the right of scolding miscreants, of boxing their ears, and, perhaps, of thrashing them. The basis of his authority lay in his military leadership. . . . [T]he power of the War chief has diminished until his position today is entirely devoted to ceremonial observances. (Titiev 1944:65-66)

Titiev identifies Qöyangayniwa of the Badger clan as War Chief in the 1890s, apparently considering that the position of *qaleetaqa,* "guardian," "sergeant-at-arms," in the *Soyalangw* ceremony was the same as village *Qaletaqmongwi*. It is very likely that this duplication of roles was the case prior to the disputes that eventuated in the split. However,

Qöyangayniwa's tenure of the *Soyalangw qaleetaqa* position seems to have been the result of the factional division.

The *Qaletaqmongwi* was head of the *Momtsit,* or "Warriors," ritual sodality. It is clear from documents of the 1880s and 1890s that the *Qaletaqmongwi* position rested in the *Kookop* clan (a major seat of Hostile faction leadership), and Titiev (1944:156) affirms that the *Momtsit* was owned jointly by the *Kookop* and Spider clans. The incumbent in the 1890s was Heevi'yma, of the core *Kookop* segment; Heevi'yma was consistently referred to as *the* leader of the Hostile faction in the early 1890s (see Whiteley 1983:160-63). The *Qaletaqmongwi* was the earthly representative of *Pöqangwhoya,* the elder of the "War Twins," and was often assisted by a representative of *Palöngawhoya,* the younger brother. (Fewkes [1922], for example, describes the initial ritual stages of a declaration of war, by Orayvi Hostiles against U.S. troops, involving both the *Qaletaqmongwi* and his assistant.) The historical record reveals several cases where it seems clear that the *Qaletaqmongwi* was vested with responsibility for the negotiation of political relationships with outsiders. For example, Escalante recorded a meeting with Orayvi leaders in 1776:

> I sent for the cacique [i.e., *Kikmongwi*] and captains to prepare them for the sermon I wanted to preach to them the next day. Only the chief captain [*Qaletaqmongwi*] and his lieutenant or companion came, with some old men. . . . The chief captain (with obstinacy) said that he was superior to all, that the cacique would approve whatever he might decide, and that if I did not state my purpose in coming then and there they would not come to meet me again. (Adams 1963:124-25)

The opposition between *Kikmongwi* and *Qaletaqmongwi* in the Orayvi split is a complex issue that I have discussed elsewhere (1988).[6] For the present I simply want to note that the underestimation of the War Chief's role results in a skewed interpretation of the structure of political power in Orayvi. While the evidence is insufficient for conclusive proof, I believe that the status of *Qaletaqmongwi* was complementary to that of the *Kikmongwi,* with the War Chief principally responsible for the protection of the village from external forces. His coercive physical authority in internal affairs seems to have been very limited, and it by no means constituted a systematic regime of discipline and punishment. A useful analogy to the complementary roles of *Kikmongwi* and *Qaletaqmongwi* may be drawn from a number of ceremonies that have both a *mongwi* and a *qaleetaqa,* a "chief-priest," a "sergeant-at-arms." In the Snake-Antelope and Flute ceremonies, for example, the *qaleetaqa* serves as a guardian of the participants, protecting them from external intrusion or harm; the *mongwi* directs the performance and ensures that everything goes well *within* the ceremony. Thus, the *Kikmongwi* is to the *Qaletaqmongwi* as an "inside chief" is to an "outside chief." In times of peace and harmony, the *Kikmongwi*'s role is considerably more significant; in times of external stress and/or internal crisis, the *Qaletaqmongwi* assumes a prominent role.

In sum, Titiev's emphasis on the *Kikmongwi*'s direct group of supporting officers in the *Soyalangw* ceremony as the "most important officials in the pueblo" provides a partial and insufficient view of Hopi political offices. The *Qaletaqmongwi* and the other *Wimmomngwit* were formally instituted positions and were centrally important constituents of the *pavansinom* category.

POWER, SECRECY, KNOWLEDGE, AND TRUTH

The primary source of power in Hopi society lies in esoteric ritual knowledge. Initiation into ritual sodalities confers power on "lay" members, but the greatest proportion adheres to the *momngwit*, "chief-priests." Their knowledge of an essential core of rites is kept with strict secrecy from lay members, who are taught only the general features of the sodality's ceremony. Hopi ritual practice is highly secretive. Even older men not initiated into a particular sodality are only familiar with its overt practices (and by all accounts, this is not simply a social fiction). Secrecy is strictly enjoined on all initiates and breaches meet with severe social and supernatural sanctions. The pattern is again parallel to ritual secrecy among the Pueblos in general: "The genesis of secrecy lies in the nature of religious societies, their ritual and political functions, and the fact that all esoteric and much secular knowledge is communicated through speech in the Pueblos" (E. Brandt 1980:123–24). Secrecy serves to keep valued knowledge, in this oral culture, exclusively in the hands of an elite group of ritual specialists.

Through secrecy, knowledge takes on the character of property. Material property is insignificant as an index of inequality in Hopi society—the reason, I believe, for some observers' conclusions of egalitarianism. From a Hopi perspective, the valued resource lies not in material conditions, but in the ability to transform these through supernatural skills. Anthropologists of many persuasions have been reluctant to grant profound societal effects to cultural systems of value not embedded (proximately or ultimately) in material things. But control of material wealth is simply not the measure of power in the Pueblos (cf. E. Brandt 1985). Ritual knowledge serves as the scheme of value, the "currency," perhaps, of power. Bunzel notes for Zuni:

> There are societies, like Zuni, where wealth and power are kept distinct. Wealth is desirable there because it contributes to comfortable living. It gives no control over others. Power, by which is always meant knowledge ritualistically acquired . . . is supernatural and dangerous. (Bunzel 1938:336, quoted in Pandey 1977:195)

In his classic analysis of secrecy, Simmel compares secret knowledge to property ownership (1950:332) and suggests that when institutionalized, it acquires an aura of mystery and danger that constitutes a great source of power for those who control access to it. With this perspective, secret knowledge can be used, then, as a medium of social value and a calculus of social differentiation.[7]

In Hopi society generally, a paradigm of secrecy articulates the sociology of knowledge. Over the course of an individual's life, progressive initiations and increasing experience in the ritual sodalities gradually open levels of secret knowledge—rather like the Chinese boxes of Barth's (1975) analogy to Baktaman ritual knowledge. The aged are generally held to control more knowledge than the young, but the distinctions of *pavansinom* and *sukavungsinom* continue to apply in the upper age range. Chief-priests tend to be the oldest functioning members of the ceremony-owning lineage segment. Since knowledge confers authority and is acquired through progressive maturation, old *pavansinom* have most authority—at least until decrepitude renders this impracticable.

Pavansinom are treated with deference, respect, and fear for their mastery of forces that cause changes in the state of life forms, both human and nonhuman. They are also attributed with control over highly valued truth. In everyday Hopi discourse, one of the most distinguished terms for a man is *navoti'ytaqa,* "a man of knowledge." Conversely, an oft-heard comment is that an opinion deserves no attention because its bearer is *pas qanavoti'ytaqa,* "really not a man of knowledge." *Navoti'ytaqa* is an informal designation of one with authoritative wisdom, whether this pertains to ritual, history, ecology, geography, or other valued domains of understanding. Typically, such an individual is one whose age, status in his kin group, ceremonial position, and demonstrated facilities with oral tradition, denote an unimpeachable control of truth. Foucault elucidates the relationship between truth and the social order:

> Truth is a thing of this world: it is produced only by virtue of multiple forms of constraint. And it induces regular effects of power. Each society has its regime of truth, its "general politics" of truth . . . including the status of those who are charged with saying what counts as true. (Foucault 1980:131)

In sum, in Hopi society socially valued knowledge serves to demarcate statuses of distinction and an authority concomitant with the degree of secrecy. Secret ritual knowledge both configures the structuring of hierarchy and provides the idiom of political action.

COERCION AND CONSENT

Valued knowledge concerns the ability to influence, create or transform events in the world. *Pavansinom* can control events in both the natural and social environments. The Hopi universe (cf. Whorf 1956) is far from the Western conception of an intentionless arrangement of material phenomena where many events are held to occur at random. Rather, it is filled with intentional forces of which mankind is a part. *Pavansinom* have the knowledge to tap into these intentional forces to affect the course of events.

As in many societies, such transformative power is ambiguous— chiefs can destroy their people (with pestilence, crop failure, by treacherous invitations of enemy warfare, etc.), curers can kill, rain-makers can cause drought. *Pavansinom* are respected for their abilities but simultaneously feared as potential *popwaqt* who may cause great harm. The veil of secrecy implicitly lends itself to suspicion: "Although the secret has no immediate connection with evil, evil has an immediate connection with secrecy: the immoral hides itself for obvious reasons" (Simmel 1950:331). Power itself is intrinsically neither good nor evil from a Hopi viewpoint: Its use depends on the intentions of the user. This explains why *pavansinom* are frequently the subjects of witchcraft suspicion. For example, a great deal of witchcraft accusation occurred during the time of the Orayvi split; the primary suspects were the ritual sodality leaders, who were simultaneously factional leaders.

The authority of *pavansinom,* then, is predicated on the collective belief that they can either benefit or destroy life. Such collective belief bespeaks a paradigm for interpreting events—of causes and effects, and of practical means to promote or avoid consequences—that is, a view of *power,* in which the individual, through correct conduct, can ensure benefits rather than suffer penalties. In Hopi, this paradigm is perhaps best identified by *maqastutavo* (literally, "fear teaching"), a fundamental doctrine that prescribes adherence to behavioral norms. Lack of adherence causes supernatural sanctions, which usually involve sickness or death for the transgressor or a close relative. In the words of an older Hopi man, "*maqastutavo* is very powerful. It is the equivalent of the white man's law."

The threat of sickness or death by supernatural means, and the allocation of responsibility in the explanation of individual deaths, are prominent subjects of Hopi discourse. Two contemporary examples will serve to illustrate:

Example A. Over the past few years, clusters of modern dwellings have been constructed by various government programs in the valleys below the mesa-top villages. Frequently, there have been severe disputes (which go far back into mythological/historical times) over site-ownership, who gave permission for the government to build, etc. Many families have refrained from moving into one of these houses for fear of public opprobrium (see Cox 1970 on the effectiveness of Hopi gossip). Against the wishes of a senior family member, one young couple moved into such a house. Before long, the husband died. The senior family member allocated blame not to the wife, but to her mother, for allowing the daughter to make the move. Naturally, in a time of family grief and with tightly knit residential proximity, such an accusation, not in the least discordant with Hopi beliefs, had a powerful and damaging effect.

Example B. Two men, both advanced in age, have been planting corn next to each other for many years. Gradually their fields have become closer and there is a continuing dispute over encroachment. The older man, who is initiated into a first-order ritual sodality, informs the younger that he will use his *wiimi,* "ritual power/knowledge," against him. The younger, not initiated into a first-order society but a veteran of the Second World War and renowned for his valor in dispatching numerous enemy soldiers, replies that he will use his own *mongko* (usually a staff of office, but here used to denote an emblem of power, i.e., his war experience) in return. They conclude an encounter: "All right. We'll see who dies first."

Inherent in these two examples is a community of belief in supernatural causes of suffering and death, through means generalized and indirect (Example A) and means personally controlled and direct (Example B). It is the strength of such belief, still taken as axiomatically true throughout contemporary Hopi society, that renders *maqastutavo* more than simply an ethical system, but an instituted mode of thought that fosters social conformity through fear of supernatural action.

Coercion and consent are central problems in any consideration of political power. Such concepts have almost invariably presupposed a control of the means of physical violence by the power-holders, and anthropologists have been unwilling to recognize practices as political that do not rest upon such control (cf. Clastres 1977:14). In the Hopi case, the internal use of brute force is, and was, rare. By Titiev's account (quoted above), the *Qaletaqmongwi*'s rights of corporal punishment were very limited, and certain disciplinary Kachinas had the right to use yucca whips to encourage (though not force) engagement in occasional communal work parties—to harvest the *Kikmongwi*'s field, clean out springs, etc. But such isolated practices hardly constitute a regime of physical coercion. Rather, in the Hopi system, coercive force is transfigured into covert, mystical action. But how does this operate to produce consent to authority? With what "locutions" (following Geertz) can we intelligibly render *maqastutavo*?

In Gramsci's extended sense (e.g., 1970), "hegemony" can explain consent to authority without physical coercion, "rule" or "domination." Hegemony functions, in these terms, as a regime of consciousness that is culturally entrenched and inherent in praxis. Williams encapsulates this Gramscian sense of hegemony—distinguished from "ideology" and "world-view"—superbly:

> It is a whole body of practices and expectations, over the whole of living: our senses and assignments of energy, our shaping perceptions of ourselves and of our world. It is a lived system of values—constitutive and constituting—which as they are experienced as practices appear as reciprocally confirming. It thus constitutes a sense of reality for most people in society, a sense of absolute because experienced reality beyond which it is very difficult for most members of the society to move, in most areas of their lives. (Williams 1977:110)

Seen in this light, *maqastutavo* is not an inert ethical doctrine, but an active component of political praxis. The supernatural capabilities accruing to *pavansinom* are not mere superstructural symbolism, but hegemonically constitutive of the field of power sui generis.

The ingrained notion that brute violence is a necessary condition of political power may be simply too narrow. It ignores the palpable lack of dualistic distinctions between supernatural/natural and mental/material in many societies. My point is that in a society where it is collectively believed that individuals can control the causes of sickness, death, famine, and so forth, through supernatural means, the boundaries drawn between "supernatural" and "political" power dissolve into irrelevance. In the community of belief, fear of witchcraft is at least as effective a deterrent as fear of the electric chair.[8]

PRACTICE

The practice of power in Hopi society has legitimate and nonlegitimate contexts, although the lines cannot be sharply drawn. The most legitimate context is formal ceremony, correctly performed with purity of intention ("pure hearts"). Here, the forces controlled by the sodality heads are ritually channeled to produce benefit for mankind and the world in general; rain for the crops, fertility both human and animal, and health and happiness for the people. On an individual level, the medical practices of a *tuuhikya* are usually thought of as legitimate, though they are more subject to ambiguous interpretation.

The most nonlegitimate context is the maleficent exercise of power by *popwaqt* at secret meetings. The main location for these, Palangwu, is unknown, of course, except to *popwaqt*. There, it is held, they meet in a kiva to plan the prolongation of their own lives at the expense of others, particularly their own relatives, and to foster ill for the world in general (a mirror image of the legitimate ceremonial practices of ritual sodalities). A *powaqa* can also practice his or her evil craft (access to illegitimate power is more sexually equal) on an individual basis, mirroring a *tuuhikya*'s practice. Such mirror images form a set that illustrates the intrinsically ambiguous nature of power and its exercise.

Ceremonial contexts, especially those aspects involving secret kiva rituals, are also regarded as a primary locus of elite decision-making. This is particularly true with the First-Order societies of *Wuwtsim* and *Soyalangw,* which bring together the chief-priests of the most important societies to plan out a scheme of events for the following year. Such plans follow the model of secretive action: They are clandestine, conspiratorial, and hedged about with much mystery. Outside formal ceremonial contexts, they take place in private meetings under cover of night, in someone's house or in other concealed quarters of the village, such as underground tunnels.[9] Typically, the protagonists arrive in stealth and are blanketed to obscure their identity, though they often comprise the *Kikmongwi* and other *Wimmomngwit*.

Such planning is referred to as *pasiwni*. *Pasiwni* implies the "planning of destiny" and is connected with the conception that the life of the Hopi people (and even of all mankind) is part of a grand design. Interpreted politically, *pasiwni* refers to the process of decision-making. Decisions are ritually "sealed" in such a way that their planned consequences are inevitable: "Once something is planned that way, it *has* to happen." (For a more detailed account of this concept, see Whiteley 1988; and see Chapter 1). *Pasiwni* takes its form against the background of a shared cosmology. Plans concern not merely human society, but also climate, ecology, and "man in nature." The planning of a bountiful harvest or, conversely, of adverse weather conditions is, because of the effects on the life of man, a political act. Such effects are often explained as the results of intentional actions by *pavansinom*, and may be interpreted as a reward or punishment for collective behavior.

An informative analogy to Hopi political praxis was offered by an older consultant:

> Hopis are like clowns and Kachinas—they plot what's going to happen, they plan out life. This is what the chief-priests do in real life as well. . . . Remember in the Hopi way everything is done through *pasiwni* by the chiefs—once planned, once the wheels have been set in motion, the ends *have* to occur. This is how Hopi politics and society works.

The analogy refers to a segment of the two-day clown ceremony. It involves the clown chief (*tsukumongwi*) bargaining with the chief of a group of masked Warrior Kachinas. Toward the end of the first day the clowns are approached by Warrior Kachinas and warned about their excessive, outrageous behavior. The clown chief tries to persuade the Warrior Kachina chief (usually a *Mongwu,* or "Great Horned Owl Kachina," the use of which may well involve a ritual pun, i.e., between *mongwu* and *mongwi*) to spare his people (i.e., his fellow clowns) from dreadful punishment, including the threat of death. During the remainder of the ceremony, several times the clown chief is seen squatting down to one side of the plaza in discussion with the Warrior Kachina chief. He is rebuked for his failure to produce an improvement in the

Figure 3.2. *Hopi Clowns and Kachinas,* by Otis Polelonema (Lomadamocvia), no date. *Tsutskut,* "the clowns," are idlike tricksters who portray untamed human desire and self-interest. The psychosocial contract is enforced (to pursue the Freudian allusion) by superego-like Warrior kachinas, led by *Mongwu,* "Great-horned Owl" (at left in the background), and his lieutenant, *Angwusi,* "Crow/Raven" (at right). The stage depicted is prior to the final disciplining and redemption of the clowns plotted by *Mongwu* and the clown chief. Photograph by Blair Clark. Courtesy School of American Research Collections in the Museum of New Mexico.

clowns' behavior and so offers increasingly persuasive blandishments to plead mercy for the clowns, finally presenting a turquoise necklace as a sort of mortgage on their lives. During the last of the four negotiations, especially, the other clowns look on suspiciously at what they take—quite rightly—to be a conspiracy about their own destiny, between their leader (whose role represents the *Kikmongwi*) and the Warrior Kachina chief.

Clowns represent mankind in a pre-moral state, where basic Hopi values—self-control in eating, decorous and respectful interpersonal relations, nonaggression, nonacquisitiveness, noninquisitiveness, sexual modesty, etc.—are overturned, reversed, and burlesqued in the typical fashion of inversionary ritual. Hopi clowns are gluttonous, uncouth, aggressive, grasping, intrusive, prying, obscene (and extremely funny). This is part of their purpose: to stand the world on its head in order to

99

reveal its rules and their necessity against chaos. The Warrior Kachinas, as the clowns' adversaries, represent the moralizing influence of pre-scribed behavioral values and the upholding of these with severe super-natural sanctions. Eventually, the clowns are stripped, doused with gallons of water, whipped with willow branches, and forced to go through what amounts to a public confessional, before reintegration into their everyday social identities.

In sum, the clown analogy indicates that, from a Hopi perspective, leaders plan the future of society; political decision-making is secret and has a conspiratorial character; and the ritual sealing of decisions (i.e., inter alia, with the turquoise necklace) makes their realization cosmo-logically inevitable. Further, the ceremony concretizes the conscious-ness of political structure in ritual drama. Here some of the punitive supernatural devices are realized as figured entities—taken from the *conscience collective* and given representational shape and substance—their power, intentions, and concerns made manifest.

THE EXPLANATION OF MARKED EVENTS

Space does not allow an analysis of marked political events. Elsewhere (Whiteley 1988) I have given an interpretation of the Orayvi split deriving from Hopi analyses. Here I simply wish to summarize a few points of Hopi explanation of political process.

Characteristically, Hopis explain the Orayvi split with a paradigm that is similarly applied to other major political events in Hopi history, includ-ing the demise of the villages of Awat'ovi, Pivanhonkyapi, Sikyatki, and Palatkwapi, and even of the third world, below the present one (cf. Voth 1905). Signs of corruption and decadence, frequently indicated by im-moral or antisocial behavior, begin to be noticed by the village leaders. After admonitions to improve behavior fall on deaf ears, the leaders convene in secret and ritually formalize a plan to destroy the social system in the village—including their own leadership.

Often, the plan is realized indirectly, via the deliberate manipulation of other social issues altogether. For example, regarding the Orayvi split, the issue of enforced Government schooling, it is held, was used by *pavansinom* to manipulate *sukavungsinom* sentiments into such antagonistic positions that the split was achieved. But the leaders' true reasons were quite different (see Whiteley 1988). One consultant re-ferred to this process as dramatizing things, or "faking it," for the *sukavungsinom,* in order to foment actions proximately unrelated but ultimately conducive to the leaders' ends. In other instances, village leaders persuade the leaders of other Hopi villages, or sometimes Navajo or Ute leaders, to attack their own village and kill off the male population—including themselves ("fatalism" is a label often attached to Hopi thought). In such cases, the means of physical violence is clearly appropriated by leadership, but indirectly and with the curious additional twist of self-immolation.

In these examples, the radical abolition of the status quo is achieved, in order to promote social renascence. In a very real sense, such events are revolutions in Hopi history, and are interpreted not as the anarchic products of an insufficiently integrated social system (as Titiev [1944:96–99] has suggested), but as the results of high-level politico-religious deliberation in a thoroughly orchestrated social process.

TWENTIETH-CENTURY CHANGE AND PERSISTENCE

As I emphasized at the beginning, the ethnographic focus of this chapter is Third Mesa society at the turn of the century. It will have been evident, however, from contemporary analogies and references, that aspects of this system still obtain. Third Mesa no longer has First and Second Order ritual sodalities, although there are still many individual initiated members. With the split of Orayvi in 1906, the basic politico-religious structure collapsed and was not completely reconstituted in any of the villages founded subsequently. At Third Mesa it has slowly eroded as a system of government. Since the death of Tawakwaptiwa in 1960, there have been no *Kikmongwi*s in the traditional sense, although several individuals have laid claim to such a title in some villages. Similarly, the *Qaletaqmongwi* and most other *Wimmomngwit* are no longer operational offices, although heads of recently defunct sodalities may still be referred to by their official titles.

The overlay of institutions from the dominant society has extensively altered political organization. A thorough analysis of these is beyond my present scope, because of their sheer complexity, both in structure and in interaction with traditional Hopi forms. Introduced institutions include: schools; a hospital; missionary churches; trading posts/supermarkets; the Bureau of Indian Affairs Agency; the Tribal Police and Court; village governing bodies—usually a "governor" and "board of directors"—in some villages; and above all the creation of a pan-Hopi Tribal Council (which now has several separate departments) as a result of the Wheeler-Howard Act of 1934 (again, see Whiteley 1988).

Reaction to these structures has been various. The majority are at least partially accepted nowadays, and they impinge upon many spheres of Hopi life. Nevertheless, the Tribal Council has met with fluctuating and limited success in replacing the traditional political forms. It has been, and often still is, unable to establish a quorum, because traditional village leaders sometimes refuse to certify elected representatives (a prerogative established in the Tribal Constitution). Further, an anti-Council "Traditionalist" movement has become increasingly organized since the 1940s (cf. Clemmer 1978, 1982). The interaction of all these forces (and others) takes different forms in different villages and among different groups within the same village—hence the complexity.

Nevertheless, despite dramatic changes in Hopi life in the present century, the community of belief and numerous features of the politico-religious system described above persist. As a scheme for the enforcement of social conformity, *maqastutavo* is still very active, although not perhaps so pervasively as in the past. When the Tribal Council was bewitched (allegedly by the Traditionalist faction) in 1980, supposedly progressive members of the Tribal organization rapidly evacuated the building, and a *tuuhikya* was called in to purify the place. Supernaturally induced benefits and sanctions remain prominent features of Hopi discourse. The term *pavansinom* continues in use and, as Nagata points out (above), may be applied to Tribal Council officials.

There is an enduring belief in the elevated status and capacities of lineage-members in which power was traditionally vested. It was still a significant act in 1980 for a man, frustrated with his village's modern-style governing body, to appeal to men of the Bear and Spider clans to resume their traditional mandates as societal leaders (which had not been formally operative for seventy years). Similarly, it is not uncommon for members of old *pavansinom* lineage-segments to be elected to modern offices, with explicit suggestions that their suitability is sanctioned by traditional associations.

CONCLUSION

I hope to have demonstrated that there is a significant division in Hopi society into those who have power and those who do not—*pavansinom* and *sukavungsinom*. Moreover, this division includes an institutionalized authority structure where legitimate leadership roles are inherited within matrilineage segments. Power is fundamentally equated with elite access to specialized secret knowledge that enables the bearer to induce significant transformations in the world. Ritual knowledge is the "strategic resource"; material entities are not the medium of power differentials. The structure of ritual leadership is simultaneously the structure of political leadership. Political action on the part of the *pavansinom* is homologous with, and ultimately inseparable from, ritual action: secretive and conspiratorial, and directed towards the planning of society's future. Ritual has an instrumental mode that transforms the world's conditions. Coercion mostly takes a supernatural form, and consent to authority is based on fear of supernatural sanctions. Explanations of marked societal events identify deliberate execution of joint elite decisions toward preconceived ends.

All of which seems to indicate that the Hopi are clearly as engaged in "political" action and social inequality as "we" are. Why the contradictions, then, with which I began? Egalitarian? Hierarchical? "Tribal"? The problem, I maintain, lies not with Hopi society, but with theoretical premises that restrict the identification of political power to a rationalist interpretation of human motivations wedded to a materialist conception of the means of production and a physicalist conception of the means of coercion. That such premises underlie basic Western notions of human action is a cultural datum, not a guarantee of self-evident truth. Political power has been treated as a species of behavior between independent wills rationally interacting in a free competitive market (cf. Colson 1977:376). Power is thus seen "not as an entity in itself, but as the ability to bend others to one's ends" (ibid.). In such conceptions, there is no notion that power can inhere in the mechanics of the cosmos, processes of socialization, ideas of the self, or transcendent forms of experience.

Such strictures have impeded the understanding of differing political systems cross-culturally, and, in particular, of the Hopi system. If we are willing to listen, the explanations of our consultants can greatly help to construct meaningful interpretations of politics *as practiced in* other societies, rather than as theoretically preconceived by formalist categories deriving originally from "European folk-theories" (Schneider 1984:184). I am in complete sympathy with Fredrik Barth's exhortation:

> We should capitalize on our unique advantage: that our "object of study" can help us actively to transcend our categories by teaching us their own. This means recognizing that the actors' categories provide a way to understand reality, *as well as* being part of that reality. In prac-

tice, probably most of the productivity of the anthropologist derives from this source, even though his arrogance as a professional academic, and his defensiveness when his *own* reality is being threatened by the enchanted world of another culture, both militate against such learning. (Barth 1981:9–10)

Lest this approach endanger us toward excessive particularism, we can balance it by expanding our basic premises from another direction simultaneously. In particular, Foucault extends the study of power into a much broader and deeper social field than that generally considered in political anthropology:

> . . . a whole series of power networks . . . invest the body, sexuality, the family, kinship, knowledge, technology, and so forth. True, these networks stand in a conditioning-conditioned relationship to a kind of "meta-power" which is structured essentially round a certain number of great prohibition functions; but this meta-power with its prohibitions can only take and secure its footing where it is rooted in a whole series of multiple and indefinite power relations that supply the necessary basis for the great negative forms of power. (Foucault 1980:122)

> In itself the exercise of power is not violence; nor is it a consent which, implicitly, is renewable. It is a total structure of actions brought to bear on possible actions; it incites, it induces, it seduces, it makes easier or more difficult; in the extreme it constrains or forbids absolutely; it is nevertheless always a way of acting upon an acting subject or acting subjects by virtue of their acting or being capable of action. A set of actions upon other actions. (Foucault 1982:220)

The development of such a thoroughgoing and multifaceted conception of the ways of power in society may allow a way out of the quagmire of category-mistakes afflicting the intercultural interpretation of political systems.

4

HOPITUTUNGWNI
"Hopi Names" as Literature

INTRODUCTION (1997)

From Chapters 2 and 3, Hopi society emerges as a set of structural tendencies and ideational forms that are acted with and upon by individual persons and by groups. Here, my discussion of Hopi naming practices extends the focus on cultural structures to their poetic production of distinctive selves and persons. Names mark subjects with the imaged forms and elements that are the grounds of clan, ritual, and environmental conceptualization. We thus pass from some collective dimensions of Hopi social philosophy and metaphysics applied to the world, via Hopi aesthetics and phenomenology, to more interior applications. Some of the cultural categories explored in Chapters 2 and 3 (and taken up in Chapter 7) are reflected here in a poetics and aesthetics at the heart of Hopi practice. In this chapter, ethnography is sited at the borders of another epistemological negotiation—with Western paradigms of poetics (particularly with regard to authorial intentions and textual "meaning") and subjectivity (particularly regarding Mauss's sense of Pueblo persons).

Over the last few years, there has been a marked increase in Hopis rejecting inherited patronymics and legally replacing surnames with their Hopi birth or initiation names. Every recent issue of *Hopi Tutuveni* (the Tribal newspaper) carries a series of name-change petitions to Hopi Tribal Court to this effect.

◆

[N]o proper name of place or person names any place or person as such; it names *in the first instance* only *for* those who are members of some particular linguistic and cultural community, by identifying places and persons in terms of the scheme of identifications shared by, and perhaps partially constitutive of, that community. The relation of a proper name to its bearer cannot be elucidated without reference to such identifying functions.

Alasdair MacIntyre (1985:7)

The old pond;
A frog jumps in,—
The sound of the water.[1]
Basho

If the naming of cats is a difficult matter, the naming of persons is assuredly more so.[2] Naming practices vary widely across cultures. From an anthropological perspective, names may individuate "persons"; they may designate positions in a social order; they may class individuals into social groups; or, in use, they may serve performative negotiations of personal identities and relationships.[3]

The idea that personal names might comprise a literary genre in some cultural contexts does not seem immediately obvious. In the "West," personal names have generally been regarded as signs without semantic content. John Stuart Mill's view that "proper names are meaningless marks set upon things and persons to distinguish them from one another" retains currency in philosophical and linguistic inquiry (Willis 1982:227; Basso 1988:103). Within anthropology, Lévi-Strauss's interpretation (1966:172–216) of names in "primitive" societies as instruments of social classification has been very influential. Consequently, in those societies where personal names have individual meanings, their full interpretive potential remains largely unplumbed.[4] In many instances Native American personal names carry semantic content that narratively denotes cultural or natural occurrences, or historical or mythological events.[5] Moreover, name-composition may reflect a formal poetics; some Hopi names, I shall argue, are "tiny imagist poems." As narrative figures poetically composed, such names are oral texts, and "require exegesis in addition to translation" (Kendall 1980:261). Hopi personal names do a number of things simultaneously. First, since they derive from totemically named clans (albeit indirectly—see below), they reflect a pattern of social relations that articulates with the kinship and ritual systems. Second, names serve to individuate persons—each name is unique and confers a unique identity on the bearer.[6] Third, and my central concern here, Hopi names are individually authored poetic compositions that comprise a literary genre. In concert, these three aspects bespeak a Hopi conception of their society as comprised of conscious individual agents who use the figures that are names to construct personal identity, cultural meaning, and interpersonal relations—within, of course, received structures of social (and natural) organization.[7] Let me begin with the social background.

THE SOCIAL CONTEXT OF HOPI NAMING

In August 1989, in order to supplement other accounts I had gathered over the years, I asked Herschel Talashoma from Paaqavi to provide a formal account in Hopi on naming practices. We then produced a translation, mostly in his own English idioms. Part of this discourse (which I will explicate subsequently) went as follows:

Nu' hapi Niiti'yvaya. Ina hapi tapwungwa. Pu' inay oovi angqwat put sinomat puma ikyam. Pu' puma hapi hakiy tungwayangwu hakiy inayat angqwat. Niiqe oovi pu' puma nuy pan tungwaya nuy tiitiwaqw, nuy sunattaqw, Niiti'yvaya. Pumuy nu' oovi kyamuy'ta tapngyamuy. . . .

My name is Niiti'yvaya[8]—it means "brought a lot." My father is a Rabbit clan. So from my father's side, his relatives, they are my aunties. They are the ones that name you, from your father's side. And so, they are the ones who named me when I was born, when I made the twenty days—Those are the ones who are my (naming) aunts, the Rabbit clan. . . .

Noq put yu'at itanay hapi pam oovi yu'at pu' itaakya yu'at pam nuy yaw pan tungwa, Niiti'yvaya. Pu' pam pi tapwungwa niiqe pu' pam oovi put aqw taykyangw naatoylay aw taykyangw: yaw maqwise' a'ani qöqöye' ahoy ökye' pu' taataptuy, sowituy niiti'yvayangwu. Put nu' aw Niiti'yvaya.

It was my father's mother who named me, and my auntie's mother who named me that, "brought a lot." Because she was a Rabbit clan, so she was looking up to that, her clan [-totem]: when they go out hunting, and if they kill a lot, and come back with a lot of cottontails and jackrabbits. That is the reason why she named me "brought a lot."

Pantikyangw pu' paasat hak piw naat wimkyatingwu, wimkyate', paasat pu' piw aqw naat pas sukwat piw aqw naat nay'tangwu, nay'vangwu. Pu' nu' pantiqe' paasat pu' nu' tsu'ngyamuy, tsu'wungwat nu' nay'taqe aw paasat pu' tsu'ngyam ikyam piw. Pu' puma piw nuy oovi tungwaya. Pu' pam pay naap hiisa'niiqam hakiy asnayangwu: pay pi naamahin sen piw suukyaningwu, piw qa suukya, lööyöm, paayom, pam pay qa tuwaniy'tangwu. Puma piw paasat pu' hakiy tuwat naatoylay panwat tungwayangwu. Noq pu' pay pi itam soosoyam Hopisinom naatoylay'ngwu—*hiihiita*. Pu' peetu pay himu naatoyla pay piw pay sukw amumningwu puma pay naama yantaningwu. Kur nu' uumi pangqawni nu' honanwungwa; itam poovolwungwat enangwye'. . . .

After that, then you have to be initiated. When you are initiated then you have to have another father, you will be given another father. After that I received a father from the Snake clan, a Snake clan man. So, from there on, my aunties were the Snake clan. So they named me also. There is no set number of them who will wash your hair: it could be one, not just one, it could be two, three, there is no limit to that. Then they name you according to their clan-totem. And then, all of us Hopis, we have clans—*all* kinds. And also some of these clans can join together, they go along with each other. For example, let me tell you, I'm a Badger; we go along, we also have Butterfly with it.

Pu' niikyangw itam Hopiit pay aqw sutsep yuy amumningwu hakiy yu'at himuwungwa niqw pay hak put amumningwu. Pay qahisat hopiitsay haqam nay amum. . . .

But us Hopis all the time, whatever your mother's clan is, you go along with that clan, you go with your mother's clan. Never a Hopi child goes along with his father's clan. . . .

Paasat pu' nu' oovi wimkyatiq paasat pu' puma tsu'ngyam puma paasat pu' pi nuy tuwat asnaya, nuy wimkyate'. Paasat pu' puma pi tsu'ngyam niiqe pu' puma naatoylay oovi pu' pi aw nuy tuwat tungwaya. Pu' put nu' hakiy nu' Joseph nay'ta, katsinnay'ta, put niqw put oovi

So that's why when I was initiated, it was them, the Snake clan, who washed my hair then, when I was initiated. And since they were the Snake clan, they named me according to their clan. And so, from there on my god-father was someone by the name of Joseph, he was my

pas yu'at ephaqam naat qatu,
hak Nasiwunqa pam nuy
Tahooya yan tungwa, ispi naat
nu' ephaqam pay naat tsayniqw
oovi hoyat pam aw nuy tungwa
Tahooya. Noq pu' paasat i'i pas
naap ina niiqe pu' pamwa pu'
nuy Tsu'leetsiwma yan tungwa.
. . . Pu' paasat i'qööqa'at inay
qööqa'at pam pu' nuy paasat
Tsuu'a yan tungwa.

katsina god-father. At that time,
his real mother, Nasiwunqa, was
still living; it was her who named
me "little blue racer snake," because at that time I was still a
young one, and small, so she
named me "*little* blue racer
snake." And then my god-father
himself named me "Snake-danc-
ers in line." And then my god-
father's older sister [later
amended to younger sister]
named me "rattlesnake."

Hopis are given names in a sequence of ritual initiations through life.
Hopi is a matrilineal society, that is, clan membership is inherited from
the mother.[9] But a baby's name givers are female members of its father's
clan (Niiti'yvaya's "aunties"), not of its own clan; in fact you never
receive a name from your own clan. Gathering in the house of the
newborn (traditionally twenty, but nowadays often only ten days after
birth), several paternal clanswomen each bestow a name associated
with their clan. Typically, a child receives half a dozen different names,
only one of which will *huurta,* "stick."

At about ages six to ten, every Hopi child is initiated into either the
Katsina or the *Powamuy* ritual society—a practice still strongly maintained at all three Hopi Mesas. (For summary accounts of the Hopi
ritual order, see Frigout 1979, or Whiteley 1987.) If male, new names
are conferred by an initiating "godfather" and his close female relatives; if female, by a "godmother" and her close female relatives.
Naming and initiation by a "godparent" create formal relationships
with another clan (and group of clans, or phratry); the named now
applies the appropriate (patrilateral) kin terms and role behavior to
members of this clan (and phratry), who reciprocate in kind. Moreover,
the godparent-godchild relationship is more than notional; the godparent holds a tutelary role in the child's learning of ritual knowledge,
especially.

The new namegivers must be of another clan than *either* of the child's
parents.[10] Still at Second Mesa, and formerly at First and Third Mesas,
a male receives an "adult" name on initiation by a godfather into one
of the four *Wuwtsim,* "Manhood Initiation," societies. This godfather
may be the same person as the Katsina godfather, but sometimes

another individual, perhaps from a different clan again, is chosen. Yet other names will be conferred if a boy is inducted into one of several "Second Order" religious societies (notably, Blue Flute, Drab Flute, Antelope, Rattlesnake). Likewise, if a girl is initiated into one of the three women's societies (*Mamrawt, Lalkont, Owaqölt*)—and most were in the past initiated into at least one (the same Mesa breakdown applies here, too)—she receives a new name.

There are other occasions for name-giving as well—such as being accidentally doused with someone's wash-water or urine. In the past, a boy also received a name at his first participation in a hunt, and a girl at her puberty initiation; Orayvi men returning from a (post-*Wuwtsim* initiation) salt expedition to the Grand Canyon received new names; and at death, clan "aunts" conferred new names, preparatory to the "soul's" (*hikwsi,* literally "breath") journey to Maski, the home of the dead.[11]

Names are conferred ritually while the subject's hair is washed in yucca suds. An ear of corn is wafted over him or her, and the namegiver enunciates the name in a short ritual formula (Voth 1905b provides a detailed account). The name a male receives during *Wuwtsim* initiation supersedes all others, marking the assumption of adult status. With the end of *Wuwtsim,* of the Second Order societies, and of the women's societies (the *Owaqölt* persists in modified form) at Third Mesa (Whiteley 1988), child-names or names conferred *at Katsina/Powamuy* initiation remain operative in those contexts where Hopi names are used. These contexts are principally in ritual, and as terms of third-person reference in everyday discourse. Kin terms, English names, nicknames, or abbreviated versions of formal names are the usual forms for address, and English names serve bureaucratic requirements, such as school and Tribal enrollments.

THE POETICS OF NAMING

All formal Hopi names refer to clan associations of the namegiver. Naming images are myriad. A proliferation of associations—by no means limited to finite repertoires—with one's *naatoyla,* "clan emblem" or "totem," are drawn upon from the name-giver's clan or phratry. Some names are straightforward clan eponyms: for example, *Hoonaw,* "bear," *Taawa,* "sun," *Koyongo,* "turkey," (associated with the Eagle clan), *Honani,* "badger," *Kuukutsi* "lizard," or *Tsuu'a,* "rattlesnake." A few others metaphorically combine a totemic species with an observed personal characteristic, as in Herschel Talashoma's explanation of *Tahooya* (*taaho,* "a whipsnake or blue racer"—a totemic association of the *tsu'ngyam,* [Rattle]snake clan plus -*hoya,* a diminutive suffix, apt because of his age and size). But more often, the namegiver has a specific event or instance in mind that is not semantically presented in full in the lexical components of the name. Meaning is thus typically oblique, and not inferable from literal translation. A name's sense may not be widely known beyond the particular donor and receiver. Asked the meaning of certain names, my consultants often indicated that this was impossible to discern from the morphemes themselves, though these were easy enough to identify; the *express intentions* of the namegiver would have to be known (cf. Voth 1905b:68).

Let me provide some examples (see Voth 1905b for many more). *Lomayayva* literally means "beautiful climbed (pl.)" or "beautifully ascended" from *lolma,* "beautiful" or "beautifully" and *yayva,* "climbed," "ascended (pl.)." This name belonged to an Orayvi Lizard clan man. There is absolutely no way to infer phenomenal sense from the literal translation (it could refer to any number of entities ascending something) or to ascertain the clan-identity of the name-giver. In the concrete case, it is a Badger clan name—though, I hasten to add, it does not refer to "climbing badgers." As part of its ritual prerogatives, the Badger clan "owns" the *Powamuy* ceremony—a grand February pageant featuring numerous different *katsinam* (masked representations of spirits, in this case). A connected ceremony, *Patsavu,*[12] is performed at the end of *Powamuy* when there have been initiations into the *Wuwtsim* societies the previous November. During *Patsavu,* an elaborate procession of many different kinds of *katsinam* ascended into the village of Orayvi, in the afternoon, along a path from below the southwest side of the mesa on which Orayvi sits. "Beautifully ascended" refers to the aesthetic splendor—in terms of color, costume, and movement—of the procession of *katsinam* at *Patsavu* coming up into Orayvi as seen from the perspective of someone standing on the mesa.[13]

The condensed evocation this name conjures—a typical feature—displays the same quality that Keith Basso (1988:126, n.17), borrowing from Edward Sapir, attributes to Western Apache place-names, as "tiny imagist poems." The almost photographic quality of the captured image and the emphasis on process and movement are also reminiscent of some Japanese haiku.[14] But the poetic form of Hopi names is even

Figure 4.1. Lomayayva, "beautifully ascended." Procession of kachinas at the *Patsavu* ceremony, led by Ewtoto, the Bear clan chief of all the kachinas, and Aholi, the chief kachina of the Corn clan (with high-peaked head), ascending into Orayvi, probably 1910, following the *Wuwtsim* initiations of 1909. Photograph by Kate Cory. Courtesy of a private collection.

more compact than haiku. Maria Chona's remark about Papago songs that "the song is very short because we understand so much" (Underhill 1979:51, cited in Krupat 1989:47) illustrates a widespread tendency toward condensation in some Native American narrative genres. This is very markedly the case with Hopi names.

Syntactically, and this, too, is a common feature, the name is elliptical: a compacted phrase in which the subject (the *katsinam*) is suppressed, leaving a predicate composed of a contraction of verb and adverb ("ascended" and "beautifully") to accomplish the poetic task.[15] Meaningful translation thus hinges, in the first place, on the identification of a lexically absent subject.

Another example: a widely known name, *Sikyakwaptiwa*,[16] is similarly oblique in denotation. Morphemically, it is composed of *sikyangpu*, "yellow," "yellowness," *kwapta*, "he/she put some things (pl.) above on high," and *-tiwa*, a male name suffix.[17] "He/she put yellows above on high" may be a reasonable translation. The name-giver's clan was Coyote, and the reference is to *sikyaatayo*, "yellow fox," or, as C. and F. Voegelin (1957:18) record it, "brown, colorful fox with white-tip on tail"; I mention this for the acuteness of Hopi perceptual distinctions it reveals, a quality echoed in the strong visual emphasis of many name-images (see below). *Sikyaatayo's* color and habits are associated in Hopi thought and tradition with the appearance of *sikyangnuptu,* a perceptually discrete stage of yellowish dawn light that follows *qöyangnuptu,* first gray light of dawn, and precedes *taalawva,* full daylight. The name, then, images the distant eastern appearance of a yellow fox in the completed act of putting the yellowness of postcrepuscular auroral light up onto the sky.[18]

If William Carlos Williams is "correct" that, "so much depends upon a red wheelbarrow glazed with rain water beside the white chickens," then a "yellow fox putting up the yellow dawn light" similarly speaks of as it celebrates a powerful aesthetics that centrally animates Hopi cognition and cultural values. A "pure" translation of the morphemes would miss not only the intended meaning but also the aesthetic force of the poetic image.

Associations between this name and some traditional concepts occur in myths referring to sunrise. The personified (male) sun, Taawa, rises by climbing out of a kiva in the east. At the top of the kiva ladder, he puts on a gray foxskin tied to one of the ladder-poles, at which point the gray dawn light appears. He then puts on, from its position on the ladder pole, a yellow foxskin, creating the yellow dawn light, before beginning his journey across the sky to a western kiva, into which he descends at dusk (Voth 1903:351; 1905:1). Voth (1903:351 n.1) records a further association in this context with the two Flute societies (which have a ritual concern with the sun's movements); according to myth, the Drab Flute (*Masilelent*) society was brought to the Hopi mesas from its original location in the eastern kiva where the sun rises, and the Blue Flute (*Sakwalelent*) from the western kiva where it sets. The gray foxskin is the *naa'tsi,* "ritual standard," of the Blue Flutes, and the yellow foxskin that of the Drab Flutes; these standards are tied to the ladder-poles of the societies' respective kivas when they are in session. The mythological prototypes of the Flute societies continue to perform in the sunrise and sunset kivas, but instead of putting up foxskins on the kiva ladder-poles, they magically raise up the live animals. I have not been able to discover any specific connection between these myths and the namegiver's intention, but clearly a nexus of mythological ideas associating yellow foxskins and yellow dawn light informs the name.

In this way, then, names may excerpt an image from an ideational complex more fully embodied in mythological narratives. Moreover, Hopi myth and ritual are mutually integral (as above with the Flute societies). Name images evoking ritual activities simultaneously invoke correlated myths. *Lomayayva* may be further unpacked by reference to the *Patsavu* ritual's accompanying mythology. The ascent of the *katsinam* into Orayvi in part reenacts the original arrival of the Badger clan. Each Orayvi clan, having completed its migrations undertaken after emergence from the "third" world below, had to seek entry to the village from the first arrivals, the Bear clan, and in particular their leader, the *Kikmongwi,* "village chief." Each clan had to demonstrate special ritual or other abilities before the *Kikmongwi* would accept them. At first the Badger clan, whose skills pertained to medicine and seed-fertility, were refused admission and went off to live at Tuuwanasavi ("earth-center place"), a few miles south in the Orayvi Valley. Finally, the *Kikmongwi* decided he needed their skills, and went four times (the archetypal number in Hopi sacred narrative, but, in this case, also because the Badgers were miffed by their earlier rejection) to persuade them to move into the village. To mark the significance of the event, the Badger clan entered Orayvi dressed as *katsinam,* along the same route from below that is retraced in the *Patsavu* ritual. To translate the name *Lomayayva,* then, is to image a moment of the *Patsavu* ritual, and simultaneously to evoke and recapitulate the Badger clan's mythological narrative of arrival.

Lévi-Strauss's structuralist approach to Amerindian myth, widely influential as it has been, has tended to obscure some vital connections with ritual. In many instances, of course, ritual enactments of myths are no longer observable in North American social life. Likewise, myths, recorded in written texts, or recalled in oral traditions, often no longer speak directly to ritual practice. All I am suggesting is that in those cultures, and Hopi is one, where many ritual practices are still very much alive, a major dimension of mythological meaning will be located in ritual performance. Translating names that evoke ritual and myth together requires an explicit attention to particular forms of this interplay.

A similar neglect of ethnographic context characterizes some recent literary treatments of North American mythological narratives (e.g., Ramsey 1983). It seems to me that any separation of myth from its empirical grounding in social, cultural, and historical contexts seriously vitiates culturally significant interpretation.[19] What holds for myth is true of the densely laconic narratives in Hopi names, as Alasdair MacIntyre's epigraph to this chapter is intended to highlight. Accordingly, my claim for interpreting Hopi names as literature is also diametrically opposed to various poststructural theoretical emphases on the free play of signifiers that give no import to authorial intention, no possibility of language as referential, and no relevance to the sociocultural and historical sites of the literary production. For *"Lomayayva,"* without a basic knowledge of the namegiver's intention, or of the *Patsavu* ritual and the Badger clan migration myth (and of the Hopi linguistic practices, naming conventions, clan and ritual system, and natural environment, in which name, ritual, and myth are constructed)—but *with* only an oblique, silent subject—"beautifully ascended" is utterly fathomless, even to the most linguistically competent translator.

Although many Hopi names are composed, like *Sikya-kwap-tiwa,* of three morphemes, complex events may be rendered by a simple lexeme. For example, Voth records a name *U'na*[20] that literally just means "recall it," "remember it." In the specific case, it was given by a Coyote clan member, and the intended image is a coyote's habit of burying tidbits of food in different locations. The name denotes a coyote in the mental and physical act of remembering the locations of buried food.

We can take this example, *U'na,* to highlight the multiplicity of possible connotations if the namegiver's intention were not known. Let me turn to a conversation with Herschel Talashoma of the Badger clan:

PW: You also said that, for example, that name *"U'na"* could be a Badger clan name and it could refer to a badger going and remembering medicine plants.

HT: Where he got his medicine the previous, the last time.

PW: That's because a badger is a *tuuhikya* ("medicine man")?

HT: Yes. yes.

PW: And is in charge of *ngahu* ("medicine").

HT: Right. [Pause] *Or,* where he ate the last corn!—at which field! Because, well, according to a porcupine it would work, because a porcupine really does that.

PW: So a porcupine could be *"U'na"*?

HT: *"U'na,"* right: "Oh! I remember that—that's where I got the last good corn!"

Porcupines lie within the Badger clan's totemic compass. The porcupine is notorious among Hopi farmers for descending upon cornfields toward the end of the labor-intensive four or five months it has taken to produce a crop. It may be the most wasteful—as well as, perhaps, the most heartbreaking for the farmer—of crop pests, since it goes from clump to clump of corn breaking off the ears and stripping away the husks in search of a few ripe ones. In this way, a single porcupine can devastate a large field in one night's work. Many a Hopi farmer at this time of the year (August and September) spreads his traps well and spends night after night in a field house with his shotgun. The porcupine's memory, then, is a matter of vital concern!

Speculative play with the conceivable meanings of names, or with how a name might be applied from a particular clan's perspective (i.e., possibly entailing a free play of signifiers), nonetheless takes its place within an entrenched, observed convention that the name as given means something specific. As such, the convention dictates that the grounds of its meaning shall not be trespassed upon, during the life of the individual to whom the name has stuck, by any additional application of the same lexical combination to another individual.

Female names are as imagistic and unique as the male names in the foregoing examples, equivalently *poems*, so to speak, in themselves. For instance, *Qöyangöynöm* is composed of *qöya*, "light gray," *ngöyta*, "he/she/it keeps chasing [it]," and *-nöm*, a female name suffix. This was conferred by a member of the *Piikyas-Patki*, "Young Corn" and "Divided Water," phratry, whose totemic sphere includes clouds. The image is of two small gray clouds, one chasing the other across the sky.

Talashongsi, a female name conferred by a Badger clan-member, displays another dimension of the breadth of potential imagery available to this clan. The components are: *talasi*, "pollen," *hoongi*, "standing (pl.)," and *-si*, a female name suffix. The sense is of a pollen-laden flower standing up straight. The association with the Badger clan is via its consociate Butterfly clan; the perspective is that of a butterfly's interest in a pollen-laden flower. In this example, as is perhaps most clearly the case with *Lomayayva*, the visual (or perhaps "apperceptive" is better for a butterfly) perspective is intrinsic to the image. But simultaneously, the name evokes a double identification: with the butterfly and its "eye-view" of the pollen, and with a viewer's witnessing of this scene. This is also the case with the mind's (and stomach's) eye of the coyote in *U'na*. Again, a "pure" translation is inadequate for this perspectival dimension of the image too.

The aesthetics of sensory, especially visual, imagery are key features in name composition; upon learning the sense of a name, Hopis often comment on its relative "beauty." So *Puhuhoynöm*, a Rabbit clan name, refers to the perception of the beauty of a newly made rabbit-fur blanket. Nowhere in the morphemes themselves is there a direct reference to either rabbit fur or a blanket. *Puhu-* (*puuhu* in noncombinatory

Figure 4.2 *Poovoli,* "butterflies," appear in a variety of Hopi aesthetic, cognitive, and metaphorical contexts. Some songs image the ground covered with butterflies, reflected sunlight shimmering from their wings. The opening and closing of butterfly wings is metaphorized to flower petals that open when prayed-for rain arrives. Unmarried girls with "butterfly-whorl" hairdos are even more explicitly metaphorized as butterflies in *Poliitiikive,* the "Butterfly Dance" (usually held in August), at which they are the key performers. *Poliingyam,* the "Butterfly clan," looks to the butterfly as its *wu'ya,* "clan ancient." Varicolored butterflies are associated with the six Hopi cardinal directions—a probable meaning of the six butterflies surrounding the lip of this Sikyatki polychrome storage jar. Department of Anthropology, Smithsonian Institution, neg. #155681.

form) means "new" or "newly," *hoy-* comes from *hooyi* meaning "separated," "taken off," and *-nöm* is the same female name suffix as above. The reference is to the cottontail and jackrabbit skins that have been newly taken off the animals' bodies in the process of making a blanket. The visual beauty Hopis associate with fresh rabbit fur is foregrounded in the image. Or, in Herschel Talashoma's words, "After when they are finished with a blanket, new blanket from all the rabbit fur, I guess it's pretty, that's why she is called Puhuhoynöm, 'newly made rabbit-fur blanket.'"

Hopis no longer make rabbit-fur blankets, and as I indicated above, at Third Mesa they no longer practice the central *Wuwtsim,* or indeed Snake-Antelope, Flute, *Maraw,* or *Lakon* rituals. In some instances, oral narratives commemorating practices formerly central to Hopi life provide a storehouse of name-giving imagery that no longer directly reflects experience. But in many cases, the passing of traditional quotidian or ritual practices has seriously curtailed the variety of possible images, and so, of names. When discussing with younger Hopis a name, the meaning of which I had learned from an older person or from a written source, several times the response I received was a nostalgic delight at the "beauty" of the name and a wistful observation that nowadays people had lost the ability to invent such beautiful names. But while the variety of available images has receded somewhat, names—at least in my (outsider's) impression of some recently conferred ones—continue to be richly imagistic, indeed poetic in the "West's" sense of the term.

The literary qualities of some Hopi names should by now be apparent in several respects. First, names constitute a marked use of language that involves an intentional construction of imagery that exceeds ordinary discourse. This "surplus of signification" calls conscious attention to the image depicted, as, for example, in "My love is like a red, red, rose." This is true with Hopi names, despite the fact that signification is formally opaque without a knowledge of the namegiver's intentions. Of course, *any* perception of "surplus signification" will depend on the cultural context of language usages. In the context of Hopi discourse, the surplus of signification in a name is ineluctably bound to a determinate "meaning"—in E. D. Hirsch's (e.g., 1976, 1984) terms—dependent on authorial intention, and independent of its farther fields of extratextual (or extracultural) "significance." Second, names are individually authored creative "texts" that have in mind a "readership"— at least of the name-receiver. Third, there is a central element of delight, enchantment, or aesthetic pleasure in many names—a key criterion of "literature," as Arnold Krupat (1989:39) points out: "Poetry, by its rhyme and meter, or—this is the case in literary prose—by its figures and structure—delights us; it is pleasurable beyond what can be accounted for rationally." And fourth, another axis of the "literary," Hopi names *instruct*—about clan tradition, ritual, myth, natural event, even about a particular kind of perceptual perspective. Moreover, they instruct reflexively—for the namer in fixing an image—as well as for the "reader" (i.e., the name-receiver or another who learns the name's sense). Again, following Krupat (1989:40), "the surplus of signification, the excess that pleased, ha[s] cognitive value."

The conjunction of aesthetic and cognitive value is especially clear with *Talashongsi, U'na,* and *Lomayayva.* To the butterfly, the discovery of a pollen-laden flower is very pleasurable. To the Hopi viewer (especially namer and named), the captured image is beautiful to behold, and it simultaneously communicates an observation of natural history and, as with all names, an axiom of social amity (i.e., between named and namer, and namer's clan). Likewise, the coyote delights in remembering the food burials, and the intended Hopi imaginer of this scene should find it intriguing and delightful (and perhaps on reflection, though here I am speculating, also amusing and morally instructive, in that Coyote as Trickster—an idea complex that is not at all exclusive to the Coyote clan, but that significantly informs its totemic associations—serves as a hilarious exemplar against, among other things, self-serving canniness and gluttony). And again, the viewer on the mesa top will be enchanted by the picture of *katsinam* coming up from down below, and instructed by the associated myth the name invokes—resocialized, as it were.

Many names begin with adjectival or adverbial forms that overtly signal aesthetic, especially visual, beauty. *Loma-* (from *lolma*, above) is one of these (e.g., *Lomaventiwa*, "beautifully painting," *Lomaheptiwa*, "looking for something beautiful," *Lomawayma*, "beautifully walking"). Many other names begin with *kuwan-*, "brightly and beautifully colored"—of, say, butterfly wings, parrot feathers, or coyote-pup fur. Likewise, *puhu-*, "new, fresh," often denotes beauty of something that gives the appearance of fresh color, for example, again, of young animal fur, butterfly wings (which can be thought of as "newly decorated" as in *Puhuve'yma*, "going along with freshly decorated wings"), or newly painted *katsina* masks. Specific color prefixes—*sikya-*, "yellow"; *sakw(a)-*, "blue-green"; *pala-*, "red"; *qöya-*, "light gray"; *qöma-*, "black"; *qöts(a)-*, "white"—appear in many names.

Aesthetics of motion are also commonly emphasized, presenting for the viewer a processual, rather than a static, image (a movie, if you will, rather than a still photograph).[21] In addition to the examples mentioned, other images include a sparrowhawk in flight, a spider making a web, an eagle's wings alighting, a bear walking around, a person beginning to complete a rabbit-fur blanket, the colorful movement of masked *katsinam* successively turning around in a line at a particular point in a line-dance, a rain shower "walking" across the landscape, corn tassles waving in the breeze, abruptly rising miniature columns of water produced by the force of heavy rain drops on a puddle (this last from Voth 1905b:94), and snow settling down. In each, a story is told that centrally involves action and the perception of it. Moreover, every case involves significant condensation and over-determination in both the creative practice of the story's author and the interpretive practice of its auditor/"reader."

The range of possible subjects (although to list these as such risks a misconceived emphasis on entities rather than on the actions in which they are engaged—see note 21) includes individuals, pairs, or groups of animals, insects, birds, plants, humans, clouds, rain, other meteorological phenomena, spirits, mythological figures, geographic forms, etc. More abstract notions, like a clan's reputation (e.g., *Maataq'ya*, "they are famous for it" [i.e., a specific behavioral trait or traditional practice]), also appear.

Finally, humans are not the only creatures who are regularly and poetically named. Eagles are gathered in late spring, and kept on house-tops until the *Niman*, "home-going," ceremony in July, when the *katsinam* depart for their spiritual homes around Hopi country. The captured eagles are "baptized" and named after the clan of the namegiver, just like human children. Eagle names reflect the same conventions as human names, and unless given by a member of the Eagle clan, may refer to numerous other species and practices. For example, one recorded eagle name given by a member of the Spider clan is *Hayyiwma*, "coming down," the sense denoting a spider descending on a single filament (Page and Page 1982:194).[22]

POESIS AND CONSCIOUSNESS, SELFHOOD AND THE SOCIAL ORDER

Hopi names derive from the clan-system and are thus integral to the social structure. Name senses represent aspects of Hopi "totemic" classes and processes. For the name-receiver the totemic figure of the name is a mental image evoking a natural and social association of the (paternal or godparental) clan the name ties him or her to. The social relationship is thus culturally enframed in a narrative "picture" that lives and resonates in the mind of the named.[23] In this nonliterate society, the name is a poetic sign instantiating attributes of Hopi traditional knowledge—about the environment, ritual practices, clan histories, and so forth—that are inseparable from the organization of society. Reflection on a name's form and meaning thus serves to re-delight and re-teach an aspect of Hopi knowledge. Effective translation must address this range of social, cultural, and cognitive contexts in which names have their meanings constituted.

The classifying function of personal names that Lévi-Strauss (1966) postulates (one of his principal examples is Hopi) seems borne out by the totemic references. But the great degree of authorial latitude and creativity within totemic spheres, on the one hand, and the intentional uniqueness of each name, on the other, add strongly individuating elements simultaneously for namer and named. The namegiver is a genuine author, who, in inventing a new name, inscribes, as it were, his or her personal "signature" onto it. Moreover, the esoteric nature of meaning produced simply by the frequent (though not prescribed) absence of public explications of exact sense, keeps the names "special"; the mystery produced merely from denotative opacity, vouchsafes the individuality of the name and its author. Authorial individuality, as it must do elsewhere, takes its place within an "intertextual" context of other images and other authors. Appropriate imagery derives from a collective consciousness of the general parameters of totemic associations. If one were to take all the names conferred by members, or individual "authors," of a particular clan, these would constitute a canonical genre of the narrative depictions of clan tradition.

For the receiver, a name confers a unique individual identity, in addition to the roles ascribed by kin, clan, and sodality membership. Within a Mesa group of villages, no two individuals will share the same name. There is a clear desire to avoid duplicates—even of homonyms— which, conferred by members of different clans, would have entirely different meanings (cf. Voth 1905b:69). For example, *Lomavuyawma*, "beautifully going along flapping," could be conferred by members of any clan with totemic interests in birds, in each case referring to a different image. But if one person had been given this name, specifically, say, referring to an eagle flying high in the sky easterly in the morning sunlight, another would not choose the same lexeme, even if the reference intended would be, for example, to a duck flying low over a specific lake away from the viewer in the afternoon, or to a roadrunner in flight. The resultant individuation of identity names serve to mark, and partially constitute, is pronounced.

The effect of names that individuate both authors and subjects, selves and others, is well drawn by David Parkin (1982:xxxix, implicitly critiquing Lévi-Strauss 1966:181) discussing Fipa and Omaha personal naming systems:

> [T]he choices made by a namer reflect on himself as well as on the bearer and those who may or may not use the name. Naming then defines selfhood as well as others' personhood. Putting this another way, the subject objectifies himself through the act of defining or objectifying another.

In the first three decades of this century, government officials, missionaries, and schoolteachers insisted that Hopi children adopt English forenames and their fathers' names (in a few cases, mothers' names)—in
many instances butchered by Anglo pronunciations—as hereditary patronymics. So in *Herschel Talashoma, Talashoma* is a corruption of his
father's father's Hopi name, *Talashoyiwma*. (In *Talashoma* principal
stress falls on the third syllable, and *sh* is a single phoneme, as in English
ship; in *Talashoyiwma* principal stress falls on the second syllable—the
usual case with Hopi polysyllabic names—and the *sh* is two phonemes
as in English *mishap*). The clan association of the original namegiver
and her or his relationship to the original name bearer are entirely
confounded by this process. Moreover, the name's intended meaning is
often simply lost. Many seemingly Hopi names have thus become English names, as Hopis describe this, and are now the untranslatable,
"meaningless marks" of Mill's depiction. Some Hopis have taken on
English surnames, or used their fathers' English forenames (Sidney,
George, Charlie, etc.) as surnames, because of the difficulty non-Hopis
experience with Hopi phonology and morphology. Nonetheless, each
child also still receives several ("true") Hopi names, which are generally
not used for the dominant society's bureaucratic purposes that require
a "forename" and "surname." Some people, conscious of the hegemony
present in accepting the national society's naming conventions, have
rejected inherited patronymics and substituted their own Hopi names as
surnames. Thomas Banyacya (or *Paangaqwya* according to the orthography I follow), for example, the widely known spokesman for the
Traditionalist movement, replaced the surname *Jenkins* that his father
had adopted with his own *katsina* initiation name.

   The avoidance of duplicating Hopi names is pursued also with English forenames, resulting in an extraordinary range and variety;
Aquila, Lemuel, Starley, Ebin, Orin, Lovina, Kylene, Marietta, Char-
metria, Aldena are just a few. Here again, the sense aspect of a Hopi
name is absent, but in order to maintain the individuative function,
Hopis have purposefully found access to a store of English, and some
Spanish, names that greatly outstretch the average name list in the
Anglo Southwest. Sometimes English forenames are passed on to the
next generation, or after a gap of one or two generations, and the
intention is to foreground the relationship of the name holders. But
often the name spelling is deliberately changed, or the name is applied
to a member of the opposite sex, in order to differentiate as well as
associate; never is the name regarded as reincarnating a social person.

In addition to both individuated Hopi and English names, most people have at least one nickname, which is commonly used for address and reference in ordinary conversation. Nicknames are often mildly insulting. They may poke fun at personal habits or appearances; for example, *Kutuksona,* "parched-corn craver"; *Kwaa'töqti,* "eagle's call," the name of the Hopi newspaper (for a gossip); *Tseemoni,* "Germany" (for a person who worked for the German Mennonite missionaries); *Wunavutsqasi,* "planklike thighs." Also, child-names are sometimes long remembered and used as quasi nicknames, especially by the namegiver and his or her close relatives, after the acquisition of initiation names.

CONCLUDING REMARKS

"Literature," as Arnold Krupat (1989:43) puts it, "is that mode of discourse which foremost seeks to enact and perform its insights, insisting that we understand with affect, feel with comprehension." Partially constituted in a naming genre that seems genuinely literary in its imagistic qualities, Hopi selves are consciously marked in the intersubjective naming process that links an individual namegiver and a name-receiver. Hopi names provide vivid images and tell stories that commemorate their storytellers, and individuate and identify the sites of their telling, that is, the named subjects. Elsewhere (Whiteley 1988a:2), I have drawn attention to a Hopi conception of marked narrative form as an active mnemonic device for important events and traditions, or "Making a story out of it, to remember it by." This, it seems to me, is what Hopi names do for Hopi persons: "tiny imagist poems" or narrative mental-pictures through which the subject as author delightfully and instructively marks the individual identity of another subject. And, in turn, Hopi persons thus marked are walking poetic metaphors of cultural, social, and natural experience:

Pay yan itam it ayangqaqw
yuupahaqaqw tumalay'ngwu.
Niiqe oovi hak naatoylay aw
hakiy tungwangwu; meh, nu'
honanwungwa, pu' kur nu'
hakiy tungwanik pu' nu' in-
aatoylay aw taykyangw pu' nu'
hakiy tungwani. Pu' son nu'
hakiy naatoylayat aw hakiy

This is how we've been doing it
all the way along from the past.
And so you name a person according to your clan-totem; see,
I'm a Badger clan, so if I want to
name someone, I would have to
look at my own clan in order to
name someone in a certain way. I
will not name anyone looking at

tungwantani, nawusni himuy'sa aw put taykyangw hakiy tungwamantani.

someone else's clan-totem; I will only look at my own clan's prerogatives in order to name that person, give that person a name.

5

BURNING CULTURE
Auto-da-fé at Orayvi

The theme of the subject in the structure, addressed in Chapter 4, and how individual agency and intentionality operate, are amplified in this chapter's analysis of a historical transformation. The empirical focus is on cultural transvaluation through time (i.e., historically) in an event where a key ritual nexus was destroyed by a (Hopi) priest, and the effects of this on Hopi society and collective consciousness through the twentieth century. Again my ethnographic negotiation is epistemological, addressing especially Hopi intentionality and action.

Determinist models and totalizing social theories, as I discuss in Chapter 1, are constitutively unenamored of individualist, intentionalist perspectives on history or sociocultural change. Individual actions are mostly regarded as having unintended consequences (see below), and abstract forces are privileged as the determining engines of history. But this neglects the reality of planned agential engagements in the world by individual persons, some of which, on some occasions, have envisioned transformative effects. This, I argue, is what occurred in K. T. Johnson's burning of the Two-Horn altar. He acted as an intentional agent of change, according to situated Hopi perspectives on the state of the world.

Anthropological explanation might well profit from some recent wrestling in history with the problems produced by overstructured determinations, of the Annaliste type, which frequently mask an un-stated analytical dependency on individual agency:

> It is no simple matter to establish the micro-macro link at any level in a complex society, but the historical interest lavished on the role of lead-ers in the formulation and execution of policies eases the historian's challenge of resolving distinct problems, such as the origins and con-duct of World War II or the origins, scope, and character of the Great Purges of 1936-39. Whether or not they have a theory explaining these events, historians usually situate Stalin and Hitler in various schemes of causation, in which individual agency plays a greater or lesser role. (Pomper 1996:283)

Philip Pomper surveys a series of theoretical positions in historical analysis in which individual agency is effaced in the interests of para-digmatic explanation, and, their antithesis, the explanatorily excoriated Great Man theories. For those who foreground intentionalism in his-torical analyses more effectively, Pomper cites a series of "non-revision-ist" students of Hitler and Stalin "who make a strenuous effort to connect a given policy and its execution precisely to the ideas, inten-tions, and actions of individual agents" (Pomper 1996:304 n.94). The opposition between "holism" and "individualism" in historical expla-nation, Pomper argues, is mediated by Christopher Lloyd's method-ological structurism (Lloyd 1993) and Giddens's structuration theory. Lloyd emphasizes a dialectics of structure and agency: "persons have agential power, structures have conditioning power" (Lloyd 1993:46).

The point for the anthropology of both history and subjectivity is that the erasure of individual conscious agency is now being found analytically paralyzing and explanatorily inadequate in Western histor-ical theory.

The sufficient conditions of agency are simply:

> . . . that actions be *effective* in changing material or cultural conditions, that they be *intentional*, sufficiently *unconstrained* that actions are not perfectly predictable and that the actor possesses the ability to observe the consequences of an action and to be *reflexive* in evaluating them. (Dietz and Burns 1992:194, in Pomper 1996:283)

But while actions cannot be "perfectly predictable," the frequent (im-possible) determinist demand that they should be so, if intentionalism is to be worthy of serious explanatory consideration, rests upon what I shall call the fallacy of overdetermining unintentional consequences:

> It is, of course, unreasonable to require as a test for agential power that leaders formulate their policies down to the last detail, that the policies be fully rational (in an instrumental sense), that the leaders systematically micromanage their execution, and that the outcomes line up precisely with the leaders' intentions. With respect to the last issue, Dray wrote: "For holding that a person causes what he intends need not commit us to the absurd idea that a causally significant intention must itself be a sufficient condition of what it causes. It is quite enough that it be a necessary one." (Pomper 1996:306 n.98, quoting Dray 1978:152)

It is a similar perspective on the interpretation of intentions that Richard Wollheim (below) articulates so effectively.

The questioning of "inner states" and intendings in Other cultures, as I noted in Chapter 1, also comes into play here. K. T. Johnson's own statements (as translated in the appendix at the end of the chapter) should defer such questions in the present context. Roy Wagner (1995:164-75) argues that identification of intentions often follows performance in Daribi ritual. Similarly, Hopi ritual performances are frequently followed by social critique and identification of the intentions of the *tunatyaytaqa*, "the intending one" or "sponsor." Indeed these may well be discernible only after the fact, indexed to weather conditions. If the wind blows cold and there is no rain, this may mark ineffectual or even ill intentions on the sponsor's part (cf. D. Eggan 1943). Often Hopis comment on the ineffectuality of ritual in other villages, suggesting that those people lack the power to focus their thoughts and prayers in such a way as to produce consequential results (by contrast to those of *our* village).

Such retroactive attributions of intent, however, operate more effectively in relation to programmatic, stereotyped performances; they do not work so well when the event at issue is singular, like Johnson's action.

What we have learned during the past year (the most unusual in the forty-four years of my life) is that there is no determinism in history, that *our history depends far more on ourselves, on our will and our decisions* than any of us thought.

Adam Michnik (1990, emphasis added)

When we ask why someone acted as he did, we want to be provided
with an interpretation. . . . When we learn his reason we have an interpretation, a new description of what he did, which fits it into a familiar
picture. The picture includes some of the agent's beliefs and attitudes;
perhaps also goals, ends, principles, general character traits, virtues or
vices. Beyond this the redescription of an action afforded by a reason
may place the action in a wider social, economic, linguistic, or evalua-
tive context. *To learn, through learning the reason, that the agent con-*
ceived his action as a lie, a repayment of a debt, an insult, the fulfilment
of an avuncular obligation, or a knight's gambit is to grasp the point of
the action in its setting of rules, practices, conventions, and expectations.
Donald Davidson (1980 [1963]:9-10, emphasis added)

SOCIETY, HISTORY, AND INDIVIDUAL ACTION

Critical oppositions in recent social theory—between structure and
agency, structure and event, and culture and agency[1]—revisit a vener-
able problem in ethnographic explanation: how to account for historical changes in the cultural and social orders articulating individual
lives. Past solutions have tended either to deny the problem's
significance (as in the synchronic emphasis of structural-functionalism,
the "cold societies" of structuralism, or the "closed systems" of the
neo-rationalists) or to seek causes of change in external, impersonal
phenomena—material conditions, structural contradictions, intercultural influence (from diffusion to conquest), and so forth. But the
"problem of history"[2] in non-Western societies has intruded more and
more into the anthropological consciousness:

> Anthropologists are discovering that history is not just something im-
> posed on native populations from the outside . . . but is also an essen-
> tial feature of native peoples' own creative efforts within the contexts,
> contradictions, and conflicts of their own cultures and societies. (Med-
> ick and Sabean 1984:4)

When these contexts, contradictions, and conflicts encounter those of
a supervening dominant society of entirely different cultural background, indigenous historical consciousness and its active creative efforts are conjuncturally transformed, but by no means, I shall argue,
just abandoned.

Oppositions engendered by the problem of history—particularly
with respect to transformative events—may be seen to rest on another,
perhaps more fundamental opposition: between society and the indi-

vidual (cf. Boudon 1982:153-205). Individuals, insofar as they are recognized in (determinist) social theory, are largely held to play out received social and cultural protocols—mere *"paroles"* to the *"langue,"* "practicing the structure," etc.—rather than as being conscious agents who may have determinate effects upon the sociocultural order: Individual action may produce changes, but these are largely by-products of the agent's intentions (e.g., Boudon 1982, Ortner 1984:157; Tambiah 1990:119), not direct results. "Structure," "society," or "culture"—transformed, "reproduced," perhaps dialectically modified by impersonal events—always predominates over individual action, which remains *explanandum* rather than *explanans,* anomaly rather than regularity.

Now all of this is in many respects as it should be. If anthropology is to persist as any sort of rigorous social inquiry (rather than descending into an ironic play of tropes, a "fantasy reality of a reality fantasy" [Tyler 1986:134] or some such), then the guiding metanarrative must privilege regularity over idiosyncrasy; intersubjective convention over subjective invention; order, in short, over individualist anarchy. Likewise for history: Fogelson (1989:135) points out that histories that constitute the individual as "the ultimate locus and transmitter of historical change" have been found radically wanting by Annaliste critique. I do not mean, then, to champion a socially naive voluntarism over a systematic concern with structural regularities; for individuals to consciously produce transformative change, they must possess the socially constituted, and unequally distributed, power to so act. I want merely to argue that individuals, as intentional agents, may on occasion, in addition to reproducing preexisting cultural and social orders, act to change these orders in ways they explicitly conceive (as well as in ways they do not).

This emphasis is closely allied to Fredrik Barth's transactionalism (e.g., 1981). But the methodological individualism associated with that approach (e.g., Kapferer 1976, Evens 1977)—that all social process is the aggregation of individuals' self-interested actions—deleteriously deemphasizes structure. Moreover, Barth's antipathy to history (1981:6) would seem to disenable a "historical transactionalism." Marshall Sahlins (1981, 1985) has cogently demonstrated the indispensability of "structure" for a thoroughgoing historical anthropology. Yet his analyses of historico-structural transformations, for example in Hawaii, deemphasize the effects of individual action in social process, by treating it as systemic sign rather than endemic force.

I want to tread a middle path: to keep both *structure* and *the individual* for a historical anthropology, and to suggest that self-interest is only a partial account of individual action. We should see individual action as ongoing positional negotiation (i.e., with group interests also in mind, with contingent, random, habitus-inspired actions, as well as consciously deliberated ones) with received cultural and social structures.

PERSON, INDIVIDUAL, SELF

An immediate problem is the anthropological doubt that individual persons as conscious intentional agents exist in non-Western societies (e.g., C. Geertz 1974; Shweder and Bourne 1984, Carrithers et al. 1985:passim). If the *person*—in Mauss's (1985:22) sense "the engine of every act of consciousness . . . of all science and all action"—is in doubt, individual agency can have little meaning. I cannot pretend to solve transcultural questions of "individual," "person," and "self," but my argument requires some statement of position (and see also Chapter 1).

Anthropological inquiries into persons and selves have, in my view, often failed to separate out complex and contested philosophical, psychological, and ideological strands that comprise these conceptions in Western thought.[3] For my purposes, intentionality and agency are the essential conditions of persons and selves cross-culturally: As Glover (1988:97) puts it, "[t]he rational will . . . is the ego applied to action."[4] Intentionality is predicated upon consciousness; indeed, for philosophers like Dennett (1987), this is its essential index: "[T]he intentional strategy consists of treating the object whose behavior you want to predict as a rational agent with beliefs and desires and other mental stages exhibiting what Brentano and others call *intentionality*" (ibid.:15). Intention and agency may thus be treated as diagnostic of self-conscious personhood (and see Glover 1988:59–97). I will return to intentions, actions, and interpretations when I have framed the practical context.

For now, the following seems to me unobjectionable as a universal proposition:

> One of the distinctive things about human beings . . . is that normally we know what we are doing in our activities and why. . . . In addition human actors have reasons for their actions, reasons that consistently inform the flow of day-to-day activities. . . . [A]gents virtually all the time know what their actions are, under some description, and why it is they carry them out.[5] (Giddens 1987:2–3)

I propose further that all societies recognize a relative uniqueness and actional autonomy of individual moral subjects, as well as imposing sociocultural roles that specifically and hegemonically restrict actional autonomy, and differentially enable social agency. I thus take Geertz's (1974) argument about Balinese persons and selves, or Mauss's (1985) about the lack of selves and self-conscious agents among the Pueblos, Kwakiutl, et al.,[6] to address cultural *ideologies* (the former Balinese, the latter 1930s French bourgeois) that impose upon individual conscious energies and capacities (cf. Shweder 1984:12-17).

Doubts about individuals make structured systems more persuasive as the only true candidate for comparative inquiry. But the widespread suggestion that structure is all is to reduce our subject—human beings, their actions and interactions—to a perpetual cultural chess game, with individual pieces condemned to stereotypical behavior by the superordinate codes that govern them: They may reproduce or transform, to use favored terms, but never fundamentally shift the ground or its rules. It is this overemphasis on structure, to the exclusion of individual action (particularly in small-scale societies), I believe, that has made the explanation of historical change so problematic.

EVENTS

Processes of social and cultural change are realized in particular events. "Event," Sahlins (1985:153) notes, "is the empirical form of system . . . a relation between a certain happening and a given symbolic system." More concretely, events are composed of the actions and interpretations of individuals (and groups of individuals) who participate in them—as protagonists, observers, meaning-makers, or what have you. "Society," "culture," "system" do not participate directly in events; people—that is, conscious, judging subjects, intentional actors—do. A selective focus on individuals and particular events they participate in—on their intentions, correspondent actions, and interpretations—then, may allow a practical synthesis of society, culture, and history.

HISTORY AND CULTURAL CHANGE

"Culture," anthropology's central trope, remains fiercely contested conceptually (e.g., R. Rosaldo 1989). For my present purpose, Clifford Geertz's general view—that culture is a system of symbols with shared meanings—will suffice. Transformative cultural changes should, then, reorient, refigure, or otherwise significantly alter existing structures of cultural symbols and their social correlates. "Religious" symbols, and here I follow Geertz's specific definition (1966:4),[7] are particularly powerful concentrations of cultural attention; major changes to central religious symbols will have correspondingly powerful effects in other dimensions of the sociocultural order.

In the case in question, a key symbolic complex (a religious altar) was deliberately destroyed—a rather radical form of cultural refiguring. The altar served as a metonymic centerpiece in the Hopi ritual system. I have argued elsewhere (Chapter 3, and Whiteley 1988) that this system was simultaneously religious and political—a "total social fact," in Mauss's terms—the central structural engine articulating Hopi society.

Conventional approaches to historical change in Native American societies have successively adhered to, first, acculturation (tragic), and second, persistence (triumphal) narratives (Bruner 1986). In either instance, the rationale de-emphasizes individual action: No specific consciousness within social processes is sought for, merely the sociocultural organism's relative capacity to decline or persist. The present case may be interpretable as an acculturation process; an ostensible context for the altar-burning was Christian conversion. But as we shall see, this ignores complexities introduced by Hopi perspectives.

NARRATIVE AND INTERPRETATION

My focus on the event is through a textual record in part authored by the leading actors. Owing to the text's length, my explanatory narrative is interspersed throughout. The immediate meaning of the actions, I shall argue, is to be found in the actors' intentions. The text records some of these intentions directly (rationalization and the text's proselytizing purpose do not, I think, obscure them). I want further to situate the actors' interpretations and representations of intention (a) in biographical features supplemental to the text, (b) in subsequent interpretations by other Hopis, and (c) in the relevant documentary record.

TEXT AND CONTEXTS

On 27 August 1922, K. T. Johnson, Bow clan, heir to the chiefship of Orayvi's *Aa'alt,* "Two-Horn sodality," set up his altar *(Alvongya)* in public and burned it.[8] Not long before, he had converted to the Mennonite Church. The Church, notorious for its lack of success, was established at Orayvi in 1893. U.S. Government hegemony, particularly

A HOPI INDIAN FINDS
CHRIST

The Experience of Mr. K. T. Johnson

and

His Judgment on Idolatry

Mr. K. T. Johnson

Prepared by

Rev. John P. Suderman

Missionary to the Hopi Indians

Oraibi, Arizona

Figure 5.1. Cover page of the text in question. Courtesy of the Mennonite Library and Archives, Bethel College, North Newton, Kansas.

in the form of an Indian Agency and schools, also intervened in the late nineteenth century. This intercultural conjuncture thus provided a major context. But Hopi interpretations, including Johnson's own, suggest more than simply the piety of a new convert. They invoke: the 1906 Orayvi split and its enduring politics; a hermeneutics of prophecy; historical attitudes to conversion; and a complex internal sociology of knowledge and practice.

The text is a Mennonite pamphlet authored by Johnson and Otto Lomavitu, another Orayvi Christian, under the auspices of John P. Suderman, missionary at Third Mesa from circa 1929 to 1953.[9] The first chapter (see Chapter 5 Appendix) contains Johnson's account of his conversion. Chapter 2, "The Judgment Upon Idolatry (Written by Otto Lomavitu)," opens as follows:

> Aug. 22.—On the evening of this day I called upon Johnson in company with my wife. After a few introductory words Johnson spoke and said, "Otto, I have something upon my heart which I would like for you to consider and pass your judgment upon.
>
> "My aunt died today and the fire of our clanship is extinguished. We have in our possession the Al-vo-na (the altar and the idol of the Horned-ones, a foremost secret order or ceremony) and I have been minded to burn them. I have thought of bringing these things down from the upper village [Orayvi] and have them displayed before the public on this coming Sunday afternoon prior to burning them. Before doing this, however, I would be glad to know whether it would be scriptural or not."

Johnson's aunt was not the last woman of the Bow clan, but her death seemed to signal the clan's demise, and indeed it is now extinct.[10] His foregrounding of this event problematizes Christian conversion as prime motive. Many Hopi deaths are attributed to witchcraft. Witchcraft works principally within a clan or phratry and may utilize (corruptly), or even autonomically proceed from, supernatural powers governed by the clan. According to Waters (30 November 1960), Johnson reported a specific Bow clan *mongko,* staff of ritual office, to have "killed all women in his family."[11]

The *Awatngyam,* "Bow clan," in Orayvi (its only village location in recent history) was powerful. In one tradition, this clan held overall chieftainship in the "third world" below. Owing to systemic corruption, that world was abandoned (e.g., Voth 1905:16–26) and upon emergence to the "fourth world," the Bow ceded leadership to the Bear clan.[12] Historically, Bow was also the preeminent clan at Awat'ovi, "bow on top (village)," until its destruction by internecine attack from other villages in 1700 (e.g., Montgomery et al. 1949; Whiteley 1988a:22).[13]

In Orayvi the Bow clan controlled prominent ritual knowledge. According to my consultants, this clan first organized *wiimi,* the "higher-order ritual system"; previously, ritual sodalities had practiced,

Figure 5.2. *Wuwtsim* ceremonies at Walpi, with a long line of *Aa'alt*, the "Two Horn society," in the foreground. Photograph by Kate Cory, between 1905 and 1912. Courtesy of a private collection.

but without the efficacy achieved by Bow clan systematization. This refers especially to *Wuwtsim*, a ritual complex conducted by four sodalities: *Aa'alt*, "Two-Horn"; *Kwaakwant*, "One-Horn"; *Taatawkyam*, "Singers"; and *Wuwtsimt* (untranslatable). I have argued (Chapter 3, and Whiteley 1988) for the surpassing sociopolitical importance of these sodalities. The Bow clan "owned" *Aa'alt*, and curated its central sacra, the *Alvongya*. The *Aa'alt* held a superordinate role within *Wuwtsim*; one older consultant characterized them, in English, as the "philosophical society" with specialized insight into "psychology, emotionalism and individual ambitions." Only the *Aa'alt* were allowed unrestricted access to the other three sodalities' private rituals, and thus only they are regarded as formally comprehending and supernaturally coordinating the whole ritual scheme (cf. Titiev 1944:137).

Additionally, the Bow clan owned *Sa'lako* (Voth 1905:24), a rare and powerful Kachina ceremony linked with *Wuwtsim* initiation.[14] Titiev (1944:137 n.54) records that the Bow clan was in "'charge' of all weapons" in Orayvi.[15] And another tradition is that only Bow among

Hopi clans regularly practiced human sacrifice in earlier times. All these ritual prerogatives entailed a rather awesome reputation: "If you get in trouble with the Bow clan (which controls important ceremonies), you might do nothing. You can't face them; you can't get even with them. They could kill you. I'd let it go. . . . The Bow clan is powerful" (Brandt 1954:181–82).

More particularly, in recent history, several Bow people were widely regarded as *hoonaqti*, "crazy," *popwaqt*, "witches, sorcerers," or both, as a direct result of their *wu'ya*, clan "totem" or "ancient."[16] Accounts of madness and witchcraft are not unusual in Hopi discourse, but the high concentration of them for the Bow clan definitely is. The clan's demographic demise is specifically attributed to internal sorcery. Johnson's death in the 1960s left one clan member remaining, who died shortly thereafter.

The narrative continues:

> I assured him that I believe it to be scriptural and that it would no doubt prove itself of greater blessing to our people. That besides this there would no doubt be a good number of white tourists out for the snake dance which was to take place on the coming Saturday in Hotevilla, a village that is eight miles north of Oraibi. Accordingly we referred this matter to the native Christians at the prayer meeting and a warm discussion followed. The oldest man and the very first convert to Christianity, and a noted hero who had made himself famous by going single handed to Santa Fe, N.M., after the captives of the Hopi children by the Mexicans and succeeded in bringing them back, was asked first to give his opinion and he answered in part:
>
> "I have done away with idolatry many years ago and therefore I have nothing to put away." This man is an ex-priest of one of the religious ceremonies. Wik-va-ya. (It means Brought-back.)
>
> Ta-las-nom-ti-wa the blind man and also a former priest, but now a priest unto God, was next asked being the oldest. He said in part, "I have no idols to put away. I had to do with living men, making men play the part of gods. I cannot burn them but they can burn themselves."
>
> A long discussion followed in which it was decided that the idols should be publicly burned.

Timing the altar-burning to coincide with the (Hotvela) Snake Dance adds significance. Since the 1890s the Snake Dance has attracted myriad tourists.[17] In turn-of-the-century Orayvi, the rituals were a major nexus of contention between "Hostile" and "Friendly" factions. The

Hostiles took control of both sodalities, Snake and Antelope, that jointly perform. Each performance became an enactment of Hostile sociopolitical power, with the Friendlies inhibited from contestation by the tourist presence. The Orayvi split took place a day and a half after the 1906 performance, and the timing was not coincidental (Whiteley 1988:107). For the Christian convert, the Snake Dance, condemned by the missionaries but condoned by so many other whites, became a cause célèbre in this conflict of values. Johnson himself was a *tsu'wimkya*, Snake initiate, who, immediately following his conversion, destroyed his sodality insignia (see Chapter 5 Appendix).

The burning was thus designed as a spectacle for an intercultural audience. This element implicates the additional motive of political maneuver: a brinkmanship stratagem to performatively demonstrate *new* authority, as well as attack the old. The Orayvi split and its aftermaths (Whiteley 1988) ruptured the leadership at Third Mesa, in some ways leaving a power vacuum, while the Indian Agency continued to expand its influence over Hopi life. At Orayvi and Hotvela, leaders variously refused to recognize or negotiate with Government authority (e.g., Crane 1925:passim). At Kiqötsmovi (New Oraibi), still technically under the Orayvi *Kikmongwi*, "village chief," efforts were made to form a secular political council. Johnson's later involvement with this (e.g., Fredericks et al., 7 March 1934) and in other activities (see below) suggest neopolitical aspirations. In this respect, his actions do conform to the transactionalist emphasis on self-interested stratagems.

Of the protagonists mentioned, we know some relevant biographical details. Johnson, Hopi name Tuwaletstiwa, was born circa 1876 (Hopi Hearings 1955:168).[18] By his own account, he was to succeed to *Al-mongwi*, "*Aa'alt* chief," at around the age of forty (i.e., c.1916), (see Chapter 5 Appendix). In another register of social prominence, during the allotment program of 1908 to 1911, he led a movement (eventually aborted)—subscribed to by some thirty others—to found a new village on the Dinnebito Wash (Lawshe, 6 December 1910).

Some leadership patterns were markedly shifting toward younger individuals during this period. Titiev (1944:72) describes *Kikmongwi* Loololma (d. c.1904), because of his juniority, as under the "regency" of his father until, inferably, he was in his fifties. Likewise, Loololma's "Hostile" rivals were, following the norm, older leaders; indeed Yukiwma (below) did not emerge as leader until his fifties. Yet Tawakwaptiwa succeeded Loololma at roughly thirty, and Kuwannömtiwa (below), who did establish a village, rose to prominence when he was

in his early thirties. Johnson's move to head a new village, then, occurred during a crisis of leadership and a climate of great social flux
(1906-10; see Whiteley 1988), in which other younger men—of the
same age cohort—asserted authority.[19]

In 1920 Johnson dated his conversion to about six years earlier
(Duberman et al. 1979:113), though before this he was involved with
the mission, as occasional caretaker (Frey, 6 December 1909). Conversion itself was highly fraught politically, as I shall pursue further
below. Johnson was also one of the first few children from Orayvi sent
in 1889 to school at Keam's Canyon (Friesen 1923:11; Hopi Hearings
1955:168)—an event that exploded factional controversies (Whiteley
1988:74-83). This is a clear indication that his parents were very close
allies of *Kikmongwi* Loololma. He attended for two and a half years,
learning to speak English quite well (Friesen 1923:11). Thus, from
early on, Johnson was at a leading edge in the emergent encounter
with U.S. society.

Otto Lomavitu (Rabbit clan) was an early student convert and well-
known "progressive"; as early as 1916 he tried to organize a secular
council (Keam's Canyon Office Diary, 1 May 1916). By the early 1930s,
he was "President of Hopi Council" in Kiqötsmovi (Miller, 10 January
1931), and became in 1937 first chairman of the Hopi Tribal Council
(Adams n.d.), instituted after the Indian Reorganization Act of 1934.
Oliver La Farge (1937:17), author of the Tribal Constitution, described
him as:

> . . . an outstanding Christian and perhaps the best educated man on
> the reservation. Otto has slowly evolved from an early phase of violent
> hostility to all things Hopi into a relatively moderate and balanced pro-
> gressive. . . . He has the general reputation of being an absolutely hon-
> est interpreter with a remarkable command of Hopi as well as of En-
> glish.

The next named individual, Wikvaya, the first "native Christian" asked
for comment on the planned auto-da-fé, was Lizard clan head, and had
been *Marawmongwi,* male head of the *Mamrawt* women's sodality, his
clan's principal ritual prerogative.[20] He held another special distinction:
"In the year 1909 the first convert from among the so-called 'raw'
heathen was baptised, the elderly priest Wikwaya, one of the chiefs. A
few young people in or from schools were baptised before that" (Epp
1923:7).

Talasnömtiwa was head of the Sparrowhawk clan (Titiev n.d.:29) and had been *Wuwtsimmongwi,* chief of Orayvi's *Wuwtsimt* sodality (Titiev 1944:242). His consent to the burning is particularly significant because of his clan position and his former office. The rightful heads of two of Orayvi's four *Wuwtsim* societies, then, were principally involved.

Determinate planning in a private meeting is very similar to orthodox ritual practice, where a formative "plan," or *tiingavi,* is made for the overall performance. In seeking whether the act would be "scriptural," Johnson mirrors the role of a *tunatyaytaqa,* "the one who intends," or "the sponsor," aligning his specific plans with the ritual paradigm. Although Johnson assumes principal responsibility, formal approval by his cohort (just as in ordinary sodality practice) is a prerequisite. In short, the pattern of deliberation follows the protocols of traditional politico-religious leadership.

Aug.25.—In the meantime Johnson had learned that the Al-vo-na had been taken to Hotevilla, a hostile village, by chief Yu-kiw-ma, a man who had no title to the idols in question. Upon Johnson's request, he and I went there towards evening. Upon our arrival there, we were told that Yu-kiw-ma was in the kiva, (an underground association room) performing the rituals of the snake dancers. Johnson called him out and soon brought me word that all was favorable. He said however, that the chief had stubbornly refused to let him have them to which Johnson replied, "I shall enter your house myself for them."

We went on to his house where the idols and the altar were kept. Soon the chief came and said to his sister, "Have you the key with you? Open the door and let them enter." This done we followed him through several rooms until we were in the innermost room. The room was dingy and small and we had to stoop much. The altar and the idols were there.

Yukiwma then laid his hand on the bundle of altar pieces which were hanging from the ceiling. But instead of taking it down he scrutinized us intently as though he wished to detect treachery. He then asked, "Now, who are you?" Johnson introduced us. The chief asked this not so much to know our names but to ascertain whether or not we belonged to the clanship worthy of consideration. Being satisfied as to who we were, he then proceeded to ask, "And who has sent you here? By what authority do you intend to take these things? I have doubts concerning your adventure. Has Washington or the missionaries sent you? What will you do with them?"

Johnson answered and said that he had come of his own accord. A long talk then followed in which the chief emphasized the predominance of this altar and how it got that place. Johnson then asked him two definite questions which were, a—What good or bad have you found in these idols that has prompted you to take them away, and, b—What advantage is there in these?

The chief replied that the altar and the idols were good but that the people were bad. "If our hearts are good," he said, "we should see the desire of our heart, that is, goodness. But if our hearts are not right evil will result." (That is to say, in plain language, that the idols and the altar play no important part in the religious life of the Hopi.[21] Why should men set these up and worship them in fear if they play no part as to results? As well leave them out and afflict themselves with the hope of obtaining their end.)

He then said in tones of deepest feeling, "Alas! it has come, but so must it be. By destroying these things you will have DESTROYED the very foundation of our ceremonies. The conflagration must spread. Take these and do as you have said." (Johnson had told him that he was going to burn them.)

We then took up our trophies and wended our way out. We could not help but feel the very presence of our Lord Jesus and no sooner had we laid our hand on the altar and idols when Johnson triumphantly cried, "The blood of Jesus Christ, God's Son, cleanseth us from all sin" to which I responded with my heartfelt amen. We then went home and had them deposited in the back rooms of the chapel where we left them to wait for their trial on serious charges of murder! These helpless creatures, helpless, though gods, in the house of Almighty God.

Yukiwma (*Kookopwungwa*, "Fire" clan), Hostile leader at Orayvi and founder of Hotvela, was a Two-Horn initiate. How he had charge of the altar was addressed by an older Paaqavi consultant:

So, it was decided to do the *Wuwtsim* ceremony at Hotvela. But as we know, before that happened Yukiwma and Nakwavey'ma stole the *Alvongya* from Orayvi. Shortly thereafter, Tsonsi [Johnson] came up here to Kuwannömtiwa's place and asked his advice.[22] "What do you think I should do about this, for they have stolen our altars from Orayvi?" Kuwannömtiwa said to him, "Go get your altar back from them. It is your altar, it is yours." So Tsonsi went up to Hotvela and asked for the altar and took it back. (Translated from the Hopi)

According to consultants, Yukiwma did not want Hotvela to resume *Wuwtsim* initiations, but bowed to popular demand (Whiteley

1988:279). The fact that Yukiwma and Nakwavey'ma are credited with appropriating the altar, however, and that Yukiwma himself was curating it, is interesting. Nakwavey'ma (Eagle clan) was a prominent Hostile at Orayvi and later, at Hotvela, was Yukiwma's "lieutenant"; he was also an *Aalaytaqa,* Two-Horn initiate. Yukiwma's son, Qötshongva, and nephew, Pongyayawma, long-time rivals for the chief-ship of Hotvela after Yukiwma's death in 1929, were both *Aa'alt.* Nakwavey'ma's nephew and chosen heir as Eagle clan leader, Lomakwahu, another prominent man in Hotvela later, was an *Aa'alt* initiate too. In short, central leadership in Hotevilla was becoming partly constellated around the *Aa'alt* sodality. Yukiwma et al. may have been trying to ritually constitute their legitimacy (key in Hopi politics) in the *Aa'alt,* transforming this sodality into a new context of social power. (Yukiwma could not become a true *Kikmongwi,* since he was not Bear clan.) Johnson's reappropriation and destruction is thus a direct attack on the Hotvela leadership and the emergent ritual grounds of its authority.

Johnson and Lomavitu arrived on the day of the Antelope Dance (a day before the Snake). Yukiwma was also an Antelope initiate, which explains his presence in the kiva. The Orayvi Snake-Antelope rituals had, to all intents and purposes, been transferred to Hotvela after the split and remained a political, as well as a religious, enactment. The kiva would have been Naasavi, home at Hotvela (as at Orayvi) of both the Antelope sodality (owned by the Spider clan, another key nexus in Hotvela leadership) and the *Aa'alt,* and also Yukiwma's home kiva— for all these reasons, then, a major political center.

Yukiwma's inquiry as to the "clanship worthy of consideration" (Bow) and his eventual cession of the altar indicates the persistent legitimacy of Bow clan control despite Johnson's conversion and the severe fission at Orayvi, which placed the two at political loggerheads. (Yukiwma's attempt to refigure structure into a new pattern clashed with Johnson's reasserted reproduction of the sign's old value.) But as a Christian convert and prominent figure in Kiqötsmovi, emergent center of "progressivism," Johnson's position was directly antithetical to Yukiwma's vaunted arch-conservatism (reversing the structure-value interplay from the previous instantiation).

Yukiwma's reported reaction, "Alas! It has come, but so must it be. By destroying these things you will have DESTROYED the very founda-tion of our ceremonies. The conflagration must spread," suggests sev-eral important elements. First, there is a definite sense of inevitability, very probably enframed as prior "prophecy" (*navoti,* also translated as "theory").[23] Invocation of prophecy remains central in Hopi etiological discourse: "structure"—re-cognized tradition—is actualized to comprehend unfolding events (cf. Sahlins 1985). The prophetic aspect is clearly evident in a later account by Johnson:

> It was told to us by our forefathers that this religious setup [*sic*] was to disintegrate the people here at Oraibi and the time would come when we as Hopis would all come to the point of following the Holy One.
>
> I was once in the position of authority, the authority of this clan. Its leadership was once in my hand and those who passed it on to me told me that this was ours to use in this village [Orayvi] and that it would be up to me to decide in what manner this should be destroyed when this leadership, the authority, was placed into my hands, knowing what had been handed down to me, knowing that this which had been placed into my hand was the root of this religious pattern, knowing of its evils and all that was involved, I took them and burned them. (Hopi Hearings 1955:174)

Yukiwma's reported assessment of the "predominance of this altar," and that burning it would destroy "the very foundation," underscores the *Alvongya*'s central ritual force in *Wuwtsim* symbology, a view confirmed by Johnson's characterization of it as "the root of this religious pattern." The prediction that "the conflagration must spread" confirms the protagonists' intention to terminate the ritual system: Destruction of this manifestly potent symbolic core would infect (indeed "epidemiologically," to use Sperber's [1985] metaphor) the whole complex of ritual representations.[24]

Johnson's timing is interesting in another respect. In spite of the attempt at the Orayvi split to terminate *Wuwtsim,* as mentioned, a desire emerged at Hotvela to reconstruct the ritual order.[25] According to several older consultants, Hotvela had not held a *Wuwtsim natnga* (initiation) prior to 1922, but plans to do so were clearly afoot. One man specifically recalled that the first one occurred in 1923.[26] So another important motive is indicated here: to forestall or undermine Hotvela's plans to resume initiations, negating both ritual efficacy and the planned reconstitution of paradigmatic power structures.[27]

The idea of *Wuwtsim* initiations at Third Mesa had become extremely controversial. The last in Orayvi were held in 1909, causing much turmoil that resulted—at a critical stage in the ritual process—in a second dramatic village fission (Whiteley 1988a:70). *Wuwtsim,* which begins the Hopi year, is associated in Hopi historical discourse with prior crises. Awat'ovi was destroyed during *Wuwtsim* (note 13), and some accounts of emergence indicate a timing during this ritual period. Initiation includes reenactment of emergence by initiates under great psychological stress; there is a clear association with cosmic death and rebirth, with rupture in an epochal order. But beyond this, I cannot illuminate further the intersection of *Wuwtsim* with historical crises, apart from restating the absolute centrality—political and metaphysical—of this sodality system in the Hopi social order (cf. Chapter 3).

Lomavitu's reference to the altar's "murderous" power contrasts strikingly with his earlier remarks on its unimportance, although his precise meaning is difficult to determine. It may refer specifically to the death of Johnson's aunt. Alternatively, and I think more critically, it may reflect a pervasive notion that *Wuwtsim* ritualism had become corrupt, had acquired "the character of sorcery which 'preyed' on people to the detriment of natural population growth" (Sekaquaptewa 1972:247-48). As part of its cosmic prerogatives, each sodality had the power to afflict a specific disease (e.g., Bradfield 1973:295). Such sodality *wuvaapit*, "whips," usually activated against moral impropriety or excessive population pressure, are also thought subject to abuse.[28] The "corruption" of *Wuwtsim* included the idea that *wuvaapit* were being employed capriciously, from personal and factional enmities. According to one man, the corruption was partly configured in ritual transgressions by Johnson's (Hostile) uncle, Qötsventiwa—while he was *Aa'alt* head—against *Kikmongwi* Loololma's religious leadership.[29]

Thus the desire to destroy *Wuwtsim* also takes on a prophylactic purpose: to protect against ritual forces now deemed harmful. An older consultant, addressing the leaders' refusal to initiate his cohort, spoke of an explicit rationale to save future generations from *Wuwtsim*'s corrosive supernatural dangers.

We encounter here a paradigmatic theme in Hopi historical consciousness: that the world passes through epochs that eventually decay, morally and materially, requiring a process of *naavotsiwni*, "purification." Abandonment of the "third world" is construed thus, as is the destruction of numerous former villages, historical and mythological. Purification is a prominent function in ordinary ritual practice (e.g., A. Geertz 1987:passim).[30] This metaphysical theme of renewal—particularly through the purging use of destructive fire—very probably informed Johnson's intentions.

Aug. 26—Snake dance in Hotevilla. In the evening of this day Johnson and another native Christian went to the upper village and brought down the remaining paraphernalia belonging to the captive idols which was still remaining in Johnson's house. Among them were real antlers of a deer. With these they brought down the idols which belong to the flute dancers.

The specific items burned are uncertain, although more were apparently included than appear in contemporary altar photographs (e.g., A. Geertz 1987a: plates xvii and xviii). Means (1960:126) quotes unnamed witnesses that:

> There were sticks carved to represent stalks of corn with two ripe ears, sticks cut to look like the zigzag flash of lightning, other sticks, mysterious in shape and purpose, "and strange to say many of them had a cross at one end. . . . There were two gods carved out of wood. . . . There were caps made of bent twigs with half a crook-necked gourd on each side to represent horns. Johnson told them [the onlookers] that these things were hundreds of years old, as old as the Hopi himself. Some of them were so sacred that only the priests and those who were to become priests could look upon them."[31]

Lomavitu's reference to Flute sacra must be to those of the *Masilelent,* Gray Flute sodality (and indeed the Gray Flute altar [e.g., A. Geertz 1987a: plates xxxvi and xxxvii] includes zigzag sticks that end in crosses).[32] The sodality chief-priest, Lomahongva, head of another important clan, *Patkingyam,* "Divided Water," had converted and the society had ceased to function (Parsons 1922:290). It seems certain that this chief-priest, too, was involved in the decision, but if Gray Flute sacra were in fact burnt, they receive no further mention in the text.

The "two gods" may derive from the Gray Flute altar, though several prior references to "two idols" retrieved from Hotvela suggest these were associated with *Aa'alt.* If so, they may have been *Taalawtumsi,* "dawn woman," and *Tuwapongyatumsi,* "sand altar woman," both prominent in *Wuwtsim* initiation (e.g., Bradfield 1973:96–112; see also note 24). Neither specifically belongs to *Wuwtsim* altars, but *Taalawtumsi* was brought into the kivas during *Wuwtsim* by the *Aa'alt,* with whom she had a specific relationship (Parsons 1925:119 n.182), and *Tuwapongyatumsi* was formally propitiated at her shrine. *Taalawtumsi* is the "mother of the novices" (Bradfield 1973:103) as they are reborn through initiation. If this inference is correct, it would corroborate the notion that Johnson intended to destroy not just the *Alvongya* but the *Wuwtsim* system, particularly its capacity to generate adult males ritually empowered through initiation.

The likelihood is strong that the items burnt included the Bow clan *tiiponi*. A *tiiponi* is:

> [t]he central item of every ceremonial (and consequently of every altar). Without it the society is destitute and weak, being unable to perform a vigorous ceremonial. It is owned by the clan and is used by the elder who has charge of the ceremonial. It is his symbol of authority and those who have *tiiponis* have a special relationship with the Cloud Deities. This is due to the character of the *tiiponi*. It is a very sacred object, since it was first obtained in the Underworld during mythical times. It is the mother of the people, the heart of the clan, the society palladium. (A. Geertz 1987a:17)

If the Bow clan *tiiponi* was indeed included, the event's meaning is magnified still further: Johnson would have been committing the equivalent of collective spiritual suicide/deicide on behalf of his clan—simultaneously abolishing its supernaturally instrumental power and its capacity for sociopolitical legitimation.

> Aug. 27—Sunday. Baptismal and communion service. Two young girls were baptized. After the service missionaries from other stations arrived to witness the judgment upon the wretched idols.
>
> At half past two o'clock in the afternoon, we loaded on our booty and hauled them upon a hill which is the center of the lower village. The bell was rung and a good number from other villages were assembled. We sang several songs in Hopi. A brother missionary from Hotevilla offered prayer. Our white missionary, Mr. Karl Friesen, then gave an introductory talk explaining that what was to take place soon was not due to his efforts, but that it was through the working of the Holy Spirit that this was to take place. He had known nothing about it until it was revealed to him at the prayer meeting.

Before proceeding to the finale, let me divagate from this passage to some Hopi perspectives on Christian conversion. I have noted that conversions were remarkably few: In his seven years as missionary from 1893 until 1902, H. R. Voth secured none (Voth 1923), despite his mastery of the language and his extensive acquaintance with Hopi culture. J. B. Frey recorded the first baptism—of a school student—in

1904. It, too, coincided with the Snake Dance and its seriousness in Hopi eyes prefigures that of Johnson's actions eighteen years later:

> The baptism was administered two days before the time of the big snake dance to which many tourists had come, including thirty students and two professors of Harvard University and their guides. The Hopis did not know that Lillie was to be baptized[33] and when it came to the baptism, all the women but one ran outside and stood watching from a distance. They thought that the chapel would fall down. The men too, while they did not leave the room, sat in terror not knowing what to do, for there was an old tradition[34] that from now on it would not rain any more and that the one who was baptized would die. After the baptism, when they saw that the chapel was still standing, the women returned. (Frey 1915:23)

Resistance to the Church did not abate, however. In 1906 (Epp, 18 November 1906) and again in 1909 (Frey, 19 November 1909), *Kikmongwi* Tawakwaptiwa wanted to drive the missionaries out altogether. (Missionary J. B. Epp feared seriously for his life.) Missionary Maria Schirmer was ejected from Hotvela around 1908 (Whiteley 1988a:106) and Frey was forced out of Munqapi in the 1920s (Nagata 1970:48). Moreover, the missionaries had to contend with active theological counterargument: "We are being laughed at because we speak of our dead Christ and we also say he lives" (Frey, 6 December 1909).[35] The Mennonites considered abandoning the Hopi field several times. Half a century after establishment, missionaries could still complain, "The Hopi Indian is known to be one of the most reluctant of all Indians to accept the gospel" (Mrs. John P. Suderman n.d.:7; see also Whiteley 1988:217-21).

A legacy of early experiences with Franciscans (and with Mormons, beginning in 1858) had produced institutionalized counterdiscourses to missionization (Whiteley 1988:16-29). An association between the Church and the surrender of autonomy was firmly entrenched. Fray Silvestre Vélez de Escalante, for example, after a 1775 visit, emphasized:

> . . . the inordinate religious control which the caciques and chiefs have. . . . For this reason they prevent by terrible threats any of their people from seeking conversion or even addressing a religious, or harkening to him when he preaches, reserving to themselves solely the faculty of hearing and speaking on points of religion. To disguise their ambition more

they show themselves highly interested in the infamous liberty of their pueblos, representing to them that Christianity necessarily brings intolerable bondage. (Thomas 1932:152)

As the first "raw heathen" to countenance conversion, Wikvaya (above) was daunted by prevailing sentiment. He made tentative overtures for several years, and even requested a special visit from H. R. Voth after his departure as missionary. But when Voth arrived, Wikvaya reneged:

> "Ikwatchi, (my friend) you know our ways and rules. You know, that So and So is our first chief, So and So the first priest, So and So is our war chief and then come I, now, Ikwatchi, you know that I cannot go around or past these three and be baptized first; but when they are ready I shall be ready too." (Voth 1923:6)

In short, the meaning of conversion had become overdetermined in Hopi historical consciousness and political praxis, as a threat to autonomy. The Orayvi split, however, provided a crucial rupture. Wikvaya was finally baptized on 3 January 1909 (Epp, 4 January 1909). In the two decades following, there was a small upsurge, and indeed several converts were sodality chief-priests. By 1917, the Orayvi church had seventeen members (Krehbiel 1938:84), with Johnson one of "two Hopi brothers" (Duerksen and Duerksen, March 1917). By 1926 thirty members were recorded (Stauffer 1926:25), but the tide was hardly rising at an overwhelming rate: If Johnson and Lomavitu did intend to construct a new polity on the foundation of the church, the conversion rate must have proved disappointing.

Conversion had no obvious mitigating effect on existing standards of personal evaluation. Several consultants, including some Christians, regarded Johnson as a *powaqa* (witch, sorcerer) long after his espousal of the church. One recalled that whenever "K. T." came to call, all children (especially vulnerable to sorcery) were immediately hustled out of the house.

Moreover, far from abandoning Hopi philosophical precepts, converts came to rationalize their actions by invoking traditional prophecy (cf. Johnson's 1955 account [above] and Chapter 5 Appendix):

> The Christians are really the only ones whose behavior is perfectly orthodox according to this version. They have abandoned the Hopi way, they have completely accepted the white man's path, and entirely re-

jected all vestiges of the old social organization. They themselves are keenly aware of the Hopi orthodoxy of their position, and refer to it freely in argument. Johnson, the chief of the Two-Horned . . . ceremony, was persuaded by the missionaries to burn all the paraphernalia of his ceremony in a big public function. When Mr. Hubbell[36] tried to persuade him to let this priceless material at least go to a museum he answered that the prophecy said that when the White Brother came all those things must be destroyed, and Mr. Hubbell knew that it was useless to argue with him. (La Farge 1937:32)

Conversion became cast by protagonists, then, not as transgression to an alien paradigm but as the proper transformation of structure in an autogenous process of cultural reproduction.[37]

The extent of missionary involvement in the altar-burning is unclear; obviously there was approval (and La Farge [above] suggests an active role), but Orayvi missionary Karl Friesen's disclaimer of direct influence (the text, above) is problematic. More recently, encouragement of iconoclasm by (non-Mennonite) missionaries among the neighboring Navajo is well documented (Frisbie 1987:195-216). For the Church, unilateral acts of renunciation would be highly desirable. Moreover, controversial missionary history would have made it unwise to assume an overt role. But Friesen apparently maintained his noninvolvement in a letter (written a month later and only mentioning the event in passing)—the sole record by a missionary witness so far located[38]—to his superiors in Kansas:

On the afternoon of that day [August 27] Johnson burned his idols in public. Johnson has been a Christian for many years, but these idols had been stolen from him when the reactionary element [the Hostiles] was driven out from Oraibi. Now he had found out, who in Hotevilla had them. So he had gone to claim them, brought them home, and then burned them in public, after first giving a somewhat lengthy talk in English, and a shorter one in his own language. His action unquestionably required an unusual amount of courage, and we believe that except for strength from on high, he could never have done it. (Friesen, 2 September 1922)

Other missionaries present included J. R. and Susanna Duerksen from the Paaqavi/Hotvela station (ibid.) and possibly J. B. Frey from Munqapi.

To return to the text:

While Johnson was arranging the altar and the idols I spoke a few words which were in part something like this, being addressed to the white tourists who were out for the snake dance. "—It is my purpose to speak along somewhat a different line this afternoon. . . . We, the aborigines, did not take to civilization by choice. In order that you might convert us to your ways of living, you are now paying taxes in order to have money to spend on our education for which we are very thankful. But by your presence in a barbarous ceremony, and especially like the interesting, writhing snake dance, you destroy what you have built just for the sake of a single pleasure. Some of us who have learned better through your benevolence are trying to pay our government our great debt, even though it be in a small degree, by trying to live out before our people what we have learned in school. Your presence in these occasions mean to an uneducated and a savage Indian that after all there must be something in his way of religion so that you, a person gifted with superior intelligence should even spend hundreds of dollars to witness it so that he should better shun civilization and keep his children at home. Shame on you. In order that our people may become fit for this great country they must have Christ and the Bible. If you do not need Christ in civilization do let us have him."

The contradiction between Government and Mennonite policy, on the one hand, and tourist support for tradition, on the other, together with the paradox it posed for Hopi dealings with the dominant society, resonate in Lomavitu's discourse. The intent to ideologically promote an emergent "progressivism" through the act is also clear.

It was now Johnson's turn to speak. He spoke first in English. He opened his bible to Psalm 115 and read verses 4 to 8 inclusive. Then looking upon the audience squarely, he said: (Quoted in part only.)

"We are this day gathered around these idols for the purpose of burning them. Permission will be granted you to examine them in due time.

"Look at the idols before you. They are made of wood. They have eyes but they see not. They have noses but should you pour out perfume before them they will not be able to smell it. They have hands but should you come up to them and offer them your hand they will not respond. They have ears, but they will not hear your greeting; feet have they, but they cannot walk.

"And yet these have kept me from coming to Christ for many years. They have sent hundreds of my people into perdition and, though wood, they will yet be the means of sending countless numbers of souls into hell under the power of Satan. Shall we save them? They that make them and keep them are like them. We may gain historical knowledge as has been suggested to me and know all history, but our knowledge will but drive us away from God and will never be sufficient to save us from hell. I lay myself open to consequences if there be any. I will gladly sacrifice myself in saving our people from perdition through these.

Psalm 115, whose purpose is "An exhortation to confidence in God" (King James version), disparages heathen deities. Verses 5 through 8 and part of Verse 4 are paraphrased in the latter two paragraphs of this section.

Johnson's reference to "historical knowledge" and its antithetical relation to Christianity is noteworthy. As a complex of "dominant symbols," the altar served as a mnemonic index of significant knowledge, narratively voiced in song and story and dramatized in ritual action. At Hopi, as in other nonliterate societies, ritual praxis serves multiple cognitive and archival purposes. Clan histories—recited in ritual discourses—legitimate action (they are Malinowskian "charters"). But these are more than secular histories: They encode transformative supernatural power that has guarded and guided the clan through its historical course, that originated and continuously reconstitutes clan identity, that was the precondition of the clan's acceptance into Orayvi, and that is formally invoked in the clan's ritual. Such historicized power/knowledge over fundamental ontological processes—magic, in a word—managed by clan leaders and implanted into conscious wills at initiation, vitiates the metaphysical abjection necessary to Christianity.

The reference to self-sacrifice may confirm Johnson's effective spiritual suicide on behalf of the Bow clan. It also conforms to a discourse of chiefly self-sacrifice for the health of the community (Nequatewa 1936:132 n.47), often heard, for example, in reference to the Orayvi split. Some of my consultants suggested, again in conformance with epochal prophecy, that if one of the factional leaders had sacrificed his life, the spiritual force of this would have effectively preserved Orayvi's integrity. Johnson continues:

> "Let me now tell you a story that you have never heard.
> "Once upon a time a blind boy was born to a Hopi family. His parents loved him much and so took great care in raising him up. When he was about twelve years old his father made for him a smooth stick by which he was to be led about.
> "One day he said to his father, 'Father, I want you to open my eyes. I

hear the people talk about things I do not know. I hear them talk about lightning but I do not know how it looks. I want to see the people.'

"But his father said he could not do that but that a great doctor was coming and that when he comes he would open his eyes.

"When he was thirty-six years old this doctor came and examined his eyes. He took him and performed an operation on his eyes. Oh! how much he pained him! How much pain did the medicine cause! He got angry at the doctor because he caused him such pain, but the doctor continued his operation and it was successful. And now for the first time he saw and for the first three weeks he could see only faintly. Then he went to the top of a hill and from there he saw the whole country, but he soon went up on top of a mesa from where he saw more.

"One day as he was walking he saw an object in the air which swooped down on a bad smelling thing on the road. It soon began to devour this bad smelling thing. Then it flew away evidently having been satisfied. The next day it came back but this time he brought one other with it. These two feasted on the ill smelling thing and then went away. The boy learned afterward that these two flying things were buzzards and the bad smelling thing was a dead horse. Then day by day these two buzzards came but each time bringing more until the boy could not count them all.

"Now, let me explain this allegory for such it is. The blind boy is myself. My parents loved me. When I was about twelve years old my father initiated me into this ceremony, which is likened to a smooth stick by which I was to be led about. The great doctor that was to come is the Holy Spirit, even the Lord Jesus Christ Himself. He examined my life and performed an operation. The medicine used is the gospel of Jesus Christ. How it did hurt me when it told me of my sins. I got angry at Him but He continued His work until today I can see. The hill and the mesa is the top of experience. I could only see a little at first, but when I went on the top of experience with God I learned more. Then I learned what it was the people talked about, the heavenly things which is represented by lightning. The buzzard is the first white man who came to the snake dance. The dead horse is the SNAKE DANCE. This white man first watched the snake dance and then went away. But the next time he came he brought another white man with him. This went on until the number increased until today there are so many buzzards feeding on a DEAD HORSE that it is impossible to count them! "Dear friends, feed on the Living Bread."

Johnson's allegorical style and substance—pervasive in traditional Hopi oratory, just as in Christian oratory—offers joint metaphors for the mixed audience. The lightning metaphor (simple parable of conversion for a non-Hopi), for example, has special significance for the Bow clan and *Aa'alt*. Lightning streaks are the arrows of *Sootukwnangw*, a zenith deity (arrows, naturally, are a Bow clan prerogative). A man who survived a lightning strike was healed and initiated by this sodality, after which he might become a special "lightning" shaman (Titiev 1972:22). (In 1981, while I was resident in Paaqavi, a house was struck by lightning. Everyone was confined to their houses while (evidently) three *Aa'alt* from Hotvela neutralized the area.)

> After this permission was granted to all to examine the idols. No pictures were taken.[39] By this time the lightning storm was approaching us from the east preceded by a heavy windstorm. Quickly we piled the idols and the altar pieces. After pouring some gasoline on the pile Johnson lit it. Soon the smoke arose from these wretched prisoners and amidst their smoke we sang in Hopi, "When the Roll Is Called Up Yonder" the words in Hopi being appropriate for the occasion. As the idols were reduced to ashes the storm also ceased, resulting in a particular calm as though God would have it thus.
>
> Thus passed away the most important Hopi religious ceremony. We pray God that the words of chief Yu-kiw-ma may come true that "the conflagration must spread." I have since then seen a kiva, which has been elsewhere defined, torn down by the unbelievers and made into a wagon shed. This kiva was the place where this ceremony used to be performed.
>
> Yours in our coming Lord and Savior, Otto Lomavitu.

The meteorological accompaniments are very significant in a Hopi frame of reference. All weather, but especially marked forms like lightning storms, is overdetermined sign: It is interpreted as manifest cosmic effects of the moral condition of humanity in relation to deity. And, as Armin Geertz indicates (above), a sodality leader has a special relationship with the Cloud Deities. Windstorms are often regarded as an evil force, *nukpana*. The particular associations of lightning with the *Aa'alt*, as well as the general portentousness of a lightning storm in these circumstances, must have had an acutely confirmatory effect on Hopi interpretations of the event.

According to several consultants, a younger Christian from Second Mesa was chosen to actually set light to the altar. Subsequently, this man died at an early age, reputedly surrounded by visions of *Aa'alt*.[40] The imputation is that Johnson, as a *powaqa* (sorcerer), manipulated this man in order to shield himself from supernatural consequences. If true, the event's supposedly Christian purpose and meaning become ever more doubtful. Whether true or not, the attendant skepticism of Johnson's actions reveals a wholly indigenous historical interpretation: Christian conversion is incidental event for the actualization and transformation of preexisting structure.

The tearing down of (Naasavi) kiva in Orayvi again seems, from Lomavitu's account, to proceed by contagion from the altar-burning; after the power it housed had been dissolved, its reflected potency was eviscerated; a temple become empty shell.

DISCUSSION

Antiritual and Sociohistorical Transformation

The dramatic immolation was, so to speak, illocutionary,[41] performing its task—to destroy a ritual system by attacking its metonymic core—in the process of its enactment. But it was the opposite of ritual: an "antiritual," a *dis*invention of culture. Ritual is by definition repetitive: It aims, periodically, to regenerate, restore, and reinvigorate cosmological and sociocultural order. This unique, one-time action was designed to shatter that order and to ruin ritual's structurally reproductive capacities. Its aim was not to regenerate sociocosmic structures, but to undermine their significance and power; this partly explains Johnson's enduring reputation as a *powaqa*, since sorcery similarly inverts orthodox ritual practice to produce chaos.

The event was an antiritual in other terms also. The *Alvongya*'s sanctity was marked spatially by its restriction to private kiva activity; to assemble it in public on a hill in the center of a village, in the open air—an unimaginably grave violation of ritual propriety in itself—inverted this. And the propitiatory offerings normally made to altars found their exact inverse in the application of gasoline and consuming fire.

The destruction of a key symbolic complex emphatically reaffirmed the decision to dismantle the politico-ritual system instigated at the Orayvi split.[42] Johnson's actions, in effect and probably by design, extended this leadership decision (Whiteley 1988). With Hotvela's announced intent to resume initiations as a proximate cause, his auto-da-fé was a rearguard move to reinforce that decision. As noted, several legitimate sodality chief-priests were involved in the burning: Johnson, of *Aa'alt,* Talasnömtiwa, of *Wuwtsimt,* and Wikvaya of *Mamrawt.* Additionally, it is probable that Lomahongva, chief-priest of *Masilelent,* "the Gray Flute sodality," was involved, and also Tuwahoyiwma (as Waters [30 November 1960] reports) of the Bear clan. Tuwahoyiwma was *Kikmongwi* Tawakwaptiwa's elder brother and had been first choice to succeed Loololma as *Kikmongwi* (note 8); it is likely he was also first choice for *Soyalmongwi* (head of the master ceremony *Soyalangw*). All of these *pavansinom*, "ruling people," were Christian converts, but their supreme social rank endows the altar-destruction with "legitimacy" as official prerogative, rather than aberrant unauthorized impulse.

Since the *Wuwtsim* system articulated much Hopi social action, interdigitating with the kinship system, creating fundamental differences of rank and gender, and serving both ideologically and psychologically as a critical force for integration, its elimination constituted a radical move for change. Multiple developments subsequently (Whiteley 1988) cannot be examined apart from American hegemony, but neither can their proper significance be grasped without Hopi analyses. These situate ritual abolition as the central cause of a widely ramifying pattern of sociocultural change. Abolitional acts, including Johnson's, effectively deconstructed existing "rules, practices, conventions, and expectations" (Davidson, in the epigraph), enabling the growth of others. These were reconstructions in part, but also new creations (of language, economy, polity, society, religion) from the conjuncture with the dominant society. Barth's focus on the entrepreneur as agent of change offers an instructive analogy to Johnson's actions:

> [E]ntrepreneurial successes produce new information on the interrelations of different categories of valued goods. The information produced by such activity will render false the idea that people have held till then about the relative value of goods, and can reasonably be expected to precipitate re-evaluations and modifications both of categorizations and value orientations. In other words, it changes the cultural bases that determine people's behavior, and in this way entrepreneurial activity becomes a major wellspring of cultural and social change. (Barth 1981 [1967]:111)

Johnson manipulated symbolic rather than material products, but the effects—a reordering of cultural values and categories—are identical.

Interpreting Intentions, Transculturally

What, more specifically, did Johnson do? And in doing it, what were his envisioned effects? To explain his actions requires aligning them, as far as possible, with the intentions that produced them. For this purpose I must further clarify what I mean by intentions and actions and their relationship. Let me first address this culturally.

Some features of Hopi exegesis encountered above suggest a strong idea of intentionality. A full consideration of Hopi concepts correspondent to "intending," the assignment of causes for action etc., is beyond my present scope.[43] But generally speaking, Hopis *foreground* issues of intentionality and agency in descriptions of persons and social action. As I have put it, "Hopis view their society as composed of intentional beings who construe their experience into meaningful interpretations and engage in deliberate actions with purposive consequences" (Whiteley 1988:290). Consider two examples: personal names, and a particular term, *wuuwan'ayat*. Names are uniquely individuating (Chapter 4); analyzing historical events, Hopis often refer to intentions of named agents, e.g., "Kuwannömtiwa planned it this way, that's why it happened like that." Personal names thus mark intentional agents in social process. *Wuuwan'ayat* refers to a group of advisors; it literally means "helpers with thought," serious deliberators who assist a leader in decision-making. However briefly, these two examples show that intentionality, subjectivity, and agency are not merely present in Hopi social analysis but are centrally emphasized.

Interpretation of the event may gain further illumination via Western philosophy of action. Philosophers, anthropologists well know, seldom venture far into the world, preferring constructed examples—from hypothetical tribes to hypothetical chess-games. Theories of action, from an anthropological perspective, often seem empty of real content.[44] An exception is Richard Wollheim's use of a theory of intentionality in the interpretation of paintings.

Wollheim (1987:17-18) emphasizes the multiplicity of possible descriptions that can be true of any action:

So we look out of the window, and we see a man across the street. We watch him. We follow what he does with great care, and we find that we can truly describe his action in the following ways: (one) that he walks up and down, (two) that he attracts the attention of the police, (three) that he is wearing out the soles of his shoes, (four) that he is preventing the children of the neighborhood from playing their midday game of hopscotch, (five) that he casts a sharp shadow on the pavement, and (six) that he has disturbed the old lady who lives in the front room across the street and usually sleeps late, and made her rise from her bed and pull down the blind. But, though the man certainly does all these things, he does not do them all intentionally.

He goes on (ibid.:18) to the problem of interpretation:

> Why is one description of the man's actions privileged, or how do we
> select out of the many many descriptions true of it that under which it
> is intentional? The answer I propose is this: Corresponding to each de-
> scription of an action is a thought, and an action is intentional under a
> certain description if what guides the person's action is the correspond-
> ing thought. A thought guides an action when it both causes it and
> forms its character. . . . To the question, How do we select the descrip-
> tion under which he acts intentionally, a short answer would be, We
> don't. He does. It isn't we who select the description, it is he who does.
> Everything depends on what goes on in his head.

Wollheim's interpretations of pictorial meaning treat the painter's intentions as preeminent, and he seeks to establish these through multiple
informational contexts.[45]

Historical events do not have the fixity of paintings: The finished
form of a painting is inspectable long after its production, whereas an
event is evanescent—only descriptions and interpretations persist.
Nonetheless, this event (Johnson's act)—a dramatic, intentionally exe-
cuted portrayal—may exhibit some qualities similar to the processes
Wollheim emphasizes.

From the text and other information presented, several intentions
and intentional features of the action are clear. The event was intended:

(1) first, of course, to destroy the altar;
(2) as a response to Johnson's aunt's death;
(3) as a pursuit of new-found Christian imperatives, however reinterpreted in a Hopi context;
(4) as an active fulfillment of Hopi prophecy;
(5) as a spectacle;
(6) for a joint audience of Hopis and whites;
(7) for Hopis, as a destruction of essential ritual power in the
Wuwtsim system;
(8) for the whites, as a critique of traditional ritual (the Snake Dance)
and tourist support of it.

In addition, I have inferred—from Hopi oral sources, the documentary
record, and my own deductions—some other "thoughts in Johnson's
head" (Wollheim) that motivated the action:

(1) that his aunt's death was the token of Bow clan absolute demise;

(2) that this necessitated destruction of the clan's ritual power, a sort of suicide/deicide on behalf of the clan;

(3) that this ritual power had become corrupt and was associated with evil, particularly the capacity to extinguish human life;

(4) that corruption and responsive purification conforms to a paradigmatic theme in Hopi historical consciousness;

(5) that the destruction was cooperatively planned with former chief-priests of other socially central sodalities;

(6) that this was an extension of plans to dismantle the higher-order ritual system enacted with the Orayvi split;

(7) that it was an attack on an emergent ritual legitimation of Hotvela leadership;

(8) that it was an attempt to forestall Hotvela's planned *Wuwtsim* initiations and their attendant reconstitution of a sociopolitical power paradigm;

(9) that it was a reassertion by Johnson of his legitimate ritual authority over the *Alvongya* following misappropriation by political opponents, implicating an ongoing social conflict deriving from the split;

(10) that it was an attempt to purify conditions, in order to enable new social and cultural forms to replace traditional hierarchy and its corrupt management of supernatural and social power;

(11) that it was a maneuver to gain political capital and performatively commandeer power from the disintegration produced by the split and by increasing government hegemony.

Other factors in subsequent Hopi interpretations attribute evil or madness (perverse or incomprehensible intentions) to Johnson, and associate these with inherited characteristics.

Which of these stated and inferred intentions should be included in the privileged description of Johnson's actions is problematic. I have attempted to provide relevant fragments of information without systematically adjudicating their relative validity. (Of course, what I have selected for inclusion constitutes some adjudication.) What should unequivocally form the core of the privileged description, however—and therefore attribution of intention—is that he wanted to eliminate the higher-order ritual system.

Destruction of the altar dissolved the principal focus of power for the *Aa'alt,* and a major, articulating one for *Wuwtsim* as a whole. Three sets of initiations held at Hotvela in the 1920s and 1930s are viewed, by my older consultants from across Third Mesa, as conferring diminished or flawed forms of power (Whiteley 1988:281). No initiations have been held since then at Third Mesa.[46]

It seems to me we must grant that as heir to the leadership of *Aa'alt*, Johnson was in a position to understand many of the *Wuwtsim* system's social ramifications, and that, with its elimination, it could be readily predicted that society would engage new sociocultural forms. As an agent of change, he should not be required to preconceive these new configurations exactly, in order for it to remain true that he acted in expectation of specific results. Nor should the failure of some intentions—such as the inferred interest in ongoing sociopolitical prominence—obviate the causal force of others. As Wollheim (1987:19) points out:

> A further cause of error has been to think that these mental phenomena [intentions], in order to exercise causal power, have to be assembled into some inner picture which is a complete facsimile of the picture to be. No total preconception of the picture that is independent of all engagement with the medium is a serious possibility.

Likewise complete correspondence between an agent's intentions, actions, and their predicted social consequences is not a reasonable standard for an explanation seeking the causes and effects of individual action on a sociocultural order. So, to privilege unintended consequences over intended ones is to sidestep the issue of individual agency in social process. Social theory has applied unrealistically exacting predictive standards to intentional action—standards markedly higher, for example, than are expected from our most habitual social predictors, economists.

CONCLUSION

Johnson acted on the basis of intentions formed from his interpretation of existing Hopi traditions and of the social processes he had experienced. These traditions and processes were both internal to Hopi society and constructively refigured in the conjuncture with the dominant society. The Orayvi split looms large here as the primary social response to multiple stresses—sociocultural and natural (Whiteley 1988)—impinging upon Hopi life at the turn of the century.

Johnson acted also on the basis of his socially constituted authority to make and prosecute decisions within the traditional polity. He sought to effect fundamental change in the sociocultural order by dismantling a complex of key symbols integral to its essential principles of operation. In that ritual is a fundamental source of ideology, in the Marxian sense (e.g., Bloch 1989:passim), Johnson's actions were a radical critique and subversion of the Hopi ideology of power/knowledge constituted in the traditional ritual system. Despite Christian emphases in the text, I think his ideological aim was more subversive than substitutive, though, as noted, the protagonists may well have been trying also to performatively invent a new power-base in the church.

It may be argued that underlying processes of sociocultural change would have occurred with or without Johnson's actions. But at the other two Hopi Mesas, where there have been the same external pressures for change, the traditional ritual system was not abruptly subverted and is in some cases strongly persistent.

In sum, Johnson's actions were intentionally conceived and prosecuted, and produced some consequences which may be directly linked to his intentions. Social theory that denies individual agency in historical processes, or the effects of individual intentions, is explanatorily inadequate to this case. Sahlins has effectively refigured structuralism into a historical mode; we need to conjoin this to a historically reoriented transactionalism, with its emphasis on individual action and intention in social process. Intentionality and agency, as constitutive criteria of subjectivity, may allow us to recuperate an—otherwise endangered—transcultural person, an individual moral subject.

Since we must argue, against the old prejudice, that all societies have histories, which are partly composed of the intentional engagements of individuals with received structures and impinging events, we need the individual in cultural interpretation. With a weather eye on the perils of interpretive atomism and methodological individualism (and bourgeois-individualist ideology), social and cultural theory must, insofar as s/he engages in palpably transformative actions, recover the individual in the conjunctural structure.

APPENDIX

CHAPTER I

THE EXPERIENCE OF MR. K. T. JOHNSON

Native Christian

ORAIBI, ARIZONA

(As told to Missionary J. P. Suderman)

My name is Tuwaletstewa. When I was thirty years old, I was living in the Hopi religion. My relatives wanted to put me into the ceremonies, so they prepared for them. I should not be a fornicator, a thief, nor a murderer. I learned from the chiefs about these things. When I would be forty years old, I should be the leader of my ceremony. If I would disobey my gods, they would punish me; so I tried my best.

At one time Mr. Frey came from Tuba City (about fifty miles from here) to show pictures over here. My wife went to the meetings, but I did not go. Mr. Frey had put up a tent. In the daytime he visited the Hopis. I hated the missionaries and my heart was aroused. When my wife started to go to church, she began to talk to me; but I paid no attention. Prior to the opening of the meeting, the village crier would call out for the people to come. I did not go for several days. I began, however, to think about the Hopi prophecy. It said that someone from the East should come to deliver us from our enemies and set us free.[47] He would also bring a looking-glass with him and in it we would find out what kind of a man we are. He would be somebody who would have great power. So I began to think that the prophecy is like the bible which says that when He comes, everybody would be free. The gospel must be the thing we have been waiting for. I did not know that it was the Holy Spirit talking to me, but now I know.

Now it started to work in me from both sides. I was trying to find out which was the best. I also began to realize that this was the One the Hopis were waiting for. I didn't go to church yet, but my mind began to stick to the gospel. I wanted to know more about the gospel and myself. When the last meeting in the tent came, it was at night. This time I was going to know. So I dressed myself up like a Navajo Indian. Soon there was singing in the tent. As I came to the tent, I looked for a hole where I could peep through; but I found none. So I took my knife and cut a little hole into the tent so I could look through. I tried to find out what people were there. The missionary was just showing the heart pictures and it made me angry. That evening, my wife again wanted to talk to me, but I stopped her. Mr. Frey went from here to Polacca, about seventeen miles farther east. Then I began to think more. No sleep came to me because there was a fight in me. I did not know that it was the devil and the Spirit. I did not know what to do.

At that time I was a great song-writer. They honored me by that and used these songs in the dances. I wanted to write many songs yet. I also wanted to be converted, but not baptized. In my heart I believed in the story of Jesus. I had in my mind three plans. My first plan was to write songs, but not dance, I thought I could see them, but not take part. My second plan was to be baptized, but not before my people. I thought I could be baptized at Phoenix. But then I began to think, why should I not make it public, because it was time to fulfil Hopi prophecy. Nine others were converted. I went to one of them, an old blind man,[48] and talked with him about it, and soon everything began to be very real to me. I dropped my two plans and wanted to be baptized before my people before I would be in my old ceremony. Then I began to think about my past life, about the snake dances, the Hopi medicine, to whom I had prayed, the ceremony offerings, and the unleavened bread. But now I am a new converted man. That night I went to the missionary, Mr. Duerksen.[49] I visited him, and he talked with me until I had more understanding.

I want to tell you something else. Before I was converted, I was the greatest smoker among my people. In my work I had a pile of cigarettes near me to last for the whole day. I liked smoking better than the food I ate. Smoking was to be my dessert. When my meal was not yet finished, I would start smoking cigarettes. I did not care for any fruit. It was hard to put off.

When the day of baptism came, I was also in the group. We were baptized on a Sunday afternoon. We all received the Holy Spirit and came home happy. Our burdens of sin were all rolled away. We were as if we were going out from under a heavy load. When I came back, supper was ready. I began to look around in my house, and in the corner were hanging a bunch of empty tobacco sacks. I did not know that I had my house decorated with thirty sacks of Bull Durham hanging on the wall. I put all of them into the fire. On top of the shelves were standing boxes of Prince Albert tobacco; these too went into the fire. In my closet I found the things I had used in the snake dances.[50] I took down the feathers (prayer feathers) and other ceremonial articles and made a bonfire out of them, saying, "Let it all be burned, for now I am a Christian." I believe that Jesus died for our sins, and that he rose again, went into heaven to prepare a place for His own and that He is coming again to take us home.

After that the devil picked up tobacco sacks and piled them before me that I should smoke. It was a hard temptation. I dreamed at night that I smoked. It was hard to overcome. Not a man can overcome it in his own power, but by the power of the Spirit. This is my own experience. A child of God should be clean as I understand it, "Be ye holy for I am holy. Touch not unclean things."

We Hopis have some kind of teaching of the underworld. When the Hopis were still there, they became very wicked, having many wives, practiced fornication, and became murderers. The chief wanted to punish the evil-doers and left with half of the people and came to this place. The elders warned the people of all kinds of troubles. As soon as they came here they should all live a peaceable life.[51]

Now that I am converted, I have received a better life from my Saviour. I began to live a cleaner life. The scripture says that we shall keep away from our mouth everything filthy. I am not ashamed to say that I have not gone to the dances for eighteen years, not even to the white man's dances, nor to picture shows. I have received help from the Holy Spirit to control myself not to smoke. Now I can smell people who have smoked when they are yards away. I think that is the way the Lord Jesus smells the unclean things of sin. Man must be clean and the Christian must be clean also. I could tell much, but this is all I'll say.

THE END OF ANTHROPOLOGY (AT HOPI)?

In this chapter I address the morality of the ethnographic project and its contexts in the dominant society's fields of representation and appropriation of Hopi culture. Again, a major clash lies in instrumentalist versus expressivist interpretations of image, symbol, and practice. Hopi perspectives on their situated engagements resist commodification at the same time as having to continuously negotiate commodification in their relations with the surrounding society. The "predicament of ethnography" is here seen as an outgrowth of its disengagement from the lives of its subjects and of the ambiguous nature and context of cultural representations that circulate at home as well as in the ivory tower.

The pure products of America go crazy.
William Carlos Williams (via James Clifford 1988)

SCENE I: THE RITUAL

It is August in the dusty pueblo plaza. Two lines of ritually-attired men emerge from underground kivas and make their way to an arbor. The "Antelopes," white-kilted and with white zigzags painted over a gray ground down their torsos, march past the arbor, stamping on a plank-drum, and line up in front of it. The "Snakes," brown-painted and kilted, march behind the Antelopes, stamping on the drum, and then line up to face them. A short song and dance follows. Then each Snake man goes to the arbor and procures a live snake. He places the back of its neck between his teeth and dances the snake around the plaza. At the conclusion, the Snake men set all the snakes down into a cornmeal circle, where they are sprinkled with cornmeal by Snake women; the men then pick up the snakes again and race them out of the plaza.

You thought I was talking about the Hopi Snake ceremony, right? *Pay qa pam 'i'*, "That's not it," as a Hopi clown says when he introduces his *tawi*, or pun-story, whose words depend on newly coined meaning, sometimes obscene or perverse, for existing verbal representations. No, I'm talking about the *Smoki* Snake Dance, an ersatz performance, which coins new meaning, probably obscene, certainly perverse, for Hopi ritual representations. In the *Smoki* Snake Dance, the performers are white, the "pueblo" is plywood, the snakes are all bull (rattlers are the key snakes for Hopis)—in short, the ritual is a racist parody.

Founded in 1921 by Prescott businessmen to burlesque Indian ceremonies, the Smokis soon became more earnest, initiating into a fraternal order, founding a museum with Indian artifacts and ethnographic books, and claiming to preserve Native American culture: The (racist) joke turned serious. The group has typically included men of influence in white Arizona. (Barry Goldwater was a member who performed three times [*Arizona Republic* 5 August 1990:2].)[1]

The dance itself is a mishmash. Elements are close to the Hopi original—the kilts, for example, seem probably purchased from Hopis in the past; the body paint and arbor setup are roughly accurate; some of the dance movements mimic the real thing—and my description might indeed be of the Hopi ceremony. But I was selective. I neglected to mention that the painted backdrop was illuminated by floodlights (it was night; the Hopi ritual occurs in daylight); that participants—divided into "warriors," "braves," and "squaws" under the leadership of "Chief Hairlip" [*sic*]—wore red bandannas over black long-hair wigs; that there were drummers (there are not at Hopi) dressed like Hollywood Navajos, who pounded out a Western-movie-Indian four-four bar heavy-on-the-first-beat; that the rattles were painted coffee cans; and that the "songs" (Oh! ah! oh! ah! oh! ah!) and dance movements seemed choreographed by the same characters who do "tribal" dances in Tarzan movies.

To begin, the PA system intoned a script while an elderly Smoki mimed to costumed children, and the story was enacted by other

Smokis stage-left. The story, purporting to be the snake myth, was obviously taken from Hopi ethnography, though with a heavy dose of savagist ambience: "The old Snake priest gathers his grandchildren and the children of the tribe and the story begins. Many moons ago, the chief's son, Tiyo, wondered about the universe. His father told him to go to the underworld to seek out Spiderwoman. . . ." After this, the paying audience applauded from their bleachers (payment, applause, and bleachers are absent from the original) amidst the drone of the highway (likewise) from outside the roadside arena. Then, on to the ceremony itself: "Ladies and gentlemen, the world-famous Smoki Snake Dance!" the PA boomed in Western twang.[2]

SCENE II: THE LAND

Twelve miles south of Holbrook, Arizona, rises a volcanic cinder cone known as Woodruff Butte, after a Mormon who founded a nearby settlement in the 1870s. In Hopi it is *Tsimontukwi*, "Jimson-Weed Butte," a rather important place, which has carried this name since time immemorial. It houses one of nine major shrines (*tuutuskyam*) that mark the boundaries of *Hopitutskwa*, Hopi land (Page and Page 1982; Whiteley 1989). The butte also contains clan shrines, for the Bearstrap and Water clans—both formerly lived in the vicinity—and for the *Porswiwimkyam* curing society. Some plant medicines are collected there. The two named clans also have property rights in eagles in the vicinity, which Hopis continue to gather every May. The area is partic-ularly sacred to the Water clan because of an establishing myth in which a boy and a girl were sacrificed there to appease Paalölöqangw, the Water Snake spirit of Paayu, the Little Colorado River.[3]

Tsimontukwi is not on a reservation; it has been "privately owned" by a local white family since 1935. The Bearstrap clan shrines, which used to be on top of the butte, were destroyed in the 1960s when a radio tower was erected. In September 1990, the owners leased the butte to a gravel-mining company. The Hopis protested, sending reli-gious leaders and Tribal officials. The lead owner, Norman Turley, knew of the place's significance, but apparently cared little (*New York Times* 3 January 1991), challenging the Hopis to buy him out for a million dollars. The Tribe sought a legal appraisal, which came in at $45,000, and made a counteroffer.

Meanwhile, mining went ahead. The priests, terribly concerned, con-tinued to visit the butte. While Eldridge Koinva, chief of the Antelope society (and a leader of the Bearstrap clan) from Songoopavi, looked on helplessly, the boundary shrine itself was felled by a bulldozer.

The controversy grew and mining operations ceased temporarily at various junctures during the 1990s. Tribal officials have several times met with high State of Arizona officials, including the governor (e.g., *Gallup Independent* 6 June 1992, 16 June 1992) but without any successful resolution. The owner was not amused. Angered by the Hopi counteroffer in 1991, Turley at one point threatened to blow up the whole butte rather than return it to the Hopis (telephone conversation with the Hopi Office of Cultural Preservation, July 1991). The mining area was fenced off, a large "No Trespassing" sign was put up, and to make sure the Indians got the message, a dead coyote was pinned to it. Woodruff Butte was subsequently sold to another party, and mining resumed in May 1996. A major area on top of the butte sacred to Hopis was completely destroyed. As of December 1996, the Hopi Tribe was still negotiating to preserve what was left. Again they have met with considerable resistance from the owners, who, at one point, indicated that they would cease mining if the Tribe compensated them to the tune of $2.3 million.

SCENE III: THE SACRA, OR AHÖLA'S NOSE IS OUT OF JOINT

Sotheby's auction house in New York City is in a posh setting on the Upper East Side. A sale of May 1991 featured "Fine American Indian Art" (Sotheby's 1991), including three Southwest "masks," one possibly Navajo, the other two Hopi—an *Ahöla* and a *Kooyemsi*.[4] Despite Hopi protests (*New York Newsday* 18 May 1991, 22 May 1991; *New York Times* 21 May 1991), Sotheby's insisted (Natalie Wolcott, personal communication 18 May 1991) that the masks were "legitimately acquired," although they refused to disclose the identity of the seller.

The auction room was buzzing—the press was on hand. The buyers were mostly wealthy "Indian-art" patrons, all white as far as I could see, both "old money" and arrivistes, in Madison Avenue haute couture or Santa Fe chic. Bids that outstripped most Hopi families' annual incomes were casually mounted. Finally Ahöla was swung round on a revolving platform, surrounded by a gray cloth ground—transformed into "fine art." He went for $24,200. As he came into view, I saw the nose had been dislocated, cocked slightly to one side.[5] Of course no one would care, the object's newfound commodity status, not its Hopi meaning, was the sole criterion of value. Nonetheless, the disjointed nose seemed somehow appropriate—an index of incongruities borne of the clash of cultural meanings and standards.[6]

SCENE IV: THE TEXTS

[T]he Hopi are a fascination in the public mind. More than any other group in North, Central, or South America, the Hopi have retained their aboriginal culture, with its religious expression in its purest form. And they embody a philosophy of life totally in balance with their physical and spiritual environment. . . . Within Hopi rituals and sacred ceremonies, the ancient knowledge of early humanity is deposited. It is brought to us without interruption or corruption. Most of us will go to Hopi driven by the force of the primeval need to be in communion with the source. (Boissière 1986:20-22)

North American Indians, because of their culture, hold a special place among aboriginal peoples of our world. The Hopi, in turn, are esteemed among Native North Americans. Mythology is the central feature of Hopi culture. The Hopi prophecy plays a central role within Hopi mythology. At the center of that prophecy we find Pahana, the Elder White Brother, for whose return the Hopi wait. There is thus a connection between our hopes concerning the wisdom of tribal people and the Hopi expectation for the return of Elder White Brother. (Kaiser 1991:85-86)

We have . . . a specific link between New-Age thinking and the worldview of indigenous peoples and of nature religions. We sense that our dualistic distinctions between spirit and matter, God and the world, humans and nature, subject and object, do not apply in their view of things. Instead there is an understanding of the holistic connectedness of all that exists. For a people holding such a holistic view of the world, everything would be sacred, imbued with the Spirit, part of a greater Whole, inseparably interwoven. (Ibid.:116)

These excerpts from Robert Boissière's *Meditations with the Hopi* (1986) and Rudolf Kaiser's *The Voice of the Great Spirit: Prophecies of the Hopi Indians* (1991) illustrate a wide-ranging interest by "New Age" groups from North America and Europe. The Hopi are held up as icons of spiritual wisdom, exemplars for a quest toward new meaning in the malaise of modern life (cf. A. Geertz 1987, 1994).

Popular literature on the Hopi, especially since Frank Waters's *Book of the Hopi* (1963), produced an influx of seekers and yearners in the 1960s, and while these eventually departed, the legacy has remained. During Hotvela's *Powamuy* rituals in 1981, for example, a mysterious, black-garbed German woman interrupted *Angwusnasomtaqa*'s (Crow Mother's) distribution of bean sprouts, grabbing handfuls and offering them grandiosely to spectators, before being shooed away by a Hopi woman. Another mysterious character in a red robe camped for a while by Orayvi and went round at night claiming to be *Maasaw*, a prominent Hopi deity. And recently, Hopis visiting the *sipaapuni* emergence shrine in Little Colorado River Canyon, have found, to their dismay, crystals and other pseudo-offerings.

Radically decontextualized reinterpretation of Hopi traditional and prophetic representations by New Agers and their fellow travelers has thus begotten another clash of representations between Hopi and the dominant society. The clash reached an apogee at the "Harmonic Convergence":[7]

> [L]arge numbers of people gathered at many sacred sites all over the world. . . . [i]ncluding Prophecy Rock on the Hopi reservation. A small group, between thirty and fifty people, made sacrificial offerings, drew astrological signs on the ground in front of Prophecy Rock and, at sunrise on 17 August, raised their hands toward the sky, turning east toward the rising sun, in the direction faced by Prophecy Rock for thousands of years. (Kaiser 1991:119)

None of the celebrants, so far as I am aware, was Hopi; Hopi religious leaders specifically repudiated the connection, denying any recognition of this alien convergence or its association with the so-called Prophecy Rock.[8] The Hopi meaning of this petroglyph-marked site is contested, but has been greatly reworked by Thomas Banyacya, a Hopi guru to many New Agers, and the subject of much controversy in Hopi discourse (see A. Geertz 1994:257–87).

◆

In each of these four cases, cultural conceptions that are critical to Hopi identity—religious rituals, a sacred landscape, deity masks, metaphysical beliefs—are fundamentally violated by various elements from the dominant society. Core Hopi representations and meanings are (1) directly parodied (the Smokis), (2) actively scorned and destroyed (Tsimontukwi), (3) commodified and transmuted into an alien register of value (*Ahöla*), and (4) self-servingly reimagined into the canons of a new universalizing religious cult (the New Agers).

Broadly, each case involves different interest groups, though all are predominantly white. The respective interests intersect along a number of axes, including capital gain (both material and symbolic), regional identity (particularly for the Smokis), class, and ethnic-supremacist ideology (conscious or not), among others. These cases and their attendant interests by no means exhaust the manipulation of Hopi representations by outsiders. I choose them to illustrate recent, particularly acute violations of Hopi cultural and religious sovereignty. Moreover, all occur outside the direct application of U.S. sociopolitical and ideological domination (although this serves as ultimate guarantor), such as by federal laws and BIA police, BIA schools, missionary religions, and the metropolitan economy. They involve a subtler process of cultural hegemony, a politics of representations wherein a dominant group appropriates and refigures a subaltern's cultural symbols to its own purposes (cf. Vizenor 1987, Lavie 1990, Çelik 1992).

This distortion of symbols[9] has reflexive effects back home: it conditions interactions between Hopis and non-Indians, and partly undermines the symbols' established meanings and transformative power. Tourists arrive with arrogant assumptions about heathen rituals and their rights to sample them; illegal plunder of artifacts[10] and sites proceeds apace; many items of traditional culture (notably including Kachina dolls)[11] have been commodified for the "ethnic art" market; and interference with shrines and rituals is ongoing.

A promiscuous traffic in Hopi representations thus occupies multiple nexuses of meaning. Hopi has for the last century been progressively inundated by a dominant society that has sought in myriad ways to impose its political, economic, religious, and sociocultural control. The Hopi are still technically wards of the U.S. government, "domestic dependent nations" (e.g., Deloria and Lytle 1984), their land is held in trust, and they have very limited real political sovereignty. Perpetuation of traditions must battle imposed institutions like schools and missions, supermarkets, wage-labor, television and other forms of cultural imperialism. All of this has had profound effects: Many Hopi children do not understand the Hopi language, prefer heavy-metal over Hopi songs, Coke and Big Macs over *yoyvwölö*, "rainwater," and *piiki*, "wafer bread," and expect jobs off-reservation rather than engagement in the subsistence economy.[12]

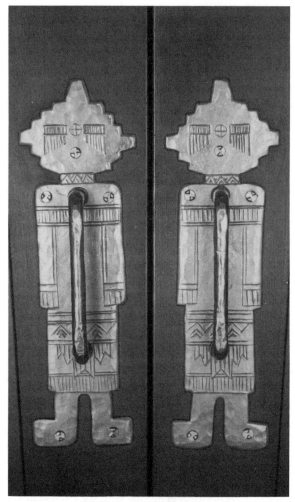

Figure 6.1. "Artistic" commodification runs from highbrow to low, regional to global. Here, the KiMo Theater in Albuquerque, built in "Pueblo Deco" style in 1927, models hybrid Pueblo-esque deity figures into lobby door handles. A recent mixed-media arts exhibit in Marugame, Japan, featured a huge kachina doll mural by Genichiro Inokuma behind mannequins in Issey Miyake clothing (*New York Times*, 17 August 1997). On a higher brow, a 1990 painting, *Paho* (i.e., *paaho*, "prayer-feather" or "prayer-stick" in Hopi—though its Hopi origin is nowhere identified in the painting description or the interpretation by Sister Wendy Beckett) by British artist Paul Hodges, depicts quasi prayer-feathers tied to bleached antlers, horns, and tusks—deforming and misinterpreting a Hopi religious device in several ways (Beckett 1992:66).

COLLECTING HOPI CULTURE

The relations of power whereby one portion of humanity can select,
value, and collect the pure products of others need to be criticized and
transformed. (Clifford 1988a:213)

At the same time as overt domination, the national society, or elements
of it, has continuously fetishized aspects of Hopi culture—especially
rituals and artifacts—into its own canons of value. Appropriation and
sale of religious objects has occurred for over a century. At Hopi,
private collectors and formal museum expeditions (especially at the
turn of the century—notably including the Smithsonian, Chicago Field
Museum, Harvard Peabody, Southwest Museum, and the Museum of
the American Indian) have made off with great quantities of artifacts,
some of irreplaceable sacred worth (e.g., Wade 1985). Recently, the
"primitive art" market has caused a renewed proliferation of pothunting and thefts. The Hopi Reservation is difficult to patrol: Some pothunters (many, apparently, northern Arizona whites) fly in by helicopter
at night, ransack sites, and are out again in no time: This is big business.
   The anthropological world has been quick to condemn pothunting,
but in its effects, the "professional" excavation of "sites" and removal
of artifacts to university museums seem hard to distinguish from the
pothunter's practice. In both cases, important materials are alienated
from Hopi, or from the collective spiritual patrimony of Hopi ancestry.
Generally speaking, Hopi belief mandates that remnants of the past be
left alone to serve as sources of power and meaning in the landscape;
eagle gatherers, for example, revisit ancient habitation sites, because
eagles who dwell there reincarnate clan ancestors. The reality that
formal archaeology may protect such sites from vandalism and theft
does not alleviate this basic contradiction to Hopi sacred values.
   For the collector, prehistoric items gain a special cachet of symbolic
capital because of their antiquity and finitude. Items in current ritual
use are also prized, partly for motives of aesthetic-primitivism (Torgovnick 1990), but also as spoils of a vicarious raid into a resistant
exotic Other's inner sanctum. Some Hopis, whose loyalties are subverted by the need for cash (cf. Price 1989:69), have dealt with the
culture-vultures, but in most cases they have no authority over, and
have effectively stolen, the sacra that they sell. Art dealer arguments
about "legitimate acquisition" thus gain credence: "This was bought
from a Hopi." Yet here again a politics of ethnic domination appears:
Vulgar stereotypes of communitarian "tribal societies"—which lack

Figure 6.2. Hegemonic ironies. Lieutenant Lewis admiring Hopi crafts in his tent, Ganado, Arizona, November 1906. Lewis was second-in-command under Captain Lucius Holbrook, who le two troops of the Fifth Cavalry from Fort Wingate to round up "Hostile" men shortly after the Orayvi split. Many were taken to Keam's Canyon and spent six months on a chain gang. Lewis run-marched twenty-eight others, several of whom were past fifty years of age, to Ganado—son eighty-five miles in all (see Whiteley 1988:112, 115; 1988a:58, 61, 62 for other photographs in the sequence). From Ganado, eighteen were sent to military prison at Fort Huachuca for a year and the rest to Carlisle Indian School for five years. Lewis is seen here holding a bowl (possibly by Nampeyo) and surrounded by First Mesa pottery and Second and Third Mesa basketry—all probably just acquired from trader Lorenzo Hubbell, with whom he is pictured in the previous image in the sequence. Collecting Hopi culture while incarcerating Hopi traditionalists echoes th simultaneous fetishization and condemnation of the Snake Dance occurring during the same period. Photograph by Jo Mora. Courtesy of John R. Wilson.

order, laws, or coherent decision-making processes—are subtextually invoked; a willful failure to recognize legitimate Hopi authorities, or whether particular individuals are adhering to Hopi religious precepts, somehow justifies expropriation.[13]

Collection of Hopi representations follows a patterned division in the commodification of "tribal art and artifacts" into, briefly, fine art, folk art/craft, and tourist art (Clifford 1988b:223–26; see also Price 1989). Though the categories overlap, this division reflects a hierarchy of interest groups in many instances coincident with class divisions in the dominant society. The panoply of cultural and social registers of interest is especially noticeable among tourists, and national class is not the only configuration of difference: Ethnicity—indigenous, national, and international—is also prominent. A typical Hopi ritual, for example, sees a multiplicity of outsiders, including: (1) *kyavakvit,* Hopis from other villages; (2) other Native Americans, especially Navajos and Pueblos—often from Zuni, Laguna, Cochiti, and Santo Domingo; (3) many non-Native Americans—the great majority white, but also Hispanics, African Americans and Asian Americans—of different classes, age groups, regions, and subethnicities; (4) Europeans, especially Germans, French, Italians, occasional British, Spanish and others; (5) Japanese and other Asians, including occasional Pakistanis, Tibetans, and Indian Sikhs;[14] (6) and perhaps the odd African, Latin American, Indonesian, white Australian, or even a Jamaican reggae entourage (see note 10). In addition to their intrinsic attraction as performers of exotic rituals and producers of acquirable tribal art, Hopis are on a major American tourist circuit because of their proximity to the Grand Canyon and Monument Valley. In short, outside interests in and valuations of Hopi people and their representations are anything but monolithic.

The invention of "tribal-art" in the dominant society into a marketable commodity (which objectifies and reflects the identity and often prestige of its owners) confounds the artifacts' indigenous meanings. Whatever it is that collectors see in Hopi artifacts, it is not their Hopi saliences. Rather, an alien code of value supervenes: that of symbolic capital and its acquisitive worth in the construction of Western selves (cf. Clifford 1988b:220). Inasmuch as Hopi objects evoke some notion of Hopiness for their collectors and observers, the cultural recognition is typically no more than "ethnocentric sentimentalism in the absence of a knowledge of what those arts are about or an understanding of the culture out of which they come" (C. Geertz 1983b:119).

As with museum objects, the artifacts of an exotic culture—or even photographs of its members—allow the metropolitan aesthetic gaze to empathize on its own terms. In earlier times, cultural exhibitions often included individual "natives," too, shipped in for display (Rydell 1984; Çelik 1992). Contemporary American Indian arts and crafts fairs perpetuate this practice in modified form. Some Hopi friends regularly demonstrate plaque-weaving and pottery in St. Louis and Washington, D.C., where they have occasionally been asked to wear buckskins and sit in front of teepees.

Modern transportation and a developed tourist industry (whether in

Papua New Guinea, the Amazon, Borneo, or the U.S. Southwest) recapitulate the self-absorbed fetishizing gaze, but in situ. At home, Hopis often don stereotypic personae for tourists, both to ensure real privacy and because it eases cash transactions for crafts (cf. Lavie 1990, on constructions of Bedouin identity).

So, graven images (in museums, private collections, or coffee-table texts),[15] briefly visited ritual performances, and staged cultural identities and practices enable outsiders, in the seclusion of their imaginations, to envisage Hopi (among other Others') experience insulated from its material realities. Psychological realization of an aesthetic impulse (involving a sort of primitivist cathexis)—through voyeuristic attributions of "beauty," "dignity," or "ingenious handiwork"—effectively discharges human obligation and diverts any real social concern. In general, aestheticization defuses social responsibility: "An aestheticizing reference to painting, sculpture or literature . . . resorts to the neutralization and distancing which bourgeois discourse about the social world requires and performs" (Bourdieu 1984:45).[16]

In some instances, fetishizers of Hopi culture have been centrally involved in overt political domination. (Snake Dance visitors at the turn of the century—a period of coercively "directed culture change"—often included political dignitaries; cf. note 1).[17] The New Agers, by contrast, ideologically (and as in the Marxist sense, with false consciousness) deny or oppose establishment values present in governmental domination: for them, fetishized Hopis become metonymic emblems of a millennarian struggle against old meanings. And haut-bourgeois art patrons, if they care, deny complicity in domination by setting their fetishism in a sublime category apart (neutralizing and distancing in Bourdieu's terms) from the grime of a material politics, that is, "Art" or "Aesthetics"—entrenched categories of bourgeois taste and self-identifaction (e.g., Williams 1977:150; Price 1989).

WRITING HOPI CULTURE

Contemporary Hopi life is indetachably positioned within the political-economic and aesthetic-cultural interests of a national polity and its local forms under the control of Anglo-Americans. Hopi perspectives on the dominant society and its interests in them are inextricably tied to contexts of interaction instanced in the above abuses of their representations.

Anthropology is deeply implicated here, both as a principal source of outside knowledge about Hopi, and as another mode of collecting, analyzing, and reordering Hopi practices to its own registers of significance. Ethnographic knowledge about the Hopi has been accumulating for more than a century (e.g., Laird 1977). The first real monograph, J. G. Bourke's *The Snake Dance of the Moqui Indians of Arizona,* appeared in 1884. Since then, ethnographic research and writing have proliferated: Every conceivable area of Hopi life—from sexuality to astronomy, herpetology to child psychology—has come under scrutiny at one point or another. Moreover, anthropologists are often indistinguishable for Hopis from other "ethnographic" inquirers, academic and otherwise:

> No ethnic group of comparable size has had as much attention trained on it as the Hopi Indians of Arizona. Ethnologists and religious specialists, linguists, art historians and collectors, hippies and "Indian-freaks," ecologists, spiritualists and pursuers of esoterica—interest in this people oscillates among extremes. (Kunze 1988:jacket, my translation)

Many Hopis are deeply suspicious of *any* graphic representations of their culture, particularly of ritual knowledge and practice. For years now, all villages have featured signs prohibiting photography, note-taking, painting, and sketching (in Hopi, the same term, *peena,* "to represent graphically," covers all these inscriptional modes). The signs may as well say "No Ethnography." While much anger is focused on Waters's *Book of the Hopi,* a great deal is directed at more serious ethnographic publications, both the older studies of esoteric ritual detail, like those of H. R. Voth, A. M. Stephen and J. W. Fewkes, and also recent works focused on religious ritual and belief.

Traditionally, academic scholars have privileged their practice and mystified its politics.[18] They do this via institutionally-supported prestige techniques and discourses, including the blanket invocation of old shibboleths—"academic freedom" (to inquire) and "freedom of speech" (to publish). Further, they distance their work from all "amateur" interests not sanctioned by the academy. So, (we) self-righteous anthropologists can be appalled by Smokis, art collectors, or New Agers, but conveniently blind ourselves to a family resemblance with our own representations of Hopi culture. In claiming an exalted ground of "pure research," scholars disavow the political situation underpinning their work, that is, the state of dominance and subordination between their society of origin and those of their subjects (cf. Asad 1973).

It is little wonder that subject societies are often unconvinced of the virtues of academic research, especially if they know that any published representations will be open to abuses impacting their cultural and political sovereignty.[19] Again, fine distinctions among serious and less serious inquiries are often irrelevant to Hopi interests. Both the scholar—whether blithely bent on "pure research,"[20] or genuinely interested in a sensitive portrayal of Hopi perspectives—and the dabbler ask similar kinds of questions, and often produce written representations with analogously disruptive effects.

Moreover, fear or dislike of *mis*representation is not the only issue. Voth's and Stephen's work (for bibliography see Laird 1977), and some recent publications on religious ritual, for example, are targeted specifically for their *accuracy*. One Hopi friend ironized after reading Voth's *The Oraibi Summer Snake Ceremony* (1903), "Thank you [to Voth, as if he were a ritual sponsor]; now I am an initiate." And others have indicated a preference for spurious, plainly inaccurate accounts, because at least these keep the reality private by misleading their audience: Truth, in this context, is held more dangerous than fiction (cf. Scott 1985).

The desire for privacy and autonomy is a function both of the inundation of inquisitors and of the internal sociology of Hopi knowledge. Knowledge conferred by initiation simultaneously endows instrumental power over actions and events in the world (see Chapter 3). Much ritual power/knowledge is held secret within specific sectors of Hopi society: Secrecy, and the attendant social care and respect accorded to esoteric knowledge, guarantees both authority (conferred by initiation) and instrumental efficacy (when the power/knowledge is activated). Prescriptions for individual conduct in ritual, namely a purity of thought, emotion, and intention, and proscriptions against the misuse of ritual knowledge, which specify supernatural retribution, are utterly central in Hopi discourse. Dissemination of ritual knowledge, either orally to unentitled parties or *ipso facto* in published accounts, violates ritual sanctity and effectiveness, and may damage the spiritual health of the community.[21]

In light of this and the abuses adumbrated above, it is not surprising that the Snake Dance has recently been closed to non-Indians, or that in 1992, for the first time ever, most villages closed down Kachina dances following an issue of Marvel Comics' (March 1992) *NFL Superpro,* which features the steroid-inflated, white superhero in a "gut-stomping" contest with named Hopi Kachinas, impersonated by a white mafioso

Figure 6.3. Kivas and kachinas (both Hopi words) are the most popularized icons of Hopi, and more broadly Pueblo, culture, some appropriated directly from ethnography. Jesse Walter Fewkes's "Hopi Kachinas Drawn by Native Artists" (from the *Annual Report of the Bureau of American Ethnology* for 1899-1900) appears now abbreviated as a sticker-book at airport news-stands, and one may also buy paper punch-out Kachina masks (a particu-larly offensive appropriation for some Hopis, see note 22). This kiva (in eastern Pueblo style) on the campus of the University of New Mexico has served since 1906 as Pi Kappa Alpha's fraternity house, where, one assumes, occur initiations of a rather different sort than in Pueblo kivas. Kiva Mort-gage and Investment Inc., Kiva Light and Freezer Inc., and Kiva Metal Arts all appear in the current Albuquerque business pages—and KYVA is still the hottest oldies station in Gallup—indicating how the Hopi sign *kiva* has been transmuted into an emblem of regional American identity. That a regional archaeology journal is also called *The Kiva*—though the borrowed signifier here operates as a more directly ostensive metonym of the journal's contents, rather than a somewhat free-floating identity metaphor—illustrates again the overlap of academic and popular transvaluations of Hopi signs. Photograph by John Martin Campbell. Courtesy of the photographer.

gambling cartel.[22] Nor, then, should it be surprising that Hopis have actively sought to prevent publication of an academic work on religious pilgrimage that identifies shrine locations (*Chronicle of Higher Education* 17 October 1990), and have resisted efforts to re-publish older Hopi ethnographic reports dealing with ritual. Tribal officials continue to de-bate specific restrictions on research; not a few argue for a total morato-rium, as Tribal Chairman Vernon Masayesva (23 January 1991) pointed out in a speech at Northern Arizona University: "As people we have been studied as "social artifacts" or quaint vestiges of a primitive existence. Our legends, handicrafts, and even the bones of our ancestors have been collected and studied outside of the subjective view of our own ways of life." He goes on to note two cases of research (by scholars from Arizona universities) Hopis found offensive, one suggesting Hopis were cannibals until the 1700s (contrary to Hopi historical knowledge), the other on the salt trail pilgrimage:

> I learned that [the] University could not take any action on my complaint since the research was protected by a sacred university tradition called "academic freedom." It is this type of research that is causing many Hopis to pressure the Hopi Tribal Council to enact an ordinance prohibiting *all* future research activities on the Hopi Reservation. . . . Although the [salt trail] research wears the cloak of scholarly enterprise, its publication denotes to us a lack of sensitivity to our religious values and the way we organize and conceptualize our sacred traditions. Research needs to be based on the reality of our existence *as we experience it,* not just from the narrow and limited view American universities carried over from the German research tradition.[23]

THE END OF ANTHROPOLOGY? OR DÉJÀ VU?

> To anthropologists I say, put your own house in order because what you may regard today as just a skirmish with Indians may tomorrow become a worldwide problem. (Ortiz 1970:91)

In 1987 Palestinian-American critic Edward Said (1989) suggested, before the American Anthropological Association, that the anthropological project itself be abandoned for its collusion with the colonial domination of its subjects. In some respects anthropology has been experiencing an ontological crisis recently, and critiques, both academic and popular, are mounting (e.g., Dwyer 1982, *Anthropology on Trial* 1984, Marcus and Fischer 1986, Sass 1986, Clifford 1988, McGrane 1989, Minh-ha 1989, Malcomson 1989, Said 1989, Torgovnick 1990). But, as with much 1980s and 1990s social analysis, there is a sense of déjà vu here.[24]

In 1969 Native American critic Vine Deloria Jr. challenged anthropologists in ways similar to Said. For a while, there was a more genuine dialogue between Native scholars, at least, and academic anthropologists (e.g., American Anthropological Association 1970), and this was associated with revisionary contemplations of the discipline's ethical foundations (e.g., *Current Anthropology* 1968, 1971, Hymes 1972). The sixties, as we nostalgically rhapsodize, were a watershed for cultural and political critique. Deloria's challenge came at a time of serious questioning more widely within and beyond the discipline. Revisionary theoretical challenge (e.g., Leach 1961) coincided with critiques of anthropology's colonial associations,[25] producing a serious examination of both the intellectual and moral condition of the discipline, and its relations with its constituted subjects. Critique of theory was explicitly associated with critique of practical political effects on subject communities.

In the 1960s the critique of anthropology had clearer theoretical and political targets in functionalism, on the one hand, and obvious colonial structures, on the other. At present, while the political (e.g., postcolonial) critique is still associated with resistance to old and neocolonial structures, it is hard to even identify a central body of theory. And perhaps, indeed, it is a question more of absence than presence. If we choose, say, postmodernism as a recent ethnographic episteme, this is less easily assailable than functionalism—as an intellectual collusion with formal power—because of its philosophical diffuseness, its emphasis on continuous deconstructing and decentering, and its own avowed critical stance on colonial structures. While the de Man affair contributed to the reawakening of a more contextualized historicism (e.g., Lehman 1991), much postmodernist critique disenables a politics of action because of its emphasis on the radical contingency of events, meanings, and perspectives. Postmodern cultural analysis depends on the same bourgeois social distance and aestheticizing valorization—but here of academic-intellectual discourse itself—present in culture collecting. If signification is only self-referential, social recommendations seem irrelevant and postmodernists may sit comfortably on their ivory fences.

If anthropology is really in crisis at present, rather than some anthropologists cultivating a fashionable, careerist neurosis, it might be hard to notice. More than twenty years ago, Asad (1973:10) noted a similar paradox:

> [T]he Association of Social Anthropologists flourishes as never before; it holds academic conferences whose proceedings are regularly published in handsome hardcover and paperback editions. Monographs, articles and text-books by writers calling themselves anthropologists appear in increasing number. . . . The subject is now being taught in more university and college departments than ever. . . . Seen in terms of its public activity there is no crisis in social anthropology.

If we change the references to a North American context in the 1990s, all of these characterizations hold true, as the American Anthropological Association annual meetings continually attest.[26]

What has changed in the last twenty years or so is the role of Native Americanists and their subjects within anthropology. Both have become marginal in critical debates and prestiged discourses of the discipline (cf. Lurie 1988)—a factor reflected in both teaching and research. In graduate level teaching of anthropological theory, contemporary texts on Native North Americans figure sparingly. Most teaching of Native American ethnography probably occurs at an undergraduate level. Moreover, undergraduate textbooks typically reproduce stereotypical vignettes of Native cultures, selected for their topical imaginative appeal, as different from, or models for, a critique of the students' own cultures. Of the Hopi, for example, undergraduates are most likely to learn that they have no concepts of time and little gender inequality.[27] Images of Native Americans constructed through canonical ethnographic texts, textbooks, and other representational modes "invent" Native Americans for their audience (cf. Deloria 1969, Vizenor 1987). Some presumptions I attributed above to New Agers derive in part from classroom inventions of Native Americans: timeless, historyless spiritualists at harmony with each other and in tune with nature. And this is the story many students continue to want to hear.

Moreover, ethnographic monographs are proving insufficient teaching tools for the interpretation of cultures. Student criticism (some of which I share) of ethnographic texts—that they are "dry," jargon-filled, and distant from the lived experience and interpretations of their subjects— causes me to assign a mix of (auto)biography and Native American literature and criticism, along with formal ethnography. A related fact is that few ethnographic texts by Native Americans are being produced, because there are very few Native ethnographers (as academics, anyway). Native American academics for the most part have pursued other disciplines, indicating, inter alia, a signal failure of anthropology in its stated goal of serving as a vehicle for genuine, usable intercultural understanding. The most interesting "ethnography" by, and to some extent of, Native Americans today is literary (Leslie Marmon Silko, Louise Erdrich), cultural critique-based (Gerald Vizenor), or visual (Victor Masayesva Jr.)[28] rather than strictly anthropological.

With respect to research, graduate students are urged to work in Papua New Guinea, Amazonia, Indonesia, or in some other, suitably exotic, overseas elsewhere. Native Americans have "lost their culture," become "proletarianized," or at any rate have been "overworked" (in the manic careerist bazaar of "original" research projects)—they have been "done" already. Central concerns in contemporary theory—like power, the self, gender, the body, discourse, agency, hierarchy, textual representation—are best worked out in those distant locales where these things are somehow more authentically constitutive of lived experience (cf. Appadurai 1986). Reciprocally, Native Americanists no longer lead in key debates, and with a few exceptions (largely in archaeology and narrative translation), inhabit the intellectual peripheries of key arguments.

This alleged marginalization may come as a shock to Hopis (and other Native peoples) who each summer—with the appropriate seasonality their "biological" worldviews are held to prescribe[29]—experience the perennial arrival of neophyte anthropologists, often from less prestigious graduate programs, and in the west, especially, from local universities. Like beaching driftwood on the flood tide of tourists, in "field schools," or just off their own bats, they appear on the reservation to investigate some "problem," usually devised without the benefit of any local input.[30] Native communities have often been proving grounds— boot camps—for apprentice researchers. That this is possible bespeaks the same political domination that underwrites the abuses of Hopi representations I began with.

The research picture is further complicated by the "blurring of genres" (C. Geertz 1983a). Anthropologists are increasingly not the only academics interested in Hopi. Occasional linguists, psychologists, and philosophers have studied there since the 1930s at least, but recently a gaggle of linguists and narratologists, students of comparative religion and art history have entered the fray, very often examining the same questions as anthropologists, but blithely unaware of the ethical standards and cultural understandings anthropology has genuinely accumulated (partly as a result of its history of interaction with Native Americans).[31] For Hopis, the many faces of research get ever muddier.

POSSIBILITIES

[I]t would be wise for anthropologists to get down from their thrones of authority and PURE research and begin helping Indian tribes instead of preying on them. (Deloria 1969:104)

[Anthropology] can be abused, but it can also be used humanely and ethically, as well as scientifically. (Ortiz 1970:87)

I had a call from a graduate student at a department quite close to Hopi that will remain nameless. He said he was writing a paper on Hopi "tipony" and did I have any advice. After I determined that he meant not a small Franglais horse, but *tiiponi*, an important ritual emblem, I suggested he go and talk to some Hopis. No, he said, he was not going to do that; he just wanted to read up on it and come to his own conclusion. He would then present his paper—on a religiously sensitive matter—to the world (actually to the AAA meetings).

I had another call from a novelist in New Jersey. He said he had read my book that focuses on the deliberacy of Hopi political decision-making (1988). He had also heard about the theft of the Taalawtumsit, very important ritual figures used in manhood initiation, from Songoopavi. Their theft in the late seventies has been deeply hurtful to Hopi sensibilities (perhaps like Catholics would feel if the Sistine Chapel were blown up by atheist terrorists), and both ritually and socially very disruptive. The novelist had an idea; he wanted to write a Tony Hillermanesque tale set at Hopi, whose plot would focus on how the Songoopavi priests deliberately got rid of these religious figures for some dark purpose. I advised him against this. The already damaged community would be gravely offended by this adding of insult to injury, and such a publication would be like pouring acid onto an open social wound.

How naive can outsiders get about the social effects of their representations? The West's liberal conscience was shocked when Ayatollah Khomeini issued a death sentence on Salman Rushdie for *The Satanic Verses*. "Freedom of speech" again was the rallying cry. But as Asad has pointed out (1990), the protests, however justified and important in one frame of reference, ignored the social context of embattled subaltern Muslim communities, particularly in Britain; the book's implicit critique of Islam—as well as the Muslim world's reaction to it—has already been transmuted into another tool of cultural oppression by the dominant white, non-Muslim majority.

While the management of Hopi representations must be partly regulated internally, it is clear that the U.S. government will put down forcible resistances—like death sentences against ethnographers or novelists—as it has repeatedly shown with numerous subaltern activist groups, from AIM to the Black Panthers. So, for their part, anthropologists must take an initiative, and decide whether they are willing to be complicit in processes of oppression or whether they will work in various ways—both in terms of their representations and their social action—for Hopi interests against this. The moral situation is, of course, more complex than this framing of choice, but not thereby grounds for its avoidance (see Maclean, Montefiore, and Winch 1990). It may already be too late: The crisis of bad faith has been compounded in so many ways that Hopis may well elect to simply exclude ethnographers (as Masayesva's speech indicates, and see A. Geertz 1996).

In the atmosphere of cultural subversion that my four initial examples point to, the question remains whether anthropology, or various sister disciplines, have any practical or intellectual utility within Hopi society or can genuinely enhance intercultural respect, appreciation, and understanding, in a way that overrides potential abuses. Anthropologists (and others) can no longer sustain the illusion that their work occurs in a political or representational vacuum. They *must* now address the likely effects of disseminating ethnography in the dominant society will have on Hopis.

As for my own work, I want mostly to leave that to the judgment of others: Emphasis on the self-scrutinizing author's voice in recent ethnographic writing seems to me mostly simple narcissism designed to obviate dialectical critique and mask unconsidered subtexts. I am concerned, however, that my representations were read by this novelist and put together into his dark little plot. And given what I have said, I think it unwise at present to publish on an area of great personal interest and substantial research over the last decade—Hopi place names; I would have to subtitle it, "A Site-guide for New Age Tourists and Pothunters." Though here again, the politics of representations are complex: If Tsimontukwi had been widely known about among those sympathetic to Hopi interests in the dominant society, it might not have been desecrated.

Postcolonial critic Trinh Minh-ha (1989:68) has characterized anthropology fundamentally as gossip. As anthropologists know, gossip can be a powerful technique for social control in any community. In the contemporary global community, if their representations are going to have any use to their subjects, anthropologists must make their gossip *more controlling on behalf of their subjects* and *less* for their subjects' oppressors. The "speaking for others" at the heart of the anthropological enterprise must come to terms with the moral responsibilities latent in all such practice (see Alcoff 1991). This will involve, in part, not just an account of resistance, but a full-blown focus on the multiple processes whereby the West has exerted its hegemony on colonized societies, forcing them to reconfigure numerous social and cultural practices and concepts (Asad 1992). If anthropologists are to survive and pursue any of their stated goals to further intercultural understanding, they must move their cultural inquiries into a different register. With regard to Hopi, first, what is badly needed in ethnographic description are Hopi perspectives—social, cultural, critical, historical, ecological, etc. It is the height of absurdity (in any event, but especially after more than a century of ethnography), for example, to read in a recent account myself cited as the authority for an observation that Hopis know they need water to grow crops (Loftin 1991:10).

Secondly, the literature already has more than enough accounts of Hopi ritual detail: We do not need to encourage "tiponyism." Regarding ritual, anthropologists should move to explaining to their audience, in a socially constructive way, how Hopis situate, evaluate, and feel about their actions in contemporary circumstances—why privacy needs to be respected, why many accounts of ritual are subversive, and that Hopis want members of the dominant society to appreciate and learn from Hopi practice but without desecrating it. In short the intersocietal environment, conditioning both Hopi and non-Hopi interpretations of ritual, needs foregrounding as the critically salient site of present cultural explanation. In many instances Hopis are glad to share their perspectives on what they perceive to be the uniquely beneficial aspects and effects of their culture's worldview. As one friend put it when discussing accounts of Hopi for the outside world, "so long as it positively enhances their lives, their understanding." In this implicit critique, Hopis see their culture not as some abstract expression, but as having instrumental effects: Ritual dramas, for example, are performed *for* the material benefit of the whole world. It is only with great reluctance and significant opposition, therefore, that, even after decades of Smoki and other kinds of abuse, the priests felt they had no alternative but to close down Snake and Kachina Dances. In other words, it runs counter to Hopi first principles to want to restrict all outside representations of them: They are simply tired of the abuses.

Thirdly, anthropologists must attend and conform to the interests of local communities in constructing research projects. The graduate school rationale of constructing "problems" in vacuo to pursue in "the field"—and here, I think, lies the epistemological key to anthropology's contemporary intellectual reproduction of colonial oppression—has just got to go. If this means giving up cherished theoretical procedures, and being skeptical of knee-jerk invocations of "academic freedom," then so be it: We stand to gain far more, for theory itself, in a discipline devoted to the study of culture, if we genuinely engage different cultural perspectives.[32]

And fourth, a corollary of the preceding, this seems the only way anthropology is going to become truly multicultural. I like to tell my undergraduate students, in the current classroom debates about culture, that anthropology is the most sophisticated potential tool for understanding cultural realities, dialogically bridging difference, and therefore engaging a truly multicultural perspective. But this remains potential. Why, after so much research for so long on Native American cultures, are there still so few Native anthropologists? It is particularly ironic, given the discipline's stated interests, to see year after year the annual meetings of the American Anthropological Association utterly dominated numerically by whites. If anthropology is to become a genuine vehicle of intercultural understanding, rather than a bourgeois language game about the oppressed, it must reform its thought and its institutional structures, both to be of interest to members of subaltern ethnicities, and to provide them formal access to its practices and discourses: In the present global society, anthropology, more than any other subject, drastically needs "affirmative action" to include practitioners from all communities.[33] For this to happen, and it sounds utopian, anthropology must not only "rethink" and "re-invent," to allude to previous efforts at revision, or "recapture," to allude to a more recent one, it must radically restructure both its thought and its institutional underpinnings.[34] If it does not make such efforts, and quickly, it will probably die a slow, lingering death from disinterest, as it becomes increasingly irrelevant to cultural interpretation in the emergent cosmopolitan order.

In terms of social action, it is easy to pontificate and issue conscious-salving hard-line calls to the barricades. But earlier attempts to do this (e.g., Moore 1971) have largely failed and it is not clear whether more recent recommendations (e.g., Scheper-Hughes 1995) will fare any better. At the same time, it seems clear that "action-oriented," activist, or applied anthropology must become a component of *all* anthropological practice, rather than being ghettoized into a subdiscipline. I do not mean to trivialize the problematics of activism and advocacy (see, e.g., Wright 1988; Hastrup and Elass 1990), but at a basic level, if anthropologists are not interested in the fates of their subjects, then what use can their knowledge have, either to the community itself, or to any genuine "science of man"? Hopis experience plenty of social and cultural problems that the particular skills of anthropologists could help with, like land loss, language loss, cultural loss, intellectual property violations, alcoholism, diabetes, all deriving from decades of U.S. cultural hegemony. But anthropologists must have the political will to do so and must show this actively if they are to be perceived as beneficial by Hopis. Again, Deloria (1969:269) pointed the way nearly three decades ago:

> If I were asked to make a list of the useful anthropologists, it would be very short. But this group of people could be critical in helping American society understand the concepts involved in equality—real equality. I believe that they should offer themselves as volunteers to the various tribes and apply their skills in research to real problems.

Some of this is taking place at present and by no means all anthropologists studying at Hopi are exclusively self-interested. Still, researchers have a long way to go, in the atmosphere I have described, to overturn Hopi impressions of cultural exploitation as the sole motive for their presence.

Let me close with some more of Vernon Masayesva's remarks (23 January 1991), which resonate with several of these arguments:

> I hope you [i.e., the academic community] can help us find common ground. Together we need to examine the issue of research and the manner in which scholars will conduct research so that Indian views will be respected. I propose an inclusive agenda . . . involving Indian people in formulating research questions. In the process you can help us become effective researchers. The inclusive agenda would involve mutual study, not just one person or group objectively studying the other. The key to our survival as Indian people is not just preserving our cultural ways, but in devising ways to effectively interact with the dominant society and other cultures with which we coexist. I believe the university has a major responsibility in sharing its academic tools with us. . . . However, let me caution you again that any university-sponsored project, regardless of how noble its aim might be will surely fail if consultation with Indian tribes is not part of the planning process from the project's inception.

EPILOGUE: THE PURE PRODUCTS GO CRAZY, #2

Lest I risk overemphasizing anthropologists' self-importance as cultural representers, it is worth recalling that they are not the only ones to practice or utilize ethnography as a medium of intercultural impression management (cf. Basso 1979, Lavie 1990). Hopis, while oppressed materially and representationally by the dominant society, are not just passive receptors of the traffic in their representations. Though I have argued that anthropologists can be of assistance in some cultural spheres, and that we need more Hopi anthropologists in a cosmopolitan program of intercultural and intersocietal studies, Hopis are working out many of their own intercultural experiences in their own traditional ethnographic modes.

It is August in the dusty pueblo plaza. . . . Well, actually it's June, but you get the picture: I am talking about a Snake Dance. But this time it *is* a Hopi plaza (Kiqötsmovi, c. 1985) with a mixed Hopi and non-Hopi audience. The performers are Hopi clowns,[35] the snakes are of the store-bought bamboo-segment variety, the songs are histrionic Hollywood-tribal, and the dance steps are, as my friend put it, "you know, white-man style" (which I took to mean, in the first place, rhythmically inept, over-gestural, and uncoordinated). They are burlesquing the Smoki Snake Dance, ridiculing its racism and incongruities, reasserting sovereignty over Hopi representations, parodically turning the parody back on itself, emptying it, for the time being at least, of its oppressive meaning and power. The Hopi part of the audience—with a trace of nervousness, because, as with much clown ethnographic allegory, this gets rather close to the bone—dissolves in laughter.

PAAVAHU AND PAANAQSO'A
The Wellsprings of Life and the Slurry of Death

PETER WHITELEY AND VERNON MASAYESVA

INTRODUCTION (1997)

Here, the social, ritual, and political structures and practices addressed
in Chapters 2 through 4 are given some environmental grounding.
Hopi conceptions and uses of natural resources provide the worldly
stage of Hopi practice in which kinship, politico-ritual, poetic, and
aesthetic structures operate and have meaning. These defining practices
are now in jeopardy, owing to the massive waste of Hopi water by
Peabody Coal Company. This chapter further seeks to enact some of
the recommendations in Chapter 6, engaging anthropological knowledge with a particular arena of Hopi interest that is causing great
concern. Its discursive style is nonacademic, reflecting the occasion for
which it was originally written (as an article for *Cultural Survival
Quarterly*).

A very long time ago there was nothing but water. In the east Hurúing
Wuhti, the deity of all hard substances, lived in the ocean. . . . The Sun
also existed at that time. . . . By and by these two deities caused some
dry land to appear in the midst of the water, the waters receding
eastward and westward. ("Origin Myth" recorded by H. R. Voth 1905)

[T]his is . . . one of the most arid countries in the world, and we need
that water. That is why we do Kachina dances in the summer, just to
get a drop of rain. And to us, this water is worth more than gold, or

the money. Maybe we cannot stop the mining of the coal, but we sure would like to stop the use of water. (Dennis Tewa, Munqapi village, at public hearings on the renewal of the Black Mesa-Kayenta mine permit, Kiqötsmovi, 9 August 1989)

HOPI SOCIETY AND ENVIRONMENTAL ADAPTATION

The Hopi Indians of northeastern Arizona are an epitome of human endurance: They are farmers without water. According to their genesis narrative, the Hopi emerged from a layer under the earth into this, the fourth, world, by climbing up inside a reed. Upon arrival, they met a deity, *Maasaw,* who presented them with a philosophy of life based on three elements: maize seeds, a planting stick, and a gourd full of water. *Qa'ö,* "maize," was the soul of the Hopi people, representing their very identity. *Sooya,* "the planting stick," represented the simple technology they should depend on: There was an explicit warning against over-dependency on technology, which had taken on a life of its own in the third world below, producing destruction through materialism, greed, and egotism. *Wikoro,* "the gourd filled with water," represented the environment—the land and all its life forms, the sign of the Creator's blessing, if the Hopis would uphold *Maasaw*'s covenant and live right. *Maasaw* told them life in this place would be arduous and daunting, but through resolute perseverance and industry, they would live long and be spiritually rich.[1]

The twelve Hopi villages lie stretched out on a generally southeast-northwest axis roughly sixty miles long as the crow flies. The villages cluster in groups around the tips of three finger-like promontories, known as the Hopi mesas, that form the southwesternmost extensions of Black Mesa, an upthrust plate of the Colorado Plateau. Black Mesa is bisected by four principal southwest-trending washes, Moenkopi, Dinnebito, Oraibi, and Polacca; all save the Moenkopi are ephemeral and only flow after significant precipitation. Smaller washes, Jeddito and Wepo near First Mesa, are also locally important. The Wepo and Oraibi Washes separate the Hopi Mesas from each other, cutting ar-royo channels in valleys some three or four hundred feet below the mesa tops on which the villages perch. The washes and their tributary fans are main areas of Hopi flood-water farming. Only the Moenkopi Wash (far removed from the central area of Hopi villages) supports irrigation, in farmlands below the villages of Upper and Lower Munqapi, which remain the most productive area of Hopi crops into the present (the name *Munqapi,* anglicized to Moenkopi, means "continuously flowing water place"—an index of its social importance). The Moenkopi Wash is fed by tributary stream flows and springs, but also directly by an aquifer in the layer of sandstone called "Navajo" that sits below the surface of Black Mesa within the hydrological province known as the Black Mesa Basin.[2]

The principal supply of drinking water is traditionally found in springs—indeed Hopi history, which focuses on centripetal migrations by independent clans from all points of the compass—specifically remarks on the abundance and reliability of water supply in the springs that stud the walls of First, Second, and Third Mesas.[3] The springs have determined Hopi settlement patterns and uses of natural resources. As Herbert Gregory, an early geologist to visit the Navajo and Hopi Reservations, pointed out:

> One of the surprises . . . is the large number of springs widely distributed over the reservation. Tucked away in alcoves in the high mesa walls or issuing from crevices in the canyon sides or bubbling up through the sands in the long wash floors, these tiny supplies of water appear to be distributed in haphazard fashion. . . . The ancient cliff dweller was well aware of the desirability of these small permanent supplies as centers for settlement, and many of the present-day Indian trails owe their position to the location of springs rather than to topography or to length of route. (Gregory 1916:132)

Insofar as the archaeological record confirms traditionary history, the period between 1300 and 1500 C.E. sees a concentric contraction of more widespread villages—from Mesa Verde, Navajo Mountain, Tsegi Canyon, the Little Colorado River, and the Hopi Buttes, into such centers as are still populated by the Hopi today.[4]

Hopi presence in the region, and engagement with its particular environmental exigencies, is thus ancient; Hopis are a Puebloan people, direct descendants of the *Anasazi* (an archaeologist's term from the Navajo word meaning "ancestors of the enemy"; Hopis, unsurprisingly, prefer *Hisatsinom*, meaning simply "ancestors"), who, between 800 and 1300 C.E. built some of the most impressive architectural structures in prehistoric North America. Chaco Canyon to the east figures in some Hopi migration legends, as does Mesa Verde to the northeast, Betatakin and Keet Seel to the north, Homol'ovi to the south, Wupatki to the southwest, and numerous other ruins throughout the greater Southwest. The common refrain of Southwestern archaeologists, "What happened to the Anasazi?" is unequivocally answered by

Hopis and other modern Pueblos: "Nothing, we are still here." In Hopi country itself, continuous occupation by sedentary agriculturalists is evident for a good 1500 years, and the Third Mesa town of Orayvi—the oldest continuously inhabited village in North America—has been dated to at least 1150 C.E.[5] In sum, the Hopis have learned to live by farming in this semi-arid environment over the course of a long presence.

Persistent occupation of the Hopi mesas for more than a millennium is both remarkable and paradoxical. Unlike the other Pueblos, with no streams or rivers to support agriculture, the Hopi subsistence economy's dependence on maize, beans, and squash must seek its water elsewhere. How Hopis get and use water is a major part of their identity, religious beliefs, ritual practices, and their daily engagements and concerns. Much of the complex Hopi religious system is devoted, in one way or another, to securing necessary blessings of water—in the form of rainfall, snow, spring replenishment, etc.—to sustain living beings, whether humans, animals, or plants. A calendar of elaborate ritual performances divides into the Kachina season (roughly from December to July) and a season (from August to December) of more esoteric practices by higher-order religious sodalities—the Snake, Flute, *Wuwtsim* ("Manhood"), and *Maraw* ("Womanhood") societies, and the *Soyalangw* festival at the Winter Solstice. All of these concentrate in some measure on ensuring beneficial environmental conditions, on keeping the world in balance. Hopis regard ritual, if performed properly—the cardinal values are pure intentions and good hearts in harmony with each other (these sentiments translate the philosophical concept *namitnangwu*)—as instrumentally efficacious ipso facto, not as mere symbolic embroidery upon a techno-rationalist means of production.

The phrase "Hopi environmentalism" is practically a redundancy.[6] So much of Hopi culture and thought, both religious and secular, revolves around an attention to balance and harmony in the forces of nature that environmental ethics are in many ways critical to the very meaning of the word "Hopi."[7] Hopi society is organized into clans (see Chapter 2), the majority of which are named after, and have specific associations with, natural species and elements, like Bear, Sun, Spider, Parrot, Badger, Corn, Butterfly, Greasewood, Tobacco, Cloud, indicating the centrality of environmental forms and ecological relationships in Hopi thought. Myriad usages of natural species and agents in Hopi religious ritual express the depth and detail of this ecological awareness and concern. A Kachina, for example, in appearance, song, and performance, typically embodies and encapsulates key vital principles of the natural world. Even a casual observation of a *Hemis* Kachina at *Niman* (the Home Dance, in July), to just take one case, discloses a being festooned with spruce branches, wild wheat, clouds, butterflies, tadpoles, seashells, and so on. The bringing together of these natural symbols is in many instances designed to both evoke and celebrate the life-giving force of water in the world.

SPRINGS, WATER, AND RAIN IN HOPI SECULAR AND RELIGIOUS PHILOSOPHY

Paahu, "natural water" or "spring," is absolutely central in Hopi social and environmental thought. Indeed, the identity of the term points to the significance springs hold: Springs are the prototypical water sources. Supplemented by wells built by the Indian Agency over the last century, springs supply drinking water and water for livestock, and they also feed a series of irrigated terraced gardens on the slopes below the mesa tops, which form another basic site of crop production, including chilis, beans, a little corn, onions, radishes, and fruit trees. The areas around the larger springs are also the only significant wetlands in much of the region. For this reason, they are also objects of religious veneration.

Even with the introduction of piped water (for the most part only within the last thirty years) springs remain critical in Hopi philosophy and practice. Springs and their immediate pond-life environs serve as the ideal model of life and growth. Such places attract denser presences of life-forms than elsewhere in the semiarid landscape. Doves, dragonflies, ducks, cranes, frogs, sand grass, cattails, reeds, cottonwoods, willow, and numerous other species concentrate at these locations—simultaneously the index and the manifestation of abundant, water-charged life. Such species serve as key symbols of the life-giving force of water in Hopi secular and religious philosophy.

It is hard to imagine anything more sacred—as substance or symbol—than water in Hopi religious thought and practice. To be sure, some elements may appear more prominent: corn, the staff of life, which is ubiquitous in Hopi religious imagery; rattlesnakes from the spectacular Snake Dance; or masked performances by Kachina spirits. But intrinsic to these, and underlying much other symbolism in the panoply of Hopi ritual, is the concern with water. Springs, water, and rain are focal themes in ritual costumes, kiva iconography, mythological narratives, personal names, and many many songs, which call the cloud chiefs from the varicolored directions to bear their fructifying essence back into the cycle of human, animal, and vegetal life. That essence—as clouds, rain, and other water forms—manifests the spirits of the dead. When people die, in part, they become clouds; songs call to the clouds as ascendant relatives. Arriving clouds are returning ancestors, their rain both communion with, and blessing of, the living. The waters of the earth (where Kachina spirits live) are, then, transubstantiated human life.

In general, springs and groundwater serve as homes for the deity *Paalölöqangw,* "Plumed Water-Snake," who is a powerful patron of the water sources of the earth and the heavens. *Paalölöqangw* is appealed to in the Snake and Flute ceremonies, and portrayed in religious puppetry during winter night dances. Springs and their immediate surroundings are places of particular religious worship in some instances, like the Flute ceremony, or during *Powamuy,* the "Bean Dance" and *Niman,* the "Home Dance." The Flute ceremony is specifically devoted to the consecration and regeneration of major springs, and the *Lenmongwi,* head of the Flute society, dives, in an archetypal gesture, to the bottom of a particularly sacred spring to plant prayer sticks for *Paalölöqangw.*

Resources from spring areas—like water, clay, reeds, or spruce branches—are gathered and taken back for use in village ceremonies, where they are deemed to draw in the life-giving power of the springs themselves. Springs as distant as one hundred miles are visited on a regular basis to bring back their sacred water for ceremonies, especially by clan descendants from former settlements adjacent to the springs. Early ethnographers Jesse Walter Fewkes and Walter Hough remarked on Hopi veneration of springs:

> In a general way every spring is supposed to be sacred and therefore a place for the deposit of prayer sticks and other offerings. . . . [E]very spring is a place of worship and hence a shrine. (Fewkes 1906:370-71)

> [N]o spring in the region is without evidence of many offerings to the deities of water. . . . Sacred Springs may . . . be regarded as altars, and the offerings as sacrifices, whose essence may be carried by the water. (Hough 1906:165)

Since time immemorial, Hopis have offered blessings of cornmeal and prayers at springs, during specific visits for the purpose or simply while passing through the landscape (say, during herding, hunting, or treks

Figure 7.1. *Flute Ceremony at Toreva Spring,* by Fred Kabotie, Hopi, circa 1940. Photograph by Blair Clark. Courtesy School of American Research Collections in the Museum of New Mexico.

to distant cornfields). When blessing a spring, typically a man also scoops a handful of water and splashes it back toward his village or fields as a way to encourage the water to transfer some of its power to where humans most need it. Springs attract the rain and snow to themselves and thus serve as powerful foci of value in Hopi thought. Indeed, this is why they are sacred places: If much of Hopi religious thought celebrates life, then springs are self-evident indexes of the dynamic process that produces and sustains life. At the winter solstice ceremonies feathered prayer sticks are placed over major springs around every Hopi village as both protection and supplication.

Among sources of water there is a quasi-magnetic relationship: the Pacific Ocean, the Colorado River, rain, underground aquifers, springs, and living plants are mutually attractive—"contagious" in the anthropological sense: "The land is a living organ, it breathes. . . . [T]he Hopis say that it is the underground water that sucks in, that breathes the rain" (Vernon Masayesva).[8] *Paatuwaqatsi,* literally "the ocean," is simultaneously a central philosophical principle denoting the universally sustaining water of life. To attract the world's powers of moisture, spring names occur frequently in ritual narrative and song: for example, *Talakwavi,* "dawn coming-up spring"; *Tsorspa,* "bluebird spring"; *Kwaava,* "eagle spring"; *Paatuwi,* "spring on the rock shelf"; *Höwiipa,* "dove spring"; *Hoonawpa,* "bear spring"; *Konva,* "squirrel spring"; *Kookyangwva,* "spider spring"; *Tsinngava,* "water droplets splashing spring"; *Söhöpva,* "cottonwood springs"; and many, many more. Springwater properly placed in one's field, mud from spring bottoms as body plaster in Kachina costumes, painted tadpoles or dragonflies on Kachina *friends* (a term Hopis prefer to "masks") all sympathetically entice the rain.

Springs themselves, like maize in fields, were originally "planted" in the earth by deities or gifted individuals. There was even a special instrument, a *paa'u'uypi,* "spring planter," known to the elect and used for this purpose. (A spring by Munqapi, for example, is said to have been planted in this way by a man named Kwaavaho—for whom the spring is named—in the late nineteenth century). Pilgrimages to reconsecrate and draw in regenerative power from especially significant springs at distant points are common in the religious calendar. Villages may be named for springs, like the mother village, *Songoopavi,* "sandgrass spring place." Some clans have exceptional responsibilities to springs, like *Patkingyam,* the "Water clan," and some springs are sacred to specific clans or religious societies at the different villages. Clan migration routes from former villages are often retraced—both literally, in pilgrimages, and figuratively, in narratives and songs—at certain times of the year. In many instances, clan associations with springs at their ruins or along the route are mentioned as locations of important historical events. So the Water clan has a series of historical points along its migration route from the south that springs frequently mark. Similarly, *Kiisiwu,* "Shady Springs," for the Badger and Butterfly clans, *Lengyanovi* for the Flute clan, *Hoonawpa* for the Bear clan, and *Leenangwva* for the Spider clan, are all memorialized in clan tradition and visited in pilgrimage. In this sense, then, the living springs embody Hopi history: They are cultural landmarks, inscribed with significance, and commemorative reminders of the continuing legitimacy of clan rights and interests in specific areas.

Springs, and the life-forms associated with them, thus occur in many Hopi stories and sacred narratives, in literary forms like personal names, and in artistic forms, like basketry, pottery, weaving, and painting. In these intellectual and aesthetic contexts, the substance and forms of springs and wetland life are described objectively and celebrated with pleasurable appreciation and spiritual gratitude. Personal names (and see Chapter 4), which are a prime form of Hopi poetic images, often reference springs and water: like *Paahongva,* "water standing up" (after the tiny columns of water that leap up from raindrops splashing on a pond or puddle); *Paanömtiwa,* "water covering up" (perhaps a cornfield after a rain); *Paatala,* "water light," referring to reflected light on the water surface, particularly in the dark. Many of the species that are the totemic emblems of Hopi clans are associated with springs— *paawiki,* "the duck," *atoko,* "the crane," *paakwa,* "the frog," *paaqavi,* "reeds," and so on. The celebration of water, its origins or results, forms a major proportion—perhaps half—of all Hopi names. So references to flowers—an explicit mark of the Creator's rain blessings—celebrate this too: like *Siitala,* "flower light," the reflected sunlight from flowers newly blossomed after a rain; *Sikyakuku,* literally "yellow foot," which refers to walking along through blossoming flowers while the pollen clings to one's moccasined feet. Or rain: *Yooyoki,* "raining"; *Yoyvwölö,* "rainwater"; lightning: *Talwiipi,* "a single lightning flash," or *Talwipta,* "lightning in the ongoing process of flashing." Even species not directly associated with water sources are frequently subjects of interest in relation to their behavior toward water. One name, "Sharp hearer," given by a Spider clan-member, refers to the fact that when rain begins to fall, certain spiders secreted inside houses, hear the rain and emerge from their cover, running out to drink from the freshly-emerging puddles.[9] Even here, then, when the species in question has no explicit conceptual links with water, Hopis often position its significance by its habitual practices in relation to water. The concern with natural water depicted in this name details a precise knowledge of a species' behavior as well as an aesthetic and creatural delight in the pleasure and happiness that the presence of water affords all the beings of the world.

In short, springs are key in Hopi social life, cultural values, and the conceptualization of the landscape—all of which form the grounds of deeper religious thought and action. Hopis smoke for rain, dance for it, sing for it, and offer many other forms of prayer for it. In the cycle of life, rainwater and snowmelt nourish the plants that feed animals and human beings. So prayers for rain are not abstract; they call the clouds to replenish the waters of the earth so that all life-forms will benefit and "be happy." Here, then, is an environment populated not by Western science's instinct-driven organisms without spirit or consciousness, but by intentional, spiritual entities which are part and parcel of the same moral system that encompasses human beings. Hopis have, so to speak, both a moral ecology and an ecological morality. As one man put it, "We pray for rain so that all the animals,

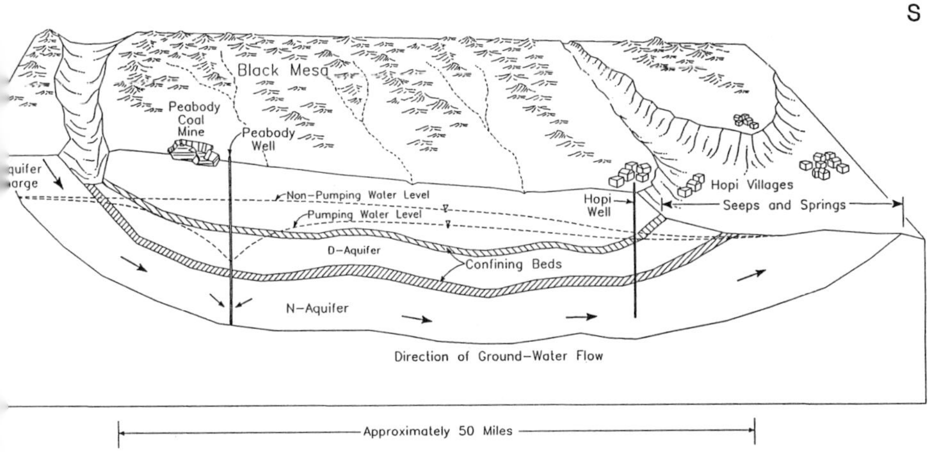

S

Figure 7.2. How Hopi springs and Peabody's wells are fed by aquifers underlying Black Mesa. (Conceptual model of groundwater flow in the N-Aquifer.) Courtesy of Water Resources Program, the Hopi Tribe.

birds, insects, and other life-forms will have enough to drink, too." The prolific complexity of Hopi ritual attends to springs specifically and in general, as sources of blessing and vehicles of prayer.

OF COAL MINES AND SLURRIES

The springs, however, are drying up, and with them the essential force of Hopi religious life and culture. Flows have been progressively declining over the last three decades. Numerous springs and seeps have ceased to produce enough water to sustain crops planted below them. The Moenkopi wash does not "continuously flow" any more and the only major Hopi farming area that depends on irrigation water is in serious jeopardy. In recent years, it has been down to a trickle by late May; not long ago Munqapi children plunged into swimming holes long into the summer. But even the trickle is supplied only by two upstream tributaries: From the mainstream itself, much of the water is channeled into impoundment ponds by Peabody Coal Company.

Peabody, which operates twenty-seven mines in the United States, is the largest private producer of coal in the world. Until recently, the company was part of the British multinational, Hanson Industries, which demerged in February 1997. Peabody then became part of the newly formed Hanson spin-off "The Energy Group PLC," but top management remains virtually identical. Peabody's total operating profit (i.e., including all its mining interests worldwide) in 1996 was $240 million, on coal sales in excess of $2 billion; Hanson's total sales, including its chemical and tobacco interests, in 1996 exceeded $19 billion, and its total after-tax profit was $2.3 billion.[10] This is no small enterprise.

Peabody's Black Mesa Mine is the only mine in the country that transports its coal by slurry. The strip-mined coal is crushed, mixed with drinking-quality water and then flushed by pipeline to the Mohave Generating Station in Laughlin, Nevada. The cities of Las Vegas and Phoenix—electric oases in the desert—buy some of the power, but most of it goes to the electric toothbrushes, garage-door openers, outsize TV sets, and other necessities of life in southern California. Most of the slurry water comes directly from the "Navajo" or N-aquifer 1,000 to 3,000 feet within the geologic formation of Black Mesa. Peabody uses approximately 3,700 acre-feet (about 1.2 billion gallons) of water per year for the slurry—ten times as much as the annual water consumption of the entire Hopi community (about 9,000 people).

The pumping, Peabody has claimed, has no effect on the Hopi springs. Those springs, it maintains, are not fed by the N-aquifer but by the overlying "Dakota" or D-aquifer, and by snowmelt. Hopis do not believe Peabody's position. But an escalating series of letters from Hopi individuals and officials, both traditional leaders and Tribal Council chairs, petitions signed by several hundred Hopis, protests in public hearings, dissenting interpretations by independent geologists,[11] repeated refusal by the Tribal Council to sanction the Department of the Interior's renewal of the mining lease, have all fallen on deaf ears. Flat rebuttals to Hopi protests continue by Peabody and Hanson representatives, and a personal invitation to Lord Hanson, Chairman of Hanson PLC, by then Tribal Chairman Ferrell Secakuku, in June 1994, to direct dialogue went ignored. In April 1994 W. Howard Carson, President of Peabody Western Coal Company, voiced the company's party line: "Changes in the flows from their springs may be the result of drought conditions in the region, and perhaps from the increased pumpage from Hopi community wells located near these springs. . . . Peabody Western's pumping from wells that are 2,500 to 3,000 feet deep does not affect these springs" (*Los Angeles Times* 30 April 1994).

Yet Peabody's characterizations of hydrological effects are eminently untrustworthy. Comments and hearings on the U.S. Office of Surface Mining and Reclamation's Draft Environmental Impact Statement (U.S. Department of the Interior 1990)[12] produced a welter of objections, both to the sociocultural and environmental effects of the mine, and to the shoddy quality of research that produced general ratings of minor or minimal environmental impacts. For example, the U.S. Environmental Protection Agency's official response noted:

We have classified the DEIS [Draft Environmental Impact Statement] as Category EO-2:[13] Environmental Objections—Insufficient Information. . . . [W]e believe the project may result in significant adverse environmental impacts to water resources and air quality that should be avoided. We have also found that the lack of sufficient information on water, air, and biotic resource conditions severely impedes evaluation of impacts, alternatives, and appropriate mitigation measures. We are particularly concerned that the DEIS lacks an alternatives analysis which would enable the Federal agencies and the public to consider less environmentally damaging actions than the preferred alternative [i.e., the slurry]. (U.S. EPA, 14 October 1989, reprinted in Department of the Interior 1990:263)

EPA's more detailed comments on hydrological compliance with the National Environmental Policy Act noted:

Conclusions based on N-aquifer modeling. While EPA accepts the approach taken in modelling hydrologic baseline conditions and impacts, the conclusiveness of this effort is undermined by lack of data. This limitation, compounded by use of material damage criteria based on thresholds much less sensitive than "significance" under NEPA, lead us to reject the evaluation of hydrologic impacts. EPA believes that the available data do not support statements in the DEIS that the cumulative effects of current and foreseeable mining and related operations (principally the coal transport slurry) are expected to result in only minor hydrological impacts. (Ibid.:267)

Six months prior to Howard Carson's 1994 statement in the Los Angeles Times (above), top U.S. Geological Survey hydrologists concluded that Peabody's ongoing analysis of water impacts was based on a wholly inadequate model. Among other shortcomings: "[T]he model is not sufficient to answer the concerns of the Hopi regarding adverse local, short-term impacts on wetlands, riparian wildlife habitat, and spring flow at individual springs" (Nichols, 28 October 1993). Recent figures (USGS 1995) suggest that declines in water level (ranging from 30 feet to 97 feet from 1965 to 1993) of area wells are up to two-thirds caused by the mine's pumping. Peabody's claim that throughout the thirty-five-year life of the mine it would use one tenth of one percent of N-aquifer water, which would naturally recharge itself, is seriously questioned by a USGS recharge study in 1995, which charted a recharge rate 85 percent less than Peabody's estimate.[14] (It has been suggested that Peabody has tried to suppress public release of these discrepant figures since, if verified, the company would be contractually obligated, according to the terms of the lease, to post a bond for aquifer restoration.)

It seems evident, too, that depletion of the N-aquifer has had serious impacts on the D-aquifer, and on the springs themselves; the Moenkopi Wash is directly affected since it is supplied by N-aquifer seepage, and since Peabody impounds surface water (at a rate surpassing 1,800 acre-feet per year) that would otherwise directly flow into the Moenkopi Wash.[15] USGS computer simulations predict total drying of some major Hopi wells beginning in the year 2011. Upstream Navajo communities are also significantly affected by the drying and by deteriorating water quality: Forest Lake has been particularly hard hit. In recent documents, Peabody has finally acknowledged that it takes water not only from the N-aquifer but also from other aquifers present, including the D-aquifer. This has come as no surprise to Hopis. But as Nat Nutongla, head of the Hopi Water Resources Office, puts it, "the elders regard all water as sacred. It doesn't matter whether the springs are supplied directly by the D-aquifer or the N-aquifer or whatever; they represent ALL sources of water" (personal communication to Whiteley, 1995).

Peabody's position that declines in Hopi springs derive from increased domestic and municipal consumption, reflecting population growth (principally Navajo) and water development by the Navajo and Hopi Tribes, is not entirely untrue. Tuba City wells and significant increase in local population since the 1960s directly impinge on Munqapi area springs. Hopi use of domestic water has definitely expanded since newer villages adopted indoor plumbing over the last thirty years. But these changes, Hopis argue, are all the more reason not to waste the reserves of N-aquifer water. As coauthor and former Tribal Chairman Vernon Masayesva has put it elsewhere:

> I believe there is a water crisis. Peabody Mining Company says that if there is a lowering of the water in the wells, it's because of domestic uses, and not as a result of their pumping. And to that, I simply said, "All the more reason why you should not be pumping that water, because the do-

mestic users are already having a significant impact on that N-aquifer water." So why throw away the savings? I see aquifers as money in the bank, in a savings account. So why are we dipping into it?[16]

A serious, compromising quandary is that 80 percent of the Hopi Tribe's annual operating revenues are supplied by coal royalties and water lease fees from Peabody. The Hopi Tribal Council (or "Tribe")— a creation of the Indian Reorganization Act of 1934—is formally supported by about half the villages, though even anti-Council traditionalists rely on numerous benefits it administers. Many people feel they were duped by the Council's attorneys when the original leases were signed in the 1960s and that some Tribal leaders were co-opted by Peabody.[17] But this is scarcely a factional issue. Hopis directly involved with the Council, including the last two Chairmen (Ferrell Secakuku and Vernon Masayesva), have strongly opposed renewal of the coal leases in lieu of an alternative means of transporting the coal. Hopis of all factions, from traditionalist *Kikmongwis,* "village chiefs," to modernist technocrats have been unanimous and clear in their opposition to the use of pristine groundwater to transport coal and in their disbelief of Peabody's denials that the pumping affects the springs. Two examples will suffice. The first is more traditionally inclined. At the public hearings in Munqapi on 8 August 1989, William Garcia recounted a childhood discussion with his grandfather, Kyarsyawma, while out herding sheep. Kyarsyawma first asked for his grandsons' impressions of the land:

[O]ur response was, "Well, it is just there. It is just there, you know, and we use it now and then, maybe to farm on and to herd our sheep. There is really nothing to it."

He said, "Look at yourself. Look at your body, what do you have? You got some parts there, it looks pretty simple on the outside, but on the inside, inside of you as a person you have a soul, you have a heart. You have some blood running through your body to keep your vital organs going," and he said, "It is the same thing with the land. The land has a soul, the land that we are on has a soul, it has a heart. It also has its own blood. The blood running through it are the streams to keep it alive, to keep us alive."

I always remember that, so to me, after I kind of learned that concept, it wasn't just there anymore. There was a purpose behind it just like there is a purpose here for each and every one of us. We are not just here. . . .

I guarantee you that if we continue to draw this lifeline from mother

Earth, then we will no longer exist, just as if someone stuck a needle in your arm and sucked out all the blood, you would be nothing, you would be dead. (Department of the Interior 1990:374–75)

Secondly, Mishongnovi Village's anti-slurry petition was worded as follows:

Be advised that we the undersigned members of the village of Mishongnovi are deeply concerned about the effects the mining of coal, by Peabody Coal Company, has had on our water resources. This is most evident in our springs drying up, our farms not producing crops, and our range wells drying up.

Our village leaders have been and are still opposed to use of our water for mining operations. Our water is our life and we stand firm with our leaders in opposition to future use of our water for this purpose. (Mishongnovi Village Petition, 1989, reprinted in U.S. Department of the Interior 1990:296)

The Tribal Council favors economic development, and does not oppose the mine as such (which some traditionalists do): Part of the allure of the mine in the first place was the promise of Hopi employment. But Hopis say Peabody has aligned itself with the Navajo Nation and ignores Hopi interests, a position borne out in employment figures. Of up to nine hundred "Native American"—a useful elision in Peabody's public pronouncements—employees, fewer than twenty are Hopis. (The great majority are Navajos, represented by the United Mine Workers Union, which enjoys a special relationship with the Navajo Labor Relations Board.)[18] The original leases guaranteed 50 percent of local employment to Hopis. And Peabody's overall attitude seems to be flagrant disdain for Hopi concerns. In Howard Carson's words, "We wouldn't (stop pumping) just to get the Hopi off our backs, because it could create another nightmare. These things snowball" (*Gallup Independent* 20 December 1993).

Several alternatives to the slurrying of aquifer water have been proposed, and progress has been made on one: another pipeline from Lake Powell that would provide domestic water for Hopis and Navajos, and industrial uses for Peabody. But Peabody, ever mindful of the bottom line, is evidently using delaying tactics, suspending negotiations and playing off the tribes against each other, despite support for the project by Interior Secretary Bruce Babbitt. Like most other negotiations involving Hopis and Navajos, this pipeline proposal is subject to the

Figure 7.3. *Nimantiikive,* the "Home Dance," with *Hemis* kachinas, by Fred Kabotie, Hopi, circa 1920. Photograph by Blair Clark. Courtesy School of American Research Collections in the Museum of New Mexico. (Formal title is recorded as *New Year's Dance.*)

cumulative politics of major land disputes between the tribes, and the Navajo Nation has sought concessions from the Hopi that it has been unable to gain otherwise. Such disputes affect Hopi interests in other ways, including religious pilgrimages to some springs. A major sacred spring, Kiisiwu, is on land partitioned to the Navajo Nation by Congress in 1974. This spring, associated with principal Kachina ceremonies, is visited by ritual-society pilgrims, especially during *Powamuy,* the "Bean Dance," and *Niman,* the "Home Dance." Formerly, local Navajos maintained a respectful distance, but younger generations are impressed less by the religious purpose and more by secular conflict. Recently, there have been physical assaults. If Kiisiwu dries up, this may solve some temporal problems between Hopis and Navajos, but at what spiritual cost?

Meanwhile, the Hopis are deeply anxious about all spring declines, for both obvious and deeper metaphysical reasons. Hopi moral philosophy, following a covenant entered into with the deity Maasaw upon emergence into the present world, charges people to take care of the earth and all its resources; indeed this is a significant measure of whether one is worthy of the name "Hopi" (see note 8). If Hopis break the covenant, cataclysm of cosmic proportions threatens. During the early 1980s when I (Whiteley) began ethnographic research at Third Mesa, Tsakwani'yma, an older Spider clan man, would sometimes talk about prophecies he had heard from his uncle, Lomayestiwa (a Hostile leader at the 1906 Orayvi split). He returned to one repeatedly; a time would come when Paalölöqangw, the water serpent deity, would turn over and lash his tail deep within the waters of the earth, and all land-life would tumble back down to the bottom of the ocean. "Can you interpret it?" he would challenge. "It means earthquake. But it's also symbolic of the life we are leading today: *koyaanisqatsi*, 'a life of chaos.'" Then in 1987 and 1988, shortly after he passed on, there were two earthquakes on Black Mesa (a rarity), which the Arizona Earthquake Information Center connects to the removal of massive quantities of coal and water. The perception of some elders that this is the result of having their souls sold out from under them—literally, in the link between groundwater and spirits of the dead—causes profound sadness and a sense of intractable religious desecration.

In addition to long-term Hopi interests, regional economic and demographic patterns make the continued pumping of more than a billion gallons of potable water every year for a coal slurry incredibly short-sighted. The coming century will undoubtedly see ever more serious problems of water supply for the rapidly growing conurbations in the West. In this light, Hopi religious concerns with springs become metaphorical of larger issues of global development and natural resource management. But while typically attuned to such universal implications, Hopis in the immediate term are concerned with basic physical, cultural, and spiritual survival. If the springs are to be saved, and along with them continued Hopi cultural and religious existence, Peabody's relentless drive toward short-term profits, at the expense of stakeholder concerns, needs a dramatic makeover in line with trends toward local-global balance pursued by more progressive multinationals.[19] In the meantime, the pumps siphon the essence of life from the water-roots of Black Mesa and the Hopi springs are withering on the vine.

STAKEHOLDERS, SHAREHOLDERS, AND REGULATORS

At the heart of this conflict over resource use is the confrontation between market capitalism and small-scale subsistence economies, or, in other terms, the opposing interests of shareholder and stakeholder. Much talk of sustainable development practices has been grounded in the inexorable logic of rationalist economics, with scant attention paid to different cultural and religious conceptions of the environment and how these might affect practical engagement with the transformation of nature for production.

In between stakeholder and shareholder interests, the powers of government to protect the former and regulate resource use are called seriously into question here. The government has a series of trust responsibilities to Indian Tribes that surpass its obligations to most other sectors of American society. There are specific provisions, like the Winters Doctrine, that could be invoked to protect Hopi and Navajo water resources and life-chances. Vernon Masayesva clearly places some of the blame in the hands of governmental agencies charged with protecting Hopi interests:

> It's a *tragic* chapter in United States–Hopi relations. *Very tragic.* They put our culture at risk, is the way I put it. The reason why Navajo aquifer water is so important is not only because, according to the Hopis, it's what sucks in the rain, but it also feeds the springs where ceremonies are occurring. It also sits in a bowl: *it's the only source of potable water available to the Hopi people.* (BBC 1995 [his emphasis])

As a concatenation of powers, the multiplicity of government branches seems to militate against effective stakeholder representation: What the left hand gives, the right will take away. So, for example, the EPA has been clear about its opposition to the mine's hydrological practices. But it is overridden by OSMRE, which, not to put too fine a point on it, has seemed to be largely a regulatory surrogate for Peabody's corporate interests. Throughout the public hearings on the DEIS at the Hopi Tribal Headquarters in Kiqötsmovi in August 1989, for example, OSMRE's representative, Peter Rutledge, seemed interested in only speaking on behalf of Peabody, and to Hopis present the difference between the two entities was not clear; I (Whiteley) was sitting next to the then *Kikmongwi* of Orayvi, Stanley Bahnimptewa, who shortly into the hearings, grew disgusted, turned to me and said "looks like we're going to be here all day," got up and left.

Recently, the OSMRE renewed Peabody's Kayenta mine permit. The Kayenta mine itself transports coal by railroad, but the two mines are linked administratively and are geographically close, so the renewal demonstrates tacit support (or, at least, benign neglect) of the Black Mesa mine operation despite the fact that the information contained in this chapter is widely known.[20] At the annual meeting of Hanson

Industries in February 1996, Hopi and Navajo protestors, along with supporters from various environmental groups, succeeded in shutting down the meeting.[21] That OSMRE would override the many Hopi protests to renew the mine permit suggests that the rules of the market, and its control by multinational capital, are so entrenched in the thinking of government and industry that, even in such a flagrant case, local constructions of environmental interest will not be heard against this tide, and possible uses by government of legal tools to protect stakeholders will go by the board.

If the imbrication of government and corporate interests in water uses seems Orwellian, the bureaucratic labyrinth overseeing regulation is positively Kafkaesque. A series of governmental agencies have made appearances in this chapter as involved at one level or another with the issues in question (and additional agencies are also involved). All told, the following are included: The Hopi Tribal Council (and various departmental agencies); the Navajo Nation (and various departmental agencies); the U.S. Secretary of the Interior; the U.S. Geological Survey, Water Resources Division; the U.S. Environmental Protection Agency; the U.S. Office of Surface Mining Reclamation and Enforcement; the U.S. Army Corps of Engineers; the U.S. Fish and Wildlife Service; the U.S. Bureau of Land Management; the U.S. Bureau of Indian Affairs; the U.S. Department of Health and Human Services (Indian Health Service); the U.S. Department of Justice; the State of Arizona; the Arizona Department of Health and Human Services; Arizona Game and Fish Department; Arizona Department of Mines and Mineral Resources. This does not include the municipal interests party to Little Colorado Basin water rights adjudications. Multilateral negotiations over these water rights—involving Hopis, Navajos, Peabody, and municipalities in northern Arizona and overseen by the U.S. Department of Justice—are ongoing as of this writing. The possibility, say, that the Hopi Tribe could sue Peabody over the environmental damage is held in abeyance by these negotiations (in which Peabody is the major player with most of the wealth) and their attachment to a web of bureaucratic strings. From this governmental quagmire, Hopis have turned recently to the environmental group, the Natural Resources Defense Council, which is supplying a hydrologist to conduct independent tests of the aquifer.

The key question for the future—how local communities can ensure basic resource needs vis-à-vis the demands of the metropolitan economy—will be played out in many contexts in the American West and elsewhere where the conflict over resource rights is exacerbated by demographic shifts, increasing urbanization, and absorption of small communities by ever more encompassing forces of market production. Global climate change will be another major factor in the capacity of small-scale indigenous societies to retain control of their environments and resources. It is quite likely that dislocations from climatically marginal areas will produce a significant tide of environmental refugees (see, e.g., Bruce et al. 1996). In those locales like the Hopi Reservation, where water supply is so limited, the threat posed by industrial exploitation of the present sort may well tip the balance prior to changes produced by longer-term impacts.

If we are genuinely committed to sustainability, it is time to expand understanding of it by listening to communities—like some Native Americans—that have practiced it for a very long time. If, to be realistic, we do not see an end to global markets as the mainspring of future economic frameworks, then the key issue is how to balance short-term profitability with long-term sustainability. The crux of that, surely, is empowering local stakeholders in the decision-making processes of companies themselves—but that will require corporate willingness to be inclusive, which may be anathema to the current ethos and praxis of the market. Without that will, the only possible hope for stakeholders is the intervention of government regulatory agencies: If OSMRE and if the bureaucratic labyrinth in which decision-making is currently trapped are anything to go by, that glimmer of hope offers precious little comfort. President Clinton announced that he would be the "Environment President." Perhaps, in the apparent failure of the Secretary of the Interior to step in here, what is needed to cut through the bureaucracy is an "Environment Czar" who could respond to stakeholder situations like the Hopi water crisis more effectively. One Hopi commentator, Rebekah Masayesva, summed up the situation with admirable conciseness, "[T]he pumping of pure underground water for slurrying of coal is unconscionable and must stop" (U.S. Department of the Interior 1990:416). Eight years on since the public hearings, the slurry, re-permitted, persists, and there is still no indication it will stop soon, no matter how environmentally damaging, socioculturally destructive, economically shortsighted, or indeed unconscionable it may be. If we can take the courage to recognize that in the long term, we are all stakeholders, the question for both industry and government is, "why not?"

EPILOGUE
Fin-de-Siècle

Less than Angels (1955), Barbara Pym's marvelously prescient romance of anthropological crisis (begun in 1953, the year of my birth), portrays representational anxiety, disciplinary identity questions, ethnographic and political self-doubt, and indeed the very relevance of anthropological knowledge—in the vexed fate of a trunkload of fieldnotes. Catherine, the central character, a journalist romantically attached to one or another of the anthropologists, is the novel's only realist. The anthropologists are all faintly ridiculous romantics, idealists, or both (all are white, largely middle-class Britons).

The narrative pivots on two emblematic anthropological deaths. The first is Tom, a charismatic young professor in the throes of his fieldwork, who dies while participating in a political demonstration in a West African city on behalf of "his people" (when was the last time that phrase was uttered without irony?). Catherine turns to Alaric, a withdrawn, dyspeptic character, defined by the talismanic residue of eleven years' fieldwork—the moldering trunk of fieldnotes. Alaric is incapable of publishing anything—except virulent expostulations in reviews of others' ethnography—owing to a surfeit of ethnographic knowledge that transforms into a sort of intercultural nausea. The relationship between culture (small *c*) and imperialism (the reference, of course, is to Said [1993]) at this midtwentieth century moment— which present-day anthropologists are apt to look back upon as halcyon days—has taken rather a shabby detour into the inherently liminal byways of ethnography.

The second death, at the dénouement, is a delicious "goodbye to all that": Alaric and Catherine take the trunk into the suburban back yard and, in a sacrificial auto-da-fé, burn the lot. As ethnography expires, and its dusty, interstitial problematics disappear into the ether, life and personal redemption—reconnection to a proximate social world and letting go of a fetishized fantasy of communion with the Other—begin. Pym knows the milieu of academic anthropology well[1]—its salon politics, guild pretensions, egoistic aspirations, and celebrations of exotic difference (including the breathless excitement of a report of three peoples living on adjacent hills who speak "totally different languages!")—and draws it all with a mordant, lighthearted wit.

Has anthropology outlived its usefulness? At this fin-de-siècle is it practically dead? The characters who persist (in Pym's novel) in anthropology beyond its crisis of worldly engagement are cartoonish marginal dilettantes, perhaps painfully anticipating the postmodern solipsistic moment. The essays I have collected here were written over the decade from the mid-1980s to the mid-1990s, covering a period that has seen the discipline increasingly define itself, perhaps even neurotically, by this sense of crisis—whether the crisis is of "ethnographic authority," or of appropriate positioning in the contemporary world, or, perhaps most neurotically, of "representations"—of the possibility that anything can be said about anything.

If Pym's perspectival moment is anything to go by, however, this identity crisis is in many respects intrinsic to the ethnographic project, and the current crisis is, as I have noted elsewhere (1988:44), merely a "gathering of speed." Anthropologists, at least those with a smidgen of sensitivity, hover at the borders: of society, culture, understanding, and praxis. In this lies their primary usefulness, as agents of plural translation. Yet in this very liminality lie the seeds of both the genuine transformation of worldly understanding and epistemological autodestruction. The move toward progressive pluralism is clearly present, though often unconsciously so, as a result of ethnographic, as well as other intercultural, moves toward interpretation and approximation. The self-immolating tendencies of anthropological theory—of, say, totemism, kinship, the self, and of course "culture" (that insidious deceiver that has occupied anthropology from Tylor and Boas's time on)—reproduce a cultural critique of western academic and other epistemologies that has resulted in multiple reflexive transformations. But this, again, is to be celebrated, rather than denied or obviated.

Philosophically, then, ethnography stands in the interstices, continuously critiquing, mirroring, showing arbitrariness and relative value. Like clowning or pollution, such liminality can be dangerous and subversive, but it is a primary source of cultural production and transformation. It is my hope that these essays, which attempt in their various ways to negotiate the liminal positionalities of anthropology among cultural discourses, practices, and representations, can lead toward a more genuinely plural space of understanding—with both the proximate and ultimate goal of greater social equity. This, it seems to me, should be the general charge for anthropology in the future.

Anthropologists are positioned particularly well to act as agents of transformation—discursively and practically. But if anthropology cannot realize its inevitable moral implication in the human condition and act to honor moral conjuncture, its recession into discursive marginality will continue. That realization fundamentally entails recognizing the common humanity of our subjects, their consciousness, embodiment of agency as selves, their suffering, and the fact that they think about their world in ways that can transform understanding rather than as cognitive objects for imperial ivory-tower analysis. Without the moral commitment to this shared interest in human freedom, anthropologists should perhaps all retire to our backyards and do away with our dusty discipline. But with it, the possibilities for global change are genuinely present.

NOTES

1. INTRODUCTION

1. Navajo ritual knowledge, saleable and evidently fluidly transmissible, offers a signal difference in this respect.

2. Academic commodifications of Hopi culture (see below in the text) continue to circulate in a largely restricted system, owing to the specialized discourses, and protocols of entry and engagement, that characterize the academy.

3. Hotvela, long considered one of the most traditional villages, and the most resistant to external hegemony, now has its own home page on the Internet, where political affairs are publicized and disputed. Many houses in Hotvela and Orayvi (another staunchly conservative village) now feature solar cells on the rooftops, nicely illustrating that resistance is not to alien ideas or techniques per se, but to the cession of autonomy these entail when attached to government or corporate control.

4. Intellectual property rights are of widespread interest among, and on behalf of, indigenous peoples worldwide as means of protecting and capitalizing on local knowledge; see, for instance, Greaves 1994, or recent issues of *Cultural Survival Quarterly*.

5. The "Hopi Tribe" is the official governing body and administrative unit of the Hopi people, created as a result of the Indian Reorganization Act of 1934. I use "Tribe" and "Tribal" (with initial capital *T*s) always in reference to this organ of government. It houses the Hopi Tribal Council, and some writers tend to refer to the whole organization by that name. But this does not reflect local usage, and it fails to recognize the extensive growth,

over the last three decades, of departments—Education, Health, Lands, Water Resources, etc.—which, in many respects, comprise a civil service independent of the particular elected officials of the Council. All of these collectively are referred to locally as "the Hopi Tribe." The Council itself—an elected body, comprising a chairman, vice-chairman, and village representatives—remains only partly representative of the Hopi people, with several villages refusing to participate. Although there have been strenuous moves recently by some groups to send representatives from Hotvela, Songoopavi, and Lower Munqapi (the first two comprise two of the largest population centers), this is still resisted by many who refuse to recognize the Council. But anti-Council traditionalists often have extensive dealings with branches of the civil-service side of Tribal government, which are housed in the same complex of buildings in Kiqötsmovi. "The Hopi Tribe" is often used to refer to this physical complex of buildings as well.

6. Arnold Krupat's (1996) discussion of cultural, political, and intellectual sovereignty, and its associations with separatism and essentialization of Native identities and narratives, is highly pertinent here. Anthropologists would do well to enter more fully into the fray of interdisciplinary relationships with emergent ethnic (here Native American) studies, and their poetics and politics.

7. The reference, of course, is to Eve Sedgwick's (1990) lucid account of the cyclic reproduction of ignorance and effacement of homosexual life in American and European society.

8. For a penetrating inquiry into the presence and reception of anthropologists at Zuni, see Pandey 1972.

9. The fieldwork employed several Hopi researchers, some of whom subsequently became well-known figures, including the painter Fred Kabotie, and Elizabeth White (Polingaysi Qoyawayma), who wrote a well-known autobiography (1964), and who acted as host to later parties of visiting anthropologists at her house in Kiqötsmovi. Like Kabotie, White was a major figure in Hopi arts, storied for her innovative pottery. For the outside world—which frequently fetishizes Indianness through primitivist projections of craft-art (see Chapter 6)—these artistic practices form their principal identities; within the community, each was prominent in various other social fields (see also Kabotie 1977).

10. I just include those Hopi scholars with formal academic attachments: Sekaquaptewa is a cultural and linguistic anthropologist, Jeanne is a linguist, Dukepoo is a geneticist, Lomawaima is a cultural historian and museologist.

11. Durkheim and Mauss's chief example, drawing upon Cushing's work, is Zuni, "because it has been the best and most completely observed among them," but they explicitly include Hopi, too (1963:54 n.1). Mauss's fondness for Cushing's analyses of Zuni (e.g., Mauss 1938), throughout a period when they were marginalized in American anthropological circles, persisted

into later French anthropology, notably by Lévi-Strauss (see below), who treats Hopi totemic ideology as a transformation of Zuni (e.g., Lévi-Strauss 1955, 1966).

12. Zuni, of course, is Benedict's primary Pueblo example. But she discusses Hopi practices in several passages of "The Pueblos of New Mexico" in *Patterns of Culture* (Benedict 1934:passim). Hopi Kachina initiation served as a primary example of un-Apollonian Pueblo tendencies in criticisms of Benedict by other Pueblo specialists (Barnouw 1963:46). Again, the Hopi have often been lumped with Zuni and other Pueblos in general analyses.

13. Both these works have received more than usual attention outside the field of Hopi studies. Alice Schlegel's characterizations of Hopi gender equality caught a tide of feminist interest in identifying non-Western counter-patriarchies. Ramón Gutiérrez's more recent work on Pueblo versus Hispanic gender and power, is storied among historians (it has garnered numerous major awards) and Pueblos alike; though the latter (including Pueblo women, who apparently hound him at conferences) react with less favor (see Native American Studies Center 1993). Its academic success is baffling, given its fantastical ethnohistoric reconstruction of Pueblo libidinous female sociosexual power and male blood-cultism (his main references to Pueblo warfare are borrowed from Plains ethnography, and to penile bloodletting, from Maya ethnohistory), and its seriously flawed ethnography, notably here of Hopi ideas about kachinas, political leadership, and marriage (Gutierrez 1991:3-36, passim).

14. I cannot exclude myself here either. Following the Musangnuvi Home Dance a few years back, I was quietly wending my way down the hill-path from the village, when an earnest, not in the least subdued, voice shattered my contemplations with "Excuse me, excuse me! Are you an anthropologist?" I shrank into the pathway, seeking to avoid overt identification by a phrase that can be the local equivalent of "Are you a leper?" From my bemused state of invaded privacy, I brushed him off, not without some inner irony, "No, I am just a tourist, like you." Like some of Barbara Tedlock's (1992) encounters with other outsiders at Zuni, he had cracked my delicate shell of self-identification as "the culturally sensitive outsider." In hindsight, I wanted to say to him, "Yes, I am, but I am not like those other anthropologists." For some Hopis, I am indeed like any other anthropologist who has "made a career off Hopi culture," and occasionally I am bluntly reminded of this.

15. Just some of these are: (1) monographs: Clemmer 1978, 1995; Malotki, 1983; Malotki and Lomatuway'ma 1987, 1987a; A. Geertz 1987, 1987a, 1994; Whiteley 1988, 1988a; Loftin 1991; Wyckoff 1990; Adams 1991; Levy 1992; Wright 1994; (2) coffee-table and photographic books: Page and Page 1982, Webb and Weinstein 1987 [1973], Wright et al. 1986, Casagrande and Bourns 1983, Long 1992; (3) reprints of older ethnograph-

ies: Bourke 1884, Titiev 1944, Fewkes (several, e.g., 1903, 1926), Bradfield 1995 [1973]; (4) dissertations and theses: Malotki (published in 1979), Jeanne 1978, Whiteley 1983, Sanner 1992, Brenton 1994, McLeod 1994.

16. The Hopi Tribe's Cultural Preservation Office sought for a considerable time to prevent publication of the dictionary.

17. See, for example, Kammer 1980, Benedek 1992, Aberle 1993, Brugge 1994, American Anthropological Association 1986-92; some of the AAA Navajo-Hopi Land Dispute Panel's reports are more evenhanded, though the leaning has been more toward the problems of Navajo relocatees than toward Hopi losses of lands and resources to Navajo expropriation. One of the few pro-Hopi assessments is Feher-Elston 1988; the apparent temerity of espousing such a view called forth a virulent response from Navajo scholars (Brugge 1994).

18. This brought Fred Eggan, Edward Spicer, Watson Smith, Emory Sekaquaptewa, Alice Schlegel, Louis Hieb, and others to speak to an audience of sometimes polite, sometimes dissenting Hopis at the Civic Center in Kiqötsmovi. A particularly interesting interchange between Fred Eggan and Fred Kabotie, his long-term acquaintance (who had worked with anthropologists on the Peabody Museum's excavation of Awat'ovi, as well as on Laura Thompson's personality study), showed that Hopi critiques of anthropological interpretations of their life are by no means new.

19. This was led by Fred Eggan and Richard Clemmer, and included Charles Adams, Richard Ford, John and Carlotta Connelly, Ekkehart Malotki, Shuichi Nagata, Alfonso Ortiz, Alice Schlegel, Barton Wright, Robert Rhodes, and myself. The papers presented at the seminar have never been published as a collection, though several have appeared individually.

20. E.g., SITES 1979; Washburn 1980, 1995; Bean 1989; Kunze 1988.

21. Notably by Helga Teiwes of Arizona State Museum, Susanne Page (e.g., Page and Page 1982), Jens Jensen of the Danish National Museum, and Victor Masayesva (e.g., Masayesva and Younger 1983).

22. These include: *Hopi: Songs of the Fourth World* (1984, Pat Ferrero), *Broken Rainbow* (1986, by Victoria Mudd), *Techqua Ikachi,* (1989, Anka Schmidt), *The Hopi Way* (1995, overseen by David Wason), and *Hisatsinmuy Navoti'am/Words of Our Ancients* (1997, Paige Martinez).

23. Masayesva's films include *Hopiit, Itam Hakim Hopiit, Ritual Clowns, Pott Starr,* and *Imagining Indians.*

24. This is Hillerman's *The Dark Wind,* which Robert Redford subsequently made into a feature film, partly shot on the Hopi Reservation with some Hopi extras. The dissonance of Hopi and Hollywood views on that film is one of Victor Masayesva's themes in *Imagining Indians.*

25. Beginning in 1975, publication of the Traditionalist newsletter *Techqua Ikachi: Land and Life* by James Koots from Hotvela, and its recent transformation onto the Internet (http://www.timesoft.com/hopi/tech-

qua.htm), has particularly appealed to young, mystically inclined whites, by reworking traditional Hopi knowledge into a universalist frame. (Thomas Banyacya has been especially instrumental in this regard also; see A. Geertz 1994.)

26. Such Othering has historically defined "the rest" often by an absence—as opposed to presence in "the West"—of language, souls, science, history, religion, and so forth. Othering of the New World has a distinguished genealogy, from Columbus through Montaigne and Locke to Todorov. And to the old absences—*sans roi, sans foi, sans loi*—recent anthropology seems to be adding another: *sans soi*.

27. By privileging "experience" I am opening myself to criticism for essentializing and naturalizing here too. Joan Scott's problematization (1991) of "experience" is pertinent in this regard. But the road of anti-essentialism and anti-naturalism is, I fear, the path of infinite regress, bestrewn only with corpses (denaturalized, of course!).

28. The marginalization of Native Americans from the field of anthropology (Chapter 6) is mirrored in the frequent marginalization of "post-Indian" critics from contemporary high-critical discourse, where the four non-Natives mentioned are systematically and regularly cited, whereas Native critics are, what?—insufficiently Other in academic fashion ratings?

29. For a series of arguments on relations between the "Native" and the "anthropological" see Biolsi and Zimmerman 1997.

30. I do not mean to single out either Radcliffe-Brown or Crapanzano as particular targets; both represent general disciplinary trends of their historical moments. And both have redeeming features: Radcliffe-Brown's functionalist rigor, for example, and Crapanzano's thoroughgoing attention to complexities in Western senses of the self (unlike other recent anthropologists—see below).

31. Some that continue to inspire are: Basso 1996, Brightman 1993, Brody 1981, Lavie 1990, Meigs 1983, Price 1983, Tsing 1993.

32. Crapanzano (1992:333-34 n.1), like many other university anthropologists, entirely neglects practicing anthropology, privileging the academic sphere as definitive of disciplinary praxis (his contrast is with psychoanalysis).

33. *The Tewa World* (1969) continues to shine an anthropological beacon in this regard.

34. This was somewhat prior to the transformation of the New Mexico populace by the major influx of Hollywood, Texas, and New York wealth, and a concomitantly intensified commodification of local culture, that took off in the 1980s. While the long-term romanticization of the Southwest, associated with Mary Austin, Mabel Dodge Luhan, and the Taos artists, was well under way by the early twentieth century, this was a trickle compared to the recent deluge of haut-bourgeois Anglos, especially to Santa Fe.

35. I was officially attached to the Department of Ethnology and Prehis-

tory in the Pitt-Rivers Museum, but all classes took place at the Institute, and they have since combined more formally. I did, however, benefit—by magical contagion, as it were—from close association with the colonial anthropology of General Pitt-Rivers: I was assigned an office in his field caravan, which the museum maintained on its grounds.

36. Among legions of commentators, Theodore Roosevelt, hardly a novice traveler, noted, in a letter (4 September 1913) to Henry Cabot Lodge, "I have never seen anything more absorbingly interesting than the ceremonies attending the Snake Dance" (Roosevelt 1925, ii:437).

37. The macho explorer ethic of fieldwork, ritually requiring work in some remote locale preferably infested with virulent undiscovered parasites, mystically glorifies privation and suffering, crucial for the rite of passage to be deemed a success. Well, true enough, I did not come down with African river blindness or even a mild bout of malaria in Arizona (though bubonic plague was on the rise and hantavirus came along later—I did not get these either, however). I did spend a good deal of time recovering from various gastrointestinal afflictions probably caused by eating by hand from communal food bowls around which a fly or two had chanced to land. A particularly memorable occasion involved a mile of crawling home on hands and knees in the dark to Paaqavi along the frozen February ground, following *Powamuy* night dances at Hotvela, retching all the way from too much *haru'kwivi* (*Powamuy* bean stew).

38. "Grandfather David," an astute politician and skilled rhetorician within the Traditionalist faction (of which Harry was deeply skeptical), served as guru to many young whites at the time, and was often seen around Hotvela supported by young white acolytes (see A. Geertz 1987b).

39. One of the more striking memories is of Harry and I watching the attempted assassination of Ronald Reagan in 1981 on his television set, in company with a medicine-man from Kiqötsmovi. Profoundly concerned about a society that could repeatedly do this to its leaders—the same society whose Agency schoolteacher had tied him, when he was a child, to the porch frame of the Paaqavi BIA schoolhouse and publicly flogged him for truancy (beginning a long line of racist derogations both on and off the Reservation)—he was also markedly compassionate about the president's condition.

40. One of these was to compare the founding of Paaqavi to the national origin narrative of the United States. Following the Orayvi split of 1906, his people moved to Hotvela (where he was born in a lamb corral next to a crude shelter), and shortly thereafter, a portion of the Hostiles returned to Orayvi under troop escort (see Whiteley 1988, 1988a). Three years later they were again driven out of Orayvi to found Paaqavi. "It's just like the pilgrims," Harry would say. "First they were forced out of England and went to Holland. Then they had to leave there and went back to England, before finally leaving to come to America." The several ironies of this analog (in-

cluding telling it to an Englishman) do not affect its explanatory virtues and the mythological sense of epochal innovation the Orayvi split holds for Third Mesa Hopi historical consciousness.

41. Again there was a virtual clairvoyance about this. I recently re-noticed, on an old tape, his remark to other Hopi elders that to begin with he had been unwilling to talk to me, but had changed his mind explicitly because he thought that I might be useful in the land dispute with the Navajos. This was seven years before my formal involvement as an expert witness in the 1934 Reservation case (see below).

42. This view of the *sipaapuni* shrine is not shared by many other Hopis, to whom it is a very sacred place (as indeed it was to Harry—he just rejected a literalist interpretation of it).

43. James Clifford's (1997) recent recommendations to replace "dwelling" as a metaphorical stance of understanding with "traveling"—a version, I presume, of "nomad thought"—reflects his identification of the "predicament of culture," in general, as a matter of fragments, borders, and unstable spaces. I do not find this adequate to cultural explanation, as my insistence on an identifiable Hopi society, culture, and history within a deeply textured dwelt-in space should suggest.

44. While I have now gathered several hundred place-names, this material will not be published until and unless the Hopi Tribe desires it. A key concern is the tourist commodification of Hopi places and place-names that would undoubtedly ensue from publication (cf. Basso 1996).

45. I take this quote of Said's from my Sarah Lawrence colleague Arnold Krupat. We have had numerous conversations on such issues, but in the present instance, I am taking the passage specifically from his quotation of it in *The Voice in the Margin* (1989:48).

46. Outsiders have typically focused on his position in the factional division of Tribal Council supporters and Traditionalists (e.g., Clemmer 1978), vilifying him and his family for their embrace of the Council, the Mormonism of his elder brother Wayne and their mother Helen, and their cattle-ranching operation. The latter involves the frankly peculiar idea that, since cattle were somehow not a part of a long-term Hopi economic pattern (which is entirely false—cattle-herding has occurred at Third Mesa since the seventeenth century, following introduction by Franciscan priests—see Whiteley 1988:144), this represented the Sekaquaptewas's commitment to unmodified progressivism. Some (e.g., Benedek 1992:145) have suggested that the Sekaquaptewas's interests in cattle were a prime motive for the Hopi drive to regain access to the Joint Use Area of the 1882 Hopi Reservation—an argument I find about as plausible as the idea that the Gulf War owed to George Bush's personal stock options.

47. Lévi-Strauss's notorious enslavement to Saussurean synchrony via the logical privileging of *langue* over *parole* has fixed structure unnecessarily.

And his reduction of culture to a system of communicative exchanges—of messages (in language, myth, and ritual), women (in kinship and marriage), and goods (in economics)—is not the aspect of his approach that I find useful. But his multiplex attention to levels of cultural signification (sociological, cosmological, economic, technical, geographic, etc.), their mutuality and reciprocal fields of reference (e.g., 1966, 1968, 1970, 1995), inspires the possibility for analytical holism that I am recommending. And his overall neglect by fin-de-siècle American anthropologists—scared off, perhaps, by Derrida's (1977) philosophically hermetic, decidedly unethnographic critique—is a tragic, needless loss to serious anthropological thought.

48. In trying to locate my arguments at an extremity, some critics (e.g., Clemmer 1995, Levy 1992) have suggested that my critique of Eggan's analyses is encompassing. It is not. Both *Social Organization of the Western Pueblos* and Titiev's *Old Oraibi* remain enormous contributions to the understanding of Hopi social order. My engagement with the ideas of these texts is toward critical improvement rather than wholesale displacement.

49. Kluckhohn and Leighton's work on the Navajo (1946) has held a more enduring legacy.

50. I largely stay with Thompson's 1945 article "Logico-Aesthetic Integration in Hopi Culture," although substantial passages recur almost verbatim in her popular level text (Thompson and Joseph 1944), and in her monograph (1950). In both instances, greater generalization elides some salient specificities present in her 1945 article.

51. I am least satisfied with Thompson's characterization of Hopi conceptions of nature; it seems to me that she attributes an autonomous mechanism to natural processes that is unwarranted by Hopi talk about, and action in relation to, different species. In my experience, Hopis may attribute intentionality (and thus optation) to other species, including eagles, burros, coyotes, ravens, etc., and to the subsistent forms of the spirits of the dead. It is interesting to note that while much of this passage survived unaltered into *Culture in Crisis* (Thompson 1950:133-34), the "reciprocity principle" gets transformed into "the rhythmic correlativity principle," perhaps suggesting doubt about what was identified. Again, in my understanding, if ritual is performed correctly, it works, not as the mechanical compulsion of determinate natural reciprocities, but more by performed persuasion of intentional supernatural forces, i.e., that the ritual is being properly, prayerfully, and humbly conducted, and therefore deserving of the requested response (by animate cloud beings, etc.).

52. The term is *naawakna* (Thompson and Joseph 1944:138 n.2, citing Kennard 1937). *Naawakna* is also "to want," as in *pahannaanawaknaqam*, "those willing/wanting the white man's way," a main Hopi term for "Friendlies" or "progressives" and its opposite *qapahannaanawaknaqam*, "Hostiles" or "traditionalists."

53. And indeed the same is true for Navajo traditional thought (e.g., Witherspoon 1977; Ladd 1957)—another philosophical island in a sea of Western influence.

54. Indeed this is so despite Dorinne Kondo's (1990:38) admonition about the cultural embeddedness of "subjectivity" in Western metaphysical conceptions.

55. Battaglia (1995:8) identifies the problematics of this opposition, and several contributions to that volume work to critique it, identifying relational selfhoods in various Western contexts. Nonetheless, the reader is left with a sense that the opposition persists—it has simply been shifted to a more abstract, nonlocational "center" versus "periphery" axis of cultural identifications.

56. The 1979 revision of "Rite One" deleted "which is," rendering the emphasis on dividual sociality somewhat less transparent. Some more conservative churches continue to use the 1928 version. But the same sentiments are also clearly present in the modernized alternative postcommunion prayer of "Rite Two," a liturgical innovation ratified in 1979: ". . . that we are living members of the Body of your Son . . ." (Episcopal Church 1979:366).

57. Collectivist sociality in the military is another prime example.

58. Interestingly enough, the earlier formations of cultural studies (particularly in Richard Hoggart's influence) placed a strong value on the creativity and imagination of the "individual as the agency of history" (Grossberg 1993:37). But in the typical late twentieth-century theoretical move away from individuality to totality as the locus of significant agency, "postmodern cultural studies" now produces an anonymous subject, the result of ideological effects, reflecting the diagnostic antihumanism of Foucault:

> The subject—as actor, audience, communicator or agent—is itself a construction, the articulated and articulating movement within and between apparatuses. . . . This vision of "nomadic subjectivity" existing only within the movement of and between apparatuses rejects both the existential subject who has a single unified identity, and the deconstructed, permanently fragmented subject. (Grossberg 1993:60-61)

59. Most Hopi commentators or consultants in this text remain anonymous in deference to general Hopi preferences. Recently, there has been a call by some Hopis for identification and self-identification in the texts of anthropologists, both for proper attribution to the source of information and as a check on the authority of the ideas expressed. I remain ambivalent about using personal names, however, because of the widespread antipathy toward singular identification, even though I would be pleased to do so as a guarantee of the authority of certain interpretations. I occasionally identify an individual either by a locally known Hopi name, or by a more widely

known English name, or, more occlusively, by a generic descriptor ("a Coyote clan man," etc.), but most individuals remain anonymous.

60. Whorf's analysis calls to mind Heidegger's (1962) theory of being, particularly of existence as an emergence-into-presence. A fuller explanation of the manifested-manifesting and objective-subjective premises of Hopi metaphysics may be possible with the *Dasein/Sein* analytic, although I leave this for another occasion, which will require a strenuous disengagement, if such is possible, of Heidegger's Nazism from his philosophy.

61. Whorf's own translation of *natwani* suggests the additional glosses "the practiced-upon," "the tried-for," and the "in-preparation" (Whorf 1956:149). He misses the essential emphasis on selfhood that Hopis have foregrounded in conversations with me.

62. My complaint above is not about the *concept* of dividuality, which I find important; it is about its restriction to a narrow sphere of cultural reference.

63. Malinowski's infamous diary (1967) illustrates this in negative terms, and Thomas Buckley's (1989) poignant evocation of the emotional dependency of Alfred Kroeber—that arch-scientistic ethnographer—on Yurok leader Robert Spott, is a particularly sharp portrait of the slippage between anthropology's formal reproduction of colonial relationality and the actualities of its interpersonal engagement.

2. UNPACKING HOPI "CLANS"

1. The research on which this chapter is based took place over four years beginning in 1980 with a fourteen-month period of fieldwork. The research—into the historical development of Paaqavi—was supported by: the Village of Bacavi, Sigma Xi, the Frieda Butler Foundation, Byron Harvey III, John R. Wilson, the Weatherhead Foundation, and the University of New Mexico. For most helpful comments, I would like to thank Philip K. Bock, Harry W. Basehart, and Louise Lamphere. The remaining faults are, of course, my own.

2. From east to west the mesa-top villages are arranged as follows:
First Mesa: Walpi, Sitsomovi, Tewa
Second Mesa: Songoopavi, Supawlavi, Musangnuvi
Third Mesa: Orayvi, Kiqötsmovi, Paaqavi, Hotvela
Forty-five highway miles to the west of Third Mesa lie the two villages of Upper and Lower Munqapi, which trace their principal heritage to their mother village, Orayvi.

Good general accounts of Hopi society, economy, and religion appear in the Smithsonian Institution's *Handbook of North American Indians*, vol. 9 *The Southwest*, edited by Alfonso Ortiz (1979).

3. Spelling of Hopi words follows Malotki's (1978:201-2) standardized

orthography. In Table 1, Hopi clan names have been standardized. English translations of Hopi clan names in parentheses (Fire, Water Coyote, Water-House) are those conventionally given in anthropological texts; they are not accurate translations. In particular, I disagree with "Water Coyote" for *paa'-isngyam*. *Paa'isaw*, the species referred to, is *Vulpes macrotis*, the desert fox.

4. In fact, there are several ways of referring to phratry groups in Hopi although they do not translate easily into a singular English noun. *Naanangakvim* is a term in frequent use meaning all one's phratry relatives; *amumumya*, literally "they together," refers to all the descent groups that together comprise a phratry.

5. English translations of Hopi societies are usually given as follows: *Aa'alt* = Two Horn; *Kwaakwant* = One Horn; *Taatawkyam* = Singers; *Sakwalelent* = Blue Flute; *Masilelent* = Gray (Drab) Flute; *Tsu'tsut* = Snake; *Tsöötsöpt* = Antelope; *Katsina* = Kachina. The remainder—*Wuwtsimt, Sosyalt, Mamrawt, Lalkont, Owaqölt, Powamuy*—are left untranslated.

6. "*Wuya*" (or, more accurately, *wu'ya*) is the clan's primary symbolic emblem, the "heart of the clan," and may have tangible representation in a fetish or in ritual objects of different kinds.

7. Mööyi is also the term for a grandchild, but *kya'a-mööyi* is recognized as a distinct dyad in Hopi practice.

8. Of seventy high officers listed in Titiev's Appendix 2 (1944:242–43), seven (10 percent) obtained their positions through patrilateral ties, and at least two, and probably four (5.7 percent), through affinal ties.

3. THE INTERPRETATION OF POLITICS

The research on which this chapter is based took place over five years, beginning in 1980 with a fourteen-month period of resident fieldwork. The research—into the historical development of Paaqavi—was supported by: the Village of Bacavi, Sigma Xi, the Frieda Butler Foundation, Byron Harvey III, John R. Wilson, the Weatherhead Foundation, and the University of New Mexico. An earlier version of this chapter was presented to the symposium "Inequality in Native North America: Continuity and Change," held at the Fourth International Congress of Americanists in Bogotá (1985). I am most grateful to the participants, especially Shuichi Nagata, for their comments, and to an anonymous reader for *Man*. Travel to the Congress was facilitated by a grant from the American Council of Learned Societies. While in press in 1987, the paper was presented also at the University of Chicago Department of Anthropology Faculty-Student Seminar. Particularly helpful comments, which have shaped some subsequent thinking, were provided by Marshall Sahlins, Ray Fogelson, and Terry Turner.

1. This does not mean that women are by definition debarred from access to political/supernatural power. A recent example saw Mina Lansa as

head of the village of Orayvi. Neither was this a function of social change; at the turn of the century, Nasilewnöm, a woman of the *Piikyas* clan, was titular head of the village of Munqapi. Female heads of the three women's sodalities clearly have some access to the sort of powers discussed, but all these sodalities (*Maraw, Lakon, Owaqöl*) have preeminent male heads. Further, female curers, while not common, are well-known and still practicing (in the 1980s).

2. I did not encounter this term in the field (it literally means "chiefly people"). Recent fieldworkers at Third Mesa (S. Nagata and E. Malotki, personal communications) concur that *pavansinom* is in more general use for the opposed category to *sukavungsinom*. Nequatewa (1936:125 n.1) refers to all three of these categories. He regards *mongsinom* as superior to *pavansinom*. His characterization of these two as "first class" and "middle class," respectively, and of *sukavungsinom* as "low class" is, I think, oversimplified, however.

3. This may be a reference to Yukiwma's ally, Lomahongiwma, who was put up by the Hostiles as an alternative *Kikmongwi* to Loololma in the 1890s. Lomahongiwma was head of the Spider clan and chief-priest of the Blue Flute ceremony. Part of his claim to be *Kikmongwi* rested on this ceremonial role, which the Hostiles regarded as equal in importance to the Bear clan's *Soyalangw* ceremony (both have solstitial underpinnings).

4. The War Chief is mentioned last because in Hopi mythology—particularly migration traditions—he was always supposed to bring up the rear, in order to protect the other leaders.

5. The sodalities which Yukiwma lists conform to what in Chapter 2 I term First and Second Order Societies.

6. It is possible that differing interpretations of the sources of, and solutions for, societal stress in late nineteenth-century Orayvi produced a conflict of roles between the *Kikmongwi* and the *Qaletaqmongwi*, which may have been part of the friction that led to the split.

7. The political effects of secret knowledge have received increasing attention in recent ethnography (e.g. Barth 1975; Lewis 1980; Murphy 1980; Rubinstein 1981; Bellman 1984; Lindstrom 1984; Traube n.d.; Fardon 1985a). Secrecy, of course, serves other social and personal functions, too. Luhrmann's (1986) analysis of middle-class British magical cults does much to clarify the social and psychological effects of secrecy in ritual practices. A full consideration of the effects of institutionalized secrecy in Hopi society should include an examination of the sort of psychological ramifications Luhrmann discusses. This, however, goes beyond my present scope.

8. Interestingly enough, after this chapter was first published, I learned Dorothy Eggan had used the identical metaphor (1956:362) about fear of witchcraft being even more effective in social control than fear of the electric

chair; this was mere serendipity (I had not read her article at that point), but the coincidence lends my usage welcome support.

9. Some Third Mesa people say a tunnel ran from Yukiwma's house to Loololma's (the factional leaders in 1900); there they would meet to jointly plan events connected with the Orayvi split. This may be an idealization, although tunnels are well-known in Puebloan archaeological sites.

4. HOPITUTUNGWNI

1. Translations of this famous haiku proliferate (Sato 1983); mine is taken from R. H. Blyth (ibid.:154).

2. My special thanks go to Herschel Talashoma for the text he provided for this inquiry, and for graciously putting up with me over the years. Other Hopi consultants prefer to remain anonymous. For the same reason of privacy, most of the names discussed herein are not those of living people. Earlier versions of this chapter were presented at "Persons and Selves in Pueblo and Northwest Coast Societies," a session of the 1988 American Anthropological Association annual meetings in Phoenix, and at Sarah Lawrence College in February 1990. A number of people have helped greatly to clarify some issues; in particular, remarks by discussants Alfonso Ortiz and Ray Fogelson in Phoenix, and by Lina Brock, Roland Dollinger, and Danny Kaiser at Sarah Lawrence are much appreciated. My deep thanks for extensive written comments go to Arnold Krupat (most especially), Armin Geertz, and Bob Zimmerman. None but I, however, bear the blame for what remains.

3. Recent considerations of naming practices that discuss one or more of these features and/or others include Ramos 1974; Kendall 1980; Barnes 1980, 1982; Dalforo 1982; Willis 1982; Moore 1984; the articles by Maybury-Lewis, Maxwell, Rosaldo, and Mithun in Tooker 1984; Harrison 1985; Lindstrom 1985; Glasse 1987; Revard 1987; Kuschel 1988, and several articles (among which that by Godfrey Lienhardt is particularly noteworthy) in a special issue on names of the *Journal of the Anthropological Society of Oxford,* 1988.

4. Some recent exceptions to this are to be found in the references cited in note 3. To be sure, many English names originally had denotative meaning; Peter, for example, derives from the Greek *petra,* "a rock" (and see Dunkling and Gosling 1983). And there are other exceptions. Lienhardt (1988:107) indicates women's names denoting flowers or spring and summer months and also some Puritan names with semantic content; clearly such names as Faith, Hope, and Charity betoken moral precepts. Some people name their children for sporting events or social luminaries. Likewise, writers from Shakespeare (Sir Toby Belch) to Sheridan (Mrs. Malaprop), from Joyce (Stephen Dedalus) to Pynchon (Isaiah Two Four) have used names,

often semantically significant, to evoke character, mood, or social conditions. And then there is rock star Frank Zappa's daughter, Moon Unit Two. But for the most part, it remains true that in ordinary life, proper names point out, refer to, or address; they do not denote images constituted apart from the subject's identity.

5. Two articles by R. H. Barnes (1980, 1982) are particularly useful recent treatments of Native American naming systems. And since this chapter was first published, the magisterial summary by David and Katherine French (1996) has appeared.

6. The resurrection of Marcel Mauss's 1938 essay on "the person" (Carrithers, Lukes, and Collins 1985) has renewed a misconception of naming practices in Pueblo societies. Mauss characterizes Pueblo names as drawn from a limited fund conferred by clans on their own members. Names then designate social characters in a fixed dramatis personae reproduced from one generation to the next—reflecting an underdevelopment of individuated persons and of selves as conscious agents (by contrast to the developed Western versions). Mauss's principal Pueblo examples are Zuni and Hopi, and, while he may be more accurate on Zuni names (though whether this entitles him to infer inchoate persons and selves is a different matter), he is quite wrong with regard to Hopi (this was my theme in earlier versions of this chapter)—in a way, I believe, that substantially undermines his overall argument.

7. I owe the inspiration for this emphasis on the "narrative" construction of Hopi social persons to Armin Geertz (personal communication and 1990), who, in a rather different way, has persuasively argued for "narrated ethics" in the construction of persons in ritual contexts.

8. Hopi is traditionally an unwritten language, so the kind of proper-name marking of initial capitalization is not present, as such, in Hopi discourse (cf. Mithun's [1984:40] remarks on Mohawk naming). Nonetheless, Hopi marks proper names both nominally by the term *tungwni* (pl. *tuutungwni*) "name," and verbally by *tungwa*, "to name it." *Maatsiwa*, "be named," is commonly used to identify the name of a person, e.g., *ya um/pam hin maatsiwa?*, "how are you/he/she named?" to which I would respond, *nu' Peter yan maatsiwa*, "I Peter this way am named." Likewise *maatsiwa* is used in the ritual conferring of a name, which ends with *X yan um maatsiwni*, "you will be called X" (Voth 1905a:54).

9. I have criticized conventional usages of the terms "clan" and "phratry" in Hopi ethnography (Chapter 2, and 1988). They are still useful shorthand terms for Hopi social groups, so long as the usage is not taken to imply formally and functionally discrete social-structural units.

10. Some accounts indicate a tendency to choose a member of the father's clan to serve as godfather/godmother (cf. Nagata n.d.:8 n.3). This does not correspond with my experience or with most published accounts.

11. In addition to what I have learned from Hopi consultants, I am draw-

ing here, particularly for the salt expedition and for death-names, from a very useful paper by Shuichi Nagata (n.d.a) that combines his own research with that of several prior accounts. Maitland Bradfield (1973:passim) also provides informative summary remarks of published accounts of Hopi naming. I have not personally inquired into whether name-giving at death still occurs (a sensitive ritual matter I prefer to stay away from).

12. Voth (1901:122-25) and Titiev (1944:222-26) provide the best available accounts of *Patsavu* at Orayvi.

13. This very image—a rare one indeed—is captured in a photograph by Kate Cory at Orayvi (Wright et al. 1986:photograph 4); for another photograph in this sequence, see Figure 4.1.

14. The association between imagist poetry and haiku is not accidental. Ezra Pound, for example, was explicitly influenced by Japanese styles and imagery, and was responsible for bringing some Japanese poetry to a Western audience (see, e.g., Ueda 1965).

15. Barnes (1982:221) points out a similar pattern with some Siouan names.

16. This male name (spelled Sekaquaptewa) was taken as a marital surname by the bearer's wife, Helen, the subject of a well-known autobiography (1969); it is the inherited patronymic of their sons, including Abbott, a former chairman of the Hopi Tribal Council, and Emory, an anthropologist and linguist at the University of Arizona.

17. Despite some claims that -*tiwa* is an unusual verbal form (e.g., Voth 1905b:71), I follow Malotki's position here (1979:371). I thank Armin Geertz (personal communication) for pointing out this and some other linguistic discrepancies.

18. This account of the name—the fullest I have heard—derives from the son of the name-giver, who assured me that his mother explained it to him. Slight modifications on this account exist within the extended family of those who bear the name as an inherited patronymic.

19. By leaving out here the specific performative context of myth in the telling (for which, e.g., Sherzer 1987 has so persuasively argued), I do not mean to underplay its significance. It just seems less important for the interpretation of names, which are spoken in numerous genres of discourse and depend more on the ideas of myth rather than their specific narrative utterances.

20. Voth spells it variously Úuna (1905a:59) and Úna (1905b:81).

21. Ekkehart Malotki (1983) has trenchantly critiqued Whorf's characterization of the Hopi language as "timeless." Whorf (1956:147) contends also that the Hopi language formally configures an emphasis on "events" (or "eventings") which "are expressed mainly as outlines, colors, movements, and other perceptive reports"—as opposed to the static "things" emphasized by SAE (Standard Average European) languages. While Whorf's assignment

of intrinsic perceptual qualities to the Hopi language itself is in some disrepute, the phenomenological emphasis he has identified in Hopi worldview is nonetheless clearly foregrounded in the cognitive style of name-images.

22. Voth (1905b:73) also records the formal naming of a pipe in the context of the Blue Flute ceremony. The naming of kivas shares some features of personal naming, too, but names of ritual objects and places are beyond my scope here.

23. Keith Basso's emphasis on the mental-pictorial features of Western Apache place-names (1988) is relevant here also. As one of his consultants explains (ibid.:107-8), characterizing a conversation centrally involving place-name usage:

We gave that woman . . . pictures to work on in her mind. . . . We gave her clear pictures with placenames. So her mind went to those places, standing in front of them as our ancestors did long ago. That way she could see what happened there long ago. She could hear stories in her mind, perhaps hear our ancestors speaking. She could reknow the wisdom of our ancestors.

And now see Basso 1996, which expands his account of Apache place-naming and includes the 1988 paper from which this quotation is taken.

5. BURNING CULTURE

Acknowledgments: Earlier versions of this chapter were presented at Dartmouth College in 1989, and at the 1990 Annual Meetings of the American Anthropological Association in New Orleans. I am grateful for comments at Dartmouth by Hoyt Alverson and Michael Green, and in New Orleans by William Powers. My thanks also, for valuable critiques, to Shuichi Nagata, Karl Schwerin, Arnold Krupat, and Christopher Pinney.

1. See, for example, Thompson 1978; Giddens 1979; 1984; Sahlins 1981; 1985; Archer 1988; R. Rosaldo 1980, 1989; Comaroff and Comaroff 1991.

2. By which I mean something quite different from the radical incommensurability Calvin Martin (1987) would derive from an extreme relativism.

3. A partial list of inquiries into the "person" should include, for example, Read 1955; Hallowell 1955; C. Geertz 1973a [1966]; M. Rosaldo 1980, 1984; Collins 1982; Shweder and Bourne 1984; Carrithers, Collins, and Lukes 1985; White and Kirkpatrick 1985; Battaglia 1990. Shweder (1984:12-17) includes some trenchant discussion on the cultural problematics of the self, and particularly on Geertz's notions of Balinese personhood. Sangren (n.d.) and Ewing (1990) offer powerful critiques of perspectives questioning the transcultural existence of persons and selves.

4. This view of intentionality, as index of self-conscious subjectivity, is

also the distinctive feature of personhood for Husserlian phenomenology (Rabinow and Sullivan 1987:6 n.6).

5. See also Giddens 1979:49-95.

6. I think this is also true of more recent, more inflected considerations (e.g., M. Rosaldo 1984, Battaglia 1990) that take a Hegelian, relational view of (Ilongot and Sabarl) personhood.

7. Geertz's (1966:4) definition of religion is: "(1) a system of symbols which acts to (2) establish powerful, pervasive, and long-lasting moods and motivations in men by (3) formulating conceptions of a general order of existence and (4) clothing these conceptions with such an aura of factuality that (5) the moods and motivations seems uniquely realistic."

8. The event is of ongoing remark in Hopi discourse and is recorded in print briefly by several authors, including A. Johnson (1933:174-76), Titiev (1944:208; 1972:80-81, 167), Johnson himself in *Hopi Hearings* (1955:174), Means (1960:126-28), Waters (1963:313; 1969:127-28), and Yava (1978:115). I first learned its date, which is recorded nowhere in the printed accounts, from a penciled record on the roof beam of a sheep-camp house in the Orayvi Valley. The record's author was Tuwahoyiwma, or Charles Fredericks (Bear clan), the chosen heir to succeed Loololma as *Kikmongwi*, "village chief," of Orayvi around 1904, but who withdrew in favor of his younger brother, Tawakwaptiwa. I was shown the record by Tuwahoyiwma's son, Jean Fredericks. It reads:

August 27th
1922
Johnson K
burned Alvona

9. I am most grateful to David Haury, Director and Archivist at the Mennonite Library and Archives, for permission to reprint this document, catalogue item no. M266.021356. It was printed by the General Conference of the Mennonite Church for internal church usage; it carries no date or place of publication. The first page is reproduced as figure 5.1.

I am unable to date the document specifically. Suderman's long tenure as missionary (c. 1929-53) does not help. No library accession date is marked (it was first checked out in 1949). Johnson's statement in Chapter 1 (Chapter 5 Appendix), that he had not attended a Hopi ceremony in eighteen years, may suggest the 1930s. From the precision of dates in Chapter 2, and seemingly also of Lomavitu's reportage, this part at least may have been set down close to the events themselves. A 1933 account (A. Johnson 1933:174-76) closely resembles part of the present text, but whether the author paraphrased the text itself, or Johnson's own spoken words (she was present, as a Baptist missionary), is not clear.

The text is reproduced exactly (apart from boldfaced headings): Capitalized words appear as such in the original; grammatical errors are left intact.

10. Titiev (n.d.:34) records a Bow clan woman still alive in 1932/3.

11. I am most grateful to Roxie McLeod, who has researched Waters's materials on the Hopi, for bringing this reference to my attention.

12. Interestingly enough, Johnson (Chapter 5 Appendix) uses the tradition of abandonment of the (corrupt) world below as a paradigm for his conversion: It may well have been paradigmatic, too, for the altar-burning.

13. It is highly significant, in view of what follows, that, according to Hopi historians (circumstantially supported by the available documentary record's calendrical dating to late (post-October) 1700 [Montgomery, Smith, and Brew 1949:21]) this destruction occurred during *Wuwtsim* rituals, while most of the men were in kivas.

14. Songoopavi, on Second Mesa, where the *Wuwtsim* system still thrives, has been the only village in several decades to put on *Sa'lako;* the most recent performance occurred in 1992.

15. This marks a parallel with the politically central Bow priesthood—a sodality rather than a clan—at Zuni (e.g., Eggan 1950:208).

16. Titiev's census notes of Orayvi (n.d.:34, 34a) record attributions, and specific instantiations, of witchcraft and madness to several Bow individuals.

17. This remained true until recent years; Musangnuvi and Songoopavi, the two villages where performances continue, have both closed the Snake Dance to non-Hopis since the mid-1980s.

18. He was born in mid-November (Hopi Hearings 1955:168)—probably around the time of *Wuwtsim*. Whether this influenced his later reputation is possible, although I cannot verify it. His parents were Sakwmasa, "Coyote clan" (a *Wuwtsim* and *Momtsit*, "Warriors' society" initiate) and Nakwahongqa, an officer in *Mamrawt* (the higher-order women's society) (Titiev n.d.:34).

19. My projection of ages (other than Johnson's, which he attests to himself) is based on a cross-comparison of a series of censuses beginning in 1892 (cf. Whiteley 1988:132, note).

20. He is pictured by Voth (1912:frontispiece) and in *The Mennonite* (12 April 1923:12). He led an expedition to Santa Fe in 1866–67 to seek the return of Hopi slaves taken by New Mexican raiders (e.g., Aitken 1931:378–81; Harrington 1931:227–30; the date is provided by Bailey 1966:121).

21. This orthodox Christian view of idolatry is contradicted by the (unorthodox) attribution of animacy by both Lomavitu and Johnson in subsequent paragraphs.

22. Johnson also consulted, therefore, with other leaders than among the Christian converts at Kiqötsmovi; Kuwannömtiwa was chief of Paaqavi, and a widely influential man in Hopi society more generally.

23. On *navoti* as a hermeneutic system, see Whiteley 1988:255. On Hopi

prophecy more generally, see Clemmer 1978:passim; A. Geertz 1987b, and, for a work devoted to the subject, A. Geertz 1994.

24. I disagree with Titiev's (1972:167) implication that remanufacture was easily possible. At present, thefts of prominent ritual objects sold to collectors and museums are deeply disturbing to those involved in the traditional ritual order. Since the theft of Taalawtumsi figures from Songoopavi in 1978, an event which made *Newsweek* (31 January 1983:32-33), no *Wuwtsim* initiations have been performed there (cf. *Gallup Independent* 6-18-1988:1-2), producing considerable trauma, which has manifested itself in social conflicts and deep-seated concerns over cultural preservation.

25. Elsewhere (Whiteley 1988:277-83) I have discussed some reasons for Hotvela's ritual resurrection and some Hopi interpretations of this.

26. His paternal grandfather, Qötsakwahu, was a leading officer, and his father participated—all three moved, for the purpose, from Paaqavi to Hotvela. Elsewhere (1988:277) I note the first Hotvela initiations as 1924. In going over some field notes, I located a reference to 1924 as the year *Patsavu* Kachinas were sent from Paaqavi to Hotvela (also led by Qötsakwahu). *Patsavu* occurs in the February following *Wuwtsim* initiations in November. While I cannot be certain, my inclination now is to place more reliance on this account, which would situate the initiations in 1923.

27. I have discussed (Whiteley 1988:281) the perspective—politically contested, to be sure—offered by older Third Mesa Hopis (including several from Hotvela) that rituals (specifically *Wuwtsim*) at Hotvela were merely aesthetic forms, since their essential supernatural power base had been terminated at the Orayvi split.

28. Titiev (1972:167) suggests that the power of the *wuvaapi* emanates from the altar itself. Commenting on the altar-burning, his consultant noted: ". . . Johnson displayed the objects for all to see. Orthodox Hopi were afraid to look lest they be stricken with the Al society's whip, but Christian Hopi looked freely."

29. Specific actions in private rituals are instanced, but these are—a century later—still too sensitive, from a Hopi perspective, to discuss in print (cf. Whiteley 1988:269).

30. Purification may occur by fire—the case with the villages of Awat'ovi and Pivanhonkyapi—or water: A current prophecy calls for a massive earthquake and subsequent flood caused by the deity Paalölöqangw, a water serpent, thrashing his tail (see Chapter 7). Another contemporary prophecy about *koyaanisqatsi*, "corrupt life" (a stage of moral, spiritual, and material chaos), is linked with subsequent world purification (possibly via Paalölöqangw's actions); this is a widespread idea in Hopi discourse.

31. Waters (1963:313), whose accounts of Hopi culture notoriously mix fact and fiction, lists, in addition to the altar, two elk horns and several special *mongkos*, "staffs of ritual office."

32. The Blue Flute altar, in the hands of the Hostile *Kookyangngyam,* Spider clan, was first taken to Paaqavi, and then later to Hotvela, where sodality performances continued probably into the 1940s (Whiteley 1988:199–200; 278).

33. Lillie Talavengqa, returned from Phoenix Indian School, was the novice. Frey concealed the plan to baptize, and secured Hopi presence by general invitation to a meal (Frey 1923:8).

34. In another account of the same events, Frey (1923:8) identifies this tradition specifically as *maqastutavo* ("fear tradition"). In Chapter 3 I argue that *maqastutavo,* a psychologically pervasive doctrine, is a powerful hegemonic force for social control.

35. Bourke (1884:281) records a similar Hopi sentiment in a somewhat cryptic account of the 1680 Pueblo Revolt: "He [the missionary] said that God had a Son, but couldn't tell who God's wife was, so the Moquis [Hopis] threw him over the precipice."

36. Lorenzo Hubbell Jr., of the Orayvi Trading Post.

37. Fijian conversions in the mid-nineteenth century exhibited a similarly transformative, rather than disjunctive, rationale (Sahlins 1985:37-40).

38. I am most grateful to David Haury for finding this reference.

39. Interest in preserving the objects was not limited to photography: Lorenzo Hubbell burst out of his trading post and offered him five hundred dollars for the altar. Tuwaletstiwa refused. Hubbell then offered him three hundred dollars for permission to photograph it. Again he refused. (Waters 1963:313)

40. Titiev (1972:81) also records this version (though he mistakes Johnson's son, Fred, for his father in the principal role).

41. I am following S. J. Tambiah's (e.g., 1985) extension to ritual action of J. L. Austin's (1969) analysis of linguistic forms.

42. The succession of sociocultural changes again finds a parallel in Sahlins's analysis of Hawaiian history, including an abrogation of tabus by immolatory autos-da-fé during a "cultural revolution" of 1819 (1981:56-65).

43. Some remarks, particularly on *tunatya,* "planning" or "intending," are contained in Whiteley 1988:267-68. See also Whorf 1956:61-62; Bradfield 1973:300-301; A. Geertz 1987:67 n.17. See also Chapter 1.

44. The philosophical literature on intentionality and agency is vast: see, especially, Davidson 1980 (whole volume); Putnam 1981; Searle 1983; Taylor 1985. Dennett (1987) provides a particularly lucid comparative account. Giddens's work (e.g. 1976, 1979) in sociology is also highly pertinent.

45. In choosing to follow here a decidedly non-Parisian philosophical tradition, I am disputing both structuralist and poststructuralist derogations of authorial intention in the interpretive process (see also Chapter 4).

46. A partial exception is the initiation of two men at Hotvela into the

Kwaakwant (one by his own father—a major departure from form) in the late 1950s.

47. This is the Pahaana prophecy (e.g., Whiteley 1988:270-71), which holds that at some point, Pahaana, elder brother to the *Kikmongwi,* "village chief" who led the people up into the fourth world, will return to judge which Hopis have, and which have not, held fast to aboriginal instructions. "Pahaana" is nowadays also the term for a white person. There was much debate (impinging on the factionalization of Orayvi) at the turn of the century over whether Anglo-Americans represented Pahaana. Today a distinction is made between Anglos, *pahaanam,* and the "true" *Pahaana,* whose arrival—to deliver the Hopi from current turmoil—is still anticipated by some.

48. This was very likely Talasnömtiwa, the former *Wuwtsimt* chief, who with Johnson and others, also furnished an affidavit in 1920 on the "moral character" of Hopi dances (Duberman et al. 1979:108).

49. Missionaries John R. Duerksen and his wife Susanna were based mostly at Orayvi, from 1911 (Stauffer 1926:19) to 1929 (Mennonite Encyclopedia, ii:819).

50. As a Snake initiate, Johnson's timing of the altar-burning to the day after the Snake Dance achieves an added significance.

51. Johnson is using the emergence myth as a paradigm for his own experience. By extension, it might be inferred that, with the altar-burning, he is re-enacting the pattern: destroying corruption produced under the Bow clan regime in the world below in order to purify conditions for people to build a new life after emergence. See also my remarks above on *naavotsiwni,* "purification."

6. THE END OF ANTHROPOLOGY (AT HOPI)?

Acknowledgments: Versions of this chapter were presented at a session of the 1991 American Anthropological Association meetings in Chicago on "Native Americans, Anthropology, and Ethics"; at the Royal Anthropological Institute's Third International Festival of Ethnographic Film held at Manchester University in September 1992; and to the Department of Anthropology at the City University of New York in October 1992. I am most grateful for comments and encouragement in Chicago to Leigh Jenkins, Kurt Dongoske, Roger Echohawk, and Larry Zimmerman; in Manchester to Marilyn Strathern, Paul Henley, Stephen Hugh-Jones, and Barbara Babcock; in New York to Louise Lennihan, May Ebihara, Delmos Jones, and Gerald Sider. Many thanks for comments also to Tom Biolsi, Arnold Krupat, Nicole Polier, and Hans-Ulrich Sanner. I am grateful, too, to Vernon Masayesva for permission to quote from his cited speech at Northern Arizona University.

1. The contexts of this interethnic play of identity and difference are mul-

tiple and complex, but one deserves emphasis. The Hopi Snake Dance had been since the 1880s a major feature of the Southwest tourist trade, annually drawing large parties of wealthy, socially connected tourists particularly from "back East" and Europe; Teddy Roosevelt visited in 1913; D. H. Lawrence (of course!) came in 1924 (Lawrence 1924). Frontier Anglos in Arizona were thus on one edge of an intercultural representational play: While the exoticism of local Indians was celebrated, with a quasi-erotic mixture of disgust and fascination—a look-at-the-savages-with-snakes-in-their-mouths sort of zoo-gaze—their own identity and difference with these Eastern sophisticates was equivocal. No doubt their provinciality, their Westernness as opposed to Easternness—a significant dimension of white-American class-status games—was slighted. In short, Arizona white identity was partly refracted through images of frontier otherness epitomized by the Hopi Snake Dance and its annual deluge of high-society pilgrims.

2. I should add that my ethnographer's representations are also counterfeit. I was not a "participant-observer," but watched all this on a VCR; a tape—punctuated by guffaws and wisecracks, as well as pregnant silences, from Hopi observers—was made by a Hopi videographer (Kaye 1991) as part of a large Hopi protest at the 1990 performance. My somewhat halfhearted plans to attend in 1991 were mercifully scotched by cancellation, owing to years of increasingly publicized Hopi protests (see, e.g., *Arizona Republic* 5 August 1991:1-2). For the time being at least, the Smokis have ceased their major public performances, although it is reported that they continue to march in costume in Prescott parades.

3. The area is also sacred to Zunis (Zuni's land responsibilities go south of the butte, Hopi's north), Navajos, and White Mountain Apaches (*Navajo Times* 27 December 1990).

4. For Hopis, the concept "mask"—implying representational falsity—in itself violates the item's sanctity. In English, Hopis usually refer to them as Kachina "friends" (translating from the Hopi reference *ikwaatsi,* my friend), actively avoiding "mask."

5. At the preview the nose had been correctly aligned.

6. As a result of the prior publicity, the purchaser, Elizabeth Sackler, in fact bought it with the sole intention of returning it to the Hopi people (*New York Times* 22 May 1991, *New York Newsday* 22 May 1991). While a noble enough act in itself, it scarcely solved the ironies and political-economic implications, the intercultural class and power inequities, or the clash of cultural values. The Hopi Tribe has been approached by a number of collectors seeking to return Hopi sacra—as long, of course, as they can get a tax write-off for their generosity. Sackler subsequently was a founder of the Native American Ritual Object Repatriation Foundation.

7. Kaiser (1991:118-19) explains "Harmonic Convergence" as follows: "On the basis of an intensive study of Aztec and Mayan stone calendars, he

[Jose Arguelles, an astrologer] projected the transition to the Age of Aquarius to occur during the night of the 16th to the 17th day of August 1987."

8. Armin Geertz (1994:313) claims Thomas Banyacya in fact met and led New Age acolytes in the construction of an altar at Prophecy Rock. If this is so, Banyacya must have been working both sides of the issue, since his signature appeared on circulars (posted in prominent places around the reservation prior to 16 August 1987) condemning the celebration.

9. I am utilizing a (Clifford) Geertzian conception of cultural symbols here. Unlike many (e.g., Leach 1976, Bloch 1989), however, I disavow a separation between instrumental and expressive domains of culture. The Ahöla mask is, in Hopi conceptions, inseparable from the supernatural figure it represents; the mask is not just an expression—it *embodies* the deity (cf. my remarks on the Snake Dance in Chapter 3). My use of the term "symbols," then, should not be taken to imply a denial of their intrinsic instrumental power.

10. Thefts of religious society altars, central to ritual practice, have been a particularly strong source of concern recently (see, e.g., *Tucson Weekly* 1 July 1992; my thanks to Laurel Cooper for this reference).

11. Here, too, there is a proliferation of counterfeits, including in the summer of 1991 a container-load of dolls from Hong Kong impounded by U.S. Customs in San Francisco (Leigh Jenkins, personal communication 1991).

12. More complexly, many young adults—often those without access to traditional ritual status and knowledge (because of their village or clan or family ideology)—favor an embryonic Third World/indigenist identity. This identity is socially underpinned by their experience of subalternity in the national society. It is culturally constructed, especially through the politics and music of Caribbean reggae (Hopi is a major stop on Jamaican musicians' tours), along with a rather abstract acknowledgement of the wisdom of Hopi elders.

13. This issue has complex forms when muddied by internal factionalism. Despite a long-term, society-wide ban on ritual photography, one Traditionalist spokesman submitted color footage of Hotvela rituals he had shot clandestinely since the 1960s for inclusion in a documentary film (*Techqua Ikachi* 1991). The film evoked an outcry when it was shown in Hotvela in March 1992. Hotvela, which does not send representatives to the Tribal Council, and in other respects opposes it, in this instance petitioned the Council's assistance to prevent the film's distribution. National distributors, at least for a while, shied away because of the controversy; in Europe, German and French editions of the film have been publicly available since 1989. The Swiss/German producers, approached by the Tribe's Office of Cultural Preservation, passed off responsibility for commercializing footage well-known as highly taboo throughout Hopi society (and not just from one fac-

tional standpoint) by claiming a factional allegiance to the Traditionalist group, and reasserting a challenge to the Council's legitimacy.

14. Sometimes white bourgeois Sikhs from Española, New Mexico (known in local parlance, for their white turbans, as "diaper-heads") are present, too: At a Hopi dance, transgressive postmodern identities are refracted across multiple intersecting planes.

15. On Hopi coffee-table images, cf. Whiteley 1990.

16. In an incisive critique of the same process at work in Sebastião Salgado's photography—widely acclaimed in Western bourgeois circles for its supposed social consciousness—of dying children in the Sahel, Ingrid Sischy (1991:92) points out: "[T]his beautification of tragedy results in pictures that ultimately reinforce our passivity toward the experience they reveal. To aestheticize tragedy is the fastest way to anesthetize the feelings of those who are witnessing it. Beauty is a call to admiration, not to action."

17. Foucault's analyses of power (e.g., 1978) render implausible absolute distinctions between overt political oppression and aesthetic valuation. Gramsci's concept of hegemony (e.g., 1970) also keenly demonstrates the infiltration of power structures into cognitive, including aesthetic, processes. Eagleton (1990) takes up and extends these and other arguments on the social roles and effects of aesthetics.

18. This has been pointed out by a rising tide of critics (e.g., Maquet 1964; Gough 1967; Deloria 1969; Asad 1973, 1992; Hymes 1972; Dwyer 1982; Clifford 1983; Fabian 1983; Marcus and Fischer 1986; Clifford and Marcus 1986; Said 1989; Minh-ha 1989). As Said (1989:213) puts it:

> [T]he by now massed discourses, codes, and practical traditions of anthropology, with its authorities, disciplinary rigors, genealogical maps, systems of patronage and accreditation have all been accumulated into various modes of *being anthropological*. . . . [T]he customary way of doing things both narcotizes and insulates the guild member. . . . To practice anthropology in the United States is therefore not just to be doing scholarly work investigating "otherness" and "difference" in a large country; it is to be discussing them in an enormously influential and powerful state whose global role is that of a superpower.

19. It is certain, for example, that the Smokis used ethnographic works on the Snake Dance by Voth and Fewkes, in particular.

20. Vine Deloria's witty polemic (1969:83-104) against "pure research" by anthropologists in Native American communities is still unequalled as an indictment of socially insouciant academic practice. For example:

> The anthro is usually devoted to PURE RESEARCH. Pure research is a body of knowledge absolutely devoid of useful application and incapa-

ble of meaningful digestion. Pure research is an abstraction of scholarly suspicions concerning some obscure theory originally expounded in pre-Revolutionary days and systematically checked each summer since then. A 1969 thesis restating a proposition of 1773 complete with footnotes to all material published between 1773 and 1969 is pure research. (Ibid.:85)

21. Secrecy, particularly regarding instrumentally powerful knowledge, is, of course, a universal social practice (see, e.g., Bok 1983). While in the United States, for example, academics and the press often trumpet an un-problematized version of "free speech," the same society has produced multiple secret praxes in military and other matters deemed to affect "national security." With regard to the ethnographic politics of ritual knowledge elsewhere, Australian aboriginal societies have (finally) had some particular success in persuading anthropologists to preserve secrecy (see Myers 1986).

22. One of the most acutely upsetting elements of this was that the Kachinas' masks were knocked off, revealing their human vehicles. The issue appeared on Reservation newsstands right at the time of *Powamuy* initiation, when Hopi children are supposed to be learning some of the secrets of the Kachina society in a more orthodox way. The Tribal Council's protests to Marvel Comics produced a somewhat belated and ambiguous apology, and the withdrawal (well after their peak sales period) of the remaining copies.

23. The conference "Dialogue with the Hopis" (e.g., Sanner 1996) held in Phoenix in 1995 sought to address some of these conflicting interests between Hopis and non-Hopi anthropologists. The results I heard (I did not attend) did not suggest an imminent resolution to the impasse.

24. After I had already titled this chapter I discovered, tellingly, the identical title—minus the "(at Hopi)"—in a 1966 paper by Peter Worsley. The recent debates on "endism" (e.g. Fukuyama 1989, McKibben 1989, Malcolmson 1989), from right and left, reproduce a precedent that is rather more full-bodied. Indeed compared to earlier critiques of anthropology, the later ones often seem lame—more a disengaged postmodern navel-contemplation than a call to social action.

25. For example, see Hooker 1963, Maquet 1964, Lévi-Strauss 1966, Gough 1967, Anderson 1968, *Current Anthropology* 1968, Goddard 1969, Banaji 1970, Leclerc 1972, and most especially Asad 1973, from which I take much of this history.

26. Indeed they hold less true in Britain, owing to the legacy of Margaret Thatcher's ravaging of the educational system.

27. Whorf's depictions of the Hopi language as timeless remain popular despite Malotki's (1983) careful corrective. The theme of gender equality is especially associated with Alice Schlegel's work (e.g., 1977).

28. In his film *Imagining Indians*, which appeared as the first version of

the present chapter was going to press in 1992, Victor Masayesva Jr. broaches—brilliantly, penetratingly—some of the same issues (including some of the same examples) of appropriation, fetishization, and misrepresentation of Native American cultures as are included here.

29. My gibe is intended particularly for Calvin Martin (1987).

30. Deloria's (1969:83) acid comments on this practice still hold true nearly three decades on.

31. See, for example, American Anthropological Association 1971, 1990; Fluehr-Lobban 1991; Scheper-Hughes 1995.

32. Archaeologists, for example, in both their theory and praxis, have more often than not systematically excluded the knowledge and interpretations of living Pueblo descendants—as they have with non-Western indigenous peoples worldwide (Ucko 1987, Bruguier and Zimmerman 1991; and see also Ferguson 1996). The intellectual grounds for exclusion, particularly in the now old "new archaeology," exalt cold "scientific analysis" of mute material remains over indigenous oral histories: Natives need not apply. To me, at least, this seems an appalling interpretive error (as well as a morally indefensible act in a genuinely plural society), cultural varieties of historicity notwithstanding. It is as if classical archaeologists were to simply throw out all Greek and Roman texts and deny a need to know the languages— an inconceivable circumstance. Yet I cannot think of a single Southwestern archaeologist who has taken the trouble, for example, to learn a Pueblo language.

33. The AAA's Committee on Anthropology in Predominantly Minority Institutions, founded in 1989, is a step in the right direction.

34. Neither is this recommendation new. Three decades ago (again), Delmos Jones (1970:258) put it this way: "The emergence of a native anthropology is part of an essential decolonization of anthropological knowledge and requires drastic changes in the recruitment and training of anthropologists."

35. This account is taken from a Hopi friend who participated. I did not witness the performance, though I have seen many others over the years.

7. PAAVAHU AND PAANAQSO'A

Acknowledgments: Nat Nutongla and Phillip Tuwaletstiwa of the Hopi Water Resources Office gave indispensable help and comments, and were most generous with sources.

1. See, for example, the accounts of Hopi emergence narratives in Voth (1905) or A. Geertz (1984). Nequatewa (1936) contains additional Hopi traditional narratives.

2. For a description of area hydrogeology, see Cooley et al. (1969); Greg-

ory (1916) and Hack (1942) provide more detailed local observations of the Hopi environment.

3. The most comprehensive accounts of these migrations, contested by later generations of archaeologists, but still systematically articulated by Hopi clan historians, are found in Mindeleff (1891) and Fewkes (1900).

4. See, for example, Brew 1979, Upham 1982, Cordell 1989; for more general accounts of Puebloan prehistory, see Cordell 1997, and Cordell and Gumerman 1989.

5. The other Pueblos—Zuni, Laguna, Acoma, and the Rio Grande Tewa, Tiwa, Towa, and Keres villages—also chart their migrations from some of these ancestral stone and adobe ruins.

6. Hopi attitudes toward the environment accord well with J. Baird Callicott's general meditations on Native American environmental ethics (e.g., 1982, 1996), as contrasted with European conceptions of environment. Amid often uncritical projections of the "ecologically noble savage" variety by some Western environmentalists, more careful statements on Native American attitudes toward landscape include: Momaday (1974), Vecsey (1980), Brody (1981), White (1984), Brightman (1993), Nelson (1993), and Basso (1996). The countervailing position—that Native Americans often despoiled their environments, and modified them in major ways (Calvin Martin's well-known *Keepers of the Game* [1978] is an example, and see also Redford [1991]; Denevan [1992]; Alvard [1993]; and Buege [1996])—may have some validity in specific instances. But it must be dismissed in general as motivated by the same tendency toward oppositive projection (but this time of ecologically ignoble savagery) as in the positive antithetical stereotypes. Any careful ethnographic description of Native environmental praxis typically discloses fine-grained attention to ecological concerns (cf. Lévi-Strauss 1966). For comprehensive discussions of anthropological approaches to environmentalism, see Milton (1993), and Orlove and Brush (1996).

7. *Hopi* is more than simply an ethnic-identity descriptor; in use, it carries specific implications of ethical engagement—in social action, moral thought, and religious practice. The oft-heard opposite *qahopi* ("unHopi," "badly behaved"), to chastise transgression of behavioral rules, highlights the ethical dimension of the concept of Hopiness.

8. Comments at Public Hearing, Kiqötsmovi, Arizona (9 August 1989), on the environmental impact of Black Mesa–Kayenta Mine, reprinted in U.S. Department of the Interior (1990:417). Masayesva elaborated on this perspective in the BBC film "The Hopi Way" (*Under the Sun* series, 1995), which focuses in part on the Hopi water crisis.

9. Source: Voth (1905b).

10. Source: Hanson Annual Report, 1996.

11. Examples of all these are found in Volume 2 of the Proposed Permit

Application, Black Mesa-Kayenta Mine (U.S. Department of the Interior 1990). One petition, for example, circulated among several villages:

We the members of the Hopi Tribe hereby strongly protest Peabody Coal Company's use of a valuable natural resource, water, to transport coal. We demand that Peabody Coal Company immediately cease the use of water to deliver coal to the generating plant(s) and further demand that the Hopi Tribal Council, the Office of Surface Mining and the Bureau of Indian Affairs put pressure on Peabody to immediately seek alternative means to transport coal.

Water is among our most precious resources and we feel that the millions of gallons pumped to feed the slurry lines are affecting our springs and thus impacting our cultural way of life. (Petition, 9 August 1989, reprinted in U.S. Department of the Interior 1990:261)

12. The permitting procedure for the mine is complex (see Wilkinson 1996 for the original lease history). The lessors are the Navajo Nation and the Hopi Tribe, but mining permits must be approved by a series of regulatory agencies:

(1) the Bureau of Land Management, for a life-of-mining plan (until the year 2023);

(2) the U.S. Army Corps of Engineers, for a Clean Water Act Section 404 permit;

(3) the Office of Surface Mining Reclamation and Enforcement, for a permit package that allows renewal of the mining lease, with five-yearly reviews until 2011.

(Source: U.S. Environmental Protection Agency Comments on the Proposed DEIS, U.S. Department of the Interior, 1990)

13. A source close to the process of EPA review indicated that the DEIS only received EO-2 by the skin of its teeth, and even then with some backstage arm-twisting: EPA, the source indicated, wanted to rate the DEIS EO-3 (Environmental Objections—Inadequate), which would have indicated formal failure of the DEIS to satisfy provisions of the National Environmental Policy Act, and may well have led to rejection of the permit application without further study.

14. Peabody modeled the recharge rate at 13,000 acre feet per year. The USGS study, by an Arizona office, recorded a recharge rate of 2,000 acre feet per year (figures provided by the Water Resources Office, Department of Natural Resources, the Hopi Tribe).

15. Source: EPA comments on the DEIS, reprinted in U.S. Department of the Interior 1990:268.

16. In the film "The Hopi Way," *Under the Sun* series (BBC 1995).

17. Working with Hopi Tribal Attorney John Boyden's legal files (recently made public at the University of Utah), Charles Wilkinson (1996) describes in impressive detail how Boyden was simultaneously working for the Peabody Coal Company regarding water and mineral rights on Black Mesa.

18. Robbie Honani of Supawlavi, then chairman of the Hopi Tribal Council's Resources Committee, noted at the public hearings on the DEIS:

There's less than ten Hopi people working at the Peabody mine and over 800 Navajos. Peabody has built the town of Kayenta for the Navajo and for other employees. They have erected a trailer court for its non-Indian employees and flies their top management people every day from Flagstaff, and then flies them back again. Yet there is no trailer court for the Hopi people. And there is no major road system going up to Peabody.

All taxes in the form of education monies go to the . . . Kayenta Public School District. Does the Hopi get any of these monies? No. . . . The State of Arizona receives twice as much money in taxes than the Hopi Tribe does in actual revenues. The tribe receives approximately $8 million in coal royalty, yet the State of Arizona receives between $18 to $20 million in taxes a year. Only a mere drop of that comes back to the Hopi. (U.S. Department of the Interior 1990:409)

19. See, for example, *The Economist* survey on multinationals, 24 June 1995; in a veritable tide of discussion on stakeholder questions, see for example, Altman 1994, Collins 1995. For discussions of indigenous stakeholder interests in relation to local and multinational economic development in different parts of the world, see any issue of *Cultural Survival Quarterly.*

20. Howard Carson marked this event with a two-page letter to the Hopi Tribal Newspaper, *Hopi Tutuveni* (30 December 1996), detailing the benefits the mine had brought to the community, implying that opposition to the mine was the work of cranks and extremists, and totally ignoring the widespread Hopi opposition to the slurry.

21. Source *Private Eye*, February 1996.

8. EPILOGUE

1. Pym worked for nearly thirty years (1946-74) as an editor at the International African Institute in London; this included work on the journal *Africa* (e.g., Holt 1990). For most of that period, Daryll Forde was her boss. Forde was one of the seven professors in British anthropology who "controlled the profession for two decades" at midcentury (Kuper 1973:154). (Incidentally, Forde is also one of a tiny handful of British anthropologists ever to have conducted fieldwork in North America, working at Hopi in 1929

[see Chapter 1], and also with the Yuma.) Several of Pym's other novels feature satiric asides on the anthropological predicament. Her journal for 1953 includes a favorite quote from *Notes and Queries in Anthropology* that points up her sense of the comedy of anthropological manners:

> It is important that not even the slightest expression of amusement or disapproval should ever be displayed at the description of ridiculous, impossible or disgusting features in custom, cult or legend. (Pym 1984:189)

REFERENCES

Abbreviation: MCF—Missionary Correspondence Files. Mennonite Library and Archives, Bethel College, North Newton, Kansas.

Aberle, David F. 1951. *Psychosocial Analysis of a Hopi Life-History.* Berkeley: University of California Press.

———. 1993. "The Navajo-Hopi Land Dispute and Navajo Relocation." In *Anthropological Approaches to Resettlement: Policy, Practice and Theory,* Michael Cernea and Scott Guggenheim, eds. Boulder: Westview, 153-200.

Adams, Byron P. n.d. Record of Meeting of the Hopi Tribal Council. 18 January 1937. National Archives. Record Group 75. Central Files 1907-39. Bureau of Indian Affairs. Washington, D.C.

Adams, E. Charles. 1991. *The Origin and Development of the Pueblo Katsina Cult.* Tucson: University of Arizona Press.

Adams, Eleanor B. 1963. "Fray Silvestre and the Obstinate Hopi." *New Mexico Historical Review* 28, 97-138.

Adams, Richard N. 1977. "Power in Human Societies: A Synthesis." In *The Anthropology of Power,* Raymond D. Fogelson and R. N. Adams, eds. New York: Academic Press.

Ahern, Emily M. 1981. *Chinese Ritual and Politics.* Cambridge: Cambridge University Press.

Aitken, Barbara. 1931. "Folk-History and Its Raw Material: White Men's Raids on the Hopi Villages." *New Mexico Historical Review* 6:376-82.

Alcoff, Linda. 1991. "The Problem of Speaking for Others." *Cultural Critique,* Winter 1991-92, 5-32.

Altman, John A. 1994. "Toward a Stakeholder-Based Policy Process: An Application of the Social Marketing Perspective to Environmental Policy Development." *Policy Sciences* 27:1:37–51.

Alvard, M. 1993. "Testing the 'Ecologically Noble Savage' Hypothesis: Interspecific Prey Choice by Piro Hunters of Amazonian Peru." *Human Ecology* 21:4:355–87.

American Anthropological Association. 1970. Symposium on Anthropology and the American Indian. (Published in 1973 by Indian Historian Press, San Francisco.)

———. 1971. Statement on Ethics, Principles of Professional Responsibility. Washington, D.C.

———. 1990. Amendment to AAA 1971.

Anderson, Perry. 1968. "Components of the National Culture." *New Left Review* 50:3–57.

Anthropology on Trial. 1984. Nova Videograph (WGBH). Time-Life Video New York.

Appadurai, Arjun. 1986. "Theory in Anthropology: Center and Periphery." *Comparative Studies in Society and History* 28:2:356–61.

Archer, Margaret. 1988. *Culture and Agency: The Place of Culture in Social Theory.* Cambridge: Cambridge University Press.

Arizona Republic. 1990. "Anglo 'Tribe' Dances Controversial Steps." Paul Brinkley-Rogers, 5 August 1990:A1–A2.

Asad, Talal, ed. 1973. *Anthropology and the Colonial Encounter.* London: Ithaca Press.

———. 1990. "Ethnography, Literature, and Politics: Some Readings and Uses of Salman Rushdie's *The Satanic Verses.*" *Cultural Anthropology* 5:3:239–69.

———. 1992. "Afterword: From the History of Colonial Anthropology to the Anthropology of Western Hegemony." In *Colonial Situations: Essays on the Contextualization of Ethnographic Knowledge,* George Stocking, ed. Madison: University of Wisconsin Press, 314–24.

Austin, John L. 1969. *How to Do Things with Words.* Oxford: Clarendon.

Babcock, Barbara, and Nancy Parezo. 1988. *Daughters of the Desert: Women Anthropologists and the Native American Southwest, 1880–1980.* Albuquerque: University of New Mexico Press.

Bacavi Village Census. 1977. Bacavi Village, Arizona.

Bailey, Lynn R. 1966. *Indian Slave Trade in the Southwest: A Study of Slavetaking and the Traffic of Indian Captives.* Los Angeles: Westernlore Press.

Banaji, Jairus. 1970. "The Crisis of British Anthropology." *New Left Review* 64:71–85.

Barnes, John A. 1962. "African Models in the New Guinea Highlands." *Man* 52:5–9.

Barnes, R. H. 1980. "Hidatsa Personal Names: An Interpretation." *Plains Anthropologist* 5:90:311–31.

References

————. 1982. "Personal Names and Social Classification." In *Semantic Anthropology*, D. Parkin, ed. London: Academic Press, 211-26.

Barnouw, Victor. 1963. *Culture and Personality*. Homewood, Ill.: Dorsey Press.

Barth, Fredrik. 1975. *Ritual and Knowledge among the Baktaman of New Guinea*. New Haven: Yale University Press.

————. 1981. *Process and Form in Social Life*. London: Routledge and Kegan Paul.

Basso, Keith. 1979. *Portraits of "the Whiteman": Linguistic Play and Cultural Symbols among the Western Apache*. New York: Cambridge University Press.

————. 1988. "'Speaking with Names': Language and Landscape among the Western Apache." *Cultural Anthropology* 3:2:99-130.

————. 1996. *Wisdom Sits in Places: Landscape and Language among the Western Apache*. Albuquerque: University of New Mexico Press.

Battaglia, Debbora. 1990. *On the Bones of the Serpent: Person, Memory, and Mortality in Sabarl Island Society*. Chicago: University of Chicago Press.

————. 1995. "Problematizing the Self: A Thematic Introduction." In *Rhetorics of Self-Making*, D. Battaglia, ed. Berkeley: University of California Press, 1-15.

BBC Television. 1995. "The Hopi Way." *Under the Sun* series. Manchester, U.K.

Beaglehole, Ernest. 1937. *Notes on Hopi Economic Life*. New Haven: Yale University Publications in Anthropology 15.

Bean, Lowell John, ed. 1989. *Seasons of the Kachina: Proceedings of the California State University Conference on the Western Pueblos, 1987-88*. Novato, Calif.: Ballena Press.

Beckett, Sister Wendy. 1992. *Art and the Sacred*. London: Rider Books.

Bellman, B. L. 1984. *The Language of Secrecy: Symbols and Metaphors in Poro Ritual*. New Brunswick: Rutgers University Press.

Benedek, Emily. 1992. *The Wind Won't Know Me: A History of the Navajo-Hopi Land Dispute*. New York: Knopf.

Benedict, Ruth. 1934. *Patterns of Culture*. Boston: Houghton Mifflin.

Biolsi, Thomas, and Larry Zimmerman, eds. 1997. *Indians and Anthropologists: Vine Deloria Jr. and the Critique of Anthropology*. Tucson: University of Arizona Press.

Bloch, Maurice. 1974. "Symbols, Song, Dance and Features of Articulation: Is Religion an Extreme Form of Traditional Authority?" *European Journal of Sociology* 15:55-81.

————. 1980. Ritual Symbolism and the Non-Representation of Society. In *Symbol as Sense: New Approaches to the Analysis of Meaning*, M. L. Foster and S. H. Brandes, eds. New York: Academic Press.

References

————. 1989. *Ritual, History and Power: Selected Papers in Anthropology.* London: Athlone.

Boissière, Robert. 1986. *Meditations with the Hopi.* Santa Fe: Bear and Co.

Bok, Sissela. 1983. *Secrets: On the Ethics of Concealment and Revelation.* New York: Pantheon.

Borofsky, Robert. 1997. "Cook, Lono, Obeyesekere, and Sahlins." *Current Anthropology* 38:255-82.

Boudon, Raymond. 1982. *The Unintended Consequences of Social Action.* New York: St. Martin's Press.

Bourdieu, Pierre. 1984 [1979]. *Distinction: A Social Critique of the Judgment of Taste.* Richard Nice, trans. Cambridge, Mass.: Harvard University Press.

————. 1988. *Homo Academicus.* Stanford: Stanford University Press.

Bourdieu, Pierre, Jean-Claude Passeron, and Monique de Saint Martin. 1994. *Academic Discourse: Linguistic Misunderstanding and Professorial Power,* Richard Teese, trans. Stanford: Stanford University Press.

Bourke, John Gregory. 1884. *The Snake Dance of the Moquis of Arizona.* New York: Charles Scribner's Sons.

Bradfield, R. Maitland. 1971. *The Changing Pattern of Hopi Agriculture.* London: Royal Anthropological Institute Occasional Paper 30.

————. 1973. *A Natural History of Associations: A Study in the Meaning of Community,* vol. 2. London: Duckworth.

————. 1995. *An Interpretation of Hopi Culture.* Derby, U.K.: Privately printed. (Originally published 1973 as *A Natural History of Associations,* vol. 2.)

Brandt, Elizabeth. 1980. "On Secrecy and the Control of Knowledge: Taos Pueblo." In *Secrecy: A Cross-cultural Perspective,* S. K. Tefft, ed. New York: Human Sciences Press.

————. 1985. "Internal Stratification in Pueblo Communities." Paper presented at the annual meetings of the American Anthropological Association (1985).

Brandt, Richard. 1954. *Hopi Ethics: A Theoretical Analysis.* Chicago: University of Chicago Press.

Brenton, Barrett P. 1994. "Hopi Foodways: Biocultural Perspectives on Change and Contradiction." Ph.D. diss., University of Massachusetts, Amherst.

Brew, J. O. 1979. "Hopi Prehistory and History to 1850." In *Handbook of North American Indians,* vol. 9, *The Southwest,* Alfonso Ortiz, ed. Washington, D.C.: Smithsonian Institution, 514-23.

Brightman, Robert A. 1993. *Grateful Prey: Rock Cree Human-Animal Relationships.* Berkeley: University of California Press.

Brody, Hugh. 1981. *Maps and Dreams.* New York: Pantheon.

Bruce, James P., Hoesung Lee, and Erik F. Haites, eds. 1996. *Climate*

References

Change 1995: Economic and Social Dimensions of Climate Change. New York: Cambridge University Press.

Brugge, David M. 1994. *The Navajo-Hopi Land Dispute: An American Tragedy.* Albuquerque: University of New Mexico Press.

Bruguier, Leonard R., and Larry J. Zimmerman. 1991. "Native Americans and the World Archaeological Congress Code of Ethics." Paper presented at the 1991 annual meeting of the American Anthropological Association, session on research ethics and Native American rights.

Bruner, Edward M. 1986. "Ethnography as Narrative." In *The Anthropology of Experience,* Victor Turner and Edward Bruner, eds. Urbana: University of Illinois Press, 1939-55.

Buckley, Thomas. 1989. "Suffering in the Cultural Construction of Others: Robert Spott and A. L. Kroeber." *American Indian Quarterly* 13:437-45.

Buege, D. J. 1996. "The Ecologically Noble Savage Revisited." *Environmental Ethics* 18:71-88.

Bunzel, Ruth. 1938. "The Economic Organization of Primitive Peoples." In *General Anthropology,* Franz Boas, ed. New York: Heath.

Burton, Lloyd. 1991. *American Indian Water Rights and the Limits of the Law.* Lawrence: University Press of Kansas.

Callicott, J. Baird. 1982. "Traditional American Indian and Western European Attitudes toward the Environment: An Overview." *Environmental Ethics* 4:4:293-318.

———. 1996. "American Indian Land Ethics." *Environmental Ethics* 18:4:438.

Carrithers, Michael, Steven Collins, and Steven Lukes, eds. 1985. *The Category of the Person.* Cambridge: Cambridge University Press.

Casagrande, Louis B., and Phillipa Bourns. 1983. *Side Trips: the Photography of Sumner W. Matteson, 1898-1908.* Milwaukee: Milwaukee Public Museum.

Çelik, Zeynep. 1992. *Displaying the Orient: Architecture of Islam at Nineteenth-Century World's Fairs.* Berkeley: University of California Press.

Chien, I. 1944. "The Awareness of Self and the Structure of the Ego." *Psychological Review* 51:304-414.

Chronicle of Higher Education. 1990. "Dispute Between Scholar, Tribe Leaders over Book on Hopi Ritual Raises Concerns about Censorship of Studies of American Indians." Chris Raymond, 17 October 1990, 37:7:A6, 8-9.

Clastres, Pierre. 1977. *Society against the State.* New York: Urizen Books.

Clemmer, Richard O. 1978. *Continuities of Hopi Culture Change.* Ramona, Calif.: Acoma Books.

———. 1978a. "Black Mesa and the Hopi." In *Native Americans and Energy Development,* Joseph Jorgenson, ed. Cambridge, Mass.: Anthropology Resource Center.

————. 1982. "The Hopi Traditionalist Movement." Paper presented at the School of American Research Advanced Seminar on "The Hopi Indians in the Twentieth Century." (Updated and revised, much of this is included in Clemmer 1995.)

————. 1984. "The Effects of the Energy Economy on Pueblo Peoples." In *Native Americans and Energy Development*, 2. Joseph Jorgenson, ed. Boston: Anthropology Resource Center and the Seventh Generation Fund.

————. 1995. *Roads in the Sky: The Hopi Indians in a Century of Change*. Boulder: Westview.

Clifford, James. 1983. "On Ethnographic Authority." *Representations* 1:118-46.

————. 1988. *The Predicament of Culture: Twentieth-Century Ethnography, Literature, and Art*. Cambridge, Mass.: Harvard University Press.

————. 1988a [1985]. "Histories of the Tribal and the Modern." In Clifford 1988 (q.v.), 189-214.

————. 1988b. "On Collecting Art and Culture." In Clifford 1988 (q.v.), 215-52.

————. 1997. *Routes: Travel and Translation in the Late Twentieth Century*. Cambridge, Mass.: Harvard University Press.

Clifford, James, and George Marcus, eds. 1986. *Writing Culture: The Poetics and Politics of Ethnography*. Berkeley: University of California Press.

Cohen, Abner. 1970. "The Political System." In *A Handbook of Method in Cultural Anthropology*, R. Narroll and R. Cohen, eds. Garden City: Natural History Press.

Collier, John. 1962. *On the Gleaming Way: Navajos, Eastern Pueblos, Zunis, Hopis, Apaches, and Their Land, and Their Meanings in the World*. Denver: Sage.

Collins, Dennis. 1995. "Capitalism, Environmentalism, and Mediating Structures: From Adam Smith to Stakeholder Panels." *Environmental Ethics* 17:3:227-44.

Collins, Steven. 1982. *Selfless Persons: Imagery and Thought in Theravada Buddhism*. Cambridge: Cambridge University Press.

Colson, E. 1977. "Power at Large: Meditation on the 'Symposium on Power.'" In *The Anthropology of Power*, R. D. Fogelson and R. N. Adams, eds. New York: Academic Press.

Comaroff, Jean, and John Comaroff. 1991. *Of Revelation and Revolution: Christianity, Colonialism, and Consciousness in South Africa*, vol. 1. Chicago: University of Chicago Press.

Connelly, John C. 1979. "Hopi Social Organization." In *Handbook of North American Indians*, vol. 9, *The Southwest*, Alfonso Ortiz, ed. Washington D.C.: Smithsonian Institution, 539-53.

Cook-Lynn, Elizabeth. 1997. "Who Stole Native American Studies?" *Wicazo Sa Review* 12:9-28.

Cooley, M. E., J. W. Harshbarger, J. P. Akers, and W. F. Hardt. 1969. *Regional Hydrogeology of the Navajo and Hopi Indian Reservations, Arizona, New Mexico, and Utah.* Geological Survey Professional Paper 521-A. Washington, D.C.: U.S. Government Printing Office.

Cordell, Linda. 1989. "Hopi Prehistory: Overview and Issues." In *Seasons of the Kachina,* L. Bean, ed. Proceedings of the California State University, Hayward, Conference on the Western Pueblos, 1987-88. Ballena Press.

———. 1997. *Archaeology of the Southwest.* New York: Academic Press.

Cordell, Linda, and George Gumerman, eds. 1989. *Dynamics of Southwest Prehistory.* Washington, D.C.: Smithsonian Institution Press.

Cox, Bruce. 1970. "What Is Hopi Gossip About? Information Management and Hopi Factions." *Man* (N.S.) 5, 88-98.

Crane, Leo. 1925. *Indians of the Enchanted Desert.* Boston: Little, Brown.

Crapanzano, Vincent. 1992. *Hermes' Dilemma and Hamlet's Desire: On the Epistemology of Interpretation.* Cambridge, Mass.: Harvard University Press.

Culler, Jonathan D. 1986. *Ferdinand de Saussure* (rev. ed.). Ithaca: Cornell University Press.

Current Anthropology. 1968. "Social Responsibilities Symposium" 9:5:391-435.

———. 1971. "Toward an Ethics for Anthropologists" (symposium) 12:3:321-56.

Curtis, Edward M. 1922. *The North American Indian,* vol 12. *The Hopi.* Norwood, Mass.: Plimpton Press.

Dalforo, A. T. 1982. "Logbara Personal Names and Their Relation to Religion." *Anthropos* 77:1/2:113-33.

Davidson, Donald. 1980 [1963]. "Actions, Reasons, and Causes." In *Essays on Actions and Events,* Donald Davidson. Oxford: Clarendon Press, 3-19.

Deloria, Vine, Jr. 1969. *Custer Died for Your Sins: An Indian Manifesto.* New York: MacMillan.

Deloria, Vine, Jr., and C. M. Lytle. 1984. *The Nations Within: The Past and Future of American Indian Self-Government.* New York: Pantheon.

Denevan, William. 1992. "The Pristine Myth: the Landscape of the Americas in 1492." *Annals of the Association of American Geographers* 82:369-85.

Dennett, Daniel C. 1987. *The Intentional Stance.* Cambridge, Mass.: MIT Press.

Derrida, Jacques. 1977. *Of Grammatology,* G. C. Spivak, trans. Baltimore: Johns Hopkins University Press.

Descola, Philippe. 1996. *The Spears of Twilight: Life and Death in the Amazon Jungle.* New York: New Press.

Dietz, T., and T. R. Burns. 1992. "Human Agency and the Evolutionary Dynamics of Culture." *Acta Sociologica* 35:194.

Dilworth, Leah. 1996. *Imagining Indians in the Southwest: Persistent Visions of a Primitive Past.* Washington, D.C.: Smithsonian Institution Press.

Dray, W. H. 1978. "Concepts of Causation in A. J. P. Taylor's Account of the Origins of the Second World War." *History and Theory* 17:149-74.

Duberman, Martin B., Fred Eggan, and R. O. Clemmer. 1979. "Documents in Hopi Indian Sexuality: Imperialism, Culture, and Resistance." *Radical History Review* 20:99-130.

Duerksen, J. R., and Susanna Duerksen. 1917. Correspondence to the Board of Foreign Missions, Mennonite General Conference. MCF, March 1917.

Dumars, Charles T. 1984. *Pueblo Indian Water Rights: Struggle for a Precious Resource.* Tucson: University of Arizona Press.

Dumont, Louis. 1970. *Homo Hierarchicus: An Essay on the Caste System.* Chicago: University of Chicago Press.

Dunkling, Leslie, and William Gosling. 1983. *Everyman's Dictionary of First Names.* London: Dent.

Duranti, Alessandro. 1994. *From Grammar to Politics: Linguistic Anthropology in a Western Samoan Village.* Berkeley: University of California Press.

Durkheim, Émile, and Marcel Mauss. 1963 [1908]. *Primitive Classification.* Chicago: University of Chicago Press.

Dwyer, Kevin. 1982. *Moroccan Dialogues: Anthropology in Question.* Baltimore: Johns Hopkins University Press.

Eagleton, Terry. 1990. *The Ideology of the Aesthetic.* Oxford: Blackwell.

The Economist, 1995. "Insider Trading: Multinationals Need to Become Local Insiders in Lots of Different Places." *Economist* survey on multinationals, 24 June 1995.

Eggan, Dorothy. 1943. "The General Problem of Hopi Adjustment." *American Anthropologist* 45:357-73.

———. 1956. "Instruction and Affect in Hopi Cultural Continuity." *Southwestern Journal of Anthropology* 12:347-70.

Eggan, Frederick R. 1949. "The Hopi and the Lineage Principle." In *Social Structure: Studies Presented to A. R. Radcliffe-Brown,* Meyer Fortes, ed. London: Oxford University Press, 121-44.

———. 1950. *Social Organization of the Western Pueblos.* Chicago: University of Chicago Press.

———. 1964. "Alliance and Descent in a Western Pueblo Society." In *Process and Pattern in Culture,* R. A. Manners, ed. Chicago: Aldine.

Episcopal Church. 1944 [1928]. *The Book of Common Prayer.* New York: Thomas Nelson.

———. 1979. *The Book of Common Prayer and Administration of the Sacraments and Other Rites and Ceremonies of the Church.* New York: Oxford University Press.

Epp, J. B. 1906. Report to Superintendent Matthew M. Murphy, in "Oraiba Troubles," File I. Record Group 75. Washington, D.C.: National Archives, 20 September 1906.

————. 1906a. Letter to the Board of Foreign Missions, Mennonite General Conference. MCF, 18 December 1906.

————. 1909. Letter to the Board of Foreign Missions, Mennonite General Conference. MCF, 4 January 1909.

————. 1923. "Another Period of Pioneer Work in Oraibi, 1901–1915." *The Mennonite* 12 March 1923:6-7.

Evans-Pritchard, E. E. 1940. *The Nuer.* London: Oxford University Press.

Evens, T. M. S. 1977. "The Predication of the Individual in Anthropological Interactionism." *American Anthropologist* 79:579-97.

Ewing, Katherine P. 1990. "The Illusion of Wholeness: Culture, Self, and the Experience of Inconsistency." *Ethos* 18:251-78.

Fabian, Johannes. 1983. *Time and the Other: How Anthropology Makes Its Object.* New York: Columbia University Press.

Fardon, R. 1985. "Introduction: A Sense of Relevance." In *Power and Knowledge: Anthropological and Sociological Approaches,* R. Fardon, ed. Edinburgh: Scottish Academic.

————. 1985a. "Secrecy and Sociability: Two Problems of Chamba Knowledge." In *Power and Knowledge: Anthropological and Sociological Approaches,* R. Fardon, ed. Edinburgh: Scottish Academic.

Faubion, James. 1996. "Kinship Is Dead. Long Live Kinship." *Comparative Studies in Society and History* 38:67-91.

Feher-Elston, Catherine. 1988. *Children of the Sacred Ground: America's Last Indian War.* Flagstaff: Northland Publishing.

Ferguson, T. J. 1996. "Native Americans and the Practice of Archaeology." *Annual Review of Anthropology* 25:63-79.

Fewkes, J. W. 1900. "Tusayan Migration Traditions." In *Nineteenth Annual Report of the Bureau of American Ethnology, Smithsonian Institution (1897-98).* Washington D.C.: U.S. Government Printing Office, 573-633.

————. 1903. "Hopi Katcinas Drawn by Native Artists." *Annual Reports of the Bureau of American Ethnology* 21:3-126.

————. 1906. "Hopi Shrines near the East Mesa, Arizona." *American Anthropologist* 8:346-75.

————. 1922. "Oraibi in 1890." (In *Contributions to Hopi History,* E. C. Parsons, ed.) *American Anthropologist* 24:253-98.

————. 1926. "The Katcina Altars in Hopi Worship." *Smithsonian Institution Annual Report* for the year ending 30 June 1926, 469-86.

Fluehr-Lobban, Carolyn, ed. 1991. *Ethics and the Profession of Anthropology: Dialogue for a New Era.* Philadelphia: University of Pennsylvania Press.

Fogelson, Raymond. 1989. "The Ethnohistory of Events and Non-Events." *Ethnohistory* 36:133-47.

Fontana, Benedetto. 1993. *Hegemony and Power.* Minneapolis: University of Minnesota Press.

Forde, C. D. 1931. "Hopi Agriculture and Land Ownership." *Journal of the Royal Anthropological Institute* 41:357–405.

———. 1934. *Habitat, Economy, and Society: A Geographical Introduction to Ethnology.* London: Methuen.

Fortes, Meyer. 1945. *The Dynamics of Clanship among the Tallensi.* London: Oxford University Press.

———. 1953. "The Structure of Unilineal Descent Groups." *American Anthropologist* 55:17–41.

Fortes, M., and E. E. Evans-Pritchard, eds. 1940. *African Political Systems.* London: Oxford University Press.

Foucault, Michel. 1978. *The History of Sexuality,* vol. 1, Robert Hurley, trans. New York: Pantheon.

———. 1980. "Truth and Power." In *Power/Knowledge,* Colin Gordon, ed. New York: Pantheon.

———. 1982. "The Subject and Power." In *Michel Foucault: Beyond Structuralism and Hermeneutics,* H. Dreyfus and P. Rabinow, eds. Chicago: University of Chicago Press.

Fox, J. R. 1967. *Kinship and Marriage.* Harmondsworth, U.K.: Penguin.

———. 1967a. *The Keresan Bridge.* London: Athlone.

———. 1972. "Some Unsolved Problems of Pueblo Social Organization." In *New Perspectives on the Pueblos,* Alfonso Ortiz, ed. Albuquerque: University of New Mexico Press, 71–85.

Frazer, James G. 1890. *The Golden Bough: A Study in Magic and Religion.* London: Macmillan.

———. 1910. *Totemism and Exogamy: A Treatise on Certain Early Forms of Superstition and Society.* London: Macmillan.

Fredericks, Oswald et al. (Hopi Committee). 1934. Letter to John Collier, Commissioner of Indian Affairs. Record Group 75. Washington, D.C.: National Archives, 7 March 1934.

French, David, and Katherine French. 1996. "Personal Names." In *Handbook of North American Indians,* vol. 17, *Languages,* Ives Goddard, ed. Washington, D.C.: Smithsonian Institution, 200–221.

Frey, J. B. 1909. Letter to the Board of Foreign Missions (in German). Mennonite General Conference. MCF, 19 November 1909.

———. 1909a. Letter to C. H. Wedel (in German). Mennonite General Conference. MCF, 6 December 1909.

———. 1915. "Among the Hopis of Arizona." In *Review of the Rise and Progress of the Mission Activities of the General Conference of Mennonites of North America,* Gustav Harder, ed. North Newton, Kansas: Board of Foreign Missions, 19–26.

———. 1923. "Oraibi, 1903–05." *The Mennonite* 12 April 1923, 7–8.

Fried, Morton H. 1957. "The Classification of Corporate Unilineal Descent Groups." *Journal of the Royal Anthropological Institute* 87:1–29.

————. 1967. *The Evolution of Political Society.* New York: Random House.

Friesen, Karl. 1922. Letter to P. H. Richert, Secretary. General Conference of Mennonites. MCF, 2 September 1922.

————. 1923. "The Christians at Oraibi." *The Mennonite* 12 April 1923, 11–12.

Frigout, Arlette. 1979. "Hopi Ceremonial Organization." In *Handbook of North American Indians,* vol. 9, *The Southwest,* Alfonso Ortiz, ed. Washington D.C.: Smithsonian Institution, 564–76.

Frisbie, Charlotte. 1987. *Navajo Medicine Bundles or Jish: Acquisition, Transmission, and Disposition in the Past and Present.* Albuquerque: University of New Mexico Press.

Fukuyama, Francis. 1989. "The End of History?" *The National Interest* 16:3–35.

The Gallup Independent. 1988. "Hopi Religion: Current Century Has Taken Its Toll on Tribe's Sacred Rites." Gallup, N.M. 1 June 1988, 1–2.

————. 1992. "Hopis Seek Help to Halt Woodruff Butte Mining." 6 June 1992, 1.

————. 1992a. Governor Shows Concern about Woodruff Butte." 16 June 1992, 1.

————. 1993. "Coal Mining May Threaten Hopi Water, Culture." 20 December 1993.

Gedicks, Al. 1993. *The New Resource Wars: Native and Environmental Struggles against Multinational Corporations.* Boston: South End Press.

Geertz, Armin W. 1983. "Book of the Hopi: The Hopi's Book?" *Anthropos* 78:547–56.

————. 1984. "A Reed Pierced the Sky: Hopi Indian Cosmography on Third Mesa, Arizona." *Numen* 31:2:216–41.

————. 1987. *Children of Cottonwood: Piety and Ceremonialism in Hopi Indian Puppetry.* Lincoln: University of Nebraska Press.

————. 1987a. *Hopi Indian Altar Iconography.* Leiden: E. J. Brill.

————. 1987b. "Prophets and Fools: The Rhetoric of Hopi Indian Eschatology." *European Review of Native American Studies* 1:33–45.

————. 1990. "Hopi Hermeneutics: Ritual Person among the Hopi Indians of Arizona." In *Concepts of Person in Religion and Thought,* H. K. Kippenberg, Y. B. Kuiper, and A. F. Sanders, eds. Berlin: De Gruyter, 309–36.

————. 1994. *The Invention of Prophecy: Continuity and Meaning in Hopi Indian Religion.* Berkeley: University of California Press.

————. 1996. "Contemporary Problems in the Study of Native American Religions, with Special Reference to the Hopis." *American Indian Quarterly* 20:3:393–414.

Geertz, Clifford. 1966. "Religion as a Cultural System." In *Anthropological Approaches to the Study of Religion,* Michael Banton, ed. London: Tavistock, 1–46.

———. 1973. *The Interpretation of Cultures*. New York: Basic Books.

———. 1973a [1966]. "Person, Time, and Conduct in Bali." In *The Interpretation of Cultures*, by C. Geertz. New York: Basic Books, 360-411.

———. 1974. "From the Native's Point of View'; On the Nature of Anthropological Understanding." *Bulletin of the American Academy of Arts and Sciences* 28:1.

———. 1983. *Local Knowledge*. New York: Basic Books.

———. 1983a. "Blurred Genres: The Refiguration of Social Thought." In *Local Knowledge*, C. Geertz, 19-35.

———. 1983b [1976]. "Art as a Cultural System." In *Local Knowledge*, C. Geertz, 94-120.

———. 1988. *Works and Lives: The Anthropologist as Author*. Stanford: Stanford University Press.

Giddens, Anthony. 1976. *New Rules of Sociological Method: A Positive Critique of Interpretative Sociologies*. New York: Basic Books.

———. 1979. *Central Problems in Social Theory*. Berkeley: University of California Press.

———. 1984. *The Constitution of Society: Outline of the Theory of Structuration*. Berkeley: University of California Press.

———. 1987. *Social Theory and Modern Sociology*. Cambridge: Polity Press.

Glasse, R. M. 1987. "Huli Names and Naming." *Ethnology* 23:3:201-8.

Glover, Jonathan. 1988. *I: The Philosophy and Psychology of Personal Identity*. New York: Viking Penguin.

Goddard, David. 1969. "Limits of British Anthropology." *New Left Review* 58:79-89.

Godelier, Maurice, ed. 1998. *Transformation of Kinship*. Washington, D.C.: Smithsonian Institution Press.

Goody, J. R. 1961. "The Classification of Double Descent Systems." *Current Anthropology* 2:3-25.

Gough, Kathleen. 1967. "Anthropology: Child of Imperialism." *Monthly Review* 19:11:12-27.

Graham, Laura R. 1995. *Performing Dreams: Discourses of Immortality among the Xavante of Central Brazil*. Austin: University of Texas Press.

Gramsci, Antonio. 1970. *Selections from the Prison Notebooks*, Q. Hoare and G. N. Smith, eds. New York: International Publishers.

Greaves, Tom, ed. 1994. *Intellectual Property Rights for Indigenous Peoples: A Sourcebook*. Oklahoma City: Society for Applied Anthropology.

Green, Rayna. 1988. "The Indian in Popular American Culture." In *Handbook of North American Indians*, vol. 4. *Indian-White Relations*, W. Washburn, ed. Washington, D.C.: Smithsonian Institution, 587-606.

Gregory, Herbert E. 1916. *The Navajo Country: A Geographic and Hydrographic Reconnaissance of Parts of Arizona, New Mexico, and Utah*.

References

USGS Water Supply Paper. Washington D.C.: U.S. Government Printing Office.

Grobsmith, Elizabeth. 1997. "Growing Up on Deloria: The Impact of His Work on a New Generation of Anthropologists." In *Indians and Anthropologists: Vine Deloria Jr. and the Critique of Anthropology,* Thomas Biolsi and Larry Zimmerman, eds. Tucson: University of Arizona Press, 35-49.

Grossberg, Lawrence. 1993. "The Formations of Cultural Studies: An American in Birmingham." In *Relocating Cultural Studies: Developments in Theory and Research,* Valda Blundell, John Shepherd, and Ian Taylor, eds. New York: Routledge, 21-66.

Guerrero, Marianna. 1992. "American Indian Water Rights: The Blood of Life in Native North America." In *The State of Native America: Genocide, Colonization, and Resistance,* M. Annette Jaimes, ed. Boston: South End Press.

Gutiérrez, Ramón A. 1991. *When Jesus Came, the Corn Mothers Went Away: Marriage, Sexuality, and Power in New Mexico, 1500-1846.* Stanford: Stanford University Press.

Habermas, Jurgen. 1990 [1983]. *Moral Consciousness and Communicative Action.* Cambridge, Mass.: MIT Press.

Hack, J. T. 1942. *The Changing Physical Environment of the Hopi Indians of Arizona.* Papers of the Peabody Museum of American Archaeology and Ethnology, 36:1.

Hall, Stuart. 1992 [1980]. "Two Paradigms in Cultural Studies." In *Culture, Power, History,* Nicholas Dirks, Geoff Eley, and Sherry Ortner, eds. Princeton: Princeton University Press.

Hallowell, A. Irving. 1955. "The Self and Its Behavioral Environment." In *Culture and Experience,* A. I. Hallowell, ed. Philadelphia: University of Pennsylvania Press, 75-110.

Hammond, George P., and Agapito Rey, eds. 1966. *The Rediscovery of New Mexico, 1580-1594.* Albuquerque: University of New Mexico Press.

Hanson Annual Report, 1996. Hanson PLC. London, England.

Harré, Rom. 1984. *Personal Being: A Theory for Individual Psychology.* Cambridge, Mass.: Harvard University Press.

Harrington, Isis L. 1931. "'The Good-Bringing': A Tale from the Hopi Pueblo of Oraibi." *New Mexico Historical Review* 6:227-30.

Harrison, Simon. 1985. "Names, Ghosts, and Alliance in Two Sepik River Societies." *Oceania* 56:2:138-46.

Harvey, Byron. 1972. "An Overview of Pueblo Religion." In *New Perspectives on the Pueblos,* A. Ortiz, ed. Albuquerque: University of New Mexico Press.

Hastrup, Kirsten. 1995. *A Passage to Anthropology: Between Experience and Theory.* New York: Routledge.

Hastrup, Kirsten, and Peter Elass. 1990. "Anthropological Advocacy: A Contradiction in Terms?" *Current Anthropology* 31:3:301-11.

Heidegger, Martin. 1962. *Being and Time.* New York: Harper and Row.

Hieb, Louis A. 1979. "Hopi World View." In *Handbook of North American Indians,* vol. 9, *The Southwest,* Alfonso Ortiz, ed. Washington, D.C.: Smithsonian Institution, 577-80.

———. 1979a. "The Ritual Clown: Humor and Ethics." In *Forms of Play of Native North Americans,* Edward Norbeck and Claire Farrer, eds. 1977 Proceedings of the American Ethnological Society. Saint Paul: West, 171-88.

Hillerman, Tony. 1982. *The Dark Wind.* New York: Harper and Row.

Hirsch, E. D. Jr. 1976. *The Aims of Interpretation.* Chicago: University of Chicago Press.

———. 1984. "Meaning and Significance Reinterpreted." *Critical Inquiry* 11:2:202-25.

Holt, Hazel. 1990. *A Lot to Ask: A Life of Barbara Pym.* New York: Dutton.

Hooker, J. R. 1963. "The Anthropologist's Frontier: The Last Phase of African Exploitation." *Journal of Modern African Studies* 1:455-59.

Hopi Hearings. 1955. Mimeograph. Bureau of Indian Affairs. Phoenix Area Office. Hopi Agency.

Hopi Tutuveni. 1996. Letter to the editor re: the Kayenta Coal Mine, from W. Howard Carson, President, Peabody Western Coal Company. Kykotsmovi, Arizona.

Hough, Walter. 1906. "Sacred Springs of the Southwest." *Records of the Past* 5:6:163-69.

Hymes, Dell, ed. 1972. *Reinventing Anthropology.* New York: Pantheon.

Jakobson, Roman. 1990. *On Language.* Cambridge, Mass.: Harvard University Press.

James, Harry C. 1974. *Pages from Hopi History.* Tucson: University of Arizona Press.

Jameson, Frederic. 1986. "Third World Literature in the Era of Multinational Capitalism." *Social Text* 15:65-88.

———. 1991. *Postmodernism, or, the Cultural Logic of Late Capitalism.* Durham, N.C.: Duke University Press.

Jeanne, Laverne Masayesva. 1978. "Aspects of Hopi Grammar." Ph.D. diss. Massachusetts Institute of Technology.

Johnson, Abigail F. 1933. *Beyond the Black Buttes: True Stories of Hopiland.* Kansas City: The Western Baptist Publishing Co.

Jones, Delmos. 1970. "Towards a Native Anthropology." *Human Organization* 29:4:251-59.

Kabotie, Fred. 1977. *Fred Kabotie: Hopi Indian Artist—An Autobiography Told with Bill Belknap.* Flagstaff: Northland.

References

Kaiser, Rudolf. 1991. *The Voice of the Great Spirit: Prophecies of the Hopi Indians.* Boston: Shambhala Press.

Kammer, Jerry. 1980. *The Second Long Walk: The Navajo-Hopi Land Dispute.* Albuquerque: University of New Mexico Press.

Kapferer, Bruce, ed. 1976. *Transaction and Meaning: Directions in the Anthropology of Exchange and Symbolic Behavior.* Philadelphia: ISHI.

Kaye, Merwin. 1991. Videotape of the 1990 Smoki ceremonials. Hopi Office of Cultural Preservation. Kykotsmovi, Arizona.

Keam's Canyon Office Diary. 1912–16. Record Group 75. National Archives. Laguna Niguel, Calif.

Kelly, Richard S. 1988. "Spiritueller Imperialismus oder die Vereinnahmung der Hopi." In *Hopi und Kachina: Indianische Kultur im Wandel,* Albert Kunze, ed. Munich: Trickster Verlag, 132–36.

Kendall, Martha B. 1980. "Exegesis and Translation: Northern Yuman Names as Texts." *Journal of Anthropological Research* 36:261–73.

Kennard, Edward A. 1937. "Hopi Reactions to Death." *American Anthropologist* 39:3:491–96.

———. 1979. "Hopi Economy and Subsistence." In *Handbook of North American Indians,* vol 9., *The Southwest,* Alfonso Ortiz, ed. Washington, D.C.: Smithsonian Institution, 554–63.

Kenny, Anthony J. 1979. *Aristotle's Theory of the Will.* New Haven: Yale University Press.

Kertzer, David I. 1988. *Ritual, Politics, and Power.* New Haven: Yale University Press.

Kluckhohn, Clyde. 1944. *Navaho Witchcraft.* Papers of the Peabody Museum of American Archaeology and Ethnology, 22:2. Cambridge, Mass.: Harvard University.

Kluckhohn, Clyde, and Dorothea Leighton. 1946. *The Navaho.* Cambridge: Harvard University Press.

Kondo, Dorinne K. 1990. *Crafting Selves: Power, Gender, and Discourses of Identity in a Japanese Workplace.* Chicago: University of Chicago Press.

Krehbiel, C. 1938. *History of the Mennonite General Conference,* vol. 2. Indiana: no publisher indicated.

Kroeber, A. L. 1919. "Zuni Kin and Clan." *Anthropological Papers of the American Museum of Natural History* 18(2):39–204.

Krupat, Arnold. 1989. *The Voice in the Margin: Native American Literature and the Canon.* Berkeley: University of California Press.

———. 1992. *Ethnocriticism: Ethnography, History, Literature.* Berkeley: University of California Press.

———. 1996. *The Turn to the Native: Studies in Criticism and Culture.* Lincoln: University of Nebraska Press.

Kunze, Albert, ed. 1988. *Hopi und Kachina: Indianische Kultur im Wandel.* Munich: Trickster Verlag.

Kuper, Adam. 1973. *Anthropologists and Anthropology: The British School, 1922-72.* New York: Pica Press.

———. 1982. "Lineage Theory: A Critical Retrospect." *Annual Review of Anthropology* 11:71-95.

Kurtz, Donald V. 1996. "Hegemony and Anthropology: Gramsci, Exegeses, Reinterpretations." *Critique of Anthropology* 16:2:103-35.

Kuschel, Rolf. 1988. "Cultural Reflections in Balinese Personal Names." *Journal of the Polynesian Society* 97:1:49-71.

Lacan, Jacques. 1966-71. *Écrits.* Paris: Éditions du Seuil.

Ladd, J. 1957. *The Structure of a Moral Code: A Philosophical Analysis of Ethical Discourse Applied to the Ethics of the Navaho Indians.* Cambridge: Harvard University Press.

La Farge, Oliver. 1937. "Notes for Hopi Administrators." Manuscript. Record Group 75. Washington, D.C.: National Archives.

Laird, W. David. 1977. *Hopi Bibliography: Comprehensive and Annotated.* Tucson: University of Arizona Press.

Lavie, Smadar. 1990. *The Poetics of Military Occupation: Mzeina Allegories of Bedouin Identity under Israeli and Egyptian Rule.* Berkeley: University of California Press.

Lawrence, D. H. 1924. "The Hopi Snake Dance." *Theatre Arts Monthly* 8:12:836-60.

Lawshe, Abraham L. 1910. Letter to the Commissioner of Indian Affairs. Hopi Agency Letterbooks. Keam's Canyon, Arizona, 6 December 1910.

Leach, Edmund. 1961. *Rethinking Anthropology.* London: Athlone.

———. 1976. *Culture and Communication: The Logic by Which Symbols Are Connected.* New York: Cambridge University Press.

———. 1982. *Social Anthropology.* New York: Oxford University Press.

Leclerc, G. 1972. *Anthropologie et Colonialisme.* Paris: Fayard.

Lehman, David. 1991. *Signs of the Times: Deconstruction and the Fall of Paul de Man.* New York: Poseidon.

Lévi-Strauss, Claude. 1949. *Les Structures Élémentaires de la Parenté.* Paris: Presses Universitaires de France.

———. 1955. "The Structural Study of Myth." *Journal of American Folklore* lxxviii:270:428-44.

———. 1966. *The Savage Mind.* Chicago: University of Chicago Press.

———. 1966a. "Anthropology: Its Achievements and Future." *Current Anthropology* 7:2:124-27.

———. 1968. "The Story of Asdiwal." In *The Structural Study of Myth and Totemism,* Edmund Leach, ed. London: Tavistock.

———. 1970. *The Raw and the Cooked.* London: Jonathan Cape.

———. 1995 *The Story of Lynx.* Chicago: University of Chicago Press.

Levy, Jerrold E. 1992. *Orayvi Revisited: Social Stratification in an "Egalitarian" Society.* Santa Fe: School of American Research Press.

References

Lewellen, Ted. 1983. *Political Anthropology: An Introduction.* South Hadley, Mass.: Bergin and Garvey.

Lewis, Gilbert. 1980. *Day of Shining Red.* Cambridge: Cambridge University Press.

Lienhardt, Godfrey. 1988. "Social and Cultural Implications of Some African Personal Names." *Journal of the Anthropological Society of Oxford* (special issue on names and their uses) 19:2:105-16.

Lindstrom, Lamont. 1984. "Doctor, Lawyer, Wise Man, Priest: Big Men and Knowledge in Melanesia." *Man* (n.s.) 19, 291-309.

———. 1985. "Personal Names and Social Reproduction on Tanna, Vanuatu." *Journal of the Polynesian Society* 94:1:27-45.

Littlefield, Daniel F. Jr. 1992. "American Indians, American Scholars, and the American Literary Canon." *American Studies* 33:95-111.

Lloyd, Christopher. 1993. *The Structures of History.* Cambridge, Mass.: Blackwell.

Loftin, John D. 1991. *Religion and Hopi Life in the Twentieth Century.* Bloomington: Indiana University Press.

Long, Paul V. 1992. *Big Eyes: The Southwestern Photographs of Simeon Schwemberger, 1902-1908.* Albuquerque: University of New Mexico Press.

Los Angeles Times. 1994. "Coal Mining and Hopi Water." Letter to the editor by W. Howard Carson, President, Peabody Western Coal Company, 30 April 1994.

Lowe, Lisa, and David Lloyd, eds. 1997. *The Politics of Culture in the Shadow of Capital.* Durham, N.C.: Duke University Press.

Lowie, Robert H. 1929. "Notes on Hopi Clans." *Anthropological Papers of the American Museum of Natural History* 30(6):303-60.

Luhrmann, T. M. 1986. "The Magic of Secrecy." Manuscript. (Since published in *Persuasions of the Witches' Craft.* 1989. Cambridge, Mass.: Harvard University Press.)

Lummis, Charles F. 1968 [1903]. *Bullying the Moqui.* Prescott: Prescott College Press.

Lurie, Nancy O. 1988. "Relations between Indians and Anthropologists." In *Handbook of North American Indians,* vol. 4, *Indian-White Relations,* W. Washburn, ed. Washington, D.C.: Smithsonian Institution, 548-56.

MacIntyre, Alasdair. 1985. "Relativism, Power, and Philosophy." *American Philosophical Society Proceedings,* 5-22.

MacLean, Ian, Alan Montefiore, and Peter Winch, eds. 1990. *The Political Responsibility of Intellectuals.* Cambridge: Cambridge University Press.

Mails, Thomas (with Dan Evehema). 1996. *Hotevilla: Hopi Shrine of the Covenant: Microcosm of the World.* New York: Marlowe.

———. 1996a. *The Hopi Survival Kit for Safe Passage from the Fourth to the Fifth Cycle, into the New Millennium.* New York: Welcome Rain.

Maine, H. S. 1861. *Ancient Law.* London: Murray.

Malcolmson, Scott. 1989. "How the West Was Lost: Writing at the End of the World." *Village Voice.* vol. 34. Literary Supplement 73 (April 1989):9-13.

Malinowski, Bronislaw. 1922. *Argonauts of the Western Pacific: An Account of Native Enterprise and Adventure in the Archipelagoes of Melanesian New Guinea.* London: Routledge.

———. 1967. *A Diary in the Strict Sense of the Term.* London: Routledge.

Malotki, Ekkehart. 1978. *Hopitutuwutsi-Hopi Tales: A Bilingual Collection of Hopi Indian Stories.* Flagstaff: Museum of Northern Arizona Press.

———. 1979. *Eine Sprachwissenschaftliche Analyse der Raumvorstellungen in der Hopi Sprache.* Tübingen: Gunter Narr.

———. 1983. *Hopi Time: A Linguistic Analysis of the Temporal Concepts in the Hopi Language.* Berlin: Mouton.

Malotki, Ekkehart, and Michael Lomatuway'ma. 1987. *Maasaw: Profile of a Hopi God.* Lincoln: University of Nebraska Press.

———. 1987a. *Stories of Maasaw: A Hopi God.* Lincoln: University of Nebraska Press.

Manners, Robert A. 1952. "Anthropology and 'Culture in Crisis.'" *American Anthropologist* 54:127-34.

Maquet, J. J. 1964. "Objectivity in Anthropology." *Current Anthropology* 5:1:47-57.

Marcus, George, and Michael Fischer. 1986. *Anthropology as Cultural Critique: An Experimental Moment in the Human Sciences.* Chicago: University of Chicago Press.

Martin, Calvin. 1978. *Keepers of the Game: Indian-Animal Relationships in the Fur Trade.* Berkeley: University of California Press.

———, ed. 1987. *The American Indian and the Problem of History.* New York: Oxford University Press.

Marvel Comics. 1992. NFL Superpro. New York, March 1992.

Masayesva, Vernon. 1991. "Native Peoples and the University Community." (Research on Hopi: Concerns of the Tribe.) Speech delivered at Northern Arizona University Union, 23 January 1991.

Masayesva, Victor, Jr., and Erin Younger, compilers. 1983. *Hopi Photographers, Hopi Images.* Tucson: University of Arizona Press.

Matthiessen, Peter. 1984. *Indian Country.* New York: Viking.

Mauss, Marcel. 1938. (See Mauss 1985 [1938].)

———. 1985 [1938]. "A Category of the Human Mind: The Notion of Person; The Notion of Self." In *The Category of the Person,* M. Carrithers, S. Collins, and S. Lukes, eds. Cambridge: Cambridge University Press, 1-25.

Maxwell, Allen R. 1984. "Kadayan Personal Names and Naming." In Tooker 1984 (q.v.), 25-39.

Maybury-Lewis, David. 1984. "Name, Person, and Ideology in Central Brazil." In Tooker 1984 (q.v.), 1-10.

McGrane, Bernard. 1989. *Beyond Anthropology: Society and the Other.*
New York: Columbia University Press.

McKibben, William. 1989. *The End of Nature.* New York: Random House.

McLeod, Roxie. 1994. "Dreams and Rumors: A History of *Book of the
Hopi.*" Master's thesis in religious studies, University of Colorado.

Means, Florence C. 1960. *Sunlight on the Hopi Mesas: The Story of Abigail
F. Johnson.* Philadelphia: Judson Press.

Medick, Hans, and David W. Sabean, eds. 1984. *Interest and Emotion: Essays on the Study of Family and Kinship.* Cambridge: Cambridge University Press.

Meigs, Anna S. 1983. *Food, Sex, and Pollution: A New Guinea Religion.*
New Brunswick: Rutgers University Press.

The Mennonite. 1923. "Missionary Reports: From Our Station in Arizona."
North Newton, Kans.: Mennonite Library and Archives, 12 April 1923.

Mennonite Encyclopedia. 1954-59. 4 vols. Scottdale, Pa.: Mennonite Publishing House.

Michnik, Adam. 1990. "The Two Faces of Europe." *New York Review of
Books* 37:12:7.

Miller, Edgar K. 1931. Letter to the Commissioner of Indian Affairs. Record
Group 75. Washington, D.C.: National Archives, 10 January 1931.

Milton, Kay, ed. 1993. *Environmentalism: The View from Anthropology.*
New York: Routledge.

Mindeleff, Victor. 1891. "A Study of Pueblo Architecture: Tusayan and Ci-
bola." In *Eighth Annual Report of the Bureau of American Ethnology,
Smithsonian Institution (for 1886-7).* Washington D.C.: U.S. Government
Printing Office, 3-228.

Minh-ha, Trinh T. 1989. *Woman, Native, Other: Writing Postcoloniality
and Feminism.* Bloomington: Indiana University Press.

Mithun, Marianne. 1984. "Principles of Naming in Mohawk." In Tooker
1984 (q.v.), 40-54.

Momaday, N. Scott. 1974. "Native American Attitudes to the Environment." In *Seeing with a Native Eye: Essays on Native American Religion,*
W. Capps, ed. New York: Harper and Row, 79-85.

Montgomery, Ross, Watson Smith, and J. O. Brew. 1949. *Franciscan
Awatovi: The Excavation and Conjectural Reconstruction of a Seven-
teenth-Century Spanish Mission Establishment at a Hopi Indian Town in
Northeastern Arizona.* Peabody Museum of American Archaeology and
Ethnology Papers, 36.

Moore, J. 1971. "Perspective for a Partisan Anthropology." *Liberation*
16:34-43.

Moore, John H. 1984. "Cheyenne Names and Cosmology." *American Ethnologist* 11:2:291-312.

Morgan, Lewis Henry. 1851. *League of the Ho-de'-no-sau-nee or Iroquois.* Rochester: Sage and Brother.

———. 1877. *Ancient Society; or, Researches in the Lines of Human Progress from Savagery through Barbarism to Civilization.* New York: Henry Holt.

Munn, Nancy. 1992. "The Cultural Anthropology of Time: A Critical Essay." *Annual Review of Anthropology* 21:93-123.

Murphy, William P. 1980. "Secret Knowledge as Property and Power in Kpelle Society: Elders versus Youth." *Africa* 50:207-593.

Myers, Fred. 1986. "The Politics of Representation: Anthropological Discourse and Australian Aborigines." *American Ethnologist* 13:138-53.

Nagata, Shuichi. 1970. *Modern Transformations of Moenkopi Pueblo.* Illinois University Studies in Anthropology 6. Urbana.

———. n.d. "Factionalism or Status Competition? Some Observations on Hopi Status Hierarchy." Manuscript. Paper presented at a seminar on Pueblo politics, University of California, Santa Cruz, July 1978, and to the Canadian Ethnological Society meetings, February 1979.

———. n.d.a "Being Hopi in the Twentieth Century." Manuscript. Presented to the School of American Research Advanced Seminar on "The Hopi Indians," February 1982. Santa Fe.

Native American Studies Center (University of New Mexico). 1993. "Comments on *When Jesus Came the Corn Mothers Went Away,* by Ramón A. Gutiérrez." *American Indian Culture and Research Journal* 17:3:141-77.

Navajo Times. 1990. "Apaches, Zunis Join Navajos, Hopis in Opposing Development of Sacred, Historical Landmark," George Hardeen, 27 December 1990.

Needham, Rodney. 1974. *Remarks and Inventions: Skeptical Essays about Kinship.* London: Tavistock.

Nelson, Richard. 1993. "Searching for the Lost Arrow: Physical and Spiritual Ecology in the Hunter's World." In *The Biophilia Hypothesis,* S. R. Kellert and E. O. Wilson, eds. Washington D.C.: Island Press, 201-28.

Nequatewa, Edmund. 1936. *Truth of a Hopi: Stories Relating to the Origin, Myths and Clan Histories of the Hopi.* Flagstaff: Northland.

Newsweek. 1983. "Lost Idols of Shungopavi: Pillage of Antiquities in Arizona." 31 January 1983, 32-33.

New York Newsday. 1991. "Indian Leaders Battle Auction of Sacred Items." Amei Wallach, 18 May 1991, 2.

———. 1991a. "Top Bidder to Return Sacred Indian Masks." Amei Wallach, 22 May 1991, 21.

New York Times. 1991. "Woodruff Journal: After Mining, a Furor over a Shrine." 3 January 1991, A12.

———. 1991. "Three Masks to Stay in Auction." Rita Reif, 21 May 1991, C18.

———. 1991. "Buyer Vows to Return Three Masks to Indians." Rita Reif, 22 May 1991, C11.

———. 1997. "Eastern Roots, Western Ties: A Collaboration in Japan." Peter Grilli, 17 July 1997, 2:35-36.

Nichols, William D. (Western Region Ground Water Specialist, USGS). 1993. Letter to William M. Alley (Chief, Office of Ground Water, Water Resources Division, USGS) 28 October 1993.

Obeyesekere, Gananath. 1992. *The Apotheosis of Captain Cook: European Mythmaking in the Pacific*. Princeton: Princeton University Press.

Ochs, Elinor, and Lisa Capps. 1996. "Narrating the Self." *Annual Review of Anthropology* 25:19-43.

Orlove, Benjamin S., and Stephen B. Brush. 1996. "Anthropology and the Conservation of Biodiversity." *Annual Review of Anthropology* 25:329-52.

Ortiz, Alfonso. 1969. *The Tewa World: Space, Time, Being and Becoming in a Pueblo Society*. Chicago: University of Chicago Press.

———. 1970. "An Indian Anthropologist's Perspective on Anthropology." In American Anthropological Association 1970 (q.v.), 85-92.

———. 1972. "Ritual Drama and the Pueblo World View." In *New Perspectives on the Pueblos*, A. Ortiz, ed. Albuquerque: University of New Mexico Press.

———. ed. 1979. *Handbook of North American Indians*, vol. 9, *The Southwest*. Washington D.C.: Smithsonian Institution.

Ortner, Sherry. 1984. "Theory in Anthropology since the Sixties." *Comparative Studies in Society and History* 26:126-66.

———. 1989. *High Religion: A Cultural and Political History of Sherpa Buddhism*. Princeton: Princeton University Press.

Page, Jake, and Suzanne Page. 1982. *Hopi*. New York: Harry N. Abrams.

———. 1982a. "Inside the Sacred Hopi Homeland." *National Geographic* 162:5:606-29.

Pandey, Triloki N. 1972. "Anthropologists at Zuni." *Proceedings of the American Philosophical Society* 116:321-37.

———. 1977. "Images of Power in a Southwestern Pueblo." In *The Anthropology of Power*, R. Fogelson and R. Adams, eds. New York: Academic Press.

Parkin, David. 1982. "Introduction." In *Semantic Anthropology*, D. Parkin, ed. (Association of Social Anthropologists Monograph 22) London: Academic Press, xi-li.

Parsons, Elsie Clews. 1922. "Oraibi in 1920." (In *Contributions to Hopi History*, E. C. Parsons, ed.), *American Anthropologist* 24:253-98.

———, ed. 1925. *A Pueblo Indian Journal, 1920-21*. American Anthropological Association Memoirs 32.

———. 1933. *Hopi and Zuni Ceremonialism.* American Anthropological Association Memoirs 39.

Peletz, Michael G. 1995. "Kinship Studies in Late Twentieth Century Anthropology." *Annual Review of Anthropology* 24:343-72.

Plog, Fred. 1978. "The Keresan Bridge: An Ecological and Archeological Account." In *Social Archeology: Beyond Subsistence and Dating,* Charles Redman et al., eds. New York: Academic Press, 349-72.

Pomper, Philip. 1996. Historians and Individual Agency. *History and Theory* 35:281-308.

Price, Richard. 1983. *First-Time: The Historical Vision of an Afro-American People.* Baltimore: Johns Hopkins University Press.

Price, Sally. 1989. *Primitive Art in Civilized Places.* Chicago: Chicago University Press.

Private Eye. 1996. "Hanson's Woes." February 1996, 6.

Putnam, Hilary. 1981. *Reason, Truth, and History.* New York: Cambridge University Press.

Pym, Barbara. 1955. *Less than Angels.* London: Cape.

———. 1984. *A Very Private Eye: An Autobiography in Diaries and Letters,* Hazel Holt and Hilary Pym, eds. New York: Dutton.

Qua' Töqti (The Eagle's Call). 1984. "Religious Leaders Destroy Construction Material on Ceremonial Clan Land." Kykotsmovi, Ariz.: Hopi Publishers. 22 March 1984, 1.

Rabinow, Paul, and William M. Sullivan. 1987. "The Interpretive Turn: A Second Look." In *Interpretive Social Science: A Second Look,* P. Rabinow and W. M. Sullivan, eds. Berkeley: University of California Press, 1-30.

Radcliffe-Brown, A. R. 1950. "Introduction." In *African Systems of Kinship and Marriage,* A. R. Radcliffe-Brown and Daryll Forde, eds. New York: Oxford University Press.

———. 1952. *Structure and Function in Primitive Society.* London: Cohen and West.

Ramos, Alcida. 1974. "How the Sanuma Acquire Their Names." *Ethnology* 13:171-85.

Ramsey, Jarold. 1983. *Reading the Fire: Five Essays in the Traditional Indian Literatures of the Far West.* Lincoln: University of Nebraska Press.

Read, Kenneth E. 1955. "Morality and the Concept of the Person among the Gahuku-Gama." *Oceania* 25:233-82.

Redford, K. 1991. "The Ecologically Noble Savage." *Orion* 9:24-29.

Reed, Michael C. 1997. "Nine Contemporary Anthropological Work Roles." In *Practicing Anthropology in a Postmodern World: Lessons and Insights from Federal Contract Research,* M. C. Reed, ed. National Association for the Practice of Anthropology, Bulletin 17, 11-28.

Revard, Carter. 1987. "Traditional Osage Naming Ceremonies: Entering the Circle of Being." In *Recovering the Word: Essays on Native American Lit-*

erature, B. Swann and A. Krupat, eds. Berkeley: University of California Press, 446-66.

Ricoeur, Paul. 1967. *Husserl: An Analysis of His Phenomenology.* Evanston: Northwestern University Press.

Roosevelt, Theodore. 1925. *Selections from the Correspondence of Theodore Roosevelt and Henry Cabot Lodge, 1884-1918.* New York: Charles Scribner's Sons.

Rorty, Richard. 1989. *Contingency, Irony, and Solidarity.* New York: Cambridge University Press.

Rosaldo, Michelle. 1980. *Knowledge and Passion: Ilongot Notions of Self and Social Life.* Cambridge: Cambridge University Press.

———. 1984. "Toward an Anthropology of Self and Feeling." In *Culture Theory: Essays on Mind, Self, and Emotion,* R. A. Shweder and R. A. Levine, eds. New York: Cambridge University Press, 137-57.

Rosaldo, Renato. 1980. *Ilongot Headhunting, 1873-1974: A Study in Society and History.* Stanford: Stanford University Press.

———. 1984. "Ilongot Naming: The Play of Associations." In Tooker 1984 (q.v.), 11-24.

———. 1989. *Culture and Truth: The Remaking of Social Analysis.* Boston: Beacon Press.

Rose, Wendy. 1992. "The Great Pretenders: Further Reflections on Whiteshamanism." In *The State of Native America: Genocide, Colonization, and Resistance,* M. Annette Jaimes, ed. Boston: South End Press, 403-21.

Rosen, Lawrence, ed. 1995. *Other Intentions: Cultural Contexts and the Attribution of Inner States.* Santa Fe: School of American Research Press.

Rubinstein, R. 1981. "Knowledge and Political Process on Malo." In *Vanuatu: Politics, Economics and Ritual in Island Melanesia,* M. Allen, ed. Sydney: Academic Press.

Rushforth, Scott, and Steadman Upham. 1992. *A Hopi Social History.* Austin: University of Texas Press.

Rydell, Robert. 1984. *All the World's a Fair: Visions of Empire at American International Expositions, 1876-1916.* Chicago: University of Chicago Press.

Sahlins, Marshall D. 1981. *Historical Metaphors and Mythical Realities: Structure in the Early History of the Sandwich Islands Kingdom.* Ann Arbor: University of Michigan Press.

———. 1985. *Islands of History.* Chicago: University of Chicago Press.

———. 1993. "Goodbye to Tristes Tropes: Ethnography in the Context of Modern World History." *Journal of Modern History* 65:1-25.

———. 1993a. *Waiting for Foucault.* Cambridge, Eng.: Prickly Pear Press.

———. 1995. *How "Natives" Think: About Captain Cook, for Example.* Chicago: University of Chicago Press.

———. 1996. "The Sadness of Sweetness: The Native Anthropology of Western Cosmology." *Current Anthropology* 37:395-415.

Said, Edward. 1983. *The World, the Text, and the Critic*. Cambridge, Mass.: Harvard University Press.

———. 1989. "Representing the Colonized: Anthropology's Interlocutors." *Critical Inquiry* 15:205-25.

———. 1993. *Culture and Imperialism*. New York: Knopf.

Sangren, P. Steven. n.d. "Post-Structuralist and Interpretivist Approaches to Subjectivity and Personhood: A Critique." Presented at session "The Cultural Production of the Person," annual meetings of the American Anthropological Association, New Orleans, 1990.

Sanner, Hans-Ulrich. 1992. "Tsukulalwa: die Clownzeremonie der Hopi als Spiegel Ihrer Kultur im Wandel." Ph.D. dissertation. Frankfurt: Johann Wolfgang Goethe-Universitat.

———. 1996. Gleanings from meetings: "Dialogue with the Hopis": Cultural Copyright and Research Ethics Conference, 21-23 August 1995, Phoenix. *European Review of Native American Studies* 10:1:49-50.

Sass, Louis. 1986. "Anthropology's Native Problems: Revisionism in the Field." *Harper's Magazine* May 1986, 49-57.

Sassoon, Anne Showstack. 1987. *Gramsci's Politics*. Minneapolis: University of Minnesota Press.

Sato, Hiroaki. 1983. *One Hundred Frogs: From Renga to Haiku to English*. New York: Weatherhill.

Saussure, Ferdinand de. 1966. *Course in General Linguistics*, Wade Baskin, trans. New York: McGraw-Hill.

Scheper-Hughes, Nancy. 1995. "The Primacy of the Ethical: Propositions for a Militant Anthropology." *Current Anthropology* 36:409-40.

Schlegel, Alice M. 1977. *Sexual Stratification: A Cross-Cultural View*. New York: Columbia University Press.

———. 1992. "African Political Models in the American Southwest: Hopi as an Internal Frontier Society." *American Anthropologist* 94:376-97.

Schneider, David M. 1984. *A Critique of the Study of Kinship*. Ann Arbor: University of Michigan Press.

Schneider, David M., and Kathleen Gough, eds. 1961. *Matrilineal Kinship*. Berkeley: University of California Press.

Schoolcraft, Henry Rowe, ed. 1851-57. *Historical and Statistical Information Respecting the History, Condition, and Prospects of the Indian Tribes of the United States*. Philadelphia: Lippincott, Grambo.

Scott, James C. 1985. *Weapons of the Weak: Everyday Forms of Peasant Resistance*. New Haven: Yale University Press.

Scott, Joan W. 1991. "The Evidence of Experience." *Critical Inquiry* 17:773-97.

Searle, John R. 1983. *Intentionality: An Essay in the Philosophy of Mind*. New York: Cambridge University Press.

Sedgwick, Eve K. 1990. *Epistemology of the Closet.* Berkeley: University of California Press.

Sekaquaptewa, Emory. 1972. "Preserving the Good Things of Hopi Life." In *Plural Society in the Southwest,* E. M. Spicer and R. H. Thompson, eds. Albuquerque: University of New Mexico Press, 239-60.

Sekaquaptewa, Helen. 1969. *Me and Mine,* Louise Udall, ed. Tucson: University of Arizona Press.

Sherzer, Joel. 1987. "Strategies in Text and Context: The Hot Pepper Story." In *Recovering the Word: Essays on Native American Literature,* B. Swann and A. Krupat, eds. Berkeley: University of California Press, 151-97.

Shweder, Richard. 1984. "Preview: A Colloquy of Culture Theorists." In *Culture Theory: Essays on Mind, Self, and Emotion,* R. A. Shweder and R. A. Levine, eds. New York: Cambridge University Press, 1-24.

Shweder, Richard A., and Edmund J. Bourne. 1984. "Does the Concept of the Person Vary Cross-Culturally?" In *Culture Theory: Essays on Mind, Self, and Emotion,* R. A. Shweder and R. A. Levine, eds. New York: Cambridge University Press, 158-99.

Silko, Leslie Marmon. 1991. *Almanac of the Dead.* New York: Simon and Schuster.

Simmel, Georg. 1950. "The Secret and the Secret Society." In *The Sociology of Georg Simmel,* K. Wolff, ed. New York: Free Press.

Simmons, Leo, ed. 1942. *Sun Chief: The Autobiography of a Hopi Indian.* New Haven: Yale University Press.

Sischy, Ingrid. 1991. "Photography: Good Intentions." *The New Yorker* 9 September 1991, 89-95.

SITES (Smithsonian Institution Traveling Exhibition Service). 1979. *The Year of the Hopi: Paintings and Photographs by Joseph Mora, 1904-06.* Washington D.C.: Smithsonian Institution.

Smith, M. G. 1956. "On Segmentary Lineage Systems." *Journal of the Royal Anthropological Institute* 86:39-80.

Sotheby's. 1991. *Fine American Indian Art.* Auction Catalogue, 21 May 1991. New York.

Sperber, Dan. 1985. "Anthropology and Psychology: Towards an Epidemiology of Representations." *Man* 20:73-89.

Spiro, Melford E. 1966. "Religion: Problems of Definition and Explanation." In *Anthropological Approaches to the Study of Religion,* M. Banton, ed. London: Tavistock.

———. 1996. "Postmodernist Anthropology, Subjectivity, and Social Science: a Modernist Critique." *Comparative Studies in Society and History* 38:759-80.

Stauffer, Anna G. 1926. *Mennonite Mission Study Course, Part II: Hopi Mission Field.* Newton, Kans.: Herald.

Steward, Julian H. 1937. "Ecological Aspects of Southwestern Society." *Anthropos* 32:87–104.

Strathern, Marilyn. 1988. *The Gender of the Gift: Problems with Women and Problems with Society in Melanesia.* Berkeley: University of California Press.

Suderman, Mrs. John P. n.d. (c. 1945) *Our Missions among the Hopi Indians.* No publisher indicated. Mennonite Library and Archives. Bethel College. North Newton, Kansas.

Tambiah, S. J. 1985. *Culture, Thought, and Social Action: An Anthropological Perspective.* Cambridge, Mass.: Harvard University Press.

———. 1990. *Magic, Science, Religion, and the Scope of Rationality.* Cambridge: Cambridge University Press.

Taylor, Charles. 1985. *Human Agency and Language.* New York: Cambridge University Press.

Techqua Ikachi. 1991. Film produced by Anka Schmidt, Agnes Barmettler, and James Danaqyumptewa. Mano Productions.

Tedlock, Barbara. 1992. *The Beautiful and the Dangerous: Encounters with the Zuni Indians.* New York: Viking.

Tedlock, Dennis. 1979. "Zuni Religion and World View." In *Handbook of North American Indians,* vol. 9, *The Southwest,* A. Ortiz, ed. Washington, D.C.: Smithsonian Institution, 499–508.

Thomas, Alfred Barnaby. 1932. *Forgotten Frontiers: A Study of the Spanish Indian Policy of Don Juan Bautista de Anza, Governor of New Mexico, 1777–1780.* Norman: University of Oklahoma Press.

Thompson, E. P. 1978. *The Poverty of Theory and Other Essays.* London: Merlin.

Thompson, Laura. 1945. "Logico-Aesthetic Integration in Hopi Culture." *American Anthropologist* 47:540–53.

———. 1950. *Culture in Crisis: A Study of the Hopi Indians.* New York: Harper.

Thompson, Laura, and Alice Joseph. 1944. *The Hopi Way.* Chicago: University of Chicago Press.

Titiev, Mischa. 1943. "The Influence of Common Residence on the Unilateral Classification of Kindred." *American Anthropologist* 45:511–30.

———. 1944. *Old Oraibi: A Study of the Hopi Indians of Third Mesa.* Peabody Museum of American Archaeology and Ethnology, Papers, 22 (1).

———. 1972. *The Hopi Indians of Old Oraibi: Change and Continuity.* Ann Arbor: University of Michigan Press.

———. n.d. "Census Notes from Old Oraibi." Manuscript, Peabody Museum of American Archaeology and Ethnology, Harvard University (copy courtesy of Margaret Wright).

Todorov, Tzvetan. 1984. *The Conquest of America: The Question of the Other.* New York: Harper.

Tooker, Elizabeth, ed. 1984. *Naming Systems*. Proceedings of the American Ethnological Society, 1980.

Torgovnick, Marianna. 1990. *Gone Primitive: Savage Intellects, Modern Lives*. Chicago: University of Chicago Press.

Traube, Elizabeth. n.d. "Authoritative Knowledge in an East Timorese Society." Paper presented at the annual meeting of the American Anthropological Association, Denver, 1984.

Tsing, Anna L. 1993. *In the Realm of the Diamond Queen: Marginality in an Out-of-the-way Place*. Princeton: Princeton University Press.

The Tucson Weekly. 1992. "Mystery at Second Mesa." 1 July 1992, 10-24.

Turner, Stephen. 1994. *The Social Theory of Practices: Tradition, Tacit Knowledge, and Presuppositions*. Chicago: University of Chicago Press.

Tyler, Stephen. 1986. "Post-Modern Ethnography: From Document of the Occult to Occult Document." In *Writing Culture: The Poetics and Politics of Ethnography*, James Clifford and George Marcus, eds. Berkeley: University of California Press, 122-40.

Ucko, Peter. 1987. *Academic Freedom and Apartheid: The Story of the World Archaeological Congress*. London: Duckworth.

Ueda, Makoto. 1965. *Zeami, Basho, Yeats, Pound: A Study in Japanese and American Poetics*. The Hague: Mouton.

Underhill, Ruth M. 1979 [1936]. *Papago Woman*. New York: Holt, Rinehart, Winston.

Upham, Steadman. 1982. *Polities and Power: A Social and Economic History of the Western Pueblo*. New York: Academic Press.

U.S. Department of the Interior. 1990. *Proposed Permit Application, Black Mesa-Kayenta Mine, Navajo and Hopi Indian Reservations, Arizona*, 2 vols. Final Environmental Impact Statement OSM-EIS-25. Denver: Office of Surface Mining Reclamation and Enforcement.

U.S. Geological Survey. 1995. *Results of Ground-Water, Surface-Water, and Water-Quality Monitoring, Black Mesa Area, Northeastern Arizona 1992-93*. Water Resources Investigations Report 95-4156. Tucson.

Vecsey, Christopher. 1980. "American Indian Environmental Religions." In *American Indian Environments: Ecological Issues in Native American History*, C. Vecsey and R. W. Venable, eds. Syracuse: Syracuse University Press, 1-37.

Verdon, Michel. 1983. *The Abutia Ewe of West Africa: A Chiefdom that Never Was*. Berlin: Mouton.

Vizenor, Gerald. 1987. "Socioacupuncture: Mythic Reversals and the Striptease in Four Scenes." In Martin, ed. 1987 (q.v.), 180-91.

Voegelin, Charles F., and Florence M. Voegelin. 1957. *Hopi Domains: A Lexical Approach to the Problem of Selection*. Supplement to *International Journal of American Linguistics* 23:2.

References

Voth, H. R. 1901. *The Oraibi Powamu Ceremony.* Chicago: Field Columbian Museum Publication 61, Anthropological Series, vol. iii, no. 2.
———. 1903. *The Oraibi Summer Snake Ceremony.* Chicago: Field Columbian Museum Publication 83.
———. 1905. *Traditions of the Hopi.* Chicago: Field Columbian Museum
Publication 96, Anthropological Series 8.
———. 1905a. *Oraibi Natal Customs and Ceremonies.* Chicago: Field Columbian Museum Publication 97, Anthropological Series, vol. vi, no. 2.
———. 1905b. *Hopi Proper Names.* Chicago: Field Columbian Museum
Publication 100, Anthropological Series 6:1:63-113.
———. 1912. *The Oraibi Marau Ceremony.* Chicago: Field Columbian Museum Publication 156, Anthropological Series 11 (1).
———. 1923. "Historical Notes of the First Decade of the Mennonite Mission Work among the Hopi of Arizona, 1893-1902." *The Mennonite* 12
April 1923, 3-6.
Wade, Edwin. 1985. "The Ethnic Art Market in the American Southwest,
1880-1980." In *Objects and Others: Essays on Museums and Material
Culture,* G. Stocking, ed. Madison: University of Wisconsin Press, 167-91.
Wagner, Roy. 1996. "Hazarding Intent: Why Sogo Left Hweabi." In *Other
Intentions: Cultural Contexts and the Attribution of Inner States,* Law-
rence Rosen, ed. Santa Fe: School of American Research Press, 163-75.
Warburg, Aby. 1939 [1923]. "A Lecture on Serpent Ritual." *Journal of the
Warburg Institute* 2:277-92.
Warrior, Robert A. 1994. *Tribal Secrets: Recovering American Indian Intel-
lectual Traditions.* Minneapolis: University of Minnesota Press.
Washburn, Dorothy. 1980. *Hopi Kachina: Spirit of Life: Dedicated to the
Hopi Tricentennial, 1680-1980.* San Francisco: California Academy of Sci-
ences.
———. 1995. *Living in Balance: The Universe of the Hopi, Zuni, Navajo,
and Apache.* Philadelphia: University Museum.
Waters, Frank. 1963. *Book of the Hopi.* New York: Viking Press.
———. 1969. *Pumpkin Seed Point: Being within the Hopi.* Chicago: Sage
Books.
Webb, William, and Robert A. Weinstein. 1987 [1973]. *Dwellers at the
Source: Southwestern Indian Photographs of A. C. Vroman, 1895-1904.*
Albuquerque: University of New Mexico Press.
White, Elizabeth (Polingaysi Qoyawayma). 1964. *No Turning Back.* Albu-
querque: University of New Mexico Press.
White, G. M., and J. Kirkpatrick, eds. 1985. *Person, Self, and Experience: Ex-
ploring Pacific Ethnopsychologies.* Berkeley: University of California Press.
White, Leslie A. 1935. *The Pueblo of Santo Domingo, New Mexico.* Mem-
oirs of the American Anthropological Association 43.
———. n.d. "Kinship System Charts of the Hopi (Oraibi) [by clan and lin-

eage] Noted in the 1932 Field Training Course." (Unpublished manuscript, Laboratory of Anthropology, Santa Fe.)

White, Richard. 1984. "Native Americans and the Environment." In *Scholars and the Indian Experience*, W. R. Swagerty, ed. Bloomington: University of Indiana Press, 179-204.

Whiteley, Peter M. 1983. "Third Mesa Hopi Social Structural Dynamics and Sociocultural Change: The View from Bacavi." Ph.D. diss., University of New Mexico.

————. 1987. "Southwest Indian Religions." In *The Encyclopedia of Religion*, vol. 10, Mircea Eliade, ed. New York: Macmillan and Free Press, 513-25.

————. 1988. *Deliberate Acts: Changing Hopi Culture through the Oraibi Split*. Tucson: University of Arizona Press.

————. 1988a. *Bacavi: Journey to Reed Springs*. Flagstaff: Northland Press.

————. 1989. "Hopitutskwa: An Historical and Cultural Interpretation of the Hopi Traditional Land Claim." Expert witness report presented to the district court in Arizona for *Masayesva v. Zah v. James* ("The 1934 Reservation" case).

————. 1990. Review of *Dwellers at the Source: Southwestern Photographs of A. C. Vroman, 1895-1904*, and *The Hopi Photographs, Kate Cory: 1905-1912. American Indian Quarterly* 14:3:325-26.

————. 1992. "Historic Occupation of Black Mesa." Report prepared for the Water Resources Program, the Hopi Tribe.

————. 1994. Review of *Orayvi Revisited: Social Stratification in an "Egalitarian" Society*, Jerrold Levy. *Anthropos* 89:286-87.

————. In press. "Native North American Philosophy." In *The Routledge Encyclopaedia of Philosophy*, Edward Craig, ed. London: Routledge.

Whorf, Benjamin L. 1956. *Language, Thought, and Reality*, J. B. Carroll, ed. Cambridge, Mass.: MIT Press.

Wilkinson, Charles F. 1996. "Home Dance, the Hopi, and Black Mesa Coal: Conquest and Endurance in the American Southwest." *Brigham Young University Law Review* 1996:2:449-82.

Williams, Raymond. 1977. *Marxism and Literature*. New York: Oxford University Press.

Willis, Paul. 1977. *Learning to Labor: How Working Class Kids Get Working Class Jobs*. New York: Columbia University Press.

Willis, Roy. 1982. "On a Mental Sausage Machine and Other Nominal Problems." In *Semantic Anthropology*, D. Parkin, ed. London: Academic Press, 227-40.

Winship, G. 1896. *The Coronado Expedition, 1540-1542*. Bureau of American Ethnology Annual Report, 14.

Witherspoon, Gary. 1977. *Language and Art in the Navajo Universe*. Ann Arbor: University of Michigan Press.

Wollheim, Richard. 1987. *Painting as an Art*. Princeton, N.J.: Princeton University Press.

Worsley, Peter. 1966. "The End of Anthropology?" Paper prepared for the Sociology and Social Anthropology Working Group, Sixth World Congress of Sociology.

Wright, Barton. 1994. *Clowns of the Hopi: Tradition Keepers and Delight Makers*. Flagstaff: Northland.

Wright, Barton, Marnie Gaede, and Marc Gaede. 1986. *The Hopi Photographs: Kate Cory, 1905-1912*. La Cañada, Calif.: Chaco Press.

Wright, Robin M. 1988. "Anthropological Presuppositions of Indigenous Advocacy." *Annual Review of Anthropology* 17:365-90.

Wrong, Dennis. 1961. "The Oversocialized Conception of Man in Modern Sociology." *American Sociological Review* 26:183-93.

Wyckoff, Lydia L. 1990. *Designs and Factions: Politics, Religion, and Ceramics on the Hopi Third Mesa*. Albuquerque: University of New Mexico Press.

Yava, Albert. 1978. *Big Falling Snow: A Tewa-Hopi's Life and Times and the History and Traditions of His People*, Harold Courlander, ed. New York: Crown.

WEB SITES

Hopi Information Network: http://www.infomagic.com/abyte/hopi.html
Native Americans and the Environment: http://conbio.bio.uci.edu/nae/

INDEX

Page numbers in bold indicate illustrations

Tribal Court, at Third Mesa, 101
Tribal Police, at Third Mesa, 101
Tricentennial symposium (1980), 12,
214*n*18
truth, control over attributed to the
pavansinom, 93-94
Tsimontukwi (Woodruff Butte), 165-66,
168-69, 183, 232*n*3
tsukumongwi (clown chief), 98-100
Tsu'tiikive. See Snake Dance
tsu'wimkya. See Snake society
Tuba City, 200
tunatya: in Hopi philosophy of action,
39-41, 127, 139. *See also* intentionalism
tunnels, as site for secret meetings, 98,
223*n*9
Turley, Norman, 165-66
tuuhikya ("curer"; "medicine man"), 88,
94, 97, 102, 115
Tuwahoyiwma (Charles Fredericks), 154,
227*n*8
Tuwaletstiwa. See Johnson, K. T.
Tuwapongyatumsi (sand altar woman),
144
Two-Horn sodality. *See Aa'alt* sodality

unilineal system, 51-55, 71-72, 78. *See
also* matrilineal ties
United Mine Workers, 202
universe, Hopi, 42, 94
University of Arizona, Hopi dictionary
project, 11, 214*n*16
University of Chicago, 8-9
University of New Mexico, 19-20
Upham, Steadman, 10, 68, 82
Upper Munqapi (village), 56, 189-90,
220*n*2

Vélez de Escalante, Silvestre, 146-47
verbs, in Hopi language, 33, 41
Verdon, Michel, 55
village chief. See *Kikmongwi*
violence, physical: control by means of,
96-97; use in marked political events,
101
Vizenor, Gerald, 16, 180
Voegelin, Charles, 9, 112
Voegelin, Florence, 9, 112
Voth, H. R., 88-89, 145, 147; on clan
identity, 9, 60, 62; ethnographic
work, 8, 113, 175, 176, 188,

234*n*19; on Hopi names, 111, 115,
225*n*20

Wagner, Roy, 127
Walpi (village), 12, 24, 220*n*2; Snake
Dance, 14; *Wuwtsimt* ritual, 135
War Chief *(Qaletaqmongwi),* 88-92, 96,
101, 222*nn*4, 6
Warriors *(Momtsit)* society, 70, 91, 98-
100, 228*n*18
water: importance in Hopi culture, 188-
97, 229*n*30; use by Peabody Coal
Company, 28, 188-89, 197-204,
205-6
Water clan *(Patkingyam),* 144, 165-66,
195
Waters, Frank, 12, 24, 134, 167-68,
175, 228*n*11
Wepo Wash, 189
Wheeler-Howard Act of 1934, 101
whips *(wuvaapi),* ceremonial use, 96,
143, 229*n*28
White, Elizabeth (Polingaysi
Qoyawayma), 212*n*9
White, Leslie A., 7, 8, 52, 73, 74
Whorf, Benjamin Lee, 8, 10, 42, 44; depiction of Hopi language, 31, 33,
225*n*21, 235*n*27; on meaning of
tunatya and *natwani,* 40-41, 220*n*61
wiimi. See ritual knowledge
Wikvaya *(Mamrawt* chief-priest), as first
"native Christian," 138, 147, 153,
228*n*20
Wilkinson, Charles, 239*n*17
will, human, 32-33, 35, 43, 218*n*52. *See
also* intentionalism
Williams, Raymond, 81, 96
Williams, William Carlos, 113, 163
Wimmomngwit. See chief priest(s)
wimvaavasa (ritual/ceremonial fields), 62-
68
Winship, G., 82-83
Winter Solstice, ceremonies, 191, 194
witchcraft, 36, 97; attributed to K. T.
Johnson, 147; Bow people accused of,
136, 228*n*16; deaths attributed to,
134; fear of, 94, 97, 222*n*8; *popwaqt*
as *pavansinom,* 86, 87-88, 94
Wollheim, Richard, 127, 155-56
women, Hopi, 3, 116, 221*n*1; control of
economic resources, 65-66, 85; sodalities, 110, 222*n*1